VISUAL QUICKSTART GUIDE

Microsoft Office v. X

FOR MAC OS X

Dan Henderson
Steve Schwartz

 Peachpit Press

Visual QuickStart Guide
Microsoft Office v. X for Mac OS X
Dan Henderson and Steve Schwartz

Peachpit Press

1249 Eighth Street
Berkeley, CA 94710
510/524-2178
800/283-9444
510/524-2221 (fax)

Find us on the World Wide Web at: http://www.peachpit.com.
To report errors, please send a note to errata@peachpit.com.

Peachpit Press is a division of Pearson Education.

Editor: Rebecca Gulick
Production Coordinators: Lisa Brazieal and Myrna Vladic
Copyeditor: Gail Nelson-Bonebrake
Compositors: Jerry Ballew and David Van Ness
Indexer: Karin Arrigoni
Cover design: The Visual Group

ISBN 0-201-79483-7

9 8 7 6 5 4 3 2 1

Printed and bound in the United States of America

Dedication

To the memory of Nathan Jeffrey Henderson,
who would have been 26 this year.

Acknowledgements

The authors would like to thank Rebecca Gulick, Gail Nelson-Bonebrake, Lisa Brazieal, Marjorie Baer, and Karin Arrigoni at Peachpit Press for their dedication, competence, and oft-challenged patience. Thanks also to Erik Ryan at Microsoft Corp. Dan would also like to thank all the people who were gracious when told, "No, I can't do that; I need to work on the book instead."

TABLE OF CONTENTS

TABLE OF CONTENTS

INTRODUCTION

Welcome to Microsoft Office v. X! Feel free to turn immediately to the parts of the book that will be most helpful to you. If you're the thorough type, though, you might want to take a moment to read the next few pages. They list the basic skills you'll need—skills you almost certainly have if you've used the Mac for any length of time. We'll also take a look at what's new in this edition of Microsoft Office for Macintosh.

What You Already Know

This book assumes you have a basic understanding of the following Macintosh skills:

◆ How to turn the Mac on and off.

◆ How to use the mouse (move, point, click, double-click, drag).

◆ How to use the elements of the Desktop (menus, windows, icons, Dock, Trash).

◆ How to use the common elements of applications (menus, toolbars, document windows, buttons).

◆ How to manipulate windows (open, close, move, resize, move to the Dock, switch among multiple open windows).

◆ How to manipulate files (find, open, save, close, copy, move).

◆ How to use the elements of dialog boxes (text fields, pull-down menus, check boxes, radio buttons, tabs).

◆ How to use toolbars (viewing and hiding, using the icons and drop-down menus).

✔ Tip

■ If you'd like to explore any of these skills further or learn more about what your Mac can do, we recommend *The Little Mac Book* and *The Little iMac Book*, both by Robin Williams and published (no surprise) by Peachpit Press. And if you're new to Mac OS X (the operating system for which Office v. X was designed), you might want to check out *The Little Mac OS X Book,* also by Williams, and Maria Langer's *Mac OS X: Visual QuickStart Guide.*

How to Use This Book

This is a book for beginning and intermediate users of Microsoft Office for Macintosh. If you're using Office for the first time, you're switching from a Windows version to the Macintosh version, or you just know the basics and want to get more out of your (substantial!) investment in Office, this book is for you. If you learn better from step-by-step instructions and lots of graphic examples than from reference manuals that just describe what the menu commands do, this book is also for you. Most of all, if you know what you want to do and want to get started in the shortest amount of time possible, this book is *definitely* for you.

We've worked hard to create a book that will let you turn to any step-by-step procedure, learn what it does, and do it yourself. A screen shot illustrates every significant step. Our goal is to give you all the information you need and none you don't, making you productive as quickly as possible. Along the way, you'll find tips that offer helpful information related to a given procedure.

To the best of our ability, we've designed each section to function independently; you almost never need to know one part of the subject to understand another. However, the many features common to all Office programs mean that you will quickly find yourself recognizing elements and procedures you learned for one program and applying them to the others.

About Word

Word X, the word-processing component of the Microsoft Office suite, creates letters, memos, invoices, proposals, reports, forms, brochures, catalogs, labels, envelopes, Web pages, and just about any other kind of printed or electronically distributed document.

You can type text into Word and insert almost any kind of graphic, formatting the text and graphics into sophisticated documents complete with tables, running headers and footers, footnotes, cross-references, page numbers, tables of contents, and indexes. On the other hand, you can also create simple text letters and memos with Word's easy-to-use features.

Word's approach, like that of the other applications in the Office suite, is entirely visual. As you work in a document, you see all the text, graphics, and formatting exactly as it will appear when you print it.

Word also works in concert with the other Office applications. It can display numbers from Excel and slides from PowerPoint. You can flag Word documents for follow-up in your Entourage to-do list.

About Excel

Excel X, the spreadsheet application of the Microsoft Office suite, tracks, calculates, and analyzes numbers, and creates charts to depict numbers visually.

After typing numbers into a rows-and-columns grid of cells on an Excel worksheet, you can enter formulas into adjacent cells that total, subtract, multiply, or divide the numbers. You can also enter *functions,* special Excel formulas that perform complex calculations—from simple averaging to sophisticated financial computations, such as net present value. Excel can even calculate highly involved statistics.

Excel also lets you create, maintain, and import lists and databases. You can accumulate records of both textual and numeric information, as well as sort, search for, filter, and extract data from a database. Excel works especially well with FileMaker Pro databases.

If you want to view your numbers graphically, Excel can create professional and presentable charts in dozens of different formats.

ABOUT WORD AND EXCEL

About PowerPoint

PowerPoint is the presentation-graphics component of the Microsoft Office suite. It creates charts and graphs, slides, handouts, overheads, and any other presentation materials you might use during a stand-up dog-and-pony show. PowerPoint even creates *slide shows*—electronic presentations you can run on your computer screen or on a projection device in front of an audience.

PowerPoint comes with dozens of professionally designed templates that take care of the presentation's look so you can focus on its message. It offers a selection of sample presentation outlines that help you get a start on the content.

PowerPoint's powerful arsenal includes bulleted or numbered text slides, graphs, tables, organization charts, clip art, animations and movies, and drawing tools.

If you need to convey your presentation to an even wider audience, you can convert it to a QuickTime movie or to a Web-based slide show, viewable with any Web browser.

About Entourage

Entourage helps you manage your life and your communications. Use it to send and receive email and files, read and post to discussion groups on the Internet, and maintain your calendar, address book, to-do list, and notes.

You can flag Office documents for follow-up in your to-do list, remind yourself of appointments and events, look up contact information in public directories, and easily link Entourage items to each other.

What's New in Office v. X?

Microsoft Office v. X for Macintosh has many new features. Here are the most significant ones.

What's new in all Office programs?

◆ Built for Mac OS X, Office v. X *requires* that you have OS X 10.1 or higher installed on your Mac.

◆ Office v. X offers file compatibility with Office documents created in any version of the suite since Office 97.

◆ Office bases new documents on any recently used Office document, effectively treating *all* of your documents as templates.

◆ Office lets you save any document as an Adobe Acrobat Portable Document Format (PDF) file.

◆ The AutoRecover feature allows you to avoid data loss in the event of a computer crash.

◆ AutoCorrect now includes Office's main spelling dictionary to catch additional errors.

◆ Office's new keyboard shortcuts avoid conflicts with OS X shortcuts.

◆ Office v. X includes extensive foreign-language support.

What's new in Word X?

◆ Noncontiguous text selection makes it possible to format multiple text segments simultaneously.

◆ The Clear Formatting style removes all formatting from a text selection.

◆ New, improved wizards help you create newsletters, brochures, catalogs, and menus.

◆ Word X can open AppleWorks 6 word-processing documents.

What's new in Excel X?

◆ Excel X allows you to customize your keyboard shortcuts.

◆ Excel X offers integration with REALbasic.

What's new in Entourage X?

◆ A simplified interface allows you to switch easily between Entourage components.

◆ Notification of Calendar events occurs even when no Office application is running.

◆ You can insert pictures, background pictures, sounds, and movies directly into email messages.

◆ You can clear the recently used address list or turn off the feature altogether.

◆ The Calendar supports time zones.

◆ Mac OS Keychain support allows you to store passwords.

WHAT'S NEW IN OFFICE V. X?

What's new in PowerPoint X?

◆ You can now save a presentation as a
PowerPoint Package, storing all necessary
files in a single folder. This simplifies the
transfer of a presentation to another
computer, to other users, or to a CD.

◆ Presentations saved as PowerPoint
movies can include any combination of
animations, slide transitions, and interactive features.

◆ True transparency support allows layering of objects on slides.

WHAT'S NEW IN OFFICE X?

Part I:
Introduction

ESSENTIAL OFFICE TECHNIQUES

1

Many basic operations in Office X, such as starting a new document, opening an existing document, saving your work, working with different types of content, and getting help, apply to more than one program. Rather than repeat them throughout the book, we'll cover them here.

Starting New Documents

Unless you work exclusively with documents created by others, you will need to create new documents of your own. In all Office programs, you can start a new blank document in these traditional ways:

◆ *Word:* File > New Blank Document

◆ *PowerPoint:* File > New Presentation

◆ *Excel:* File > New Workbook

◆ Press ⌘N.

A feature introduced in Office 2001 called the *Project Gallery* gives you access to standard blank documents, as well as to templates and wizards that provide a substantial amount of document formatting and content. *Templates* are formatted documents to which you add your own content. *Wizards* are short multiple-step or tabbed procedures that ask you questions about the document you want to produce and then create the document based on your answers. You can always edit the resulting document when the wizard is finished.

To use the Project Gallery:

1. Choose File > Project Gallery (or press Shift ⌘ P).

   The Project Gallery opens (**Figure 1.1**). (You may have noticed that the window also opens when you launch any Office application.)

Categories   Templates and wizards

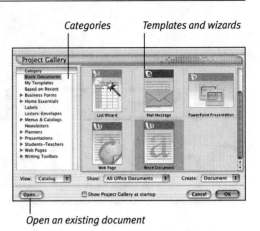

Open an existing document

Figure 1.1 Select a category in the left pane to view the available templates and wizards on the right. Or—to create a blank document—select the Blank Documents category.

*Enable or disable Project
Gallery at startup*

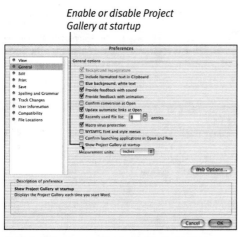

Figure 1.2 You can enable or disable the Project Gallery at startup by adding or removing the checkmark from Show Project Gallery at startup.

2. Select a category in the left pane of the Project Gallery. Click the triangles to view the subcategories.

The available templates and wizards appear in the right pane.

3. Click an icon in the right pane to select the template or wizard you want.

4. Click OK.

5. If you've chosen a wizard, provide the information it requests.

The document appears.

✔ Tips

■ You can reduce the size of the icons in the Project Gallery by choosing List instead of Catalog from the View drop-down menu.

■ You can limit the kinds of documents shown in the Project Gallery by picking a file type from the Show menu. For example, you could elect to view only Excel documents.

■ You can use the Project Gallery to open existing documents by clicking the Open button.

■ If you would rather not see the Project Gallery every time you launch an Office program, remove the checkmark from the Show Project Gallery at startup check box at the bottom of the Project Gallery window (Figure 1.1). You can also enable or disable this option in Excel's or Word's General Preferences (**Figure 1.2**).

Saving Your Work

It's a good idea to save your work frequently—to guard against unforeseen problems that require you to quit an Office program prematurely or restart your Mac.

To save your work:

1. Choose File > Save, press ⌘S, or click the Save icon on the Standard toolbar (**Figure 1.3**).

   If the document was previously saved, the new version of the file automatically overwrites the old one.

   If this is the first time you've saved this document (or if you've chosen File > Save As), a Save As dialog box appears (**Figure 1.4**). Continue with the remaining steps.

2. Enter a filename in the Save As text box.

3. Specify a file format by choosing one from the Format drop-down menu.

4. Click the Where drop-down menu to select a location in which to store the document. If you need to navigate to a drive or folder that isn't listed, click the triangle button to expand the window (**Figure 1.5**).

5. Click Save or press Return.

✔ Tips

- Each Office application proposes a default folder whenever you attempt to save your work. You can specify a different default folder in each program's Preferences.

- Word, Excel, and PowerPoint allow automatic saving of documents at user-defined intervals. In Office X, this is referred to as *AutoRecover*. To enable AutoRecover and specify a time interval, choose *program name* > Preferences and click the Save tab or category (**Figure 1.6**).

Save icon

Figure 1.3 To save the current document, choose File > Save, choose File > Save As, or click the Save icon on the Standard toolbar.

Click to expand the Where list

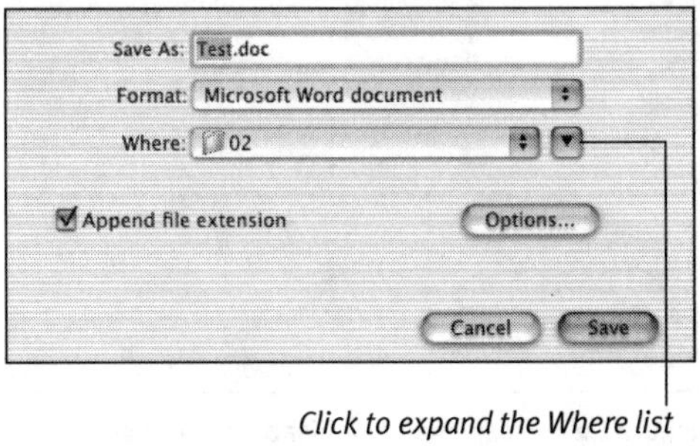

Figure 1.4 To save a new document or to save an old one using a new name or location, enter the necessary information in the Save As dialog box.

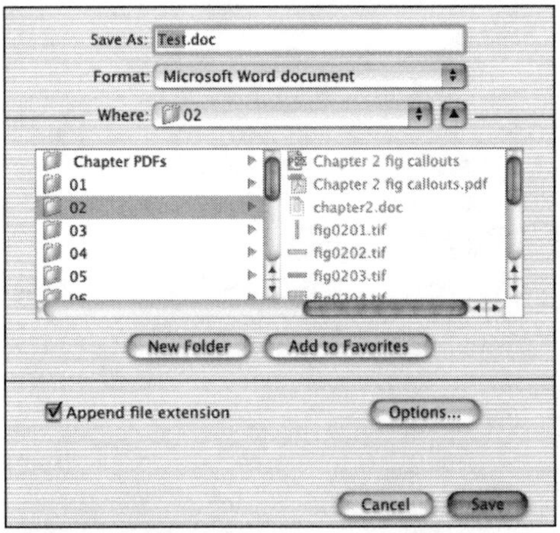

Figure 1.5 With the Where section expanded, you can choose any drive or folder in which to save the current document.

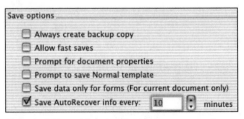

Figure 1.6 By enabling AutoRecover, you can make sure you never lose more than a few minutes of work.

SAVING YOUR WORK

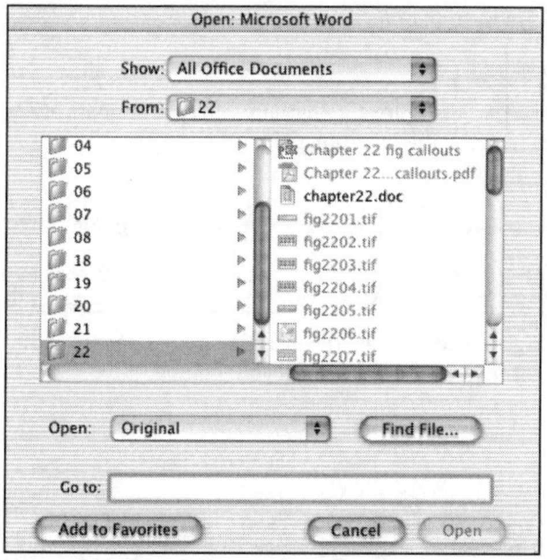

Figure 1.7 To open an existing document, choose it from the Open dialog box.

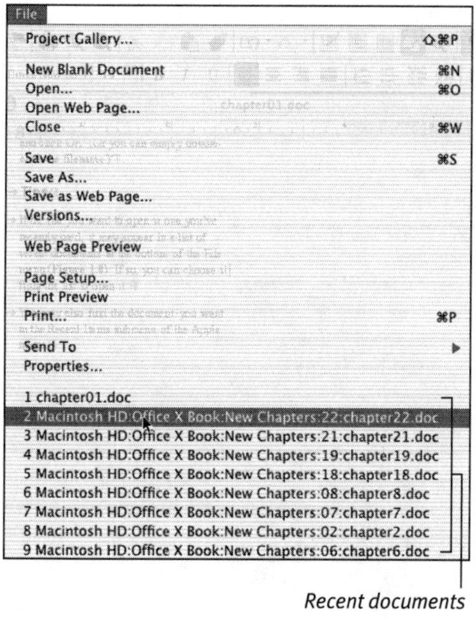

Recent documents

Figure 1.8 If you recently worked on a document, you may be able to open it again by choosing it from the bottom of the File menu.

Opening Existing Documents

Unless you use or refer to every document you create only once (a *very* unlikely occurrence), you'll need to open documents you've previously saved on disk.

To reopen a saved file:

1. You can either choose File > Open, click the Open icon on the Standard toolbar, or press ⌘O.

2. In the Open dialog box (**Figure 1.7**), navigate to the location where the file is stored.

3. To open the document, select its filename and click Open. (Or you can simply double-click the filename.)

✔ Tips

■ If the file you want to open is one you've recently used, it may appear in the list of recent documents at the bottom of the File menu (**Figure 1.8**). If so, you can choose it from the list to open it.

■ You can also open documents by choosing them from the Recent Items submenu of the Apple menu.

Working with Text

Text is an important part of most Office documents. Whenever an application is ready for you to type text, a blinking insertion point appears in the document. Whatever you type appears at the insertion point (**Figure 1.9**).

To revise or add to existing text, you must move the insertion point to the spot where you want to make the change.

To move the insertion point:

◆ Click once in the existing text where you'd like to add or edit text.

or

Press the arrow keys, Pg Up , or Pg Dn .

✔ Tips

■ In Word and PowerPoint, you can use ⌘← or ⌘→ to move the insertion point one word to the left or right, ↑ or ↓ to move it up or down one line, or ⌘↑ or ⌘↓ to move it paragraph by paragraph.

■ In Excel, the insertion point appears in the text box on the Formula Bar (**Figure 1.10**).

To select text with the mouse:

◆ Click at one end of a section of text to set the insertion point, and drag to the other end to select the text (**Figure 1.11**). A selection can be as little as one character or can contain many consecutive paragraphs.

◆ To select text on multiple consecutive lines, click to set the insertion point at the beginning of the selection and drag through the lines you want to select.

◆ You can make multiple, noncontiguous text selections in Office X. You might, for

insertion point

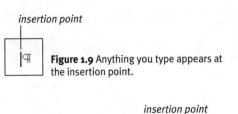

Figure 1.9 Anything you type appears at the insertion point.

insertion point

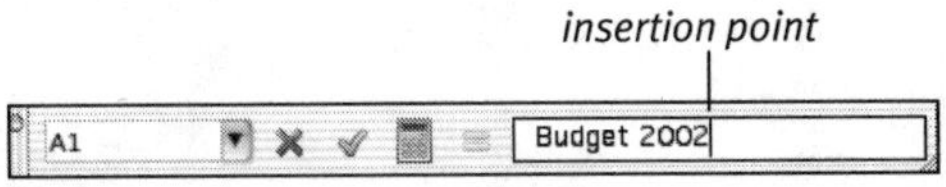

Figure 1.10 In Excel, the insertion point appears in the Formula Bar, along with all your editing.

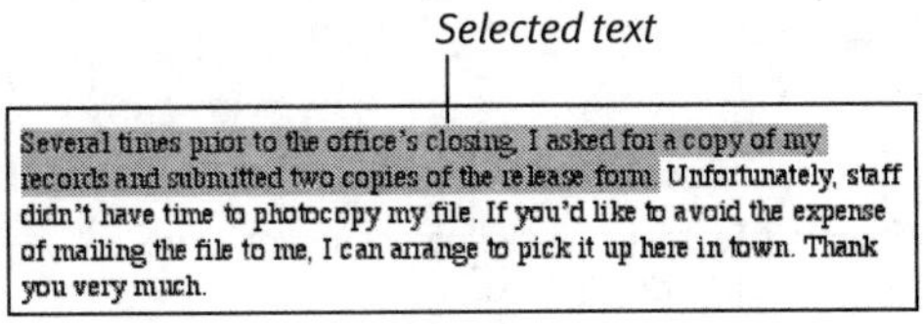

Selected text

Several times prior to the office's closing, I asked for a copy of my records and submitted two copies of the release form. Unfortunately, staff didn't have time to photocopy my file. If you'd like to avoid the expense of mailing the file to me, I can arrange to pick it up here in town. Thank you very much.

Figure 1.11 Click and drag to create a text selection.

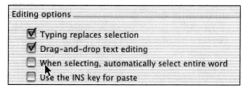

Figure 1.12 To be able to select partial words, remove the checkmark from When selecting, automatically select entire word.

example, want to select several different headings to apply the same formatting to them simultaneously. Hold down ⌘ to make multiple selections.

◆ Double-click anywhere within a word to select it.

◆ Triple-click anywhere within a paragraph to select it.

✔ Tips

■ The Automatic Word Selection prefer-ence setting ensures that the entire first and last word of the selection are high-lighted. To be able to select parts of words, choose *program name* > Prefer-ences, select the Edit heading, and remove the checkmark from When selecting, automatically select entire word (**Figure 1.12**).

■ *Mouse shortcut:* Click at the beginning of the text you wish to select, and Shift-click at the end of the selection. The text in between is selected.

■ *Word tip:* To select an entire line of text, click in the left margin of the line. To select multiple lines, click in the margin to the left of a line and then drag down through the lines.

To select text with the keyboard:

1. Use the arrow keys to position the inser-tion point in front of the first character.

2. Hold down Shift and use the arrow keys to extend the text selection.

✔ Tips

■ Use Shift ↓ to select multiple lines of text.

■ Use Shift ⌘ → or Shift ⌘ ← to select a word at a time.

(continues on next page)

WORKING WITH TEXT

Replacing text

To replace text in a document or dialog box, you can select the text and type over it. (It isn't necessary to first delete the old text.) The entire string of selected characters will be replaced when you begin typing.

Moving text

To move text in a document, you can either use the Edit > Cut and Edit > Paste commands or drag and drop. *Drag and drop* is like a simplified cut and paste, accomplished by selecting text and then dragging the text to a new location in the document. You can even drag text from one document to another or from one application window to another.

To drag and drop text:

1. Select the text to be moved.

2. Place the cursor over the selected text.

   The cursor changes to an arrow pointer (**Figure 1.13**).

3. Press and hold down the mouse button, and then drag the pointer to the desired destination.

   An insertion point indicates the spot where the dragged text will reappear (**Figure 1.14**).

4. Release the mouse button to drop the text at the new location (**Figure 1.15**).

✔ Tips

■ To copy text rather than move it (leaving the original text passage intact), press [Option] as you drag.

■ Using these techniques, you can also copy or move other kinds of objects, such as graphics and charts.

■ Since OS X doesn't support clipping files, you cannot use drag and drop to drag a text selection from Office X onto the desktop.

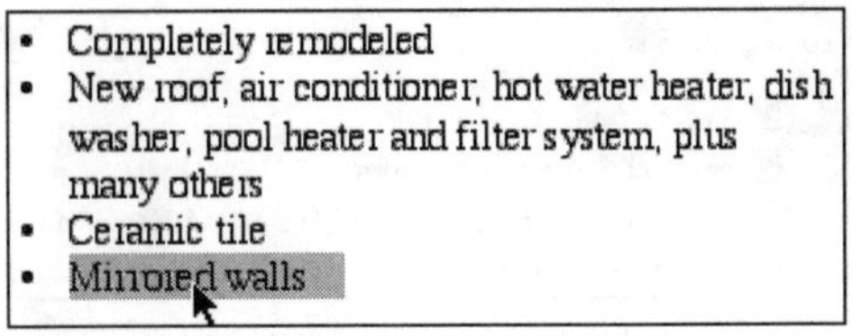

Figure 1.13 When the cursor is moved over the selected text, it changes to an arrow pointer.

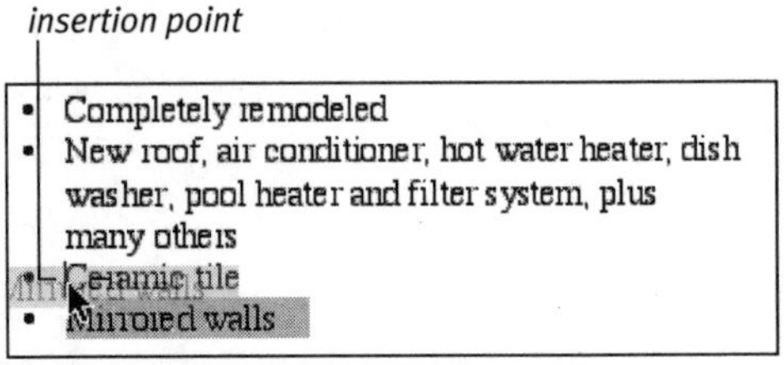

Figure 1.14 Drag the arrow pointer to the desired destination. It turns into an insertion point showing where the text will go.

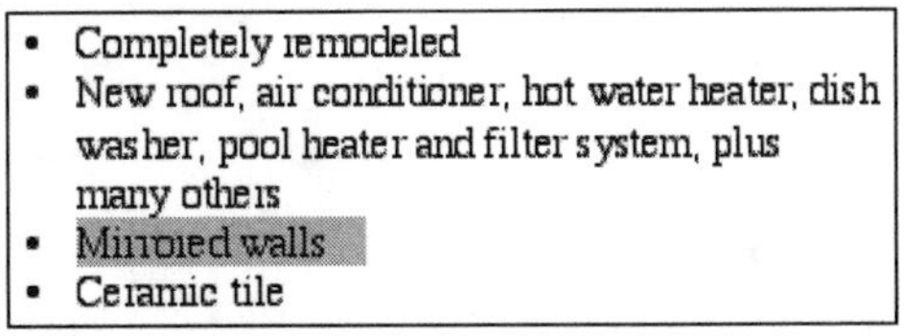

Figure 1.15 Release the mouse button to drop the text. The "Mirrored walls" bullet has been moved up one paragraph.

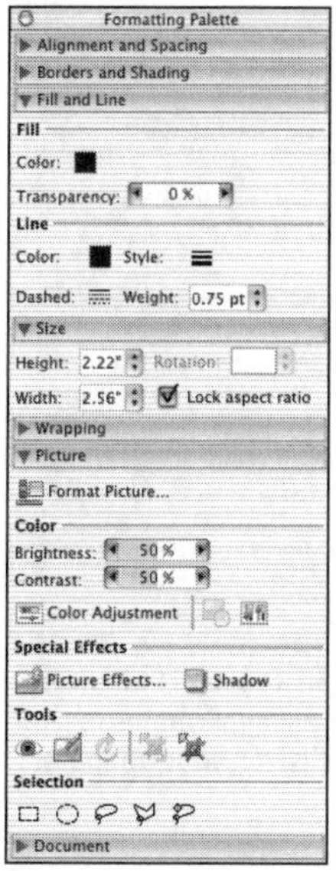

Figure 1.16 When you select an object, the Formatting Palette displays commands that are relevant to that object.

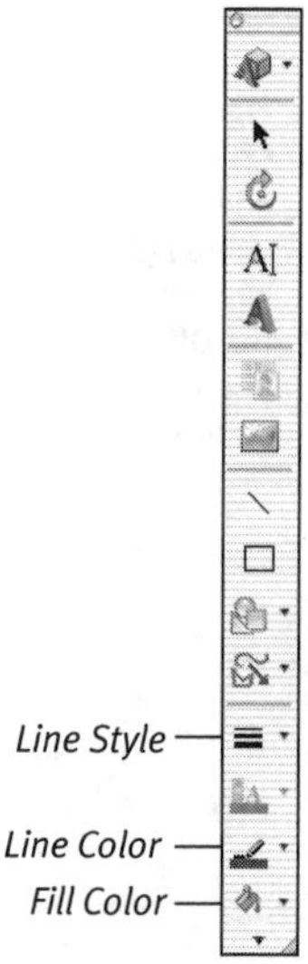

Line Style ———
Line Color ———
Fill Color ———

Figure 1.17 You can modify many objects by choosing commands and options from the Drawing toolbar.

Selected object
WordArt toolbar

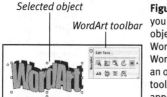

Figure 1.18 When you select an object (such as this WordArt text in a Word document), an object-specific toolbar generally appears.

Working with Pictures and Other Objects

Drawings, charts, WordArt, clip art, scanned images, and other items you can select in an Office document are called *objects*. After you've selected an object (by clicking or dragging through it), you can drag it to reposition it on the page. You can also drag objects to other documents—including documents in other applications. To copy rather than move the object, hold down [Option] as you drag.

To format an object, you must select it and then choose a formatting command.

To format an object:

1. Select the object you want to format.

2. Do one of the following:
   ◆ Choose a command or click an icon on the Formatting Palette (**Figure 1.16**), the Drawing toolbar (**Figure 1.17**), or the object-specific toolbar (**Figure 1.18**) that appears when you select the object.
   ◆ Double-click the object to bring up a relevant formatting dialog box.
   ◆ Choose an appropriate command, such as Picture, from the Format menu.

✔ Tips

■ If neither the Formatting Palette nor the necessary toolbar is visible, you can display one of them by choosing the appropriate command from the View menu.

■ For assistance with text formatting, refer to Chapter 3, Word Basics, and Chapter 5, Document and Text Formatting.

Working in Different Languages

All Office X programs support Unicode language capability. You can view and edit documents in a variety of languages, mix languages in the same document, and set program preferences to match the conventions and requirements of the various languages.

To use a foreign language:

1. Choose System Preferences from the Apple menu, and then click the International icon.

2. On the Language tab of the International dialog box (**Figure 1.19**), click the Edit button to add the desired language(s) to the Languages list (**Figure 1.20**). After adding a language, you can change the list's order by dragging items up or down in the Languages list.

3. Click the other tabs to set your preferred date, time, and number styles, as well as the keyboard layout.

4. Close the dialog box.

5. In Word, choose Word > Preferences.

6. In the Preferences dialog box, click the Spelling and Grammar heading, and then click the Dictionaries button.

   The Custom Dictionaries dialog box appears.

7. Select a language from the Languages drop-down list (**Figure 1.21**) and click OK.

8. Click OK to dismiss the Preferences dialog box.

✔ Tip

- To enter and edit Japanese text, you must install the Microsoft Language Register from the Value Pack on the Office v. X CD-ROM.

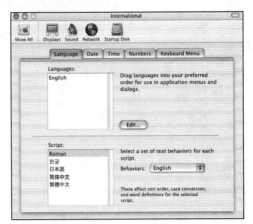

Figure 1.19 Open the International System Preferences to instruct OS X and the Office v. X applications to support languages other than English on your computer.

Figure 1.20 Check any additional languages you wish OS X and the Office applications to support.

Figure 1.21 In Word, you can select a language dictionary to use for spelling checks from this drop-down list.

Show ScreenTips

Figure 1.22 To enable or disable ScreenTips in Excel or PowerPoint, click or unclick this check box in the Customize dialog box.

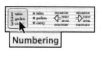

Figure 1.23 When you rest the cursor over most Office components—toolbar icons, for example—a ScreenTip pops up.

Figure 1.24 Click the Assistant to open a search dialog box. Type a question or search string and click Search.

Assistant

Getting Help

Office X provides several sources of help. You can get pop-up ScreenTips (also called ToolTips) for toolbar icons and parts of the document window; you can activate the Assistant, which responds to typed queries; you can use the detailed online help documents included with the program; and you can go to Microsoft's Web site for more extensive information.

To display a ScreenTip or ToolTip:

1. You can enable or disable ScreenTips separately for each Office program. Do one of the following:

   ◆ In Word, choose Word > Preferences, and click the View tab. Enter or remove the checkmark from ScreenTips.

   ◆ In Excel or PowerPoint, choose Tools > Customize. On the Toolbars tab of the Customize dialog box (**Figure 1.22**), enter or remove the checkmark from Show ScreenTips on toolbars. (You may also wish to check or uncheck Show shortcut keys in ScreenTips.)

   ◆ In Entourage, choose Entourage > General Preferences, click the General tab, and enter or remove the checkmark from Show ToolTips.

2. Move the pointer over any icon, button, or other Office component, and then wait a second or two.

   A yellow ScreenTip appears (**Figure 1.23**).

To use the Assistant:

1. If the Assistant isn't already visible, choose Help > Use the Office Assistant.

2. Click the Assistant to request help (**Figure 1.24**).

(continues on next page)

GETTING HELP

3. Type a question or search string, and then press Return or click Search.

The Assistant will interpret your query and present a list of options (**Figure 1.25**).

4. Click a suggested topic to open Microsoft Office Help to that subject.

To use a different Assistant:

1. Click the Assistant to open the search dialog box.

2. Click the Options button.

3. In the Office Assistant dialog box, switch to the Gallery tab. Click the Back and Next buttons to preview the installed Assistants (**Figure 1.26**).

4. When you find one you want to use, click OK.

To use onscreen help documents:

1. Choose Help > *program name* Help Contents. (If the Office Assistant isn't active, you can also open Microsoft Office Help by choosing Help > Search *program name* Help.)

The Microsoft Office Help window opens (**Figure 1.27**).

Figure 1.25 Choose from the list of proposed Help topics.

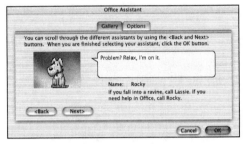

Figure 1.26 Scan through the installed Assistants by clicking the Back and Next buttons.

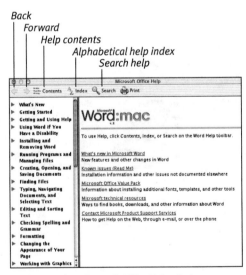

Figure 1.27 The Microsoft Office Help window opens.

GETTING HELP

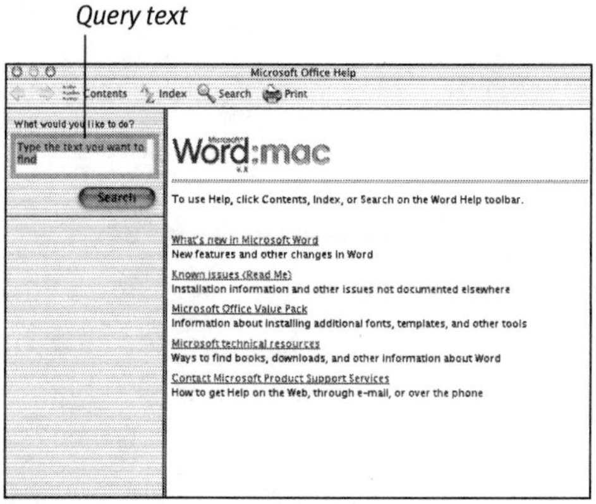

Query text

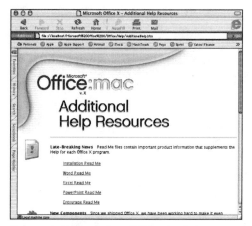

Figure 1.28 Type your question in the Help window's Search box if the Assistant isn't turned on.

Figure 1.29 Choose Help > Additional Help Resources to view helpful text in your browser.

2. Do one of the following:

♦ In the toolbar at the top of the Help window, click Contents for a list of major topics in the left pane.

♦ Click Index to get an alphabetical list of keywords.

♦ Click Search to search for keywords. If the Assistant is active, it will handle the search request; if not, the search query will appear in the left pane of the Microsoft Office Help window (**Figure 1.28**).

3. Click an item in the left pane to either bring up its help text in the right panel or expand it to display a list of subtopics, any of which you can click to view the associated help text.

4. To navigate backward and forward through multiple help screens, click the arrow icons on the Microsoft Office Help toolbar. In the body of the window, under-lined blue text represents a clickable link to another Help section. Special terms are also displayed in blue (without the under-lining); click a term to view its definition.

✔ Tips

■ The Value Pack on the Office X CD-ROM contains additional assistants you can install.

■ To view other help information in your default Web browser (**Figure 1.29**), choose Help > Additional Help Resources.

■ You can get more information, tips, templates, and software updates from Microsoft's Web site by choosing Help > Visit the Mactopia Web Site.

GETTING HELP

OFFICE V. X AND THE INTERNET

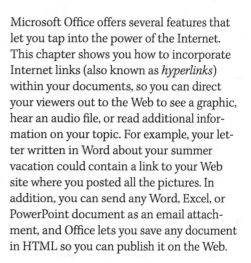

Microsoft Office offers several features that let you tap into the power of the Internet. This chapter shows you how to incorporate Internet links (also known as *hyperlinks*) within your documents, so you can direct your viewers out to the Web to see a graphic, hear an audio file, or read additional information on your topic. For example, your letter written in Word about your summer vacation could contain a link to your Web site where you posted all the pictures. In addition, you can send any Word, Excel, or PowerPoint document as an email attachment, and Office lets you save any document in HTML so you can publish it on the Web.

Adding Links

Including links to the Web within documents can be a handy way to enhance your content. Keep in mind, however, that your viewer needs to be looking at your document onscreen and on a computer that's connected to the Internet.

To create a link in a Word, Excel, or PowerPoint document:

1. Position the insertion point where you want to insert a text link.

   or

   Select the text or object that you want to designate as the link.

2. Choose Insert > Hyperlink (⌘K).

   The Insert Hyperlink dialog box appears (**Figure 2.1**). Text descriptions in the dialog box explain your options.

3. Switch to the appropriate tab and set options to link to a Web page, link to a document, or create a link that generates an email message.

4. Click OK to create the link.

   Depending on the type of link created, when it's clicked, Internet Explorer will fetch the desired Web page, Entourage will create a new preaddressed email message, or a document on your hard disk will open.

To create a link in an Entourage document:

1. Click the Insert icon on the toolbar.

2. In the drop-down menu (**Figure 2.2**), choose Hyperlink, followed by From IE Window (a page Internet Explorer is currently displaying), From IE Favorites (a saved favorite), or From IE History (a page you've recently visited).

3. Select the desired Web page (**Figure 2.3**) and click Choose.

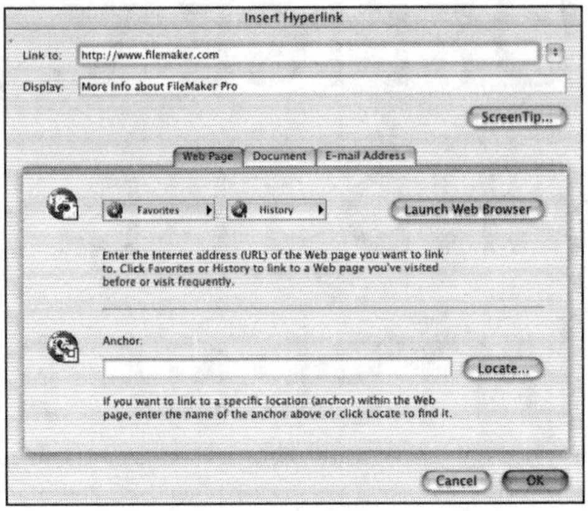

Figure 2.1 You can create a link in the current document that—when clicked—will open a Web page, a document on your hard disk, or a new email message.

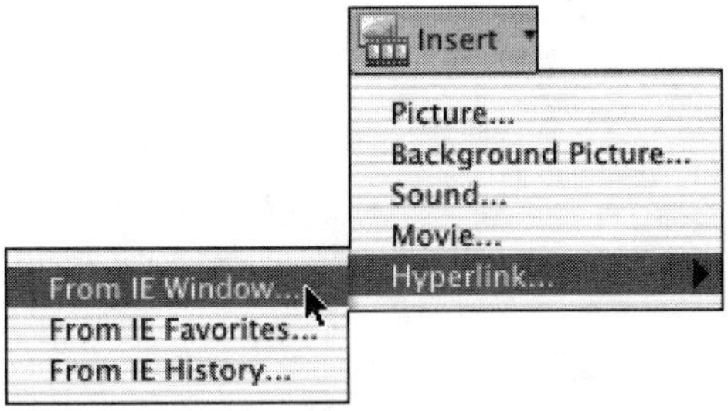

Figure 2.2 To add a Web page link to an Entourage message, click the Insert icon on the toolbar for this pop-up menu.

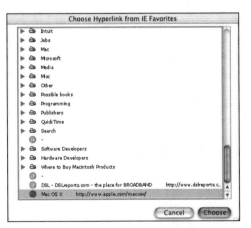

Figure 2.3 Select a Web page for the link.

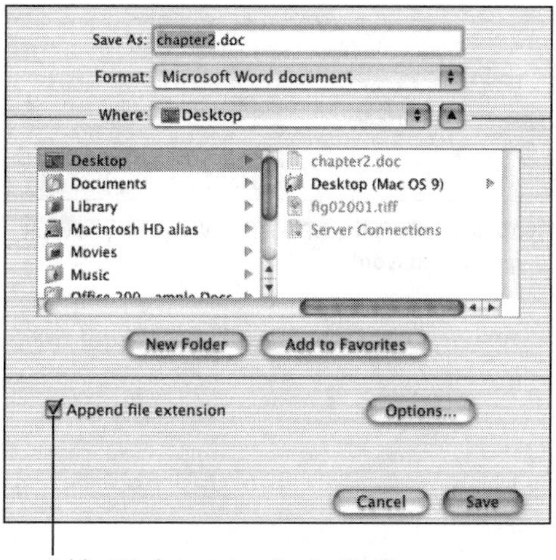

Add a Windows extension to the filename

Figure 2.4 When sending attachments to Windows Office users, click the Append file extension check box to add the appropriate extension.

Email

Entourage X is the Office v. X program for sending and receiving email. See Chapter 23, Email, for a complete introduction to using email in Entourage. In Word, PowerPoint, and Excel, you can send the current document as an email *attachment* (a file delivered with an email message).

To send an Office document as an email attachment:

1. *Optional:* Choose File > Save As to save the document. If you intend to send it to someone who is using a Windows version of Office, click the Append file extension check box (**Figure 2.4**).

2. Choose File > Send To > Mail Recipient (as Attachment).

   Your default email program launches and creates a new message with the attachment already specified.

3. Select recipients, write the email message, and send the message as usual.

✔ Tips

- The only email programs this procedure currently supports are Entourage, Apple's Mail, and Qualcomm's Eudora. If you've set a different email program as your default, the command will not be available.

- Many companies and ISPs limit the attachment size their mail servers allow. A common limitation is 1 MB. Thus, these servers may refuse large Office documents, such as PowerPoint presentations.

- If multiple people use your computer, you may need to switch identities in Entourage. Quit all other Office programs, launch Entourage, choose Entourage > Switch Identity, and click Switch in the dialog box that appears. In the next dialog box, select your identity and click OK.

Other Internet Capabilities

Office X has other Internet-related capabilities you may want to explore. Here are several of the most interesting ones:

- Using Word's File > Open Web Page command (**Figure 2.5**), you can fetch Web pages from the Internet.
- Office X lets you create Web pages from Word, PowerPoint, or Excel documents, so you can publish them on the Internet or a company intranet. If you have friends or coworkers who don't use Office, they can view the resulting Web documents in any browser. For an example of saving an Office document as a Web page, see "Publishing a Presentation on the Web" in Chapter 22, Preparing the Presentation for Viewing.
- Using the File > Web Page Preview command, you can quickly determine how the current Word, PowerPoint, or Excel document will look saved as a Web page.
- You can publish your Entourage Calendar as a series of Web pages, enabling you (and others, if you wish) to refer to it from any Internet access point—while on vacation or a business trip, for example.
- If you need to perform common Internet activities from within Word, Excel, or PowerPoint, you can display the Web toolbar (**Figure 2.6**) by choosing View > Toolbars > Web.

Open Web Page
Type the address of the Web page you want to open:
www.microsoft.com
Cancel
OK

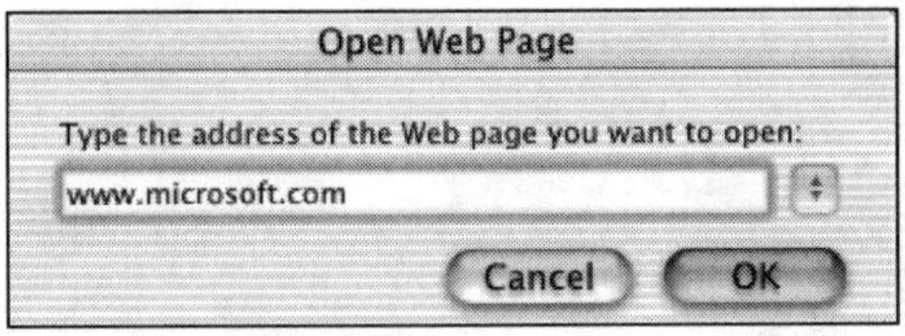

Figure 2.5 Specify the URL of the Web page you want to open within Word.

- The Help menu includes several commands that automatically launch your default browser and display information from the Web. You can also choose Tools > Tools on the Web to get assistance with Office X programs and download useful materials, such as templates.

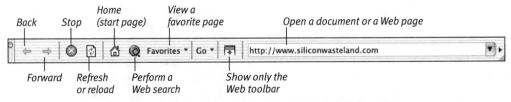

Back
Stop
Home (start page)
View a favorite page
Open a document or a Web page
Favorites
Go
http://www.siliconwasteland.com
Forward
Refresh or reload
Perform a Web search
Show only the Web toolbar

Figure 2.6 Using the Web toolbar, you can perform common Web activities in Office applications.

Part II:
Microsoft Word

WORD BASICS

This chapter provides an introduction to performing basic tasks with Word, such as creating new documents, formatting text and paragraphs, setting margins and tabs, and adding headers and footers. Even if you're new to Microsoft Word, you'll find the information in this chapter sufficient to enable you to create simple Word documents.

Other chapters in Part II explain how to perform advanced formatting techniques and how to use the many tools Word provides to create polished, professional-looking documents.

Opening a Blank Document

When you launch Word, the Project Gallery window opens, as it does when you launch any other Office application. The default option is to create a new, blank Word document, as described in the following steps.

To open a blank document:

1. Double-click the Microsoft Word icon in the Microsoft Office X folder (**Figure 3.1**).

   Word launches and the Project Gallery window opens. Blank Documents is highlighted in the Category list and the Word Document icon is selected (**Figure 3.2**).

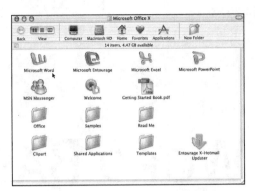

Figure 3.1 Double-click the Microsoft Word icon to launch the program.

Selected Category   Word Document

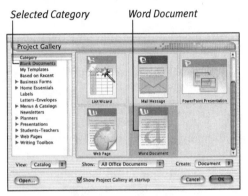

Figure 3.2 By default, Blank Documents is the selected Category and the Word Document icon is highlighted. Click OK to create a new blank document.

insertion point

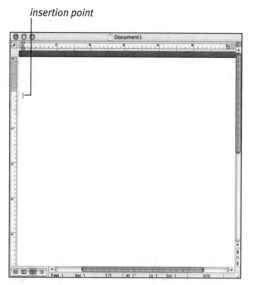

Figure 3.3 Your new blank Word document is ready for text to be entered.

2. Click OK.

A blank document named Document 1 appears, ready for you to enter text (**Figure 3.3**).

See "Working with Text" in Chapter 1, Essential Office Techniques, for details on how to enter text in Office documents.

✔ Tips

■ With Word running, you can create additional new documents by choosing File > New Blank Document, pressing ⌘Ⓝ, or clicking the New Blank Document icon on the Standard toolbar. The document number increments (Document2, Document3, and so on) to reflect the number of new documents created in the session.

■ You can disable the Project Gallery by removing the checkmark from Show Project Gallery at startup, either in the Project Gallery window (Figure 3.2) or in Word's General Preferences. In future sessions, Word will launch and automatically display a new document.

■ Much of your work in Word will involve previously saved documents—reading, printing, and modifying them. To open a saved document, choose File > Open, press ⌘Ⓞ, or click the Open icon on the Standard toolbar. For additional help with opening documents, see "To reopen a saved file" in Chapter 1.

OPENING A BLANK DOCUMENT

The Word Window

If this is your first time using Word, you
might want to familiarize yourself with the
Word window so you'll know where specific
toolbars and menus are located (**Figure 3.4**).

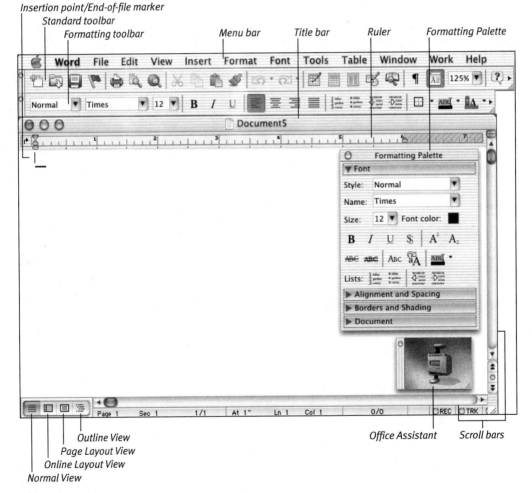

Figure 3.4 The toolbars and menus are easily accessible.

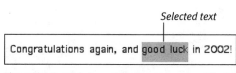

Figure 3.5 You can create documents with any combination of the fonts installed on your Mac. Text can vary in font, size, and effect (for example, bold, underlining, or small caps).

Selected text

Figure 3.6 To apply formatting to text, you must first select the text.

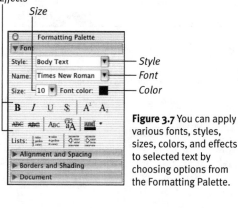

Figure 3.7 You can apply various fonts, styles, sizes, colors, and effects to selected text by choosing options from the Formatting Palette.

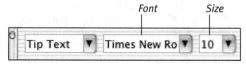

Figure 3.8 You can also choose a font or size from the pull-down menus on the Formatting toolbar.

Working with Text

You can change the look of text by applying different font formatting to it (**Figure 3.5**). This section describes text-formatting information that is unique to Word. For general information about working with text, refer to Chapter 1.

You can format text in several ways, as described below. Choose any method that's comfortable for you.

To change the font and font size:

1. Select the text you want to format (**Figure 3.6**).

2. Do one of the following:

   ◆ In the Formatting Palette, choose a font and size from the Name and Size drop-down lists (**Figure 3.7**).

   ◆ Choose a font and size from the drop-down menus on the Formatting toolbar (**Figure 3.8**).

(continues on next page)

◆ Choose Format > Font or press ⌘D. The Font dialog box appears (**Figure 3.9**). Choose a font and size to apply to the selected text, and then click OK.

✔ Tips

■ To show or hide the Formatting Palette, choose View > Formatting Palette. To show or hide the Formatting toolbar, choose View > Toolbars > Formatting.

■ To restore selected text to the standard font and size for the paragraph, select the text and choose Clear Formatting from the Style drop-down list on the Formatting Palette or Formatting toolbar.

■ To increase the font size of selected text, press ⌘ Shift >. To decrease the font size of selected text, press ⌘ Shift <.

To change the font style:

1. Select the text you want to format.

2. Do one of the following:

   ◆ Click the desired effects icons on the Formatting Palette (**Figure 3.10**) or on the Formatting toolbar (**Figure 3.11**).

   ◆ Choose Format > Font. In the Font dialog box (Figure 3.9), click the check boxes for the effects you want to apply. To set a style of underlining for the selected text, choose one from the Underline style pull-down menu.

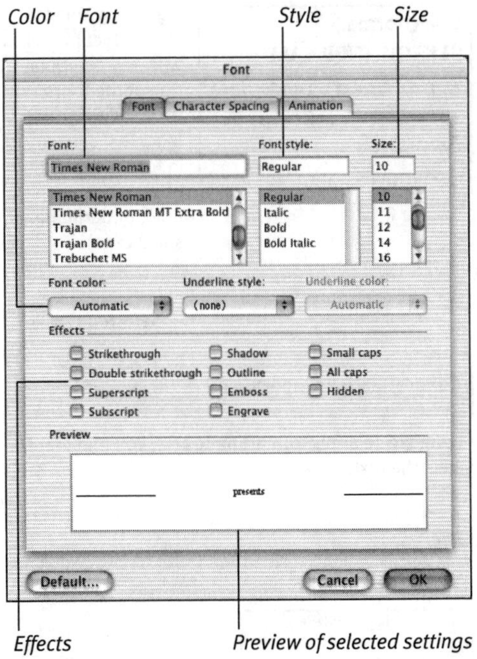

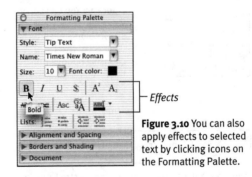

Figure 3.9 For more complex formatting needs, you can choose options from the Font dialog box.

Figure 3.10 You can also apply effects to selected text by clicking icons on the Formatting Palette.

Figure 3.11 You can also apply the three most common font effects—bold, italic, and underline—by clicking icons on the Formatting toolbar.

Figure 3.12 You can change the case of selected text by choosing an option from the Change Case dialog box. The appearance of each option shows its effect on text.

Table 3.1

Keyboard Shortcuts	
⌘ B	Bold
⌘ I	Italic
⌘ U	Underline
⌘ Shift K	Small caps
⌘ Shift A	All caps
Shift F3	Cycle through case selections

✔ Tips

■ You can use keyboard shortcuts (**Table 3.1**) to apply the most common font effects to selected text.

■ The font-effect icons (such as Bold), as well as their keyboard shortcuts, work as toggles. Click them once to turn the formatting on; click them a second time to turn it off.

■ You can change case by choosing Format > Change Case. Select an option from the Change Case dialog box (**Figure 3.12**) and click OK.

Showing/Hiding Nonprinting Characters

Nonprinting characters show where you ended a paragraph, pressed (Spacebar), or pressed (Tab) (**Figure 3.13**). You can show or hide nonprinting characters as you work on a Word document. Being able to see nonprinting characters is especially helpful when you're trying to locate multiple tab characters where only one should be or when you're looking for errant punctuation, such as extra spaces and empty paragraphs.

See **Table 3.2** for a complete list of nonprinting characters.

To show/hide nonprinting characters:

◆ Click the Show/Hide ¶ icon on the Standard toolbar (**Figure 3.14**).

   or

   In the Formatting Palette, expand the Document section and then click the Show/Hide ¶ button (**Figure 3.15**).

✔ Tip

■ The Show/Hide ¶ button is a toggle. Click it once to show nonprinting characters and a second time to hide them.

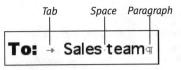

Tab   Space   Paragraph

Figure 3.13 The nonprinting characters appear in your text as you type.

Show/hide nonprinting characters

Figure 3.14 The Show/Hide ¶ icon looks like a paragraph symbol.

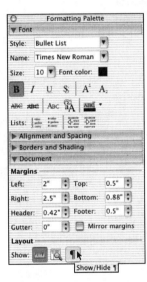

Figure 3.15 You can also show/hide nonprinting characters by clicking the Show/Hide ¶ icon at the bottom of the Formatting Palette.

Table 3.2

Nonprinting Characters	
¶	End of paragraph
· (dot)	Space
→	Tab
↵	Line break (new line, same paragraph)

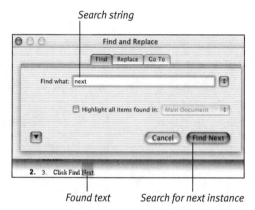

Figure 3.16 Type the text you want to find in the Find what text box.

Search string

Figure 3.17 When a Find or Find and Replace search finds its target, Word scrolls as necessary to highlight the instance of the search string.

Found text   *Search for next instance*

Finding and Replacing Text

You can instruct Word to search for and optionally replace words or phrases. For instance, if you can't remember the page on which you referred to Apple's annual report, you could perform a Find on the phrase "annual report." Or suppose your company name has recently changed from Anderson Plumbing to Widgets Inc. Using the Replace command, you could replace every instance of the old company name with the new name. Refer to **Table 3.3** for a list of special Find options.

To find text:

1. Choose Edit > Find or press ⌘F.

   The Find and Replace dialog box appears (**Figure 3.16**). The Find tab is selected.

2. Type a search string in the Find what text box.

3. Click Find Next.

   Word searches for the text string. If it finds an instance of the string, that instance is automatically highlighted in the document (**Figure 3.17**).

4. To search for the next occurrence of the search string, repeat Step 3. Otherwise, if you're done searching, click the Cancel button or the close box.

(continues on next page)

Table 3.3

Special Find Options	
Match case	Finds words that contain the same combination of upper- and lowercase characters
Find whole words only	Finds only complete words (for example, "art" finds only "art," not "artist")
Use wildcards	Allows you to enter a code to specify a special character combination to find (for example, "?" will match any single character)
Sounds like	Finds text that sounds like the search string
Find all word forms	Finds all variations of the chosen word (for example, "apple" and "apples")

To replace text:

1. Choose Edit > Replace or press [Shift][⌘][H]. The Find and Replace dialog box appears (**Figure 3.18**). The Replace tab is selected.

2. Type a search string in the Find what text box.

3. In the Replace with text box, type the replacement text string and click Find Next.

   Word searches for the text. If it finds an instance of the string, that instance is automatically highlighted in the document.

4. Click Replace to replace the text or Find Next to search for the next occurrence of the search string. Repeat this step until you're done or until Word notifies you that it has finished searching the document.

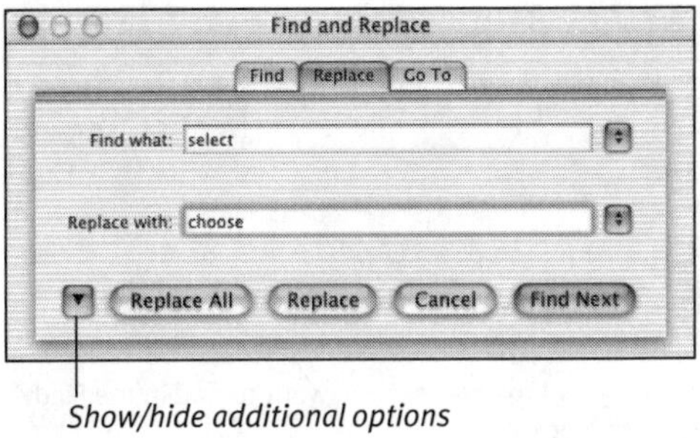

Show/hide additional options

Figure 3.18 Type the search string in the Find what box and the replacement text in the Replace with box.

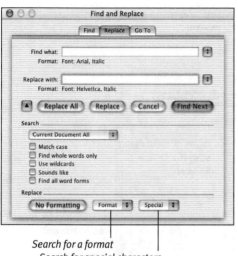

Search for a format
Search for special characters

Figure 3.19 By including only format options in the Find what and Replace with text boxes, you can replace one font with another throughout a document.

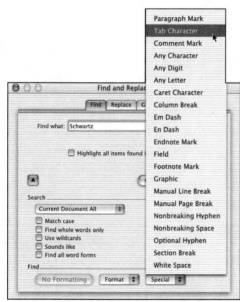

Figure 3.20 To include a special character in a Find or Replace text string, choose it from the Special pop-up menu.

✔ Tips

■ When performing a Replace, you can click Replace All to replace all occurrences of the search string with the replacement text simultaneously.

■ To search for a particular text string again, click the arrow button to the right of the Find what text box. Search terms you've previously used appear in this list.

■ Click the triangle in the bottom-left corner of the dialog box to display additional search options. For instance, Finds are normally case insensitive. If you want to find terms that match a specific capitalization, click the Match case check box. To hide the additional search options, click the triangle again.

■ You can also base a search on a particular font, effect, or style by choosing options from the Format drop-down menu. For example, you could replace all instances of Arial Italic text with Helvetica Italic (**Figure 3.19**).

■ To include a special character such as a tab or paragraph mark in a search, open the Special menu and choose a character (**Figure 3.20**). The symbol for the chosen character is automatically added to the search string. (In this example, ^t is inserted to represent a tab character.)

FINDING AND REPLACING TEXT

Using the Office Clipboard

Most Macintosh applications use a special area in system memory called the *clipboard* to store a copy of the most recent text, object, or graphic you've copied (Edit > Copy) or cut (Edit > Cut). The item is immediately available for pasting into the same document, into another document in the same application, or into documents in *other* applications. When you copy or cut another item, it replaces the item currently in the clipboard.

In Microsoft Office v. X, the Office Clipboard (**Figure 3.21**) augments the standard Mac clipboard. Instead of storing only the most recently copied or cut item, it can hold up to 60 separate items or 16 MB of data. In fact, any item copied or cut from Word, Excel, or PowerPoint can be pasted from the Office Clipboard into the same application or any other Office application.

Figure 3.21 The Office Clipboard holds cut and copied text and graphics, making them available for pasting into any Word, Excel, or PowerPoint document.

To show/hide the Office Clipboard:

1. Choose View > Office Clipboard. The Clipboard window appears.

   As long as the Office Clipboard remains open, any item you copy or cut from any Office document is automatically stored in the Office Clipboard.

2. To close the Clipboard, choose View > Office Clipboard again.

   or

   Click the close button in the top-left corner of the Office Clipboard.

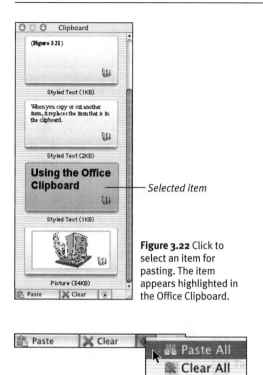

Figure 3.22 Click to select an item for pasting. The item appears highlighted in the Office Clipboard.

Figure 3.23 To paste or clear all items in the Office Clipboard simultaneously, click the button in the bottom-right corner and choose a command.

- To paste multiple—but not *all*—items simultaneously, (Shift)-click to select the items and then issue the Paste command. You can also use this technique to clear multiple items. Just (Shift)-click to select them, and then click the Clear button.

- When you exceed the Office Clipboard's storage capacity, the oldest items are removed to make room for new items.

To paste an item from the Office Clipboard:

1. Click in an active document to place the insertion point where you wish to paste the item from the Office Clipboard.

2. Click to select the item in the Clipboard that you want to paste into the current document.

   The selected item is shaded blue (**Figure 3.22**).

3. Click the Paste button at the bottom of the Clipboard window, or choose Edit > Paste, or press (⌘)(V).

   The item appears in the document at the chosen location.

✔ Tips

- You'll note that the Office Clipboard isn't visible in Entourage. Items cut or copied in Entourage are added to the Office Clipboard and are available for pasting in other Office applications, but you cannot paste *from* the Office Clipboard into an Entourage document.

- When the Office Clipboard is closed, the normal Mac clipboard is still available for storing and pasting the most recently cut or copied item.

- You can also use drag and drop to drag an item from the Office Clipboard window into place in your document. If you need to perform several paste operations, you may find this faster than having to set the insertion point repeatedly.

- To remove any item from the Office Clipboard, select the item and click the Clear button at the bottom of the window.

- To clear all items from the Office Clipboard or to paste all items at once, click the triangle button at the bottom of the Clipboard window and choose the appropriate command (**Figure 3.23**).

Setting Margins

Margins are the blank borders around the document page. Although Word has default margin settings, you can vary the margins to fit the dictates of the current document—for example, when you'll be printing on an unusual paper size or creating an elaborate layout. For example, if you intend to punch holes on the left side of the page, you might want to increase the left margin to provide room for the holes.

To change the margins:

1. Expand the Document section of the Formatting Palette.

2. In the Margins subsection (**Figure 3.24**), enter new Left, Right, Top, and/or Bottom margins. The new settings are applied immediately to the document.

3. Specify a gutter margin if you're preparing the document for binding. (The *gutter* is extra space added to the side of pages that will be bound. This prevents the binding from obscuring any of the printing.)

4. You can check the Mirror margins check box if you're printing a book, magazine, or other two-sided publication. Doing so makes the outer margin on left pages match the outer margin of the right pages, and also makes the inner margins match.

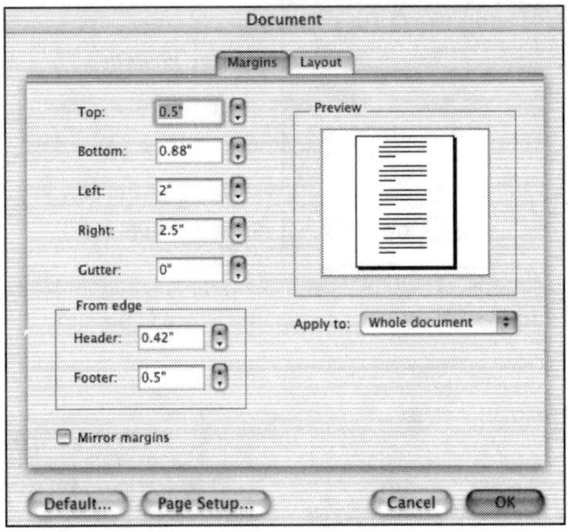

✔ Tips

■ You can also change the margins in the Document dialog box by choosing Format > Document. On the Margins tab (**Figure 3.25**), enter margin settings as you would in the Formatting Palette.

■ Headers and footers are discussed later in this chapter (see "Adding Headers and Footers"). See Chapter 4, Using Templates and Wizards, for additional document-layout instructions.

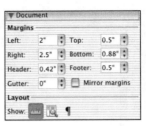

Figure 3.24 In the Document section of the Formatting Palette, you can alter the margins for selected paragraphs.

Figure 3.25 You can also set margins in the Document dialog box.

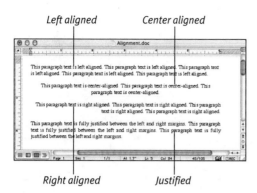

Left aligned   Center aligned

Right aligned   Justified

Figure 3.26 Word offers four paragraph-alignment styles.

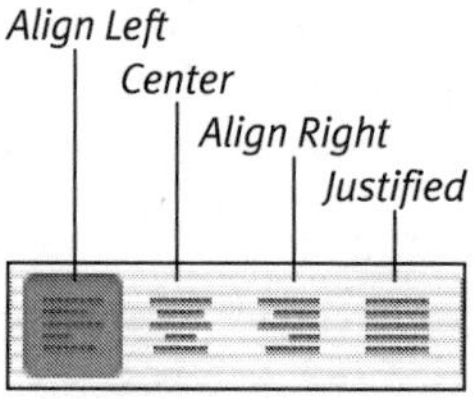

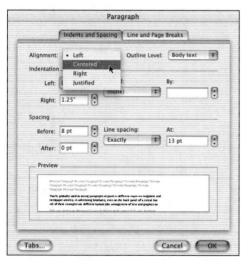

Align Left

Center

Align Right

Justified

Figure 3.27 One of the quickest ways to set the alignment for selected paragraphs is to click an icon on the Formatting toolbar.

Figure 3.28 Paragraph-alignment icons are also available on the Formatting Palette.

Figure 3.29 You can also set paragraph alignment on the Indents and Spacing tab of the Paragraph dialog box.

Aligning Paragraphs

You can align your paragraphs in various ways using Word's layout options. The following are the paragraph alignment settings offered by Word X (**Figure 3.26**):

◆ *Left* is the most common alignment setting and is the default. Text in a left-aligned paragraph is flush with the left margin and ragged on the right.

◆ *Center-aligned* paragraphs are horizontally centered between the left and right margins and are ragged on both sides. Center alignment is frequently used for titles and section heads.

◆ *Right-aligned* paragraphs are flush with the right margin and ragged on the left side.

◆ *Justified* paragraphs are aligned flush with the left and right margins; you'll often see this in a newspaper. The spacing between words is automatically adjusted as needed to maintain the flush left and right margins.

To align a paragraph:

1. Select the paragraph(s).

2. Click an alignment icon on the Formatting toolbar (**Figure 3.27**).

   or

   Expand the Alignment and Spacing section of the Formatting Palette and click an alignment icon (**Figure 3.28**).

   The selected paragraph(s) are aligned as directed.

✔ Tip

■ You can also choose Format > Paragraph to align the paragraphs. On the Indents and Spacing tab of the Paragraph dialog box, choose an option from the Alignment drop-down menu (**Figure 3.29**).

Indenting Paragraphs

There are several ways to indent paragraphs. Before setting indents, however, you must first select the paragraph(s). Selecting a paragraph for formatting is different from selecting a word. It isn't necessary to select the *entire* paragraph; it's sufficient to merely click somewhere within it.

You can manipulate the following settings to create different paragraph indents:

◆ *Left* indents the paragraph on the left side of the document.

◆ *Right* indents the paragraph on the right side of the document.

◆ *First line* indents only the first line of the paragraph.

◆ *Hanging* indents the entire paragraph except for the first line.

To indent paragraphs using the Formatting Palette:

1. Select the paragraph(s).

2. In the Formatting Palette, expand the Alignment and Spacing section.

3. In the Indentation subsection, specify the Left, Right, and/or First indents (**Figure 3.30**).

To indent paragraphs using the Paragraph dialog box:

1. Select the paragraph(s).

2. Choose Format > Paragraph or press Option ⌘ M.

   The Paragraph dialog box opens (**Figure 3.31**).

3. On the Indents and Spacing tab in the Indentation section, change the values for Left and Right.

   The numbers correspond to the ruler that appears above the document window.

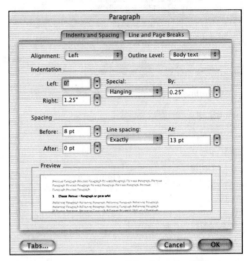

Figure 3.30 You can specify a left, right, or first-line indent in the Formatting Palette.

Figure 3.31 For greater precision in setting indents, use the options on the Indents and Spacing tab of the Paragraphs dialog box.

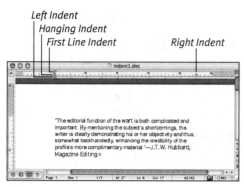

Figure 3.32 Align the main three indent markers to create a block (useful for quotations).

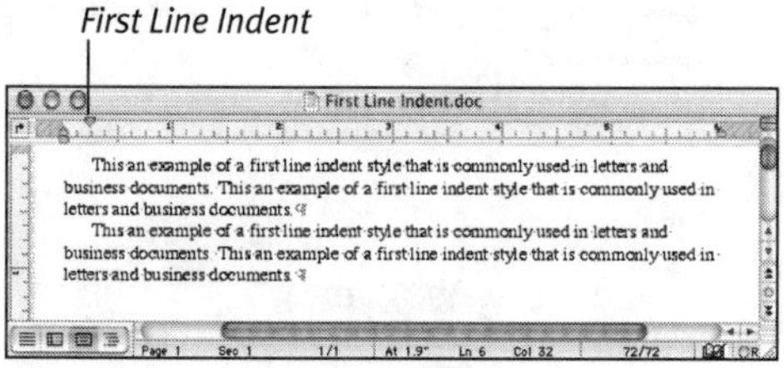

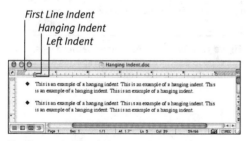

Figure 3.33 You can move the First Line Indent marker slightly to the right to create a paragraph style that is commonly used in business and education.

Figure 3.34 Hanging indents are frequently used to format items in bulleted and numbered lists.

4. *Optional:* To set a first-line or hanging indent, choose an option from the Special pop-up menu (First line or Hanging) and then enter a value in the By text box.

5. Click OK to apply the new settings to the selected paragraph(s).

To indent a paragraph using the ruler:

◆ To create a uniform or flush indent, move the First Line Indent marker so it is directly above the Hanging Indent and Left Indent markers (**Figure 3.32**). Then click and drag the square base of the Left Indent marker. All three markers will move together.

◆ To set a first-line indent, move the First Line Indent marker (**Figure 3.33**). Note that it moves independently of the other indent markers.

◆ To set a hanging indent, move the First Line Indent marker to the left of the Left Indent marker and move the Hanging Indent marker to the position where the indent will begin.

◆ To set the indent on the right side of the paragraph, move the Right Indent marker.

✔ Tips

■ Click the Decrease Indent or Increase Indent buttons on the Formatting toolbar or the same buttons on the Formatting Palette to decrease or increase the left indent.

■ The Paragraph dialog box and the Formatting Palette enable you to set precise indents.

■ When entering text for the first line of a paragraph that's formatted with a hanging indent, enter the bullet character or the number, press ⟨Tab⟩, and then type the paragraph text. If the paragraph has multiple lines, all lines after the first one will automatically align to the Hanging Indent marker (**Figure 3.34**).

INDENTING PARAGRAPHS

Setting Line Spacing

One frequently used paragraph-formatting option is *line spacing*. This option is especially useful if you're creating a document in which you have a page or space restriction, or when a document must follow specific spacing requirements set by an editor or teacher. The most common line-spacing settings are single, 1.5, and double. You can also space your paragraphs by an exact value.

Additional options are available in the Paragraph dialog box. The At least option is designed to accommodate large font sizes and graphics; it sets line spacing to the minimum amount necessary to prevent clipping the tops of text. The Exactly option generates a fixed line spacing of a specific amount. Multiple enables you to increase or decrease line spacing by a percentage. A setting of 1.2, for example, would increase line spacing by 20 percent.

To change line spacing for a paragraph:

1. Select the paragraph or paragraphs for which you want to set line spacing.

2. In the Formatting Palette, expand the Alignment and Spacing section, and then click one of the Line spacing icons (**Figure 3.35**).

   or

   Choose Format > Paragraph. The Paragraph dialog box appears. On the Indents and Spacing tab, choose a line-spacing option from the Line spacing pop-up menu (**Figure 3.36**) and click OK.

✔ Tip

■ Line spacing is a paragraph-formatting option, not a document-formatting one. When you set line spacing, it is applied only to the currently selected paragraphs. To apply the same line spacing to an entire document, choose Edit > Select All (or press ⌘A) prior to setting the line spacing.

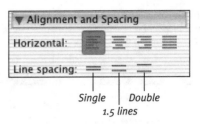

Figure 3.35 To set the line spacing for selected paragraphs, click one of these icons on the Formatting Palette.

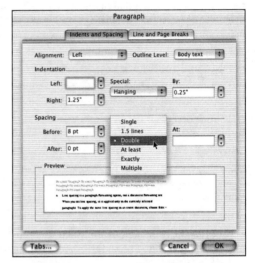

Figure 3.36 For more precise line-spacing needs, you can choose a setting from the Line spacing pop-up menu in the Paragraph dialog box.

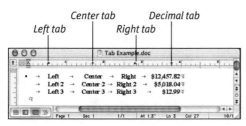

Figure 3.37 By judiciously choosing and setting tab stops, you can create impressive, perfectly aligned tables.

Figure 3.38 To set tab stops precisely or choose a leader character, use the Tabs dialog box.

Table 3.4

Tab-Alignment Markers	
⌐	Left tab
⊥	Center tab
⌐	Right tab
⊥	Decimal tab
⌐	Bar tab

Setting Tabs

Tabs can make life easier when you're formatting certain types of documents. For example, by formatting paragraphs with tabs, you can create tables of text or numbers in which the entries are aligned on their left or right edges.

To set tabs:

1. Select the paragraph(s) for which you want to add tab stops.

2. Click the tab-alignment button to the left of the ruler to select the type of tab you'd like to set. **Table 3.4** shows the types of tab-alignment markers.

3. Click the ruler to place the tab stop at the desired location (**Figure 3.37**).

   You will see the tab marker on the ruler. If the placement is off, you can click and drag the marker to another spot on the ruler.

4. To add more tab stops for the currently selected paragraph(s), repeat Steps 2 and 3.

5. If the selected paragraphs don't already contain tabs, insert them as necessary. Otherwise, affected text will automatically conform to the new tab settings.

✔ Tips

- If you want more precise tab settings, choose Format > Tabs and insert your tabs using the Tabs dialog box (**Figure 3.38**). You can also select a *leader character* (such as a string of periods) that will separate the two text strings. Leaders are frequently used in a menu to separate items from prices and in a table of contents to separate chapter titles from page numbers.

- You can remove any tab stop by dragging it off the ruler. To remove all manually placed tab stops for selected paragraphs, click Clear All in the Tabs dialog box.

- You can change the space between default tabs in the Tabs dialog box.

Creating Bulleted or Numbered Lists

Bullets help break up the text into readable chunks, making it simpler for the reader to scan through the information in a document. Word also lets you easily generate numbered lists, such as points in a contract. The procedures for adding bullets and numbers are very similar.

To create bulleted or numbered lists:

◆ To use the default bullet or numbering style for selected paragraphs, click the Bullets or Numbering icon at the bottom of the Font section of the Formatting Palette (**Figure 3.39**) or on the Formatting toolbar (**Figure 3.40**).

   or

   Choose Format > Bullets and Numbering. On the Bulleted or Numbered tab of the Bullets and Numbering dialog box (**Figure 3.41**), choose a bullet or numbering style and click OK.

   The paragraph series becomes a bulleted or numbered list (**Figure 3.42**).

✔ Tips

■ You can apply bullets and numbering to paragraphs either before or after you've typed the text.

■ You can remove the bullets or numbers by selecting the paragraphs and clicking the Bullets or Numbering icon again.

■ To use a graphic as a bullet (as is often done on Web pages), click the Picture button on the Bulleted tab and select a bullet image from the ones stored on your hard disk.

■ To choose a special bullet character or to set the bullet's distance from the text and other options, click Customize in the Bullets and Numbering dialog box.

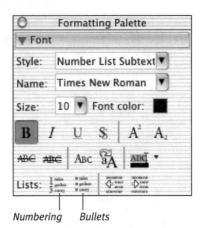

Numbering   *Bullets*

Figure 3.39 To create a simple bulleted or numbered list, click an icon on the Formatting Palette.

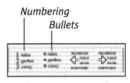

Numbering
  Bullets

Figure 3.40 You can also create a bulleted or numbered list from the Formatting toolbar.

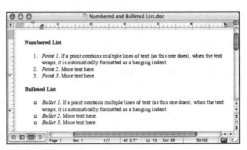

Figure 3.41 The Bullets and Numbering dialog box provides more styles and formatting options for bulleted and numbered lists.

Figure 3.42 Here are some examples of numbered and bulleted lists.

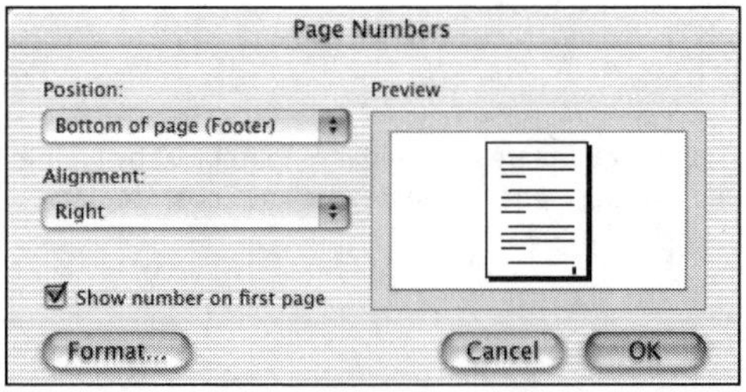

Figure 3.43 In the Page Numbers dialog box, choose where you want the page numbers, how they'll be aligned, and whether they should appear on the first page.

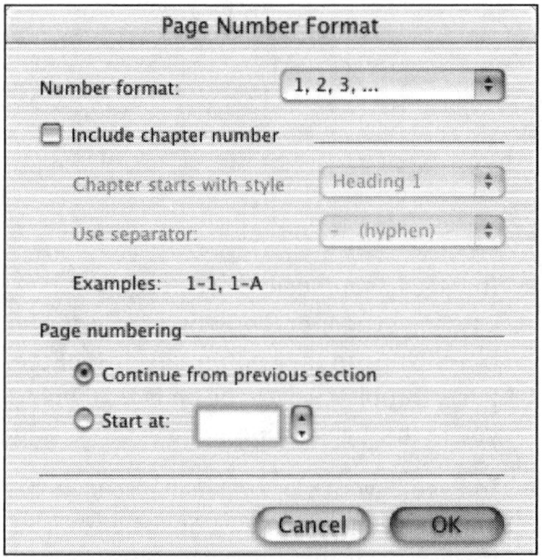

Figure 3.44 The Page Number Format dialog box provides additional options, such as whether to use chapter-relative page numbering.

Numbering Pages

Page numbers improve a document's organization and make it simpler for readers to keep their place.

To number a document's pages:

1. Choose Insert > Page Numbers.

   The Page Numbers dialog box appears (**Figure 3.43**).

2. Specify the position of the page number and its alignment.

   ◆ You can position the numbers on the top or bottom of the page (Position) and align them right, left, or center (Alignment).

   ◆ The Inside and Outside alignment choices apply if you have mirrored pages, as when you're creating a book. See Chapter 4 for more page-layout information.

3. If you want the numbering to start on the first page, click the Show number on first page check box; otherwise, numbering will begin on the second page.

4. To change the page-number format, click the Format button. The Page Number Format dialog box appears (**Figure 3.44**). You can choose a numbering style from the Number format pull-down menu. You can also choose to continue page numbering from a previous section or designate a new starting number. To use chapter-relative numbering (as in 13-1, 13-2, and so on), click the Include chapter number check box, and then choose a style and separator from the two drop-down menus.

✔ Tip

■ Page numbers are added to the document's header or footer. You can change the page number's font or formatting by selecting it on any page and then applying the desired changes to it. You can also precede the number with the word *Page*, if you wish.

Adding Headers and Footers

Headers and footers are used to display the same reference information on every page of a document at the top or bottom, respectively. You can include any information you want, such as your name, the title of the document, the date, page numbers, or a section title.

To insert headers and footers:

1. Choose View > Header and Footer.

   Word switches to Page Layout view, and the Header and Footer toolbar appears, as shown in **Figure 3.45**, at the bottom of this page. (Different views are discussed in Chapter 4.)

2. To edit the footer rather than the header, click the Switch Between Header and Footer icon on the Header and Footer toolbar.

3. A header or footer can contain any combination of text, graphics, and special features (such as page numbers and the date and time). Enter the desired text and insert any special items (**Figure 3.46**).

   To center an element, press ⸤Tab⸥ once. To right-align an element, press ⸤Tab⸥ twice.

4. Click the Close button on the Header and Footer toolbar when you're done editing.

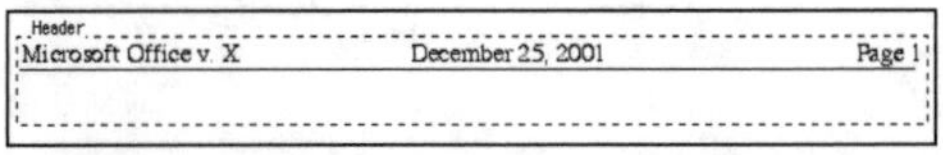

Figure 3.46 Create the header or footer text by typing and clicking icons on the Header and Footer toolbar.

✔ Tips

- In Page Layout view, you can edit an existing header or footer by simply double-clicking in the appropriate area of the page. Double-click in the body text when you're through editing.

- In Page Layout view, you can also switch between editing the header and editing the footer by clicking in the desired area.

- You can create additional room for a header or footer by adjusting the margins. See "Setting Margins," earlier in this chapter.

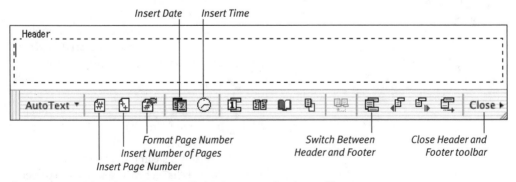

Figure 3.45 Use the Header and Footer toolbar to format page headers and footers.

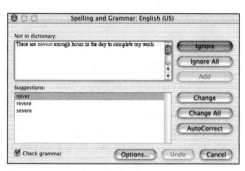

Figure 3.47 Word provides suggestions for the spelling and grammar issue it finds.

Checking Your Work

It's a good idea to check your work before letting anyone else see it. Word X provides tools you can use to check your spelling and grammar, to find synonyms when you're stuck for a word, and to look up word definitions.

To check spelling and grammar:

1. Choose Tools > Spelling and Grammar or press (Option)(⌘)(L).

   The Spelling and Grammar dialog box appears (**Figure 3.47**).

   The spelling checker searches the document for possible misspellings, and the grammar checker identifies questionable grammar.

2. As it examines the document, Word stops at each questionable word or phrase. For each instance, do one of the following:

   ◆ To accept one of the entries in the Suggestions list, highlight the suggestion and click Change.

   ◆ You can manually edit the text in the upper text box. Click Change to accept the edits or Undo Edit to revert to the original text.

   ◆ To leave the word or phrase as is and continue the spelling check, click Ignore. To ignore all instances of the word or phrase in the current document, click Ignore All.

   ◆ To add the current spelling of a flagged word to your user dictionary and simultaneously accept the new spelling as correct, click Add. (Adding a word will prevent Word from identifying it as a misspelling in all of your other documents.)

3. An alert box appears when the spelling and grammar checks are done. Click OK.

(continues on next page)

To use the Thesaurus:

1. Highlight the word you want to look up.

2. Choose Tools > Thesaurus.

   The Thesaurus dialog box appears (**Figure 3.48**) and presents a list of possible synonyms for the highlighted word.

3. Click Replace to replace your word with the highlighted synonym, or click Cancel to retain the original word.

To look up a word in the dictionary:

1. Highlight the word in your document and choose Tools > Dictionary (or Control-click the word and choose Define from the pop-up menu that appears).

   A dictionary window appears and presents a definition for the selected word (**Figure 3.49**).

2. Examine the spelling, pronunciation, and definition. Click the window's close button when you're finished.

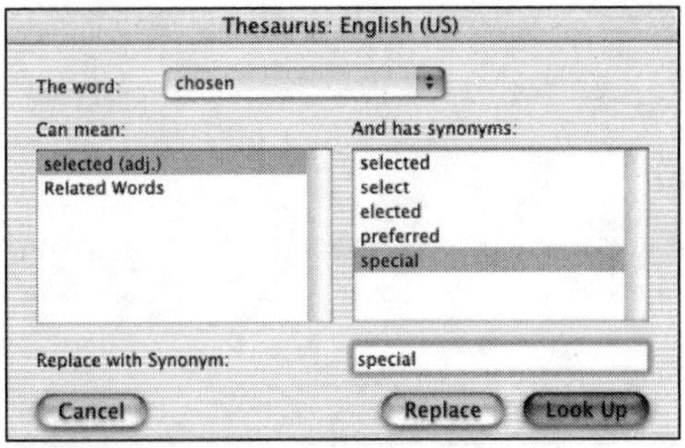

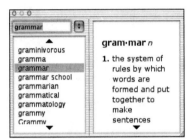

Figure 3.48 The Thesaurus lists synonyms for the word currently selected in your document. Click the Look Up button to view synonyms for any selected synonym.

Figure 3.49 You can use the dictionary to check the pronunciation and definition of any word in your document.

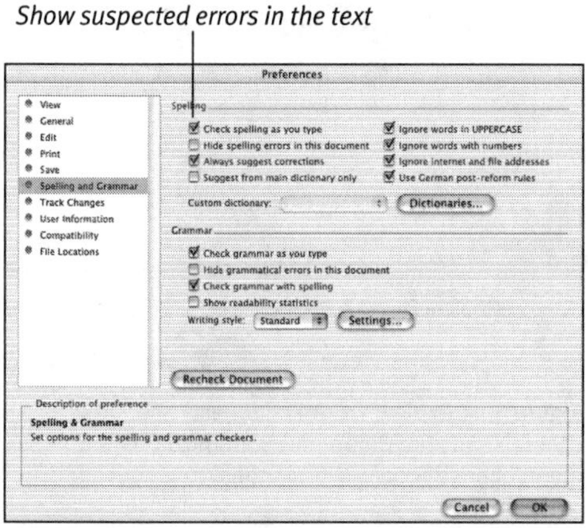

Show suspected errors in the text

Figure 3.50 If you want Office to automatically mark misspelled words as you type, make sure this Spelling Preferences item is checked.

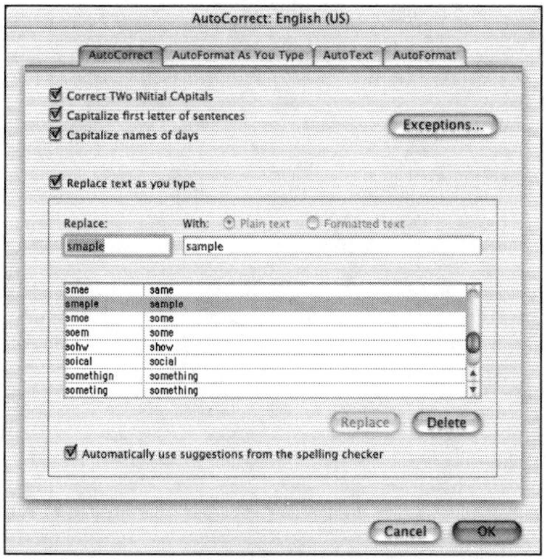

Figure 3.51 In the AutoCorrect dialog box, enter a word you tend to type incorrectly in the Replace text box and its correct spelling in the With text box.

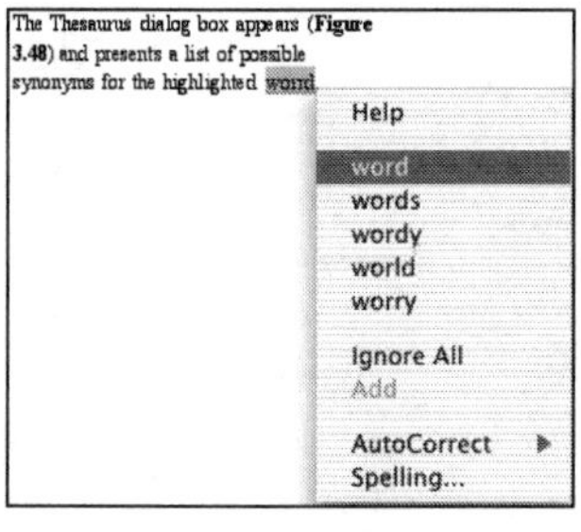

Figure 3.52 You can Control-click any word in your document to correct a spelling error or choose from a list of suggested synonyms.

✔ Tips

■ You can restrict a spelling and grammar check to selected text by selecting the text prior to choosing the Spelling and Grammar command.

■ To turn off the grammar checker, remove the checkmark from the Check grammar check box in the Spelling and Grammar dialog box. Until the checkmark is restored, Word will watch only for spelling errors.

■ Unless you've changed Spelling and Grammar's Preferences (**Figure 3.50**), Word automatically checks your spelling as you type. Suspect words are marked with squiggly red underlining.

■ As you type, Word automatically corrects common misspellings with a tool called AutoCorrect. You can add your own words to the AutoCorrect list by choosing Tools > AutoCorrect. In the AutoCorrect dialog box, enter the misspelling in the Replace box and the correctly spelled word in the With box (**Figure 3.51**).

■ You can correct misspelled words and request synonyms without displaying a dialog box. Just Control-click the word in your document and select the correct spelling or synonym from the presented suggestions (**Figure 3.52**).

Calculating the Word Count

Sometimes you'll need to know the exact word count or other general statistics about your document. For example, the word count is important when you're writing to a particular length, as is often necessary for magazine articles and homework assignments. Word can calculate this information for you.

To calculate the word count:

◆ Choose Tools > Word Count.

The Word Count dialog box appears with information about your document, including the page count and the number of words, lines, and paragraphs in your document (**Figure 3.53**).

or

Check the bottom-right corner of the document window. You'll see a pair of numbers, such as 4930/6232 (**Figure 3.54**). The first number is the word in which the insertion point is currently located (in this case, word 4,930—counting from the beginning of the document). The second number is the total number of words in the document.

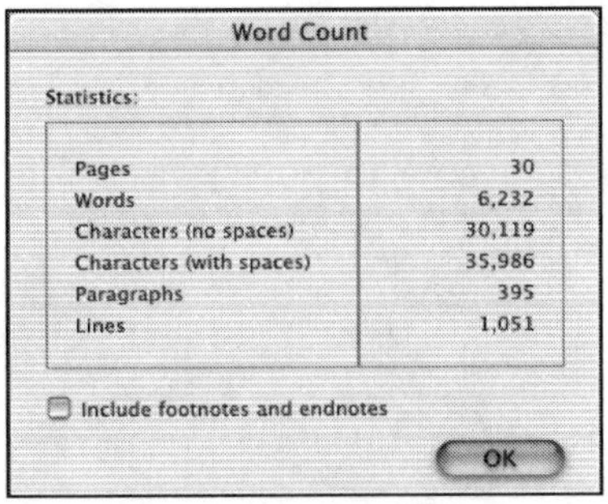

Figure 3.53 To view a word count and other useful statistics about your document, choose Tools > Word Count.

Figure 3.54 You can also see the word count by examining the bottom-right corner of any Word document.

USING TEMPLATES AND WIZARDS

If you're creating a new document, it's often best to work on the content first and worry about *formatting* (making it look good) later.

Office X offers a diverse collection of templates and wizards that allow you to enter content into preformatted documents. By using Word templates and wizards, you can easily create high-quality documents without having to become a design professional.

The procedures in this chapter assume that you already have Word launched on your computer.

✔ Tip

■ When creating a document from a template, you're always working with a *copy* of the template—not the original. To remind you, Word names the copy *Document* rather than using the template's actual name. As long as you save the copy with a new name or in a different location, any changes you make to the copy won't affect the template.

Using Templates

A *template* is a partially formed document that contains text, styles, and formatting. You can start a document with a template or wizard, and modify the formatting later, if you like. Word provides templates for letters, reports, press releases, brochures, and much more.

To use a template:

1. If the Project Gallery isn't already open, choose File > Project Gallery (Shift⌘P).

   The Project Gallery appears (**Figure 4.1**).

2. In the Category list on the left, click to select the type of document you wish to create. (To expand a category, click the triangle beside it.)

   Available choices appear in the pane on the right (**Figure 4.2**).

3. Click a choice to select it, and click OK.

   A copy of the template opens (**Figure 4.3**).

4. Fill in the content, and then save the document.

✔ Tip

■ In Word X, you can also base a new document on any of your 27 most recently used Office documents—effectively treating them as templates. In the Project Gallery's Category list, select "Based on Recent," select one of your recent documents from the ones displayed on the right, and click OK. A copy of the document opens, ready for you to edit.

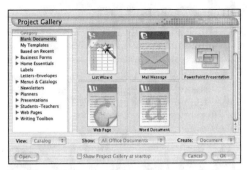

Figure 4.1 The Project Gallery offers a variety of templates.

Categories   Templates

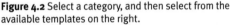
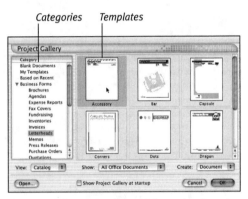

Figure 4.2 Select a category, and then select from the available templates on the right.

Figure 4.3 The template is ready for you to begin entering text.

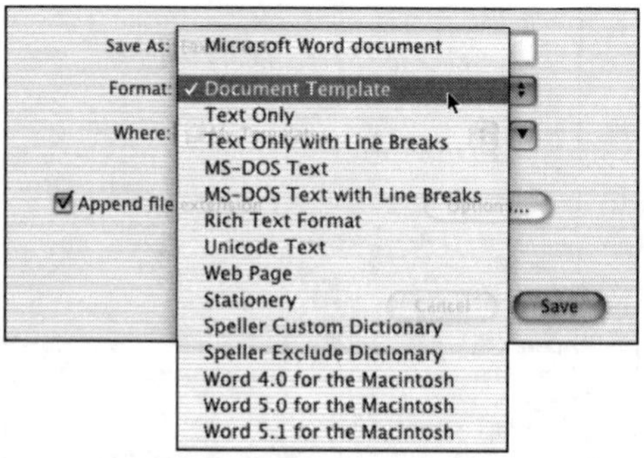

Figure 4.4 Select the Document Template format in the Save dialog box.

Saving a Document as a Template

Templates contain entire document designs, even including text in some instances. When you start a new document, you can optionally choose from among the many templates that come with Word. If none of them suit your needs, you can modify an existing template or save your own document design as a new template, and then use it to create new documents.

To save a document as a template:

1. Create a document with the desired formatting. Delete text that you don't want saved as part of the template, while retaining any text you'll want to use in new documents.

   In a fax-form template, for example, you might only leave your contact information while stripping out the message text.

2. Choose File > Save As.

3. From the Format drop-down menu on the dialog box that appears, choose Document Template (**Figure 4.4**).

4. Type a name for the template in the Save As text box.

   (continues on next page)

5. From the Where drop-down list, choose a location in which to save the template.

   Normally, you can accept the default folder (My Templates) for personal templates. To choose a different folder, click the triangle to the right of the Where drop-down list (**Figure 4.5**).

6. Click the Save button.

✔ Tip

■ AutoText entries, macros, and custom toolbars are saved in the template, so you may want to create AutoText entries and modify the toolbars before saving the document as a template. See "Automatically Entering Text" in Chapter 5 for more information.

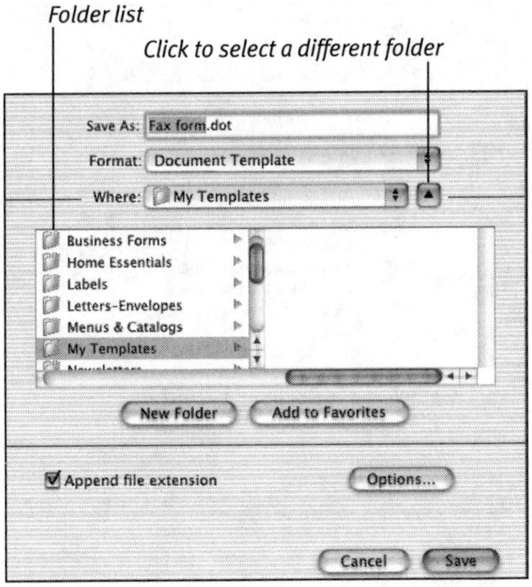

Folder list

Click to select a different folder

Figure 4.5 When you expand the sheet by clicking the triangle to the right of the Where drop-down list, you can specify a different folder in which to store the template.

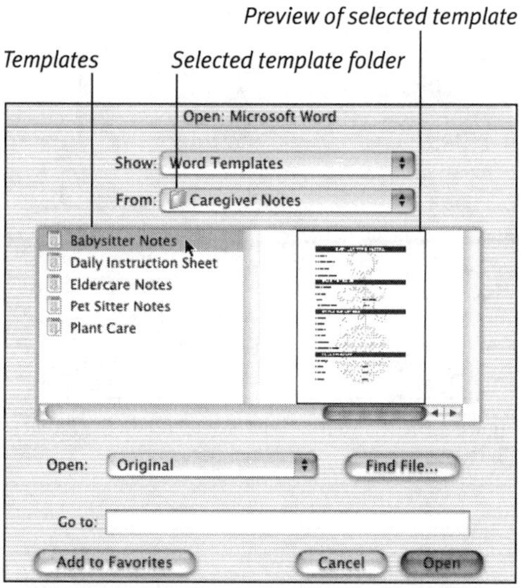

Templates

Selected template folder

Preview of selected template

Figure 4.6 Select the template you want to modify.

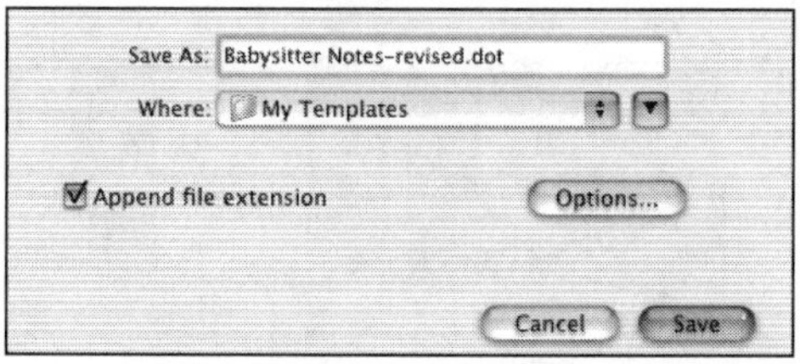

Figure 4.7 To avoid overwriting the original template, save the modified version in a different folder.

Modifying an Existing Template

You can modify any of the templates Word offers. In this way, you can create templates that better suit your purposes.

To modify a template:

1. Choose File > Open ($\mathbb{H}$$\boxed{O}$).

   The Open: Microsoft Word dialog box appears (**Figure 4.6**).

2. Choose Word Templates from the Show drop-down menu.

3. Navigate to the Templates folder within the Microsoft Office X folder. Continue opening folders until you see the template you want to change.

4. Select the template and click Open.

5. Make any necessary editing and formatting changes to the template.

6. To replace the original template with the modified one, choose File > Save ($\mathbb{H}$$\boxed{S}$).

   or

   To save the modified template without overwriting the original template, choose File > Save As, edit the template's name (if desired), and save it in the My Templates folder or some other folder of your choosing (**Figure 4.7**).

Using Wizards

Wizards walk you through the process of creating a specific type of document and provide sample text you can use. Word has wizards for creating letters, brochures, menus, catalogs, and labels.

To use a wizard:

1. If the Project Gallery window isn't open, choose File > Project Gallery (⎀Shift⎀⌘⎀P⎀).

2. Select a category from the list on the left.

3. In the pane on the right, click the wizard for the type of document you want to create, and then click OK (**Figure 4.8**). The wizard appears (**Figure 4.9**).

4. Follow the steps presented to build your document.

   Each step prompts you for more detail to help you create a customized document.

5. To complete the wizard, click Finish, Save & Exit, OK, or whatever other button is presented.

   The document now includes the information you entered and the options you selected.

6. Make any necessary changes to the document and save the file.

✔ Tips

- Many wizards—but not all—include *Wizard* as part of the name.

- The Office Assistant provides helpful hints for some wizards (**Figure 4.10**).

- You can move from one section of a multipage wizard to another by clicking Next>, <Back, or a specific tab.

Selected wizard

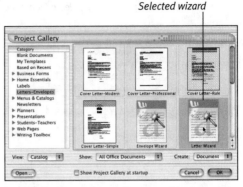

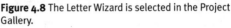

Figure 4.8 The Letter Wizard is selected in the Project Gallery.

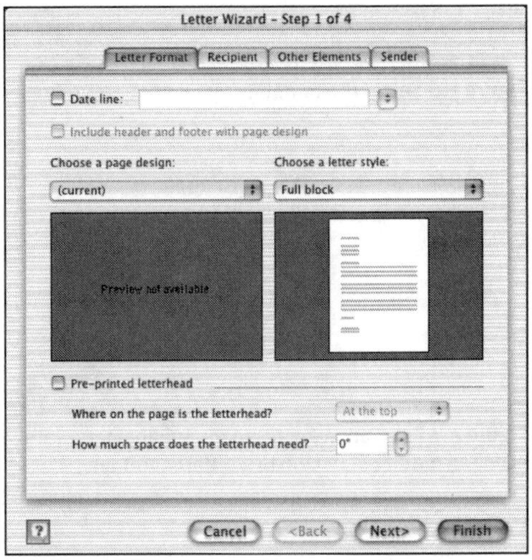

Figure 4.9 Enter any text requested by the wizard and set options as desired.

Letter Format
The options on this panel determine the general appearance and style of your letter.

HINT: Click the arrow next to each item for a list of choices.

Figure 4.10 If you're confused, the Office Assistant may have some useful advice.

DOCUMENT AND TEXT FORMATTING

Your documents can benefit from Word's many formatting options.

Document formatting gives you the freedom to create a document with the size, arrangement, and orientation that suits your needs. For example, you can alter the page orientation, set margins, or specify a special paper size on which to print an envelope or a memo. You can add columns to create a newsletter, divide a document into sections (as appropriate for a manual or a report), or force pages and columns to break exactly where you want. As you choose page-formatting settings, Word automatically adjusts the text to fit the new orientation, margins, paper size, columns, and so on.

To make it simpler to format your text consistently, you can define and apply paragraph and character styles. *Paragraph styles* define the appearance of a paragraph (indents, line spacing, and so on), as well as the default font. *Character styles* consist of font, size, and style choices you can apply to selected words within paragraphs.

In addition to discussing document, paragraph, and character formatting, this chapter also presents information about using Word's AutoText and "click and type" features.

Changing Views

Changing the layout of a document often requires that you view the document in different ways. You can select from Normal, Online Layout, Page Layout (**Figure 5.1**), Outline, and Master Document views. **Table 5.1** explains the function of each view.

To change views:

◆ Click the Normal, Online Layout, Page Layout, or Outline icon in the bottom-left corner of the document window (**Figure 5.2**).

or

Choose a view from the View menu (**Figure 5.3**).

✔ Tips

■ Master Document view is only accessible from the View menu.

■ To use Word's "click and type" (discussed later in this chapter), you must switch to Page Layout or Online Layout.

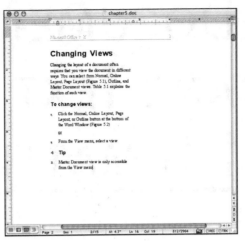

Figure 5.1 This document is shown in Page Layout view.

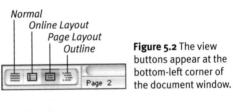

Normal
Online Layout
Page Layout
Outline

Figure 5.2 The view buttons appear at the bottom-left corner of the document window.

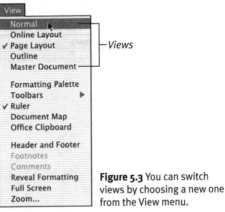

Figure 5.3 You can switch views by choosing a new one from the View menu.

Table 5.1

Views	
Normal	Shows text formatting in a simplified page layout that lends itself well to most standard writing tasks.
Outline	Shows the document's structure and allows you to rearrange text by headings.
Page Layout	Shows the document as it will look when printed, including the page borders, margins, headers and footers, columns, and frames that contain images.
Online Layout	Shows the document as it would appear in a Web browser.
Master Document	Enables you to form a compound document composed of individual documents.

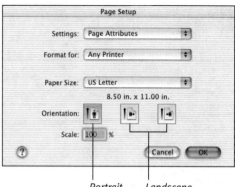

Portrait   *Landscape*

Figure 5.4 Specify a paper size and orientation in the Page Setup dialog box.

Figure 5.5 Choose a paper size or type from the Paper Size drop-down menu.

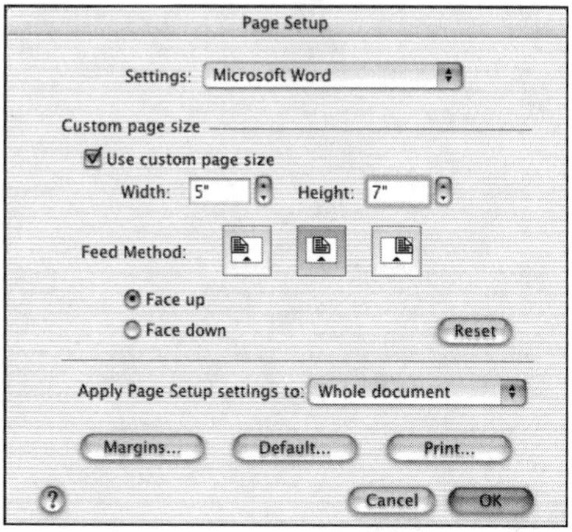

Figure 5.6 To print on an unsupported paper size, you can create a custom page size.

Changing the Paper Size and Orientation

Word's default page setting is 8½-by-11-inch portrait (vertical orientation). The choices you make for paper size and orientation are for the current document only. New documents revert to the default settings. The settings are automatically saved with each document.

To change paper size or orientation:

1. Choose File > Page Setup.

   The Page Setup dialog box appears (**Figure 5.4**).

2. To specify a standard paper size, choose Page Attributes from the Settings drop-down menu and then choose a size from the Paper Size drop-down menu (**Figure 5.5**).

   or

   To specify a nonstandard paper size, choose Microsoft Word from the Settings drop-down menu, click the Use custom page size check box, and enter the paper dimensions in the Width and Height boxes (**Figure 5.6**).

3. To set the page orientation, choose Page Attributes from the Settings drop-down menu. Click the portrait icon for a standard vertical printout or either of the landscape icons for a horizontal printout.

4. Click OK to close the dialog box.

✔ Tip

■ You can mix portrait and landscape pages in a document. Select text from the pages you want to change, choose File > Page Setup, click an orientation icon, choose Microsoft Word from the Settings drop-down menu, and choose Selected Text from the Apply Page Setup settings to drop-down menu.

Creating Multiple Sections

A document can contain multiple sections, each with different page-setup attributes: different margins, page numbering, and headers and footers. For example, an annual report might contain different sections for the title page, introduction, body, and financial information.

A new document contains only one section until you insert a section break. Then you can format the new section independently. See **Table 5.2** for Word's section-break options.

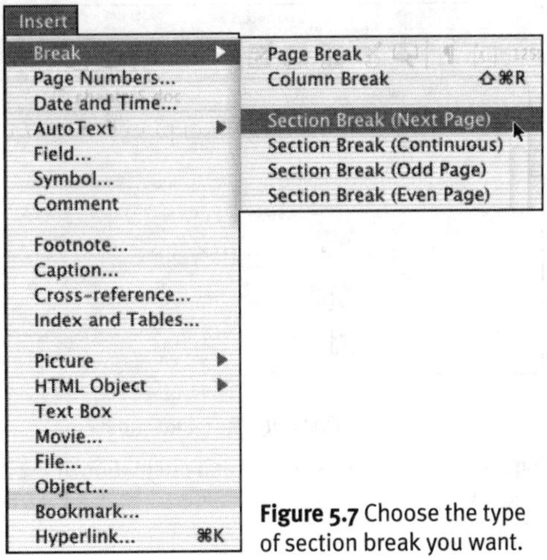

To create multiple sections:

1. Place the insertion point where you want the new section to begin.

2. Choose Insert > Break, then select one of the section-break choices from the submenu (**Figure 5.7**).

   Word inserts a double line marked with the text "Section Break," followed by the specific type of break (**Figure 5.8**).

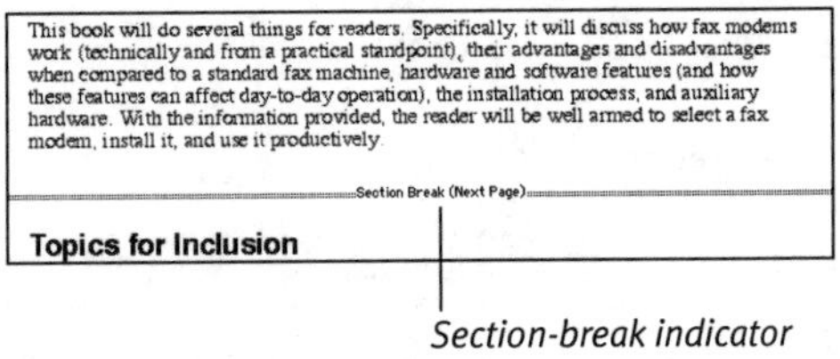

Figure 5.7 Choose the type of section break you want.

Section-break indicator

Figure 5.8 The section break appears at the insertion point.

Table 5.2

Section Breaks	
Next Page	Starts a new section at the top of the next page.
Continuous	Starts a new section without moving the text after the section break to a new page. If the previous section has multiple columns, Word evens out the column bottoms.
Odd Page	If the section break falls on an even page, Word starts the new section on the next page. Otherwise, it leaves the next even page blank and starts the new section on the next odd page.
Even Page	If the section break falls on an odd page, Word starts the new section on the next page. Otherwise, it leaves the next odd page blank and starts the new section on the next even page.

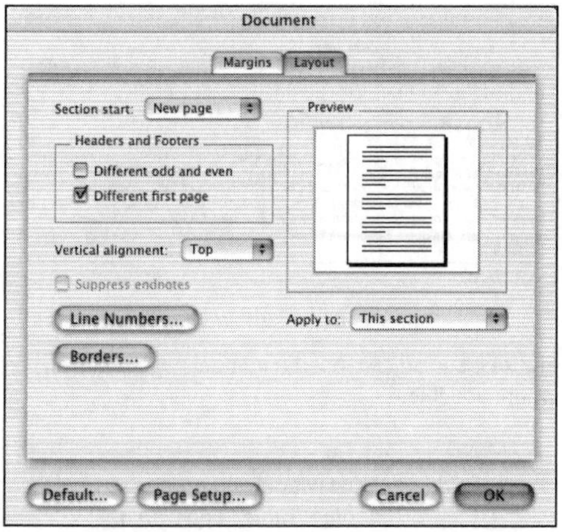

Figure 5.9 Use the Document dialog box to specify section settings.

✔ Tips

■ The "Section Break" text and double lines are only visible in Normal and Outline views.

■ To remove a section break, switch to Normal view, drag to highlight the section break, and press [Delete].

■ To format a section, select some text in the section and choose Format > Document. The Document dialog box appears (**Figure 5.9**). Specify layout and margin settings, choose This section from the Apply To drop-down menu, and click OK.

■ To bring up the Document dialog box, you can also double-click the section-break marker that ends the section you want to format.

Inserting Page Breaks

As you work in Normal view, Word enters an *automatic page break* (a dotted line across the page) whenever you fill a page. If you want to create a page break before you've filled the page, you can enter a manual page break (**Figure 5.10**).

To insert a page break:

1. Position the insertion point at the beginning of the line where you want the next page to start.

2. Choose Insert > Break > Page Break.

✔ Tips

- To delete a manual page break, select the break and press ⌐Delete⌐.

- You cannot delete or move an automatic page break. You can, however, insert a manual page break above it.

- Widow/Orphan control (set in the Paragraph dialog box shown in **Figure 5.11**) ensures that Word does not leave a single line of text at the page top or bottom when it breaks a page. Select the errant paragraph, choose Format > Paragraph, switch to the Line and Page Breaks tab, enter a checkmark in the Widow/Orphan control check box, and then click OK. Word will repaginate as necessary to eliminate the widow or orphan text.

- By switching to Page Layout view (View > Page Layout) or Print Preview mode (File > Print Preview), you can see how the text falls on pages with the current page breaks. In Page Layout view, you can enter manual page breaks.

- To keep a heading from appearing at the bottom of one page and the text that follows it at the top of the next page, select the heading, choose Format > Paragraph, switch to the Lines and Page Breaks tab, and check Keep with next (Figure 5.11).

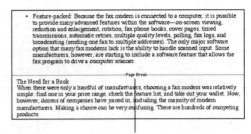

Manual page break

Figure 5.10 You can insert a manual page break anywhere you like.

Enable/disable widow and orphan control
Enable/disable keep with next

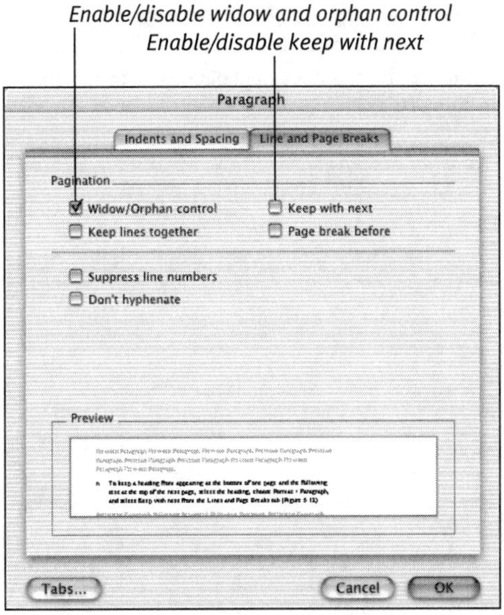

Figure 5.11 You can determine whether Word will handle or ignore widows and orphans (short lines or single words that appear in an awkward place on the page).

Enter the number of columns you want...   *...or choose one of the presets*

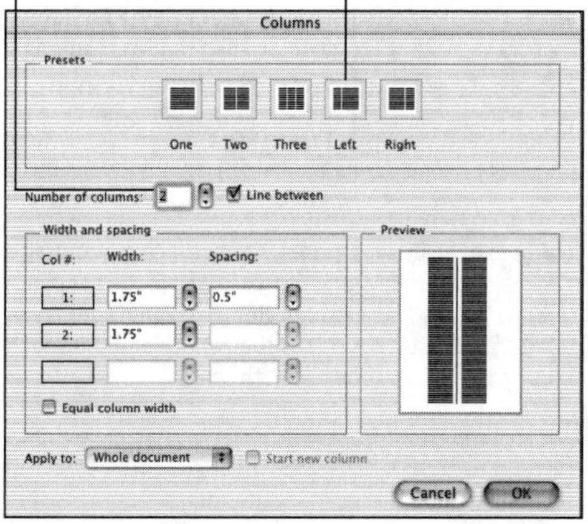

Figure 5.12 In addition to specifying the number of columns, you can set column and gutter widths in the Columns dialog box.

Using Multiple Columns

A new Word document normally starts with one large column. However, if you want to, say, create a newsletter or break up your text with pictures, you can add additional columns.

To set up multiple columns:

1. Choose Format > Columns.

   The Columns dialog box appears (**Figure 5.12**).

2. In the Columns dialog box, click one of the Presets, or enter a number in the Number of columns text box.

3. *Optional:* To display a vertical line between the columns, check the Line between check box.

4. In the Width and spacing section of the dialog box, for each column specify the width and space between. (To make all columns the same width, check the Equal column width check box.)

5. Choose an option from the Apply to drop-down menu.

   Depending on how the document is formatted, you can apply the column settings to various selections—for example, the entire document, from this point to the end of the document, or just the current section.

6. Click OK.

(continues on next page)

USING MULTIPLE COLUMNS

✔ Tips

- You can also set the number of columns by clicking the Columns icon on the Standard toolbar and then dragging until you reach the desired number of columns (**Figure 5.13**).

- After you've specified multiple columns, you can still alter the number of columns or other column-related settings by returning to the Columns dialog box.

- You can manually change the column widths or spacing by clicking and dragging icons in the horizontal ruler (**Figure 5.14**).

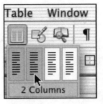

Figure 5.13 Click the Columns icon on the Standard toolbar, and drag until the desired number of columns is highlighted.

Figure 5.14 By clicking and dragging the icons above the columns, you can change column settings—such as their width and the space between them.

USING MULTIPLE COLUMNS

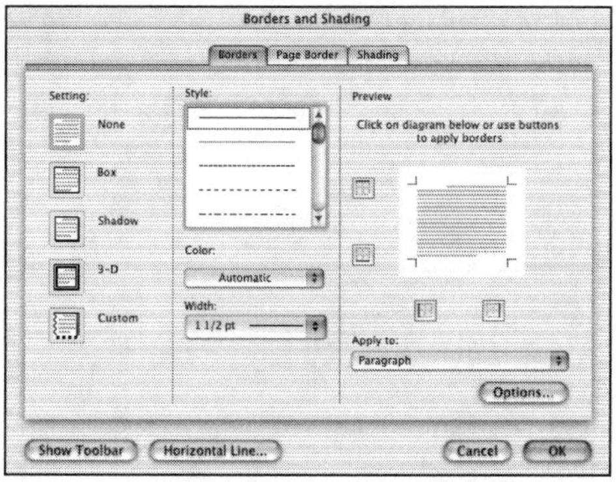

Figure 5.15 Set border and shading options in the Borders and Shading dialog box.

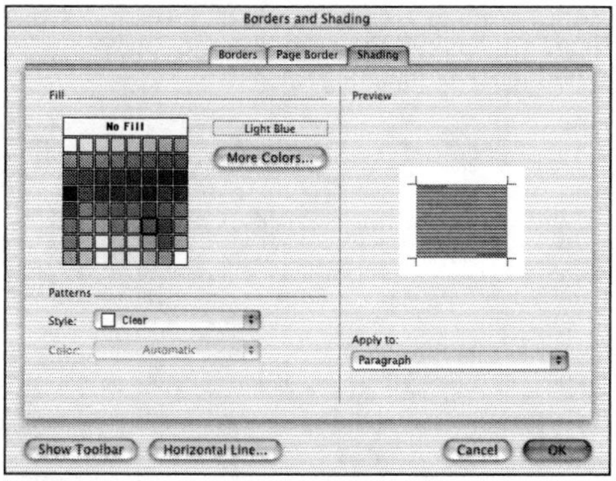

Figure 5.16 Select the shading color and choose a pattern on the Shading tab.

Applying Borders and Shading

Borders and shading add style to a document. You can set a border around selected pages, paragraphs, or text. You can do the same with shading.

To apply a border or shading:

1. Select the text to which you'd like to add a border or shading.

2. Choose Format > Borders and Shading. The Borders and Shading dialog box appears (**Figure 5.15**).

3. To add a border around selected text or selected paragraphs, click the Borders tab.

   or

   To add a border around one or more pages, click the Page Border tab.

4. Select a border type: None, Box, Shadow, 3-D, or Custom.

5. *Optional:* If you don't like the default settings, you can specify a different line style, color, and/or width for the border.

6. On the Shading tab (**Figure 5.16**), select a shading color in the Fill section and a shading pattern in the Patterns section.

7. From the Apply to drop-down menu, choose Paragraph, Text, Whole document, or This section, and then click OK.

(continues on next page)

✔ Tips

- You can also set borders and shading with the Formatting Palette (**Figure 5.17**).

- To add borders only to specific sides, switch to the Borders or Page Border tab of the Borders and Shading dialog box, and then click those sides in the Preview area. You can make each side a different line style, color, and/or width.

- You can remove any line by clicking it in the Preview area. To remove *all* borders, set Setting to None in the Borders and Shading dialog box, or set Type to No Border (click the Type icon in the Formatting Palette to see this choice).

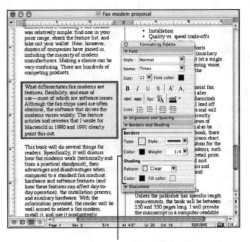

Border and shading options

Figure 5.17 You can also set border and shading options on the Formatting Palette.

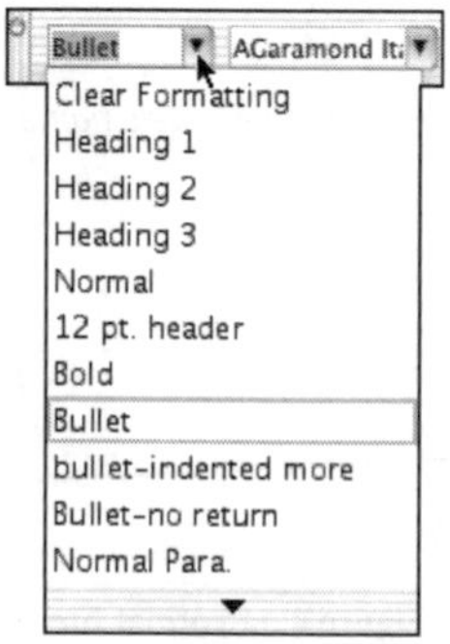

Figure 5.18 You can choose a style from the Style list on the Formatting toolbar...

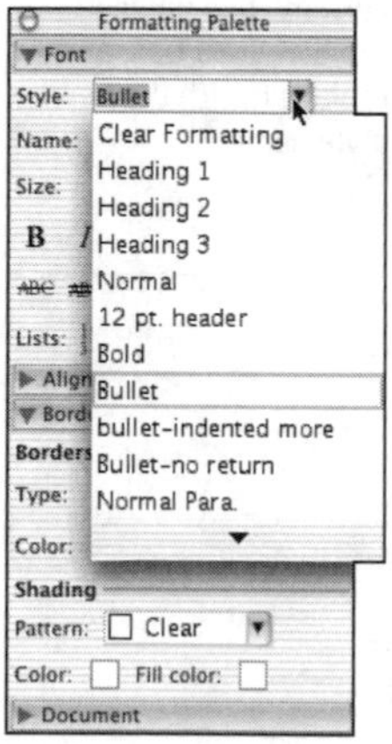

Figure 5.19 ...or from the Style list on the Formatting Palette.

Applying a Style

A *style* contains text-formatting settings. It's useful for quickly and easily applying a preset combination of formatting to characters or paragraphs. A paragraph style called Heading, for example, can contain all the formatting for one type of heading, such as its font, line spacing, and alignment. To format text as a heading, you select the heading and then choose the Heading style from the Style list.

Character styles, which can be applied to selected characters of text, contain font formatting. *Paragraph styles*, which are applied to entire paragraphs, contain both font and paragraph formatting. By default, paragraphs use the Normal style and text uses the Default Paragraph Font style.

To apply a style:

1. If neither the Formatting toolbar nor the Formatting Palette is visible, display one of them by choosing View > Toolbars > Formatting or View > Formatting Palette.

2. Select the characters or paragraphs to format.

3. On the Formatting toolbar (**Figure 5.18**) or on the Formatting Palette (**Figure 5.19**), choose a style from the Style drop-down menu.

✔ Tips

- You can make noncontiguous text selections by ⌘-clicking. Thus, to apply the same style quickly to several paragraphs, completely select the paragraphs by triple-clicking the first one, ⌘-triple-clicking the second, and so on; then select the paragraph style you wish to apply.

- To remove paragraph or character formatting quickly from selected text, choose the Clear Formatting style.

New vs. Existing Text

You can apply formats to text and paragraphs before or after you've typed them:

- ◆ When you apply a character or paragraph format to existing text, only that text is affected.

- ◆ When you apply a character format before you type, all text that follows will have the same format until you choose another character format.

- ◆ When you apply a paragraph format before you type, its style definition dictates the format of succeeding paragraphs.

Creating a Paragraph Style

It's helpful to create a paragraph style if you know you will be using the same text formatting repeatedly in the document. This section explains how to create and modify paragraph styles.

To create a paragraph style:

1. Apply font and paragraph formatting to a paragraph, and then select the paragraph.

2. In the Style list box in the Formatting toolbar or Formatting Palette, click the current style name. Then type the new style name in place of the old one and press [Enter] (**Figure 5.20**).

   This sets the selected text to the newly named style, and adds the new style to the Style list for the current document.

✔ Tip

■ You can also create a style by choosing the Format > Style command and then clicking the New button in the Style dialog box (**Figure 5.21**).

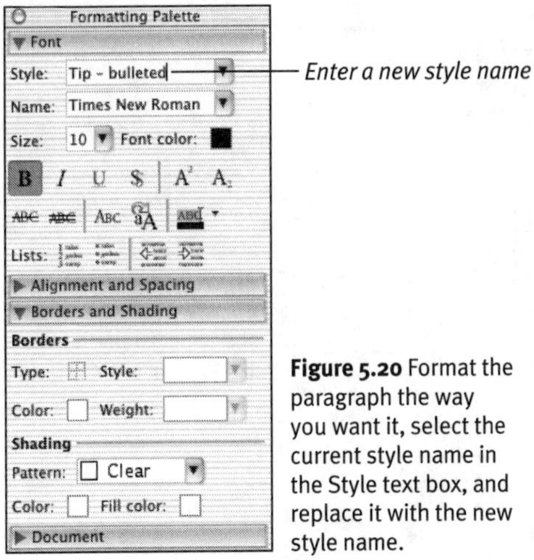

Enter a new style name

Figure 5.20 Format the paragraph the way you want it, select the current style name in the Style text box, and replace it with the new style name.

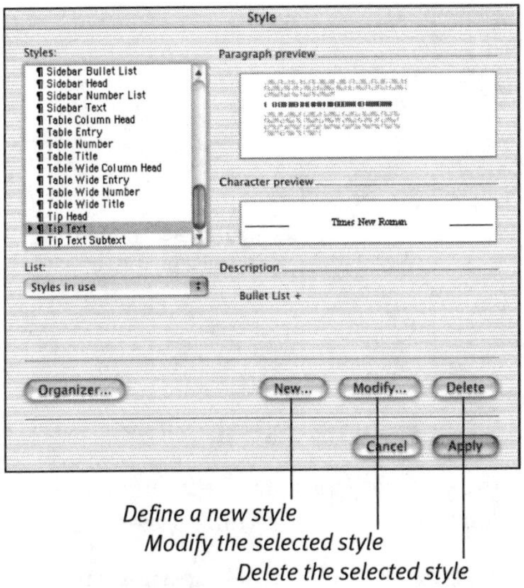

Define a new style
Modify the selected style
Delete the selected style

Figure 5.21 You can define, modify, or delete styles in the Style dialog box.

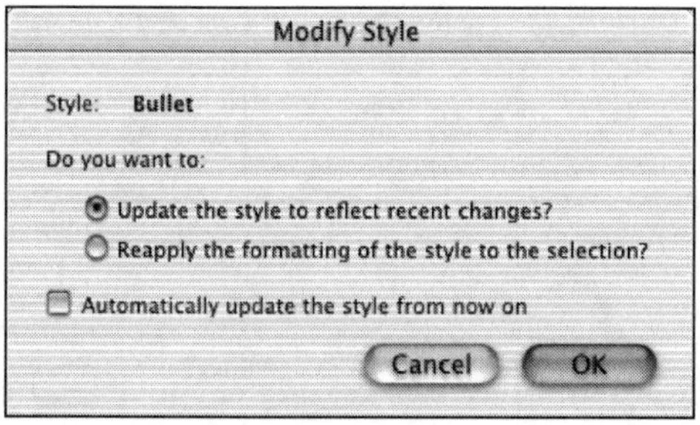

Figure 5.22 In the Modify Style dialog box, you can elect to update the style based on the currently selected text or reapply the original style to the selected text (to remove new formatting).

To modify a paragraph style:

1. Select the paragraph and apply the font- or paragraph-formatting changes.

2. Pull down the Style list and choose the previously applied style.
   The Modify Style dialog box appears (**Figure 5.22**).

3. Select the Update the style to reflect recent changes? option, and then click OK.
   Every paragraph formatted with the original style will be reformatted to match the revised style definition. Other styles based on the modified style will also change as appropriate.

✔ Tip

■ You can also modify styles in the Style dialog box (Figure 5.21).

Creating a Character Style

You can use character styles to apply consistent formatting to selected text. You can apply character styles within a paragraph that already has a paragraph style set. The style will only apply to the selected word(s) and will only add formatting, such as font, style, and size.

To create a character style:

1. Select the text for which you want to define a new style.

2. Choose Format > Style.
   The Style dialog box appears (Figure 5.21).

3. Click New to create a new style.
   The New Style dialog box appears.

4. In the Name text box, enter a name for the new style (or accept the proposed name).

5. Choose Character from the Style type drop-down menu, as shown in **Figure 5.23**.

6. Choose Font from the Format drop-down menu.
   The Font dialog box appears.

7. Specify the desired formatting (**Figure 5.24**), and then click OK to dismiss the Font dialog box.

8. Click OK to dismiss the New Style dialog box.

9. Click Apply to save the style and apply it to the selected text.

✔ Tip

■ If the selected text in Step 1 is already appropriately formatted, you may be able to skip Steps 6 and 7. By default, Word bases a new character style on the format of the selected text.

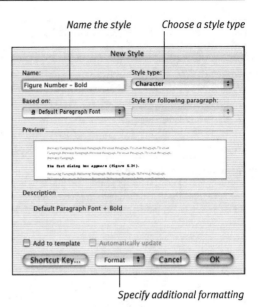

Name the style   *Choose a style type*

Specify additional formatting

Figure 5.23 Type a name for the style in the Name text box, and then choose Character from the Style type list.

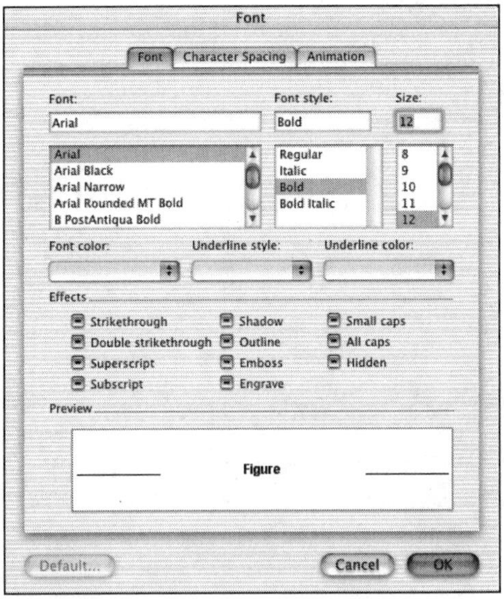

Figure 5.24 In the Font dialog box, you can choose a font, style, size, color, and effects (such as underlining or small caps).

Enable or disable click and type

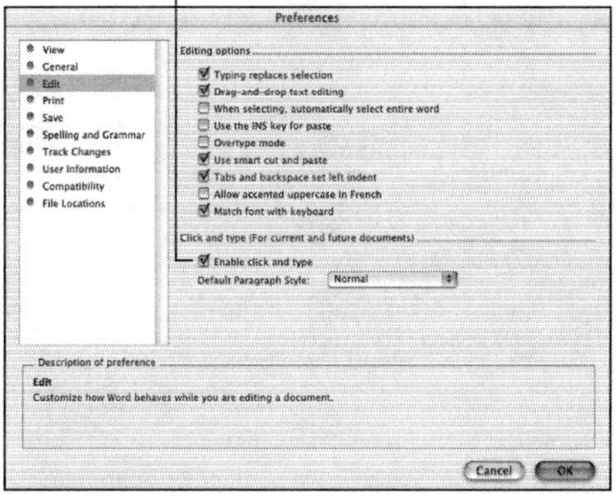

Figure 5.25 Enable click and type in the Edit section of the Preferences dialog box.

Using Click and Type

Click and type can be thought of as a form of automatic paragraph formatting. You can click in any blank area of your document to enter text at that spot. In a new document, for example, you could click near the right margin or halfway down the page. Click and type is only available in Page Layout and Online Layout views.

To enable and use click and type:

1. Choose Word > Preferences.

   The Preferences dialog box appears.

2. Select the Edit heading in the left side of the dialog box to display the Edit preferences (**Figure 5.25**).

3. Check the Enable click and type check box, and then click OK.

4. Switch to Page Layout or Online Layout view.

5. Move the cursor to a blank spot on the page where you'd like to type.

   As you move, the cursor changes shape to reflect the type of paragraph formatting that will be applied to the text. **Table 5.3** shows the different click and type cursor shapes.

6. Double-click to set the new insertion point, and then begin typing.

   Word inserts any necessary blank paragraphs and tabs to fill the document to the start of the new text.

Table 5.3

Click and Type Cursor Shapes	
I	Align left
I	Align right
I	Center
I	Left indent
I	Left text wrap
I	Right text wrap

Automatically Entering Text

AutoText saves you from repetitively typing frequently used text. With AutoText, you can quickly insert any amount of text into a document—from one word to several paragraphs.

To create an AutoText entry:

1. Select the text from which you want to create an AutoText entry (**Figure 5.26**). AutoText entries must consist of at least five characters.

2. Choose Insert > AutoText > New.

   The Create AutoText dialog box appears and suggests a name (**Figure 5.27**).

3. *Optional:* Replace the suggested name with one of your own.

   If you want to be able to insert the entry using AutoComplete, make sure the name contains at least four characters.

4. Click OK to add the text to the list of available AutoText entries.

To insert an AutoText entry:

1. As you type, Word watches for the name of an AutoText entry. When it detects one, a yellow box appears with the AutoText entry displayed (**Figure 5.28**).

2. To accept the AutoText replacement, press Enter while the yellow box is displayed.

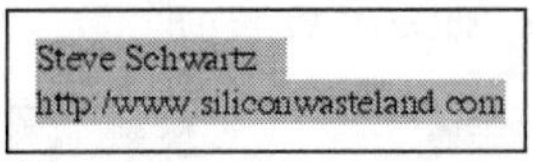

Figure 5.26 Select the text that will become an AutoText entry.

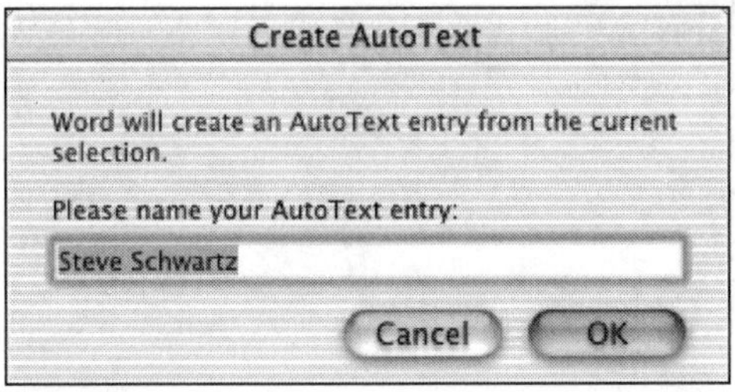

Create AutoText

Word will create an AutoText entry from the current selection.

Please name your AutoText entry:

Steve Schwartz

Cancel   OK

Figure 5.27 The Create AutoText dialog box appears with a suggested name.

Steve Schwartz
http:/www.siliconwasteland.com...
Web sign

Figure 5.28 Press Enter if you want to use the proposed AutoText entry; otherwise, just continue typing your text.

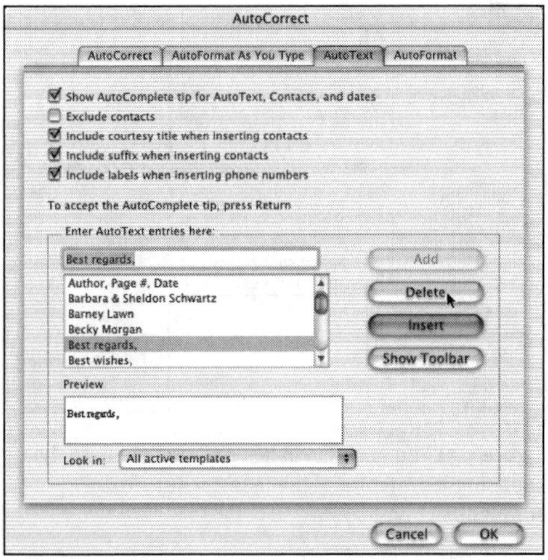

Figure 5.29 You can delete AutoText entries, as well as specify what classes of entries to use, in the AutoCorrect dialog box.

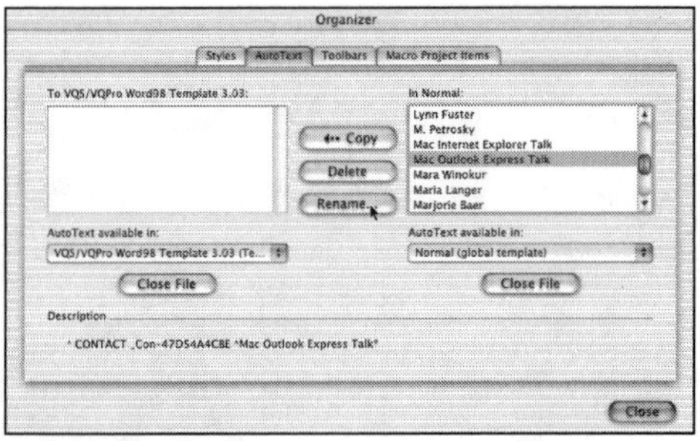

Figure 5.30 Select an AutoText entry from the list, and then click Rename.

✔ Tips

- You can use AutoText to enter lengthy medical, legal, or technical terms. AutoText is also great for writing letters that have the same opening and closing lines.

- You can include graphics in an AutoText entry. This enables you to insert a logo into your documents, for instance.

- To save a *formatted* paragraph as an AutoText entry, include the paragraph mark at the end of the paragraph in your selection. Otherwise, the entry will be inserted as plain text. (To view paragraph marks, click the Show/Hide¶ icon in the Standard toolbar.)

- To delete an AutoText entry, choose Insert > AutoText > AutoText, and—on the AutoText tab of the AutoCorrect dialog box (**Figure 5.29**)—select the entry and click Delete.

- To rename an AutoText entry, choose Tools > Templates and Add-Ins. Click the Organizer button in the Templates and Add-Ins dialog box. Click the AutoText tab (**Figure 5.30**), select the entry, and click Rename.

(continues on next page)

■ You can also make an AutoText insertion by choosing Insert > AutoText > AutoText, selecting the entry from the list in the AutoCorrect dialog box (Figure 5.29), and clicking Insert.

■ Another way to make an AutoText entry is by choosing it from any of the Insert > AutoText submenus (**Figure 5.31**). Word provides dozens of common AutoText entries to get you started. You'll find the entries you've created in the template in which they were stored; typically, this is the Normal template.

■ By default, the names of your Entourage contacts are available as AutoText entries. To exclude them, choose Insert > AutoText > AutoText, and check the Exclude contacts check box in the AutoCorrect dialog box.

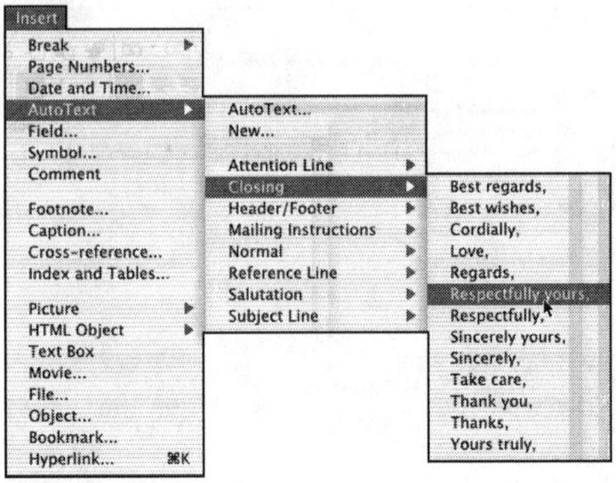

Figure 5.31 You can also insert an AutoText entry by choosing it from one of the Insert > AutoText submenus.

AUTOMATICALLY ENTERING TEXT

ADDING GRAPHICS

You can add graphics to a Word document in several ways:

- ◆ You can choose an image from the substantial clip-art collection that's part of the standard Office installation. (The Value Pack, included on the CD-ROM, offers even more art.)

- ◆ You can insert images that are stored on your hard disk, such as scans, digital photos, or pictures you've downloaded from the Web or received in e-mail.

- ◆ You can scan an image directly into a document or transfer photos from your digital camera.

- ◆ You can use Word's drawing tools to create your own graphics or add predefined shapes called *AutoShapes*.

- ◆ You can add artistic text (known as *WordArt*) to your documents.

✔ Tip

- ■ When scanning images to include in your documents, be aware that most published graphics are copyrighted and cannot be legally used without the permission of the copyright holder. Exceptions are books of royalty-free clip art, and royalty-free clip art and photographs that are distributed on disk or electronically.

Inserting Clip Art and Your Own Images

Clip art, photos, and scans can add color and visual interest to a document. Clip art is great if you're creating a brochure, advertising an event, or hosting a party. And, of course, nothing beats the realism of including your own photographs and scans in a document—whether they're inserted from disk or added directly from a connected TWAIN-compliant digital camera or scanner.

Figure 6.1 Pick from among the many high-quality images in the Clip Gallery window.

To insert clip art into a document:

1. Choose Insert > Picture > Clip Art or click the Insert Clip Art icon on the Drawing toolbar.

   The Clip Gallery window appears (**Figure 6.1**).

2. In the Clip Gallery window, choose a category from the list on the left, and then click a picture on the right.

3. *Optional:* To preview each selected image at full size in a separate window, click the Preview check box.

4. Click Insert to insert the picture into your document.

   The picture and the Picture toolbar appear in the document (**Figure 6.2**). (If the Formatting Palette is visible, the Picture toolbar won't appear. Instead, its tools are added to the Formatting Palette.)

Figure 6.2 Clicking Insert in the Clip Gallery dialog box adds the selected image to your document and displays the Picture toolbar.

To insert a picture from disk:

1. Choose Insert > Picture > From File or click the Insert Picture icon on the Drawing toolbar.

   The Choose a Picture dialog box appears.

2. Navigate to the drive and folder that contains the picture, select it (**Figure 6.3**), and click Insert.

   The image is added to the document.

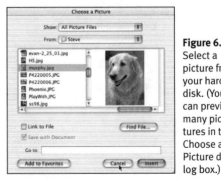

Figure 6.3 Select a picture from your hard disk. (You can preview many pictures in the Choose a Picture dialog box.)

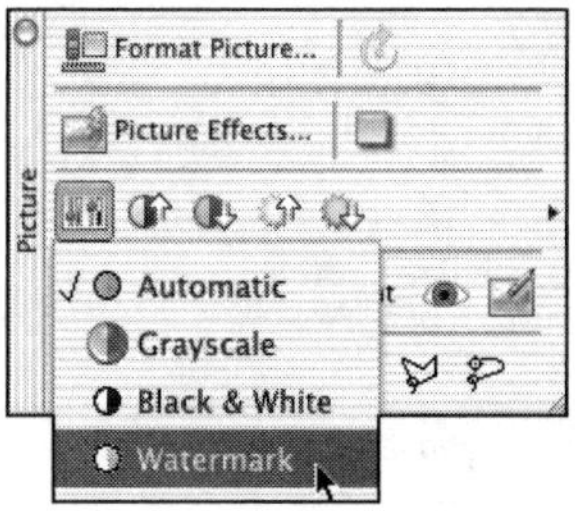

Figure 6.4 To dim the picture, click the Image Control icon on the Picture toolbar and choose Watermark from the pop-up menu.

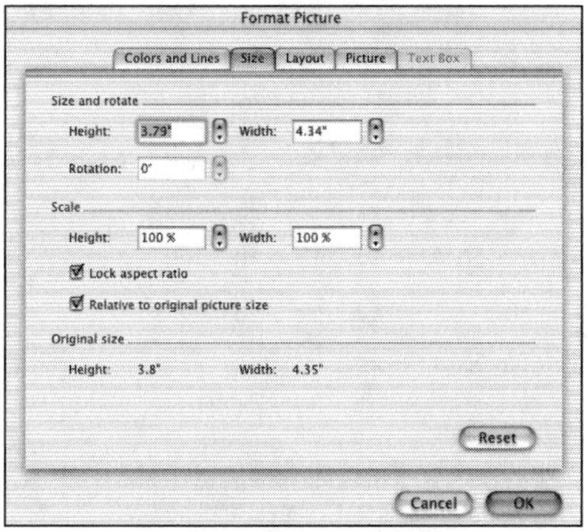

Figure 6.5 In the Format Picture dialog box, you can crop, resize, and reposition the image.

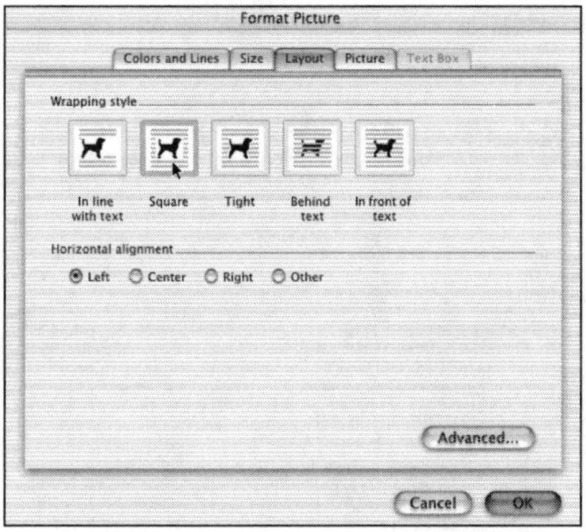

Figure 6.6 Experiment with the text-wrap options on the Layout tab of the Format Picture dialog box to see which one works best.

To insert a picture directly from a TWAIN scanner or digital camera:

1. Choose Insert > Picture > From Scanner or Camera.

2. In the Insert Picture from Scanner or Camera dialog box, select the name of your scanner or digital camera from the Device list.

3. Click the Acquire button.

   The capture or image-transfer software that came with your device will launch.

4. Scan an image as you normally would or select an image that's stored in your camera.

✔ Tips

- You can proportionately resize any image by clicking and dragging a corner handle. To resize nonproportionately, drag any middle handle.

- When inserting a picture from disk, you can filter the file list to show only pictures of a particular type (such as JPEG, TIFF, or EPS) by choosing that file format from the Show drop-down menu.

- To dim the picture's colors so it recedes into the background beneath the text, click the Image Control icon on the Picture toolbar and choose Watermark from the pop-up menu (**Figure 6.4**).

- To control the picture size and scaling precisely, click the Format Picture icon on the Picture toolbar. Switch to the Size tab in the Format Picture dialog box and set the dimensions (**Figure 6.5**).

- To specify the way that text flows on the page in relation to the picture, click the Layout tab in the Format Picture dialog box (**Figure 6.6**). You can place your picture in line with the text, behind it, or in front of it, or you can have the text wrap around the picture.

Drawing Lines

You can use lines to separate text or to begin building shapes. (We'll discuss how to make shapes in the next section, "Creating Shapes.")

To draw lines, you use the Drawing toolbar (**Figure 6.7**). To display the toolbar, choose View > Toolbars > Drawing. Keep this toolbar handy; we'll be using it throughout the chapter.

To draw lines:

1. Click the Line icon on the Drawing toolbar (**Figure 6.8**).

2. Click in your document where you want to start the line, hold down the mouse button, and drag to complete the line.

3. With the line still selected, click and hold the Line Style icon on the Drawing toolbar, and then choose from the thickness and style options (**Figure 6.9**).

✔ Tips

■ To change a line's length or direction, select the line, click a handle at either end, and drag.

■ To move a line to a new position, click and drag the middle of the line.

■ To draw a new line starting from its center (rather than from end point to end point), press Option as you drag.

■ To add arrowheads, diamonds, or circles to either or both ends of the line, click the Line Style icon in the Drawing toolbar and click More Lines. In the Format AutoShape dialog box that appears, choose an arrow style from the Colors and Lines tab. You can also select arrowheads from the Formatting Palette.

■ You can choose three basic line types (straight, single arrow, or double arrow) from the Lines icon on the Drawing toolbar.

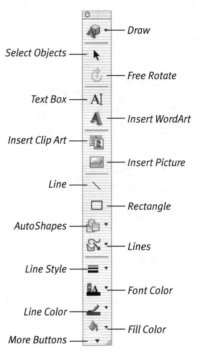

Figure 6.7 Use the Drawing toolbar to create lines and shapes, insert images, and modify graphics.

Figure 6.8 Click the Line icon, and then click and drag in your document to draw a line.

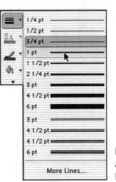

Figure 6.9 Choose a style and thickness from the Line Style pop-up menu.

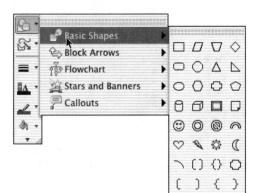

Figure 6.10 Select a shape from the AutoShape pop-up menus and palette.

Figure 6.11 Click and drag to draw a selected shape, such as this smiley face.

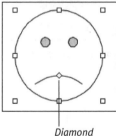

Figure 6.12 Many AutoShapes contain a yellow diamond you can drag to modify the shape. In this example, you can change the smile to a frown.

Diamond

Creating Shapes

Even if you don't know how to draw, you can readily draw interesting shapes using Word's AutoShapes.

To draw a shape:

1. To draw a predefined shape, click the AutoShapes icon on the Drawing toolbar and choose a shape from one of the submenus (**Figure 6.10**).

2. Click and drag to draw the selected shape—in this case, a smiley face (**Figure 6.11**).

✔ Tips

- To keep the shape in proportion (drawing a square or circle instead of a rectangle or oval, for example), hold down (Shift) as you drag to draw the shape.

- To draw an AutoShape from its center, hold down (Option) as you drag to draw the shape.

- By picking options from the Formatting Palette, you can change the line style and thickness, color, and angle of AutoShapes.

- Many AutoShapes contain one or more yellow diamonds that you can click and drag to change the object's shape (**Figure 6.12**).

- To delete a line, arrow, or shape, click to select it and then press (Delete).

- Another way to create an AutoShape is to choose Insert > Picture > AutoShapes. An AutoShapes toolbar appears from which you can select a shape to draw.

- You can replace one AutoShape with another. Select the shape in your document, click the Draw tool in the Drawing Toolbar, and choose Change AutoShape. Then choose a replacement AutoShape.

- You can click the Rectangle and Oval icons on the Drawing toolbar to create rectangles, squares, ovals, and circles.

CREATING SHAPES

Adding Color, Shadows, and 3D Effects

You can embellish shapes with color, shadows, and three-dimensional effects.

To color a line or shape:

1. Click a line or shape to select it.

2. Click the down arrow beside the Line Color icon on the Drawing toolbar to display a palette of line colors (**Figure 6.13**). Click to select a color.

   The color is applied to the line or the shape's outline.

3. Click the down arrow beside the Fill Color icon on the Drawing toolbar to display a palette of fill colors. Click to select a color.

   The color will fill any empty area of the selected shape.

✔ Tips

■ To add a shadow or 3D effect to a selected shape, click the More Buttons down arrow at the end of the Drawing Toolbar. Choose an option from the Shadow or 3-D menu to specify the location and direction of the shadow or effect (**Figure 6.14**).

■ The Line Color and Fill Color tools display the most recent color you've used. To apply that color to another line or shape, simply click the Line Color or Fill Color icon.

■ You can't apply both shadow and 3D effects to the same object.

■ Some shapes can take both a line and fill color; others accept only one or the other.

Figure 6.13 Select a color from the Line Color palette.

Figure 6.14 Select a shadow or 3D effect from the Shadow and 3-D pop-up palettes.

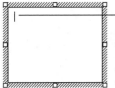

— Insertion point

Figure 6.15 The completed text box contains a blinking insertion point, indicating that it's ready to receive your text.

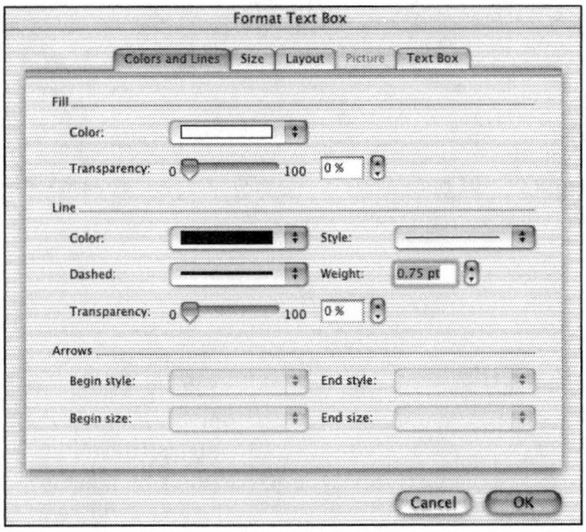

Figure 6.16 In the Format Text Box dialog box, you can adjust a text box's size, color, margins, and so on.

Adding Text as an Object

In Word, you can create text boxes that—unlike normal text—are objects. A *text box* is a rectangular or square container for text. You can edit the size, shape, color, and other aspects of a text box, just as you can do with a graphic.

To create a textbox:

1. Click the Text Box icon on the Drawing toolbar.

2. To draw a text box, click and drag from one corner to the opposite corner. When you release the mouse button, the text box is completed (**Figure 6.15**).

3. Type your text.

4. For precise control over the parameters of the text box (such as its fill and line color, word wrap, internal margins, and position), double-click one of its sides or choose Format > Text Box.

   The Format Text Box dialog box appears (**Figure 6.16**).

✔ Tips

- To create a square text box, press ⟨Shift⟩ as you draw it.

- You can change the size and shape of a text box by dragging any of its handles.

- You can change the location of a text box by moving the pointer over one of its sides and dragging.

- To delete a text box, click one of the sides so that the insertion point inside disappears, and then press ⟨Delete⟩.

- You can change the font, size, style, and color of text in a text box. Select the text and choose formatting commands from Word's menus, the Formatting toolbar, or the Formatting Palette.

ADDING TEXT AS AN OBJECT

Creating Artistic Text

WordArt is specially formatted text that Word can display in a number of preset, artistic styles. There are several tools to help you create and edit WordArt.

To insert WordArt

1. Choose Insert > Picture > WordArt or click the Insert WordArt icon on the Drawing toolbar.

2. Select a style in the WordArt Gallery window that appears (**Figure 6.17**) and click OK.

   The Edit WordArt Text dialog box appears (**Figure 6.18**).

3. Replace "Your Text Here" with your own text. Set the font, size, and style as you want and click OK.

   Your WordArt-formatted text appears, along with the WordArt toolbar (**Figure 6.19**).

✔ Tips

- You can move, resize, and reshape WordArt by dragging its handles. To move WordArt, move the pointer over the text itself. When the pointer changes to a hand, click and drag the WordArt to a new spot.

- To change the shape of the curve(s) to which the WordArt is bound, click the WordArt Shape icon and select a shape from the palette that appears (**Figure 6.20**).

- To change the angle of the WordArt, click the Free Rotate icon on the WordArt toolbar. Then drag any of the corner handles that appear around it.

- For precise control over the appearance of the WordArt, click the Format WordArt icon on the WordArt toolbar. Make any desired changes in the Format WordArt dialog box that appears.

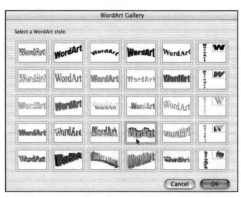

Figure 6.17 Choose one of the WordArt styles by clicking it in the WordArt Gallery window.

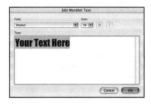

Figure 6.18 Replace "Your Text Here" with your own words. You also have the option of changing the font and size.

Figure 6.19 Your text is formatted to match the selected WordArt style.

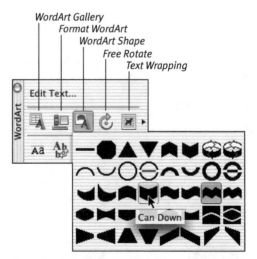

WordArt Gallery
Format WordArt
WordArt Shape
Free Rotate
Text Wrapping

Figure 6.20 Click the WordArt Shape icon on the WordArt toolbar to select a new shape for the WordArt.

CREATING TABLES

It's easy to create tables in Word documents. With the click of a button, you can create and begin entering information into a table. Tables can be included in sales reports, research projects, or data analyses. Or a table may consist of only a list of names and phone numbers. We'll discuss creating simple tables first, and then move on to building more complex tables.

The procedures in this chapter assume that you're working with an existing Word file. If you don't have a document open, choose File > Open (to add a table to an existing document) or File > New Blank Document (to create a table in a new document).

Starting a Table

You must create the table structure before entering text or data. Then you format the table.

To create a simple table:

1. Position the insertion point in your Word document where you want the table to appear.

2. Click the Insert Table icon on the Standard toolbar.

3. In the pop-up palette, drag to specify the desired number of columns and rows (**Figure 7.1**).

   An unformatted table appears (**Figure 7.2**). If you don't want to format the table immediately (or at all), you can begin entering your text and data.

4. To apply a format to the table, choose Table > Table AutoFormat.

   The Table AutoFormat dialog box appears (**Figure 7.3**).

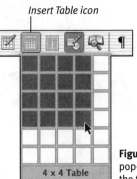

Insert Table icon

4 x 4 Table

Figure 7.1 Drag in the pop-up palette to specify the table size.

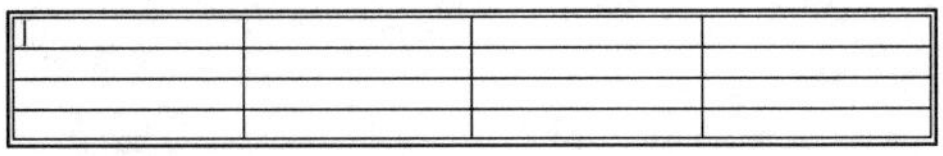

Figure 7.2 An unformatted table appears in the Word document.

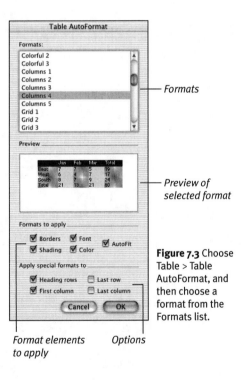

Formats

Preview of selected format

Figure 7.3 Choose Table > Table AutoFormat, and then choose a format from the Formats list.

Format elements to apply *Options*

Figure 7.4 Your formatting choices are applied to the table.

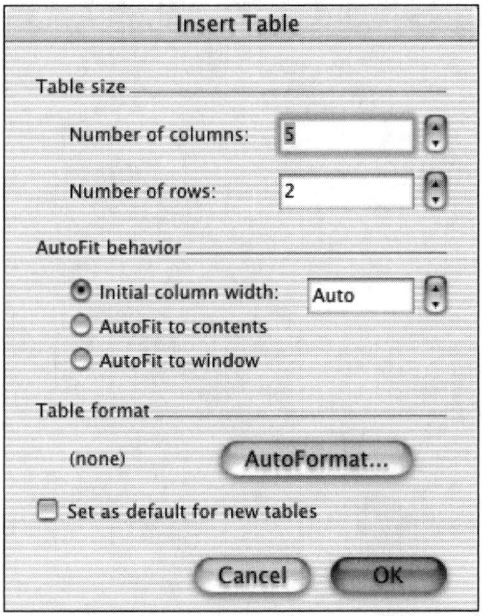

Insert Table

Table size

Number of columns: 5

Number of rows: 2

AutoFit behavior

● Initial column width: Auto
○ AutoFit to contents
○ AutoFit to window

Table format

(none)   AutoFormat...

☐ Set as default for new tables

Cancel   OK

Figure 7.5 In the Insert Table dialog box, specify the number of columns and rows for the table.

5. Scroll through the Formats list and select a table style.

You can choose from simple structures, tables with or without headers, three-dimensional tables, and colored tables. A sample of the selected style appears in the Preview window.

6. Click OK.

The formatting is applied to the table (**Figure 7.4**).

✔ Tips

■ You can simultaneously insert and format a table by choosing Table > Insert > Table. In the Insert Table dialog box (**Figure 7.5**), specify the numbers of columns and rows, and set the initial column widths. To select a table format, click the AutoFormat button.

■ You can apply table formatting at any point—regardless of whether you've begun entering the table data.

STARTING A TABLE

Entering Data

After you've placed the table in a document, you can enter your information.

To enter data in a table:

1. To insert data into a cell, click in the cell and then type.

   As you type, the text wraps within the cell as necessary. The entire row will become taller if it needs to accommodate multiple lines of text (**Figure 7.6**).

2. After completing the first cell, press Tab to move to the cell to its right, and type text in that cell.

   When you reach the rightmost cell of a row, pressing Tab moves the insertion point to the first cell of the next row.

✔ Tips

- Press Shift Tab to move back one cell.

- If there is already text in a cell when you Tab into it, the text is automatically selected. If you wish, you can delete the entire cell entry by pressing Delete or typing over it.

- You can move directly to any cell by clicking in it.

- When you finish entering data in the last cell of the table, you can press Tab to create a new row, if you wish.

Figure 7.6 If you enter text that's wider than the cell width, the row height expands as needed to display the text.

Tables and Borders toolbar   *Table outline*

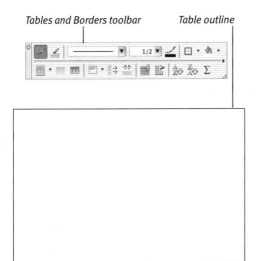

Figure 7.8 Click the Draw Table icon on the Tables and Borders toolbar, and then click and drag to create the table outline.

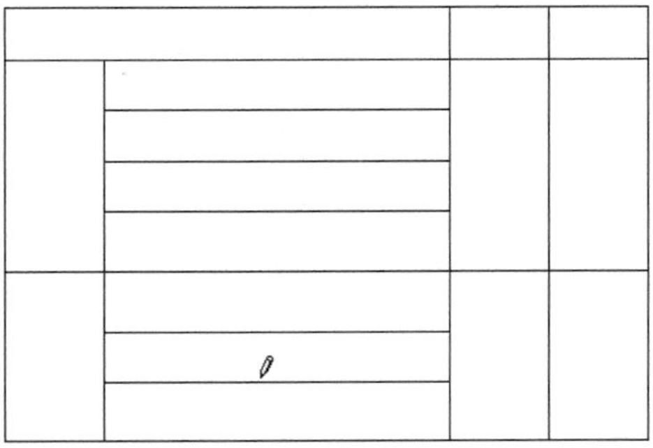

Figure 7.9 Continue drawing lines to build the structure of your table.

Building a Table from Scratch

If you have a complex table in mind, you might consider designing your own.

To build a table from scratch:

1. Choose Table > Draw Table.

   The Tables and Borders toolbar appears (**Figure 7.7**, at bottom of page).

2. Click the Draw Table icon on the toolbar, and then drag the table's outline in the document (**Figure 7.8**).

   Click where you want one corner, drag diagonally to the opposite corner, and then release the mouse button.

3. Use the Draw Table tool to draw the interior cell boundaries (**Figure 7.9**).

4. When you're done working on the table and want to begin entering text, click the Draw Table tool icon again.

   (continues on next page)

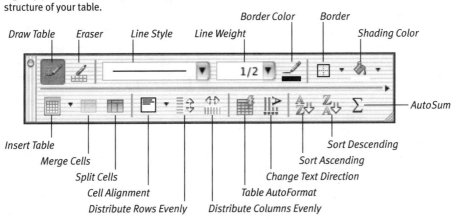

Draw Table   *Eraser*   *Line Style*   *Line Weight*   *Border Color*   *Border*   *Shading Color*

AutoSum

Insert Table
Merge Cells
Split Cells
Cell Alignment
Distribute Rows Evenly
Distribute Columns Evenly
Change Text Direction
Table AutoFormat
Sort Ascending
Sort Descending

Figure 7.7 The Tables and Borders toolbar provides the tools needed to format tables.

Chapter 7

✔ Tips

■ If the Formatting Palette is open when you choose Table > Draw Table, the Tables and Borders toolbar will *not* appear. You can close the Formatting Palette and then choose the command again, or you can open the toolbar directly, either by clicking the Tables and Borders icon on the Standard toolbar or by choosing View > Toolbars > Tables and Borders.

■ If you change your mind about a line and want to erase it, click the Eraser icon on the Tables and Borders toolbar, and then click the line you want to erase. (When drawing with the Draw Table tool, you can temporarily switch to the Eraser tool by pressing [Shift].)

■ You can use any of these methods to remove a line you've just drawn: Press [⌘][Z], choose Edit > Undo, or click the Undo icon on the Standard toolbar.

Editing the Table Structure

Once you have created the skeleton of the table, you may want to fine-tune the rows and columns. The Tables and Borders toolbar will help you.

To edit the table structure:

◆ To move a line, click and drag it to a new location (**Figure 7.10**).

◆ To change the style, width, or color of a line, choose new options from the Line Style, Line Weight, and Border Color menus on the Tables and Borders toolbar (**Figure 7.11**). Click any line in the table to apply the new settings to that line. New lines that you draw will also use those settings.

◆ To distribute cell heights or widths evenly, click outside the table to clear the tool selection. Then click and drag through the cells you want to adjust, and click the Distribute Rows Evenly or Distribute Columns Evenly icon on the Tables and Borders toolbar (**Figure 7.12**).

◆ To set row heights or column widths precisely, select the cells you want to modify and then choose Table > Table Properties. On the Row, Column, or Cell tab of the Table Properties dialog box (**Figure 7.13**), enter the preferred dimensions.

◆ You can change the table width by entering a value in the Preferred width text box on the Table tab of the Table Properties dialog box. You can also change the size of a table manually by clicking and dragging the table's bottom-right corner.

◆ To move a table, click the double-arrow symbol in its upper-left corner (**Figure 7.14**) and drag the table to its new location.

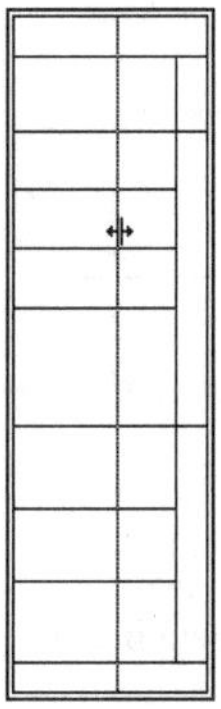

Figure 7.10 Click and drag any line to reposition it.

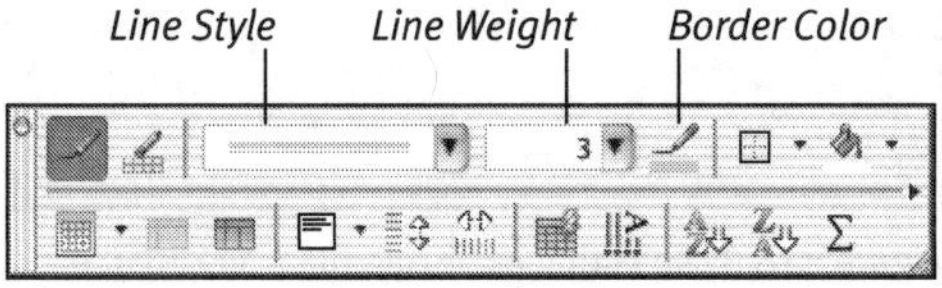

Line Style   _Line Weight_   _Border Color_

Figure 7.11 To draw or alter the lines in a table, select the desired options from the Tables and Borders toolbar.

Distribute Rows Evenly   _Distribute Columns Evenly_

Distribute Columns Evenly

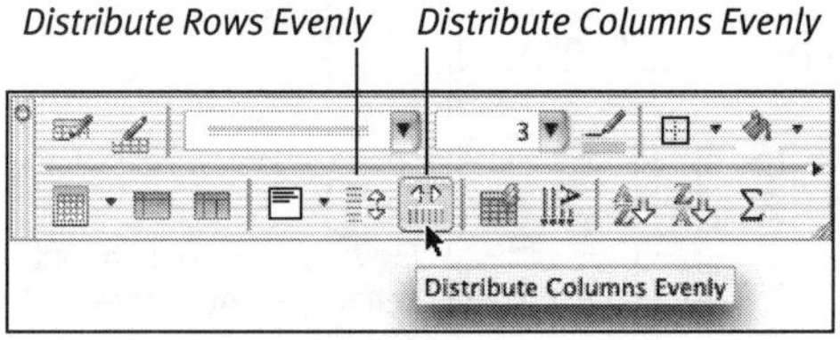

Figure 7.12 Click the Distribute Rows Evenly or Distribute Columns Evenly button in the Tables and Borders toolbar to even up the rows or columns.

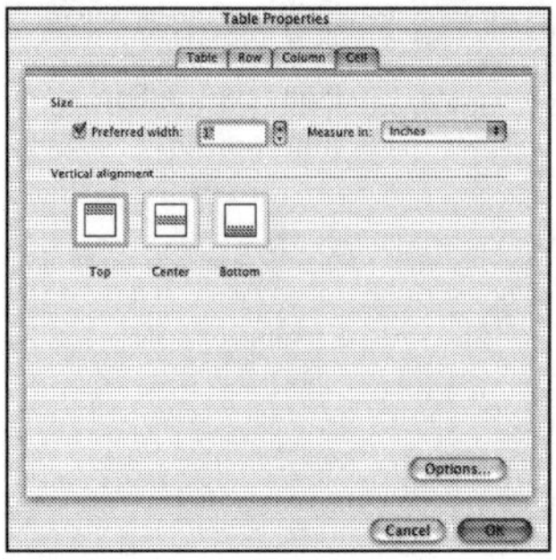

Figure 7.13 You can specify a preferred cell width in the Table Properties dialog box.

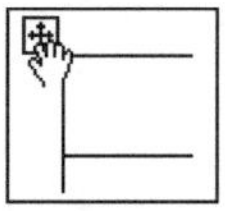

Figure 7.14 To reposition a table, move the cursor over the double-arrow symbol in the table's upper-left corner and then drag.

Aligning Table Data

Using the Tables and Borders toolbar, you can change the alignment or orientation of data.

To realign or change the orientation of cell data:

◆ To align the data within cells vertically (top, center, bottom) or horizontally (left, center, right), select the cells you want to align. Click the Cell Alignment icon on the Tables and Borders toolbar and select the desired alignment from the pop-up palette (**Figure 7.15**).

◆ To change the orientation of data within cells, select the cells you want to orient. Click the Change Text Direction icon on the Tables and Borders toolbar (**Figure 7.16**).

There are three possible text orientations (**Figure 7.17**). Click the Change Text Direction icon repeatedly until you get the desired orientation.

✔ Tip

■ You can also set the alignment of selected cells by clicking one of the four alignment icons (Align Left, Align Center, Align Right, or Justify) on the Formatting toolbar or the Formatting Palette (**Figure 7.18**).

Figure 7.15 To set the alignment for data in selected cells, choose an option from the Cell Alignment palette.

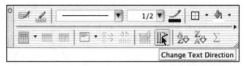

Figure 7.16 By selecting a cell and then clicking the Change Text Direction icon on the Tables and Borders toolbar, you can change the orientation of the cell's text.

Figure 7.17 You can orient cell text in any of three directions.

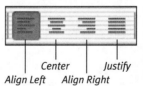

Figure 7.18 For quick-and-dirty text alignment, just click any of these alignment icons on the Formatting toolbar.

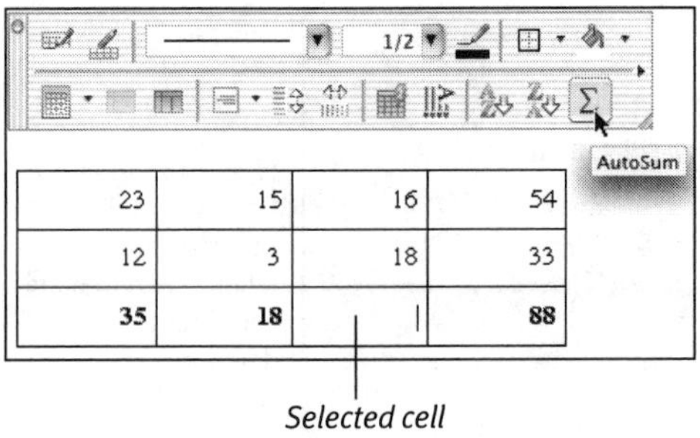

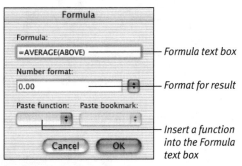

Selected cell

Figure 7.19 To create a row or column total, click in the cell to the right of the row or beneath the column, and then click the AutoSum icon on the Tables and Borders toolbar.

Figure 7.20 Choose Table > Formula, and then enter a formula in the Formula dialog box.

Working with Numeric Data

Word tables have the calculation capabilities of Excel worksheets. For example, you can use the AutoSum tool to total columns or rows of numeric values. And using the Table > Formula command, you can insert a formula into any cell.

To total a row or column:

◆ To total the values in a column, click in the cell below the numbers you're adding, and then click the AutoSum icon on the Tables and Borders toolbar (**Figure 7.19**).

◆ To total the values in a row, click in the cell to the right of the numbers you're adding, and then click the AutoSum icon on the Tables and Borders toolbar.

✔ Tips

■ You can do more complex calculations with values in a table. Click in an empty cell where you want the value, choose Table > Formula, enter a formula in the Formula dialog box (**Figure 7.20**), and click OK to insert the formula. The result of the calculation appears in the cell.

■ You can choose functions from the Paste function drop-down list in the Formula dialog box.

■ To examine the formula in any cell, select the cell and then choose Table > Formula.

■ If you alter the numeric contents of cells *after* you insert the AutoSum function or a formula, the results are not recalculated. To force a recalculation, select the result cell and reapply the AutoSum or formula.

■ If you don't have an empty row of cells that you can use as a total row, click in the last row and choose Table > Insert > Rows Below. To add an extra column, click in the rightmost column and choose Table > Insert > Columns to the Right.

WORKING WITH NUMERIC DATA

Deleting Cells

You can easily remove cells from a table. You can delete an entire table, entire rows or columns, or only selected cells.

To delete table cells:

◆ To delete an entire table, click any cell in the table and choose Table > Delete > Table.

◆ To delete entire rows or columns, select one or more cells from the row(s) or column(s), and then choose Table > Delete > Rows or Table > Delete > Columns.

◆ To delete specific cells in a table, select the cells and choose Table > Delete > Cells. The Delete Cells dialog box appears (**Figure 7.21**). You can elect to delete entire rows or columns, or to delete only the selected cells and move the rest up or left (to close up the deletion).

✔ Tips

■ Deleting a cell, row, or column is not the same as simply clearing the cells' contents. The Delete commands actually *remove* selected cells, rows, or columns from the table. To *clear* one or more cells of the data they contain, select the cells and choose Edit > Clear > Contents.

■ If you delete a table (or any part of it) by mistake, you can restore the deleted portions by immediately choosing the Edit > Undo command, pressing ⌘Z, or clicking the Undo icon on the Standard toolbar.

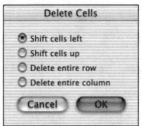

Figure 7.21 In the Delete Cells dialog box, indicate how to adjust the remaining cells following the deletion.

DELETING CELLS

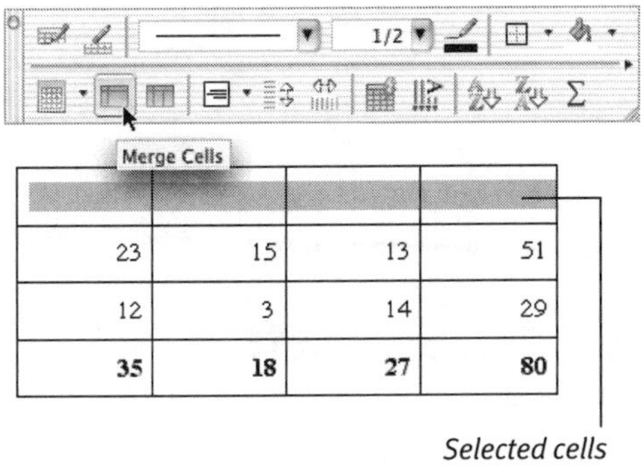

Selected cells

Figure 7.22 Select the cells you want to merge, and then click the Merge Cells icon on the Tables and Borders toolbar.

Merged cells

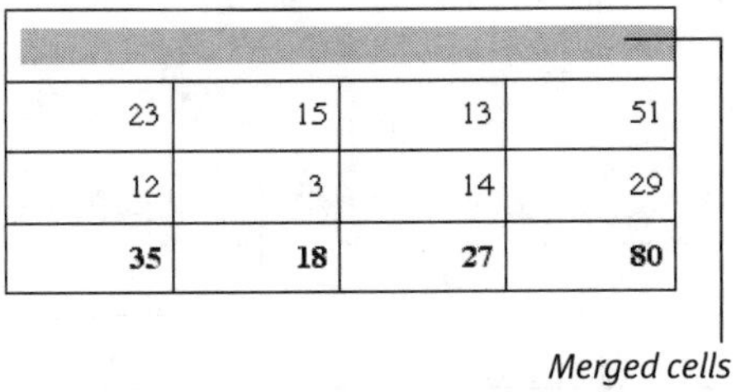

Figure 7.23 The cells merge, creating a single cell that—in this instance—can hold the table's title.

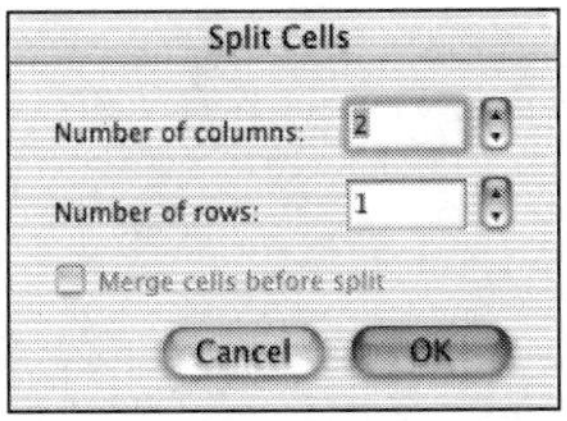

Figure 7.24 When splitting a cell, you can specify the number of resulting rows and/or columns.

Merging and Splitting Cells

Using the Merge Cells command, you can combine two or more adjacent cells into a single cell (to create column or row headings, for example). Similarly, using the Split Cells command, you can split a single cell into multiple cells. In addition to serving advanced table-formatting needs, Split Cells is useful for restoring previously merged cells to their original structure.

To merge cells:

1. Select adjacent cells to be merged (**Figure 7.22**).

2. Choose Table > Merge Cells or click the Merge Cells icon on the Tables and Borders toolbar.

   The cells merge (**Figure 7.23**).

To split a cell:

1. Select the cell you want to split into multiple cells.

2. Choose Table > Split Cells or click the Split Cells icon on the Tables and Borders toolbar.

   The Split Cells dialog box appears (**Figure 7.24**).

3. Specify the number of columns and rows into which to split the cell, and then click OK.

Adding Rows and Columns

Another way you can change a table layout is by inserting additional rows, columns, or cells.

To insert a new row:

1. Click a cell in the row that will serve as the reference for the new, blank row.

2. You can either choose Table > Insert, followed by Rows Above or Rows Below, or click the down arrow beside the Insert Table icon on the Tables and Borders toolbar, and then choose the same command (**Figure 7.25**).

   The new row appears (**Figure 7.26**).

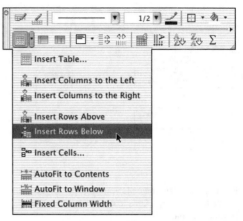

Figure 7.25 You can insert additional rows or columns by choosing a command from the Table > Insert submenu or from the Tables and Borders toolbar (click the down arrow next to the Insert Table icon).

23	15	13	51
12	3	14	29
35	18	27	80

Originally selected row
New row

Figure 7.26 In this example, the row appears above the selected row and can serve to hold column titles.

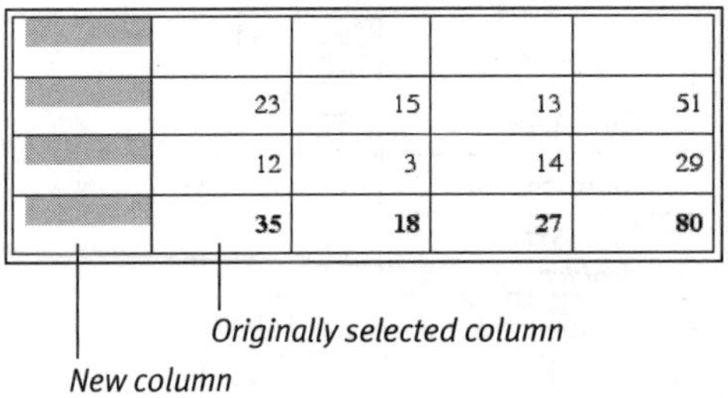

Originally selected column

New column

Figure 7.27 In this example, the new column appears to the left of the selected column and can serve to hold row titles.

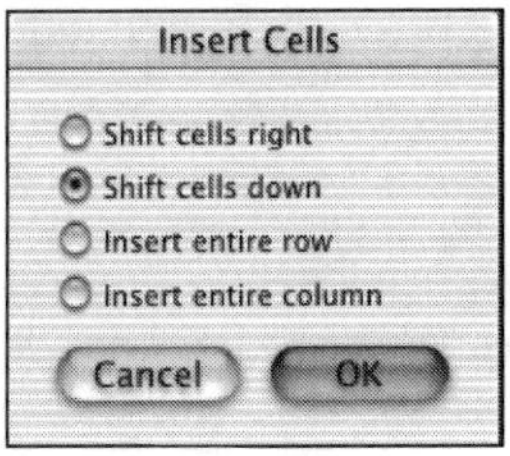

Figure 7.28 As is the case when deleting cells, when you insert new cells in a table, you must indicate how it will affect the other cells.

To insert a new column:

1. Click a cell in the column that will serve as the reference for the new, blank column.

2. Select Table > Insert, followed by Columns to the Left or Columns to the Right, or choose the same command from the Tables and Borders toolbar (Figure 7.25).

   The new column appears (**Figure 7.27**).

To insert new cells:

1. Select the cell or cells that will serve as the reference for the new, blank cell(s).

2. Choose Table > Insert > Cells, or choose the same command from the Tables and Borders toolbar (Figure 7.25).

   The Insert Cells dialog box appears (**Figure 7.28**).

3. Select an option and click OK.

   The new cells are inserted into the table, and the table is adjusted as necessary to accommodate them.

✔ Tips

- To insert multiple columns or rows, select the desired number of new columns or rows and then issue the Insert command.

- The Standard toolbar contains an Insert Table/Insert Columns/Insert Cells icon.

ADDING ROWS AND COLUMNS

Nesting Tables

Nested tables are tables within tables. They can come in useful if you have a special sub-category of information that the table needs to reflect. Inserting a nested table is similar to creating a new table.

To insert a nested table:

1. Click in your current table to select a place to insert the nested table.

2. Click the Insert Table button on the Standard toolbar.

3. In the pop-up palette, drag to specify the number of columns for the nested table.

   A nested table appears within your original table (**Figure 7.29**).

✔ Tip

■ You can also insert a nested table by choosing the Table > Insert > Table command or by clicking the Insert Table icon on the Tables and Borders toolbar. For instructions, refer to the first tip after "Starting a Table," earlier in this chapter.

Species		Jan-Jun	Jul-Dec
Cats	Abyssinian	37	42
	Burmese	19	26
Dogs	Retriever	51	54
	Golden | Blonde		
	Corgi	22	29
	Total	73	83

Nested table

Figure 7.29 The nested table is placed within the original table.

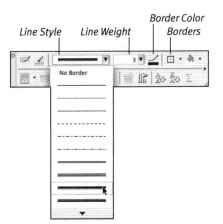

Line Style   *Line Weight*   *Border Color*   *Borders*

Figure 7.30 Choose a line weight, style, and border color from the Tables and Borders toolbar.

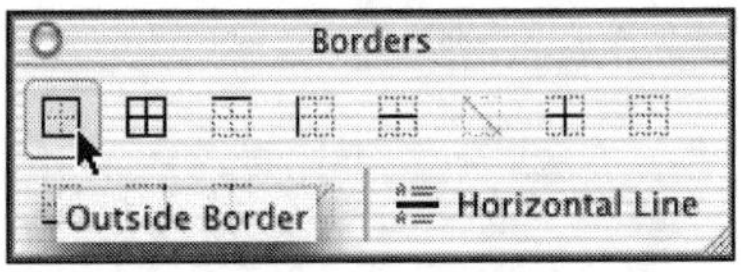

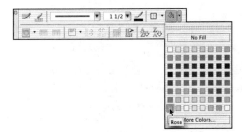

Figure 7.31 From the Borders pop-up palette (Figure 7.30), choose a border option to apply to the selected cells.

Figure 7.32 To fill selected cells with a color, pick a fill color from the Shading Color palette.

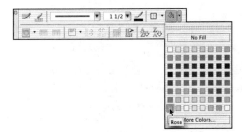

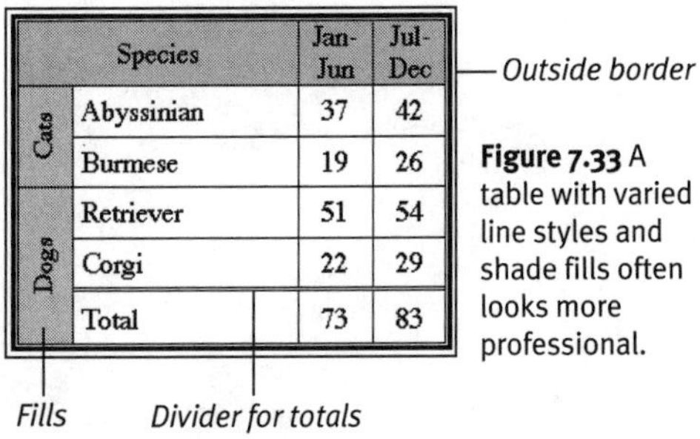

Figure 7.33 A table with varied line styles and shade fills often looks more professional.

Fills   *Divider for totals*

Setting Borders and Cell Shading

Borders are the lines surrounding cells. *Shading* is fill within the cells. The Table > Table AutoFormat command offers a collection of templates for borders and shading that you can apply to a table (discussed in the first tip after "Starting a Table," earlier in this chapter). If you prefer, you can follow the procedure below to set cell borders and shading manually.

To set borders and shading manually:

1. Select the cells whose borders or shading you want to set or change.

2. From the Tables and Borders toolbar, choose a line style, weight, and border color (**Figure 7.30**).

3. Click the Border icon on the Tables and Borders toolbar, and then pick the type of border, such as top, bottom, left, right, or outside, you wish to apply to the selected cells (**Figure 7.31**).

4. To apply shading to the selected cells, click the Shading Color icon on the Tables and Borders toolbar and choose a color from the drop-down palette (**Figure 7.32**).

    The completed table can contain any combination of borders and shading (**Figure 7.33**).

Converting Text to a Table

You can convert existing text in a Word document into a table. After you convert the text to a table, you can format it any way you like.

To convert text to a table:

1. Select the lines of existing text you want to convert into a table (**Figure 7.34**).

2. Choose Table > Convert > Convert Text to Table.

   The Convert Text to Table dialog box appears (**Figure 7.35**).

3. Specify the number of columns and rows that the resulting table will contain.

4. *Optional:* Click AutoFormat to select a format for the table.

5. Click OK to generate the table.

   The selected text is converted into a table (**Figure 7.36**). To adjust the formatting and style, see "Editing the Table Structure" and "Setting Borders and Cell Shading" earlier in this chapter.

✔ Tips

- To allow Word to convert selected text *automatically* into an appropriate table, click the Insert Table icon on the Standard toolbar.

- To convert multiple paragraphs into a table, select those paragraphs and choose Table > Convert > Convert Text to Table. Select Paragraphs as the text separator in the Convert Text to Table dialog box.

- If you're converting tab-delimited text into a table, make sure the text doesn't have multiple tab characters between items that should be in adjacent columns—even if removing the extra tabs makes the spacing look wrong.

- You can convert a table back into text by choosing Table > Convert > Convert Table to Text.

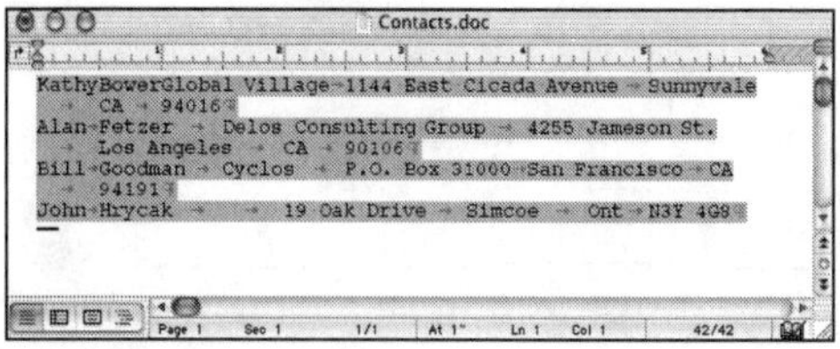

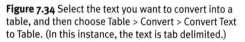

Figure 7.34 Select the text you want to convert into a table, and then choose Table > Convert > Convert Text to Table. (In this instance, the text is tab delimited.)

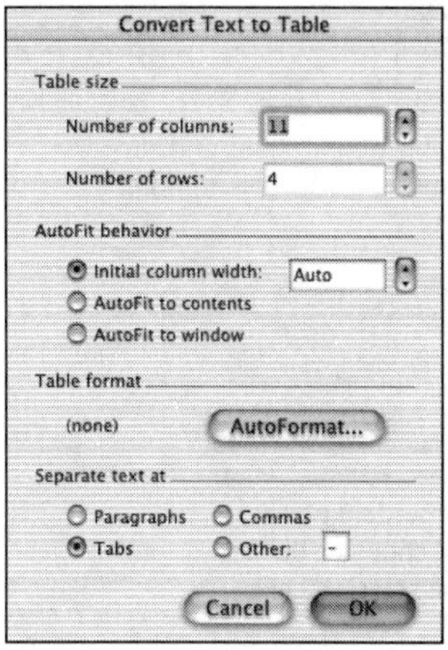

Figure 7.35 If necessary, you can set conversion options in the Convert Text to Table dialog box.

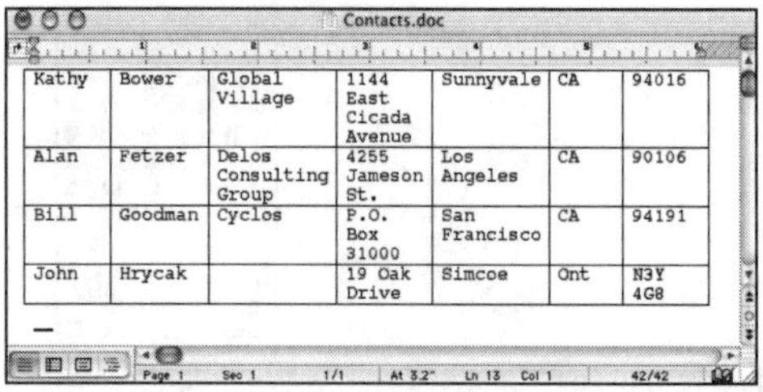

Figure 7.36 The selected text is converted into a Word table, ready for formatting.

CREATING NEWSLETTERS, LABELS, AND MORE

If you've only used Word to create simple documents like letters and memos, you might want to try some of its other diverse capabilities. This chapter explains how to create special documents, such as labels, catalogs, envelopes, and newsletters. It also discusses using the Contact toolbar to add contact information from your Office Address Book to documents, envelope-printing techniques, and using the Data Merge Manager (a tool for creating merge documents).

Using the Contact Toolbar

Using the Contact toolbar, you can quickly add name, address, and other contact information from your Office Address Book to letters, labels, and envelopes. (The Office Address Book is normally maintained in Entourage, but it's also accessible from Word.)

To use the Contact toolbar:

1. Choose View > Toolbars > Contact.
   The Contact toolbar appears above the Word window (**Figure 8.1**).

2. To insert a contact into your document, position the insertion point where you'd like to insert the contact information.

3. Choose the contact name from the Contacts pull-down menu (**Figure 8.2**). The contact's name appears in the document.

4. If you've recorded a street address, phone number, or email address for the contact, you can also insert that information into the document by clicking the Include Address, Include Phone, or Include E-mail button in the Contact toolbar.

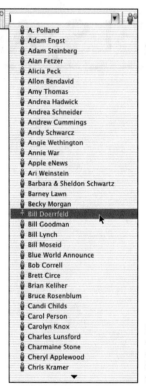

Select a contact

Create a new contact

Figure 8.1 You can use the Contact toolbar to insert contact names and other information from the Office Address Book into your documents.

Figure 8.2 Add contacts to your documents directly from the Contact toolbar.

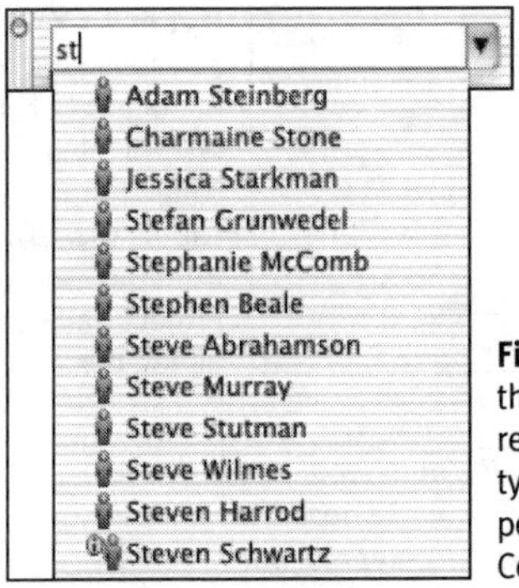

Figure 8.3 To find the desired contact record quickly, type part of the person's name in the Contacts text box.

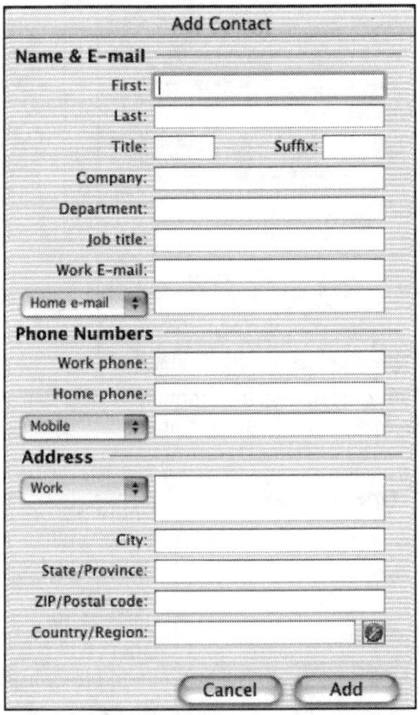

Figure 8.4 Using the Add Contact dialog box, you can create new contact records from within Word.

✔ Tips

■ You can also enter a contact's name using Word's AutoText feature. (See "Automatically Entering Text" in Chapter 5, Document and Text Formatting.) Start typing the person's name in your document. If the name is in your Address Book, Word will suggest it. Press Enter to accept the name, or continue typing if it's not the right one.

■ If you have many entries in your Address Book, the Contacts pull-down menu may not list them all. To see other entries, type part of the person's name in the Contacts text box. The contact list will show all possible matches for what you've typed, enabling you to choose the desired contact (**Figure 8.3**).

■ To create a new contact record, click the Add icon on the Contact toolbar. Enter the information in the Add Contact dialog box (**Figure 8.4**), and then click Add.

USING THE CONTACT TOOLBAR

Creating Labels

Word provides label templates that you can use to create a variety of labels, such as mailing labels, videotape labels, and name badges. Using the Labels wizard, you can generate one label or an entire sheet of the same label that will print on many manufacturers' label stock.

To create labels:

1. If the Project Gallery isn't open, choose File > Project Gallery ([Shift][⌘][P]). Choose Labels from the Category list (**Figure 8.5**), select the Mailing Label Wizard, and click OK.

   or

   Create a new document by choosing File > New Blank Document ([⌘][N]), and then choose Tools > Labels.

   The Labels wizard appears (**Figure 8.6**).

2. Click the Options button to open the Label Options window (**Figure 8.7**). Specify the type of printer you have, the label manufacturer, and the part number of the label you'll be using. Click OK.

3. Enter the address or other appropriate text in the Address text box of the Labels wizard. (To fill the text box with your own mailing address—taken from your identity in the Entourage address book—click the Use my address check box.)

4. Click a radio button to indicate the desired option, Full page of the same label or Single label. (In the latter case, you must also specify which label row and column to use.)

5. *Optional:* You can change the font, size, and style by clicking the Font button. You can set print options by clicking the Customize button.

6. Click OK.

   Your labels appear in the new document (**Figure 8.8**).

Figure 8.5 You can select the Mailing Label Wizard (also called the Labels wizard) from the Project Gallery dialog box.

Set the number of labels desired
Choose a label type
Enter the label text
Set the font

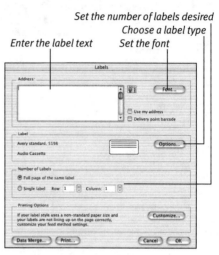

Figure 8.6 Enter the necessary information in the Labels wizard to design your label.

Specify the type of printer

Figure 8.7 In the Label Options dialog box, choose the specific label you intend to print on, as well as the type of printer you'll use.

Choose a label stock   Choose a label manufacturer

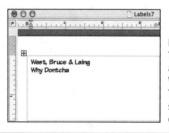

Figure 8.8 The new label appears in the Word document. This example shows a single cassette label.

CREATING LABELS

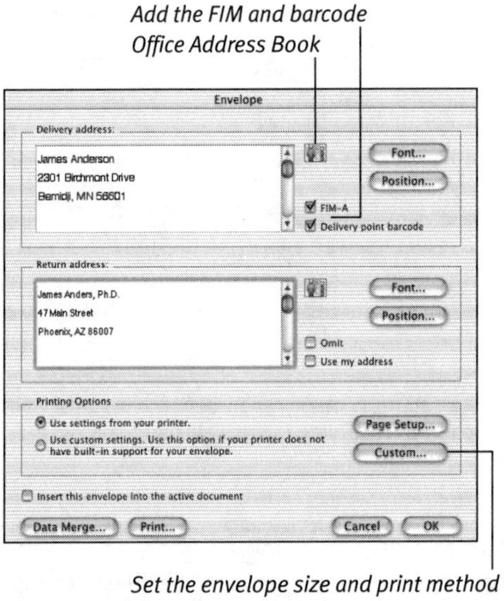

Add the FIM and barcode
Office Address Book

Set the envelope size and print method

Figure 8.9 Specify the delivery address, return address, and formatting options in the Envelope dialog box.

Printing Envelopes

The Envelope wizard can extract the mailing address from a letter and format it so you can print an envelope. Alternatively, you can use the Envelope wizard to create and print *any* envelope; it doesn't matter whether the address is extracted from an open document, chosen from the Office Address Book, or entered by hand.

To create an envelope:

1. Choose Tools > Envelopes, or from the Project Gallery choose the Letters-Envelopes category and select the Envelope Wizard.

   The Envelope Wizard appears (**Figure 8.9**).

2. If the active Word document contains a single address, the wizard automatically uses it as the delivery address.

   or

   If the active Word document doesn't contain a delivery address, you can type one in the Delivery address text box. You can also pick one from the Office Address Book by clicking the icon to the right of the text box.

3. To specify a return address, do one of the following:

   ◆ By default, your address from the Office Address Book is entered as the return address.

   ◆ To use a different return address, remove the checkmark from the Use my address check box. Then type the new return address or click the Address Book icon to select a return address from the Office Address Book.

   ◆ To omit the return address (if you're using a preprinted envelope, for example), click the Omit check box.

(continues on next page)

4. *Optional:* Click the Font and Position buttons to make any necessary changes to the format of the delivery address and return address.

5. In the Printing Options section of the wizard, click a radio button to specify whether the envelope will be printed using standard settings for your printer or, in the case of an unsupported envelope size, whether custom settings are necessary.

6. Click the Page Setup button to specify the envelope size and printer-feed method (**Figure 8.10**).

7. Click Print if you're satisfied with the formatting and print settings, and are ready to print the envelope.

or

If you want to make further changes to the envelope (reducing the line spacing in the addresses or adding a logo, for example), click OK. The envelope is displayed as a new Word document (**Figure 8.11**).

✔ Tips

■ If the active Word document contains more than one address, highlight the delivery address in it before choosing the Envelopes command or the Envelope Wizard.

■ The Delivery point barcode option in the Envelope dialog box prints a machine-readable version of the zip code on the envelope. This assists the USPS in processing the letter.

■ If you are creating reply envelopes, you can have Word print an FIM code by clicking the FIM-A check box in the Envelope dialog box. FIMs are necessary only for business-reply mail. Check with the USPS for more information.

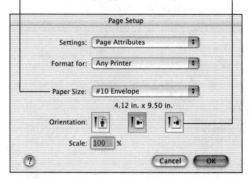

Choose an envelope type   Printer-feed methods

Figure 8.10 In the Page Setup dialog box, you can set print options.

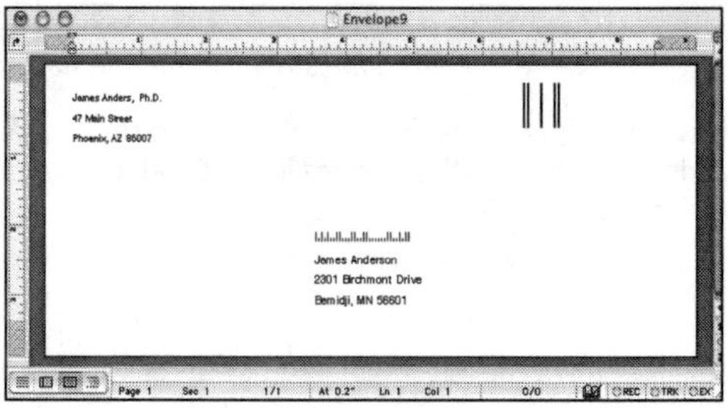

Figure 8.11 Rather than route the envelope directly to your printer, you can generate it as an editable Word document.

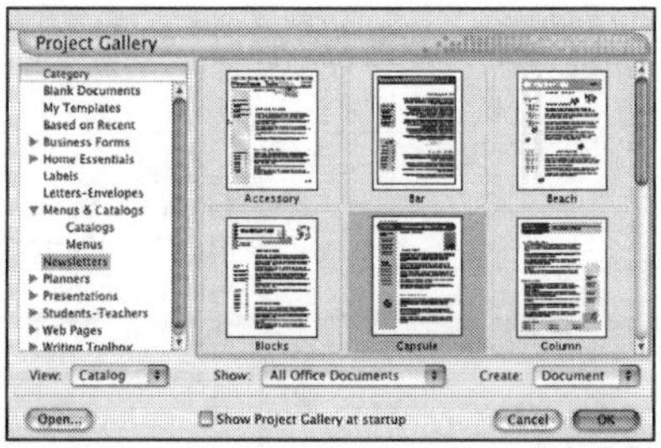

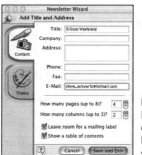

Figure 8.12 In the Project Gallery dialog box, select a newsletter, catalog, or menu layout. In this example, a newsletter template is selected.

Figure 8.13 In the Menu Wizard, enter the restaurant's name, address, and hours of operation, and indicate whether you want to add a coupon or a mailing label.

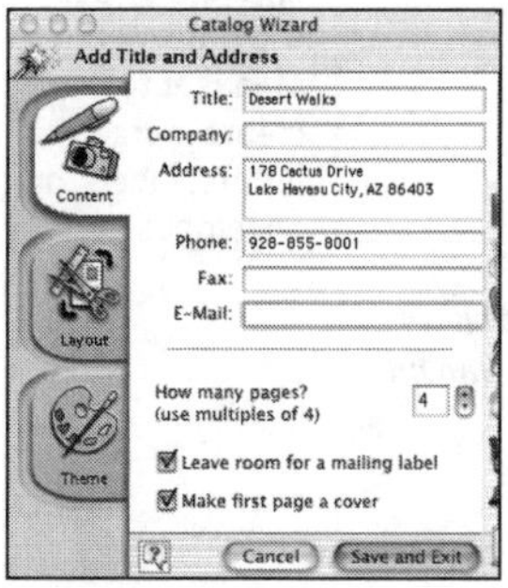

Figure 8.14 In the Catalog Wizard, enter the the catalog's title and length, along with contact information.

Figure 8.15 In the Newsletter Wizard, enter the title, length, and layout specifications.

Creating Catalogs, Menus, and Newsletters

Catalogs, menus, and newsletters are fun to work on because you can really use your creativity. Word provides wizards for creating these kinds of documents. See Chapter 4, Using Templates and Wizards, for more information about wizards and templates. You might also want to refer to Chapter 6, Adding Graphics.

To create a catalog, menu, or newsletter:

1. If you don't already have the Project Gallery open, choose File > Project Gallery (Shift ⌘ P).

2. Choose Menus & Catalogs or Newsletters from the Category list.

3. Select a template for the catalog, menu, or newsletter, and then click OK (**Figure 8.12**).

   The Catalog, Menu, or Newsletter Wizard appears (depending on the template selected).

4. Enter information in the wizard.

   ◆ For the Menu Wizard, enter the name and address of the restaurant and its hours of operation (**Figure 8.13**), and pick a color scheme (Theme tab).

   ◆ For the Catalog Wizard, enter the title and number of pages (**Figure 8.14**), specify the contents of the second page (Layout tab), and select a theme and/or color scheme (Theme tab).

   ◆ For the Newsletter Wizard, enter the title, address, and layout information (**Figure 8.15**), and select a color scheme (Theme tab).

   Now replace the text and graphic placeholders with your own material.

Using the Data Merge Manager

Word provides help for creating mail-merged letters, labels, and envelopes. It will assist you in creating the *main document* (containing placeholders for the information that changes with each copy), creating or opening the *data source* (for example, a collection of names and addresses), and printing the merged documents. In this example, we'll show you how to create form letters using records in the Office Address Book as the data to merge.

To create merged documents:

1. Create or open the document you'll use as your main document (**Figure 8.16**).

    You can use a form letter, a label layout, or an envelope layout, for example.

2. Choose Tools > Data Merge Manager. The Data Merge Manager palette opens (**Figure 8.17**).

3. Click Create in the Main Document section of the Data Merge Manager palette, and then choose a merge type (such as Form Letters) from the pop-up menu (**Figure 8.18**).

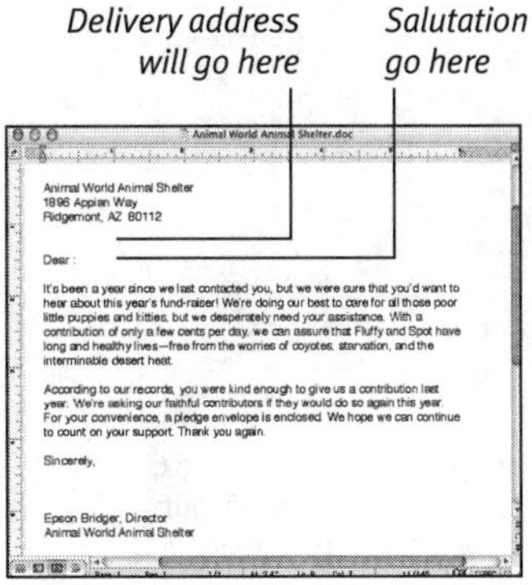

Delivery address will go here   *Salutation will go here*

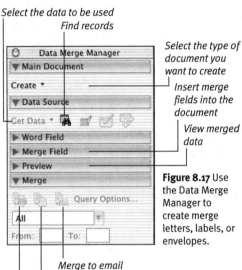

Figure 8.16 This form letter will serve as the main document. Space has been left for the delivery address and salutation.

Select the data to be used
Find records

Select the type of document you want to create

Insert merge fields into the document

View merged data

Figure 8.17 Use the Data Merge Manager to create merge letters, labels, or envelopes.

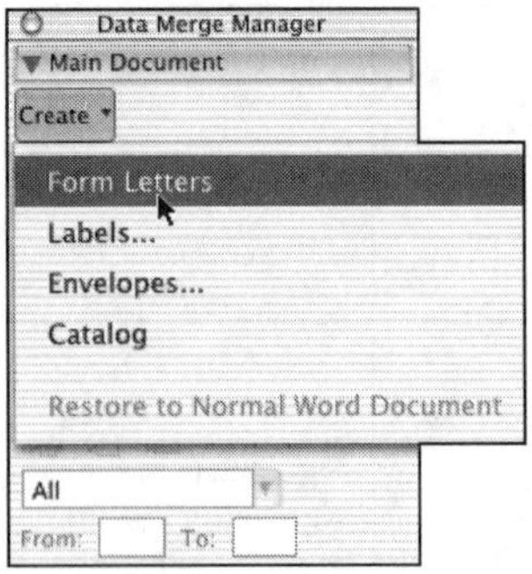

Merge to email
Merge to new document
Merge to printer

Figure 8.18 Click the Create button and choose the type of merge you want to create.

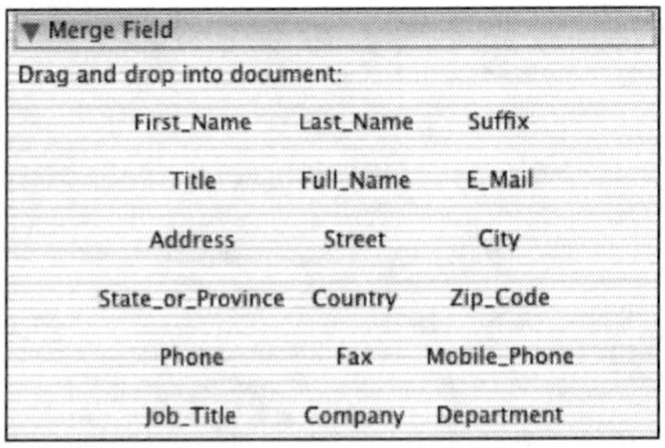

Figure 8.19 After you select the data source, a list of the merge fields it contains appears. Drag the necessary fields into the correct locations in your main document.

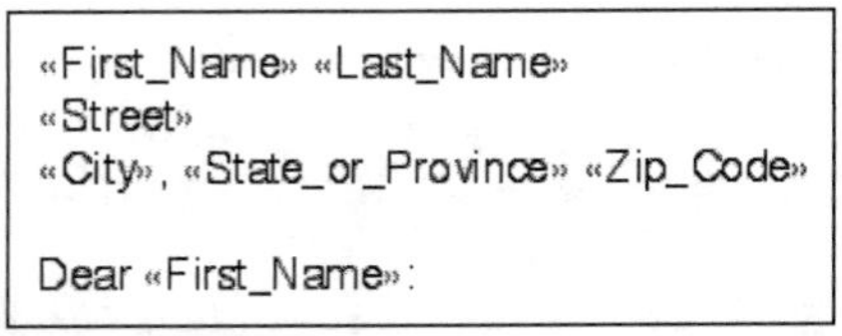

Figure 8.20 When placed in a document, field names are surrounded by brackets (« and »).

4. Click Data Source, click Get Data, and then choose one of the following from the pop-up menu:

   ◆ New Data Source steps you through the process of creating a data source from scratch.

   ◆ Open Data Source lets you use data from an existing Word or Excel document.

   ◆ Office Address Book uses contact information from your address book.

   ◆ FileMaker Pro lets you import data from selected fields in an existing FileMaker Pro database.

   After you've created or opened the data source, the Merge Field section of the Data Merge Manager expands to list the fields in the Office Address Book (**Figure 8.19**).

5. Drag the merge fields from the Data Merge Manager into the proper positions in the main document (**Figure 8.20**).

   The merge fields are placeholders for data from the data source. You can place merge fields on separate lines, together on the same line, or embedded within the text of the main document.

6. If necessary, format the merge fields and add any required spacing or punctuation.

   For example, for the final line of an address, you'd separate the City, State, and Zip merge fields with a comma and spaces, like this:

   «City», «State» «Zip »

   (continues on next page)

7. Specify which records to include in the merge by choosing an option from the Merge drop-down menu of the Data Merge Manager (**Figure 8.21**).

8. When the merge document is complete, click the Merge to printer button to print immediately, click the Merge to new document button to create a document you can print later, or click the Merge to email button to send the merge document(s) to Entourage's Outbox for sending as an email (**Figure 8.22**).

✔ Tips

■ At times, you may want to create a merge for just one record. To locate the desired record, click the Find records button in the Data Source section of the Data Merge Manager. For more complex record-selection needs, click the Query Options button in the Merge section.

■ Before completing the merge, it's a good idea to preview the data to make sure the right fields were selected and the formatting looks right. Expand the Preview section of the Data Merge Manager, depress the View merged data button, and then use the arrow buttons to review some of the records displayed as part of the main document.

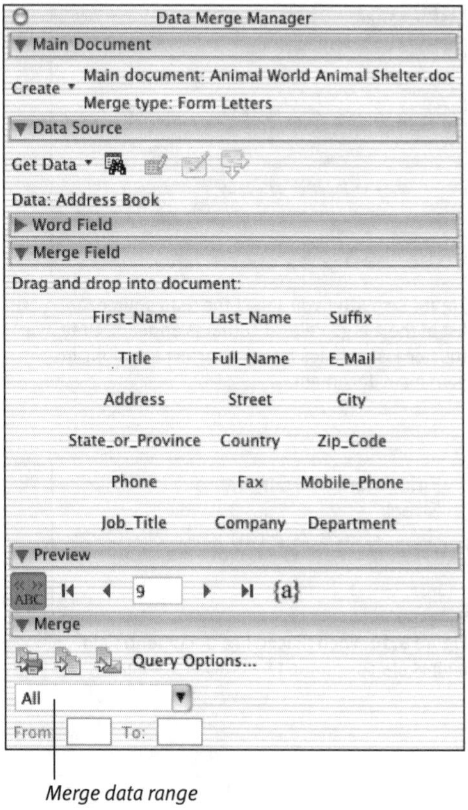

Figure 8.21 You can specify which records to use in the Merge section of the Data Merge Manager.

Figure 8.22 When you merge to email, each record generated by the merge is placed in Entourage's Outbox, ready for sending. If necessary, you can edit the messages in Entourage.

Part III: Microsoft Excel

ENTERING
INFORMATION

An important part of getting started using Excel is entering data. We'll cover the basics here: entering text and numbers and moving them around. Two special ways of working with Excel—entering lists of data and making calculations—are discussed later in their own chapters. Excel has features that help with both of those.

This chapter jumps right into working in an Excel document. For information on creating a document and using the Project Gallery, see Chapter 1.

Moving Around in a Worksheet

Excel windows work like most others in Macintosh applications, with some additional help to get you where you want to go. Note the names of the columns (letters) and rows (numbers). Specifying the column and row (for example, G4) uniquely identifies a cell. This is the cell *address*.

To move to a cell:

1. Click the cell (**Figure 9.1**). The cell address appears in the name box, and the corresponding column name and row name are highlighted.

   or

   Use keyboard shortcuts to move the cell pointer to the cell (**Table 9.1**).

   or

   Click the name box and type the destination cell address (**Figure 9.2**), then press [Enter] or [Return].

2. The cell you move to becomes the *active cell*. The new cell address appears in the name box, and the corresponding column name and row name are highlighted.

✔ Tips

- You can use the scroll bars to scroll through the document without changing the active cell.

- You can use [Control][Delete] to scroll directly to the active cell.

Figure 9.1 Click the cell you want to enter.

Figure 9.2 Click the name box, and type a cell address.

Table 9.1

Keyboard Shortcuts for Moving Within an Excel Worksheet	
SHORTCUT	**ACTION**
[↑] [↓] [←] [→]	Move to the adjacent cell up, down, left, or right
[Pg Up] [Pg Dn]	Move up or down one screenful
[Option] [Pg Up] [Option] [Pg Dn]	Move left or right one screenful
[Tab]	Move right one cell
[Shift] [Tab]	Move left one cell
[Enter]	Move down one cell
[Shift] [Enter]	Move up one cell
[Home]	Move to first cell of the row
[Control] [Home]	Move to cell A1
[Control] [End]	Move to lower-right corner of worksheet

MOVING AROUND IN A WORKSHEET

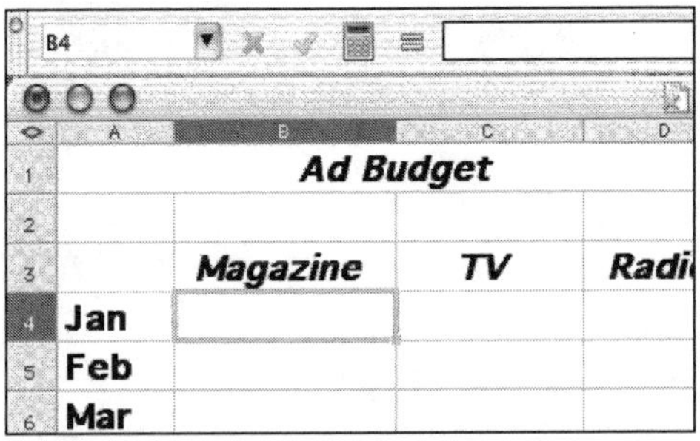

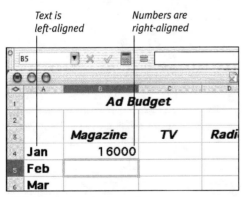

Figure 9.3 Select the cell by clicking in it.

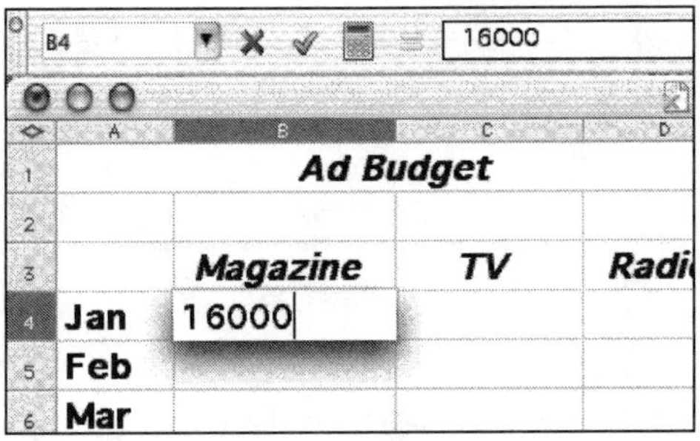

Figure 9.4 Type the contents in the cell.

Text is
left-aligned

Numbers are
right-aligned

Figure 9.5 Move to the next cell.

Typing Data into Cells

The basics are probably obvious, but here are some tips that can make it easier.

To enter data into a cell:

1. Select the cell (**Figure 9.3**).

2. Type text, a number, or a formula in the cell (**Figure 9.4**).

3. Move to the next cell (press Enter to move down or Tab to move right). The contents of the previous cell are formatted automatically (**Figure 9.5**).

✔ Tips

■ Enter and Tab are just two of the commands that will move you out of a cell. Also use any of the keyboard shortcuts to get to where you want to go next (**Table 9.1**).

■ Until you specify a different format, in cells text is automatically left-aligned and numbers are right-aligned. The format in the column headings in the figures has been changed to centered (**Figure 9.5**).

■ If you have a block of cells you want to fill, see "Filling Ranges of Cells" below for a quick way to do it.

■ If you need a series of consecutive dates or numbers for column or row headings (month names, for example), use AutoFill to enter them automatically. See "To AutoFill a range of cells" later in this chapter.

Adding Comments to Cells

In addition to entering the actual contents of a cell, you can attach a *comment* to it, which doesn't show unless you want it to. Comments are useful when you want to include a notation that explains something about the cell, or you'd like to communicate with other users about particular cells.

To create and manage comments:

1. To add a comment, click a cell and choose Insert > Comment (**Figure 9.6**).

   A text box appears. If you've filled in the User name field (Edit > Preferences > General), that name appears in the text box to identify who wrote the comment, but you can delete it if you wish.

2. Type your content in the box (**Figure 9.7**).

3. When you click any other cell, the comment text box closes, but a small triangle appears in the upper-right corner of the commented cell to indicate that it has an associated comment (**Figure 9.8**).

4. To view a cell's comment, pause the mouse pointer over that cell (**Figure 9.9**).

5. To view all the comments attached to all the cells in the worksheet, choose View > Comments (**Figure 9.10**). To hide all the comments again, choose View > Comments again.

✔ Tips

- When you choose View > Comments, the Reviewing toolbar appears (**Figure 9.11**) and lets you create, delete, edit, view, or hide comments, or email the entire workbook to someone as an attachment. You can also choose View > Toolbars > Reviewing to view or hide this toolbar.

- You can resize a comment box by dragging any of the handles that appear around it when you're editing it.

Figure 9.6 To attach a comment, first choose Insert > Comment.

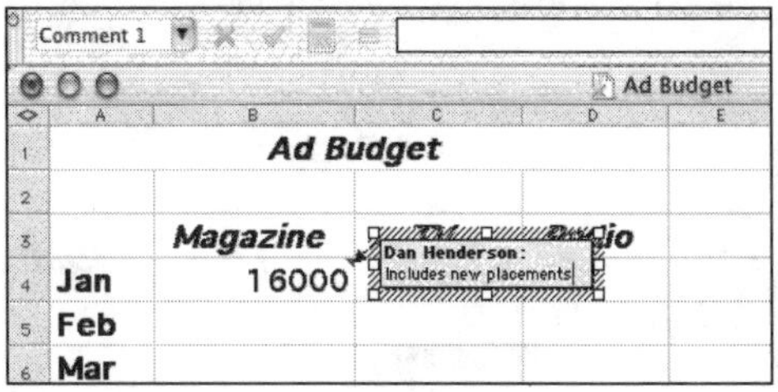

Figure 9.7 Type your comment in the text box.

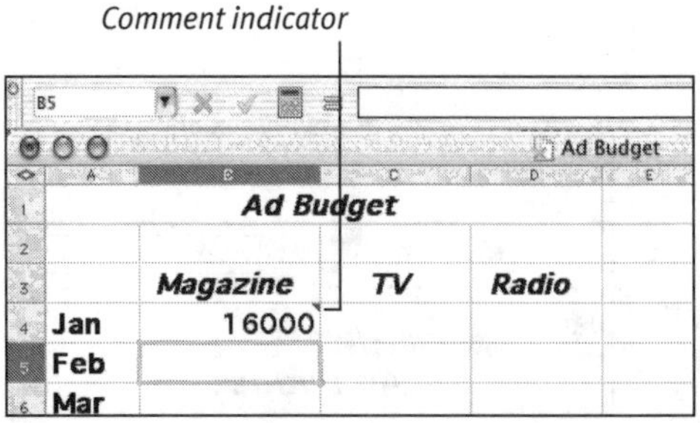

Comment indicator

Figure 9.8 The comment indicator, a small triangle, appears.

Figure 9.9 Pause the pointer over a cell to see the comment.

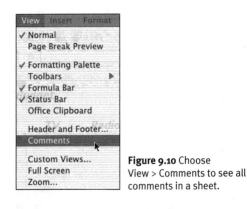

Figure 9.10 Choose View > Comments to see all comments in a sheet.

Figure 9.11 Use the Reviewing toolbar to manage comments.

B4						16000

	A	B	C	D	E
1		*Ad Budget*			
2					
3		*Magazine*	*TV*	*Radio*	
4	**Jan**	$16,000	$78,000	$8,200	
5	**Feb**	16,000	78,000	8,200	
6	**Mar**	17,500	82,500	11,000	
7	**Apr**	17,500	82,500	11,000	
8	**May**	14,000	64,000	6,700	

Figure 9.12 Select a range of cells.

Quarter 1					16000

Name Box

	A	B	C	D	E
1		*Ad Budget*			
2					
3		*Magazine*	*TV*	*Radio*	
4	**Jan**	$16,000	$78,000	$8,200	
5	**Feb**	16,000	78,000	8,200	
6	**Mar**	17,500	82,500	11,000	
7	**Apr**	17,500	82,500	11,000	
8	**May**	14,000	64,000	6,700	

Figure 9.13 Type a name for the range in the name box.

Naming Ranges of Cells

Assigning a name to a range of cells makes the range easier to refer to. For example, you could give the name "2000" to a column of numbers for the year 2000 and refer to it in a formula by that name: SUM(2000) instead of SUM(D3:D14). You can use the column head or row head as the name, or assign any name you like to a subset of a column or row, a group of cells that covers more than one column or row, or a nonadjacent group of cells.

To name a range of cells:

1. Select the range of cells (**Figure 9.12**).

2. In the name box at the left end of the formula bar, type the name you want to use (**Figure 9.13**).

3. Press (Enter) or (Return).

✔ Tips

- If you assign a name to a range of cells in one worksheet, you can refer to those cells by that name in other sheets of the workbook.

- You can assign a name to a single cell. For example, you could name one cell SalesTax, enter the current tax rate in that cell, and use SalesTax in formulas throughout the workbook without having to enter the numerical rate in each place.

- Excel won't let you name a cell while you're changing its contents.

Filling Ranges of Cells

To enter data quickly into a rectangular range of cells, create an entry range.

To type data into a block of cells:

1. Click the cell in the upper-left corner of the range (**Figure 9.14**).

2. Drag to the range's lower-right-corner cell (**Figure 9.15**).

   The active cell is the one in the entry range's upper-left corner.

3. Type data into a cell, and then press Enter.

   The cell pointer automatically moves down the column to the next cell.

4. Continue typing data into the cells, pressing Enter as you go (**Figure 9.16**).

   When the cell pointer reaches the bottom of a column, it jumps to the top of the next column within the entry range (**Figure 9.17**).

✔ Tip

- If you use the Tab key instead of the Enter or Return key between cells, the active cell moves from left to right until it gets to the end of a row within the range. Then it jumps to the first highlighted cell in the next row.

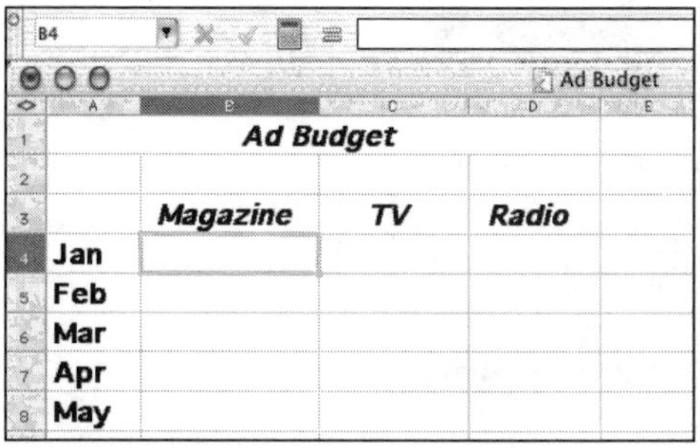

Figure 9.14 Click the upper-left cell of the range.

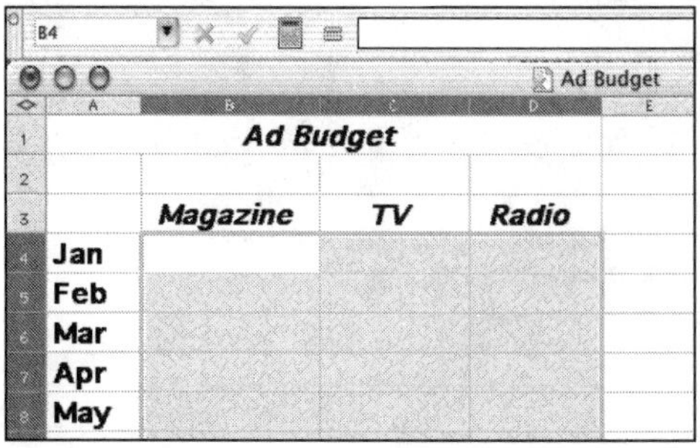

Figure 9.15 Drag to the range's lower-right cell.

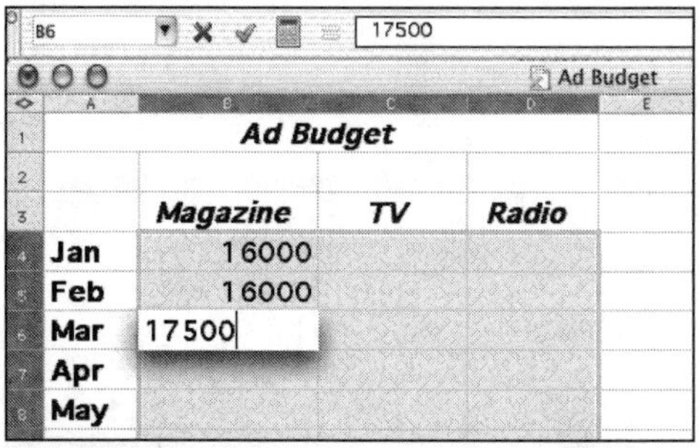

Figure 9.16 Type data into each cell, pressing Enter after each entry.

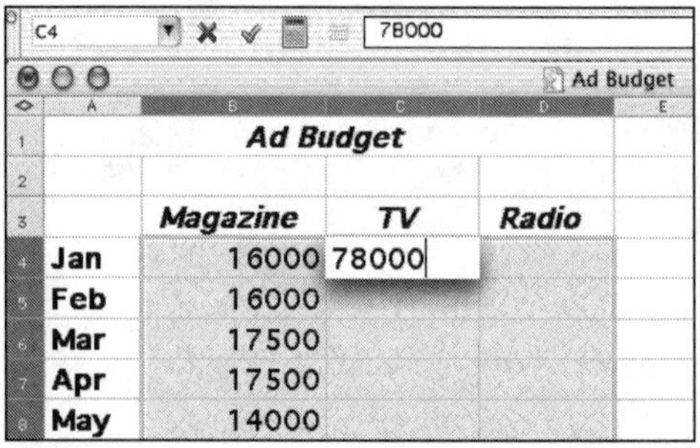

Figure 9.17 After one column is filled, the cell pointer automatically moves to the top of the next column.

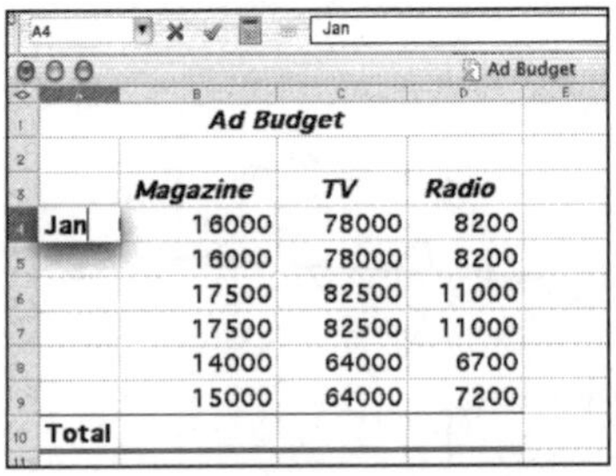

Figure 9.18
Type the first number, word, or date into the first cell in the sequence.

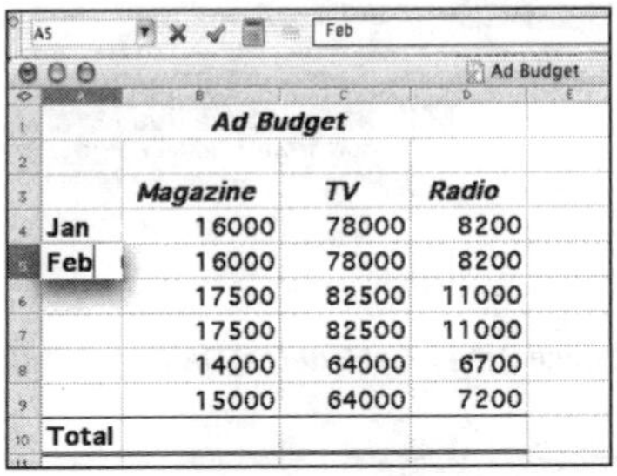

Figure 9.19
Type the next number, word, or date into the next cell in the sequence.

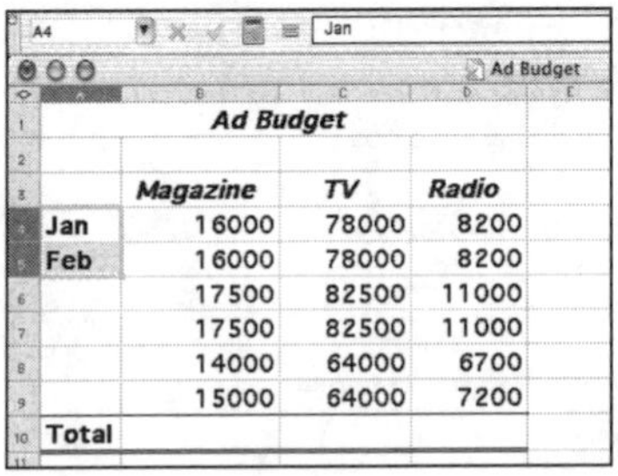

Figure 9.20
Select the two cells.

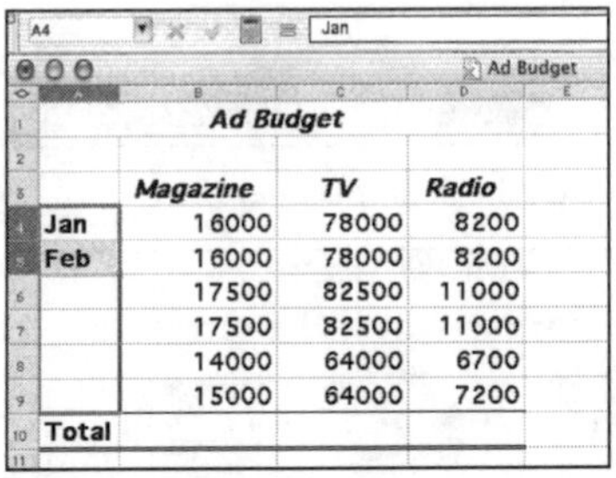

Figure 9.21
Drag the fill handle to extend the sequence.

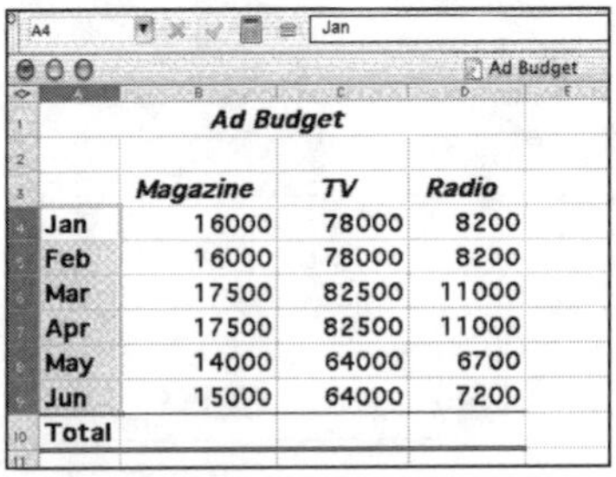

Figure 9.22
Release the mouse button.

When you want to fill a range of cells with consecutive numbers, numbers that follow a specific pattern, dates, or dates that follow a specific pattern (such as every Monday), use AutoFill as a quick and convenient method of automatically entering the sequence.

To AutoFill a range of cells:

1. In the first cell of the sequence, type the first number, word, or date (**Figure 9.18**).

2. In an adjacent cell, type the next number, word, or date (**Figure 9.19**).

3. Select the two cells (**Figure 9.20**).

4. Carefully place the mouse pointer on the fill handle at the lower-right corner of the border surrounding the two cells (the cursor changes shape) and drag the fill handle to extend the sequence (**Figure 9.21**). The sequence fills in as you drag the mouse.

5. Release the mouse button when the sequence is complete (**Figure 9.22**).

✔ Tip

■ As you drag the mouse to extend the sequence, the value of the current mouse-pointer location appears in a yellow tool tip next to the cursor.

FILLING RANGES OF CELLS

115

Bringing In Data from Outside Excel

Typing in data isn't the only way to fill cells in Excel: You can connect to an external database and import data from it (the database administrator can help with that), and you can import data from a text file.

To import data from a text file:

1. Choose Data > Get External Data > Import Text File (**Figure 9.23**).

2. Navigate to the file you want to import, select it, and click Get Data.

   The Text Import Wizard opens.

3. In Step 1 of the Wizard, in the Original data type area, tell Excel what separates the columns in your file and at which row you want to insert the imported data, and click Next (**Figure 9.24**).

   A preview of your file in the lower section of the dialog box helps you answer the questions.

4. In Step 2, Excel guesses how you want the columns interpreted. If it guesses incorrectly, you can make changes here (**Figure 9.25**), and click Next.

Figure 9.23 Choose Data > Get External Data > Import Text File.

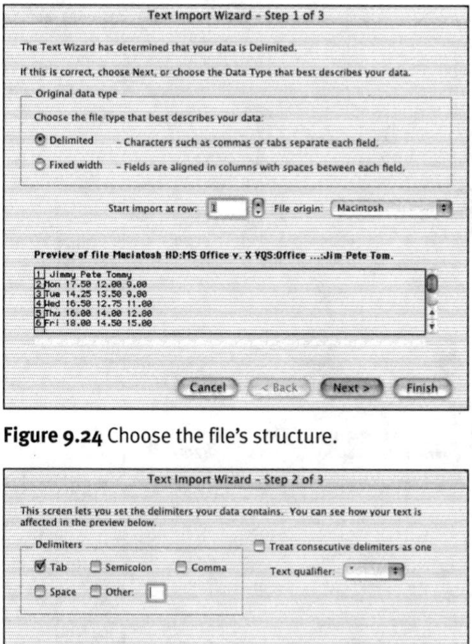

Figure 9.24 Choose the file's structure.

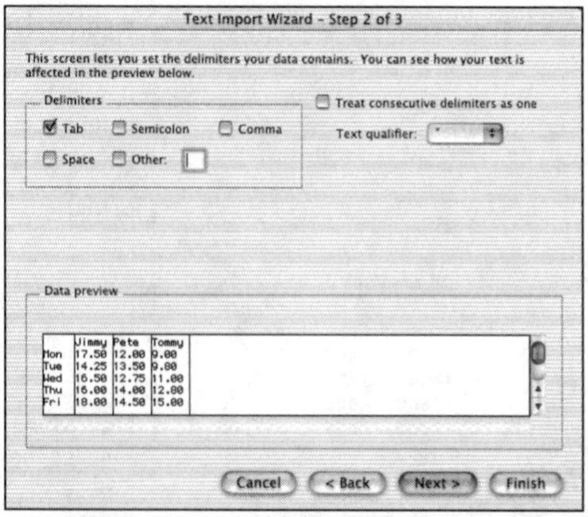

Figure 9.25 Confirm the column interpretation.

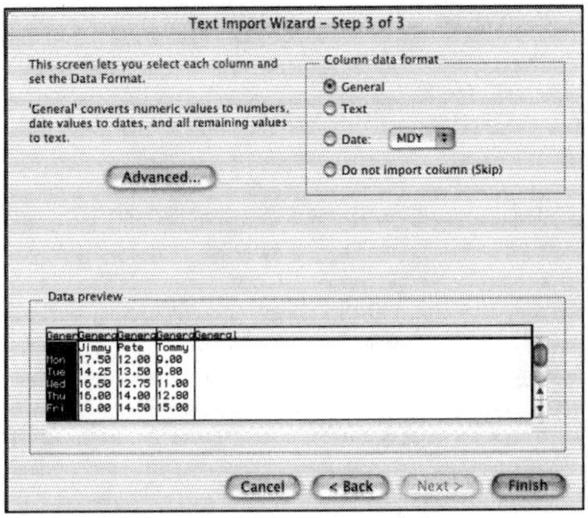

Figure 9.26 Choose column formatting.

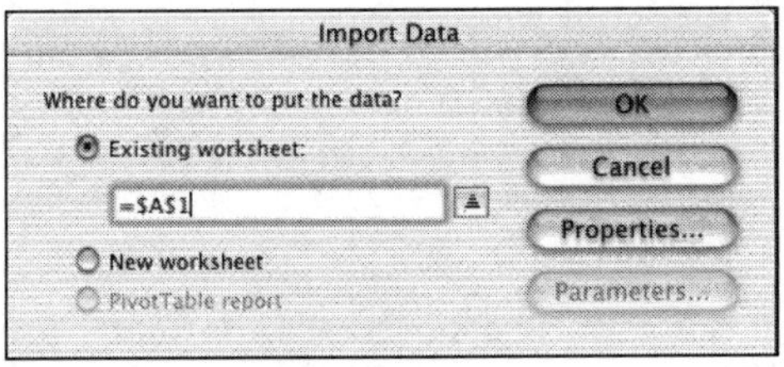

Figure 9.27 Choose the destination cell or worksheet.

5. In Step 3, you can format columns if you wish. Click each column you want to change, and choose the data format you want to assign (**Figure 9.26**). The Data Preview window shows the format name at the top of each column. Click Finish.

6. Finally, choose whether to have the imported data inserted in the current worksheet, beginning at a particular cell (the default is the currently selected cell), or to open a new worksheet to contain the data (**Figure 9.27**).

7. The data is imported as you directed, and the External Data toolbar appears.

✔ Tip

- You can use the External Data toolbar to read the current contents of the file (or all imported files) using the same settings you used before. Another tool on the toolbar allows you to change your selections in the Text Import Wizard.

Editing Cells

The easiest way to change a cell's contents is to click the cell and then type right over the words or number. But if the cell contains a formula, you may want to edit the formula instead, so you don't have to retype the whole entry.

To edit a cell:

1. Click the cell, and then type over the contents (**Figure 9.28**).

   or

   Double-click in the cell to place an insertion point in the contents.

2. Edit the contents as though you were editing text in Word. See Chapter 3.

3. Move to another cell (usually by pressing Enter or Tab) to enter the revision into the cell (**Figure 9.29**).

✔ Tips

- When you click a cell, its contents also appear in the edit line. You can click the Edit Line and edit the cell contents there (**Figure 9.30**).

- To abandon a revision and leave the original contents of a cell intact, press Esc before you press Enter or Tab to exit the cell.

- If you edit a formula, all affected cells are recalculated as soon as you move to a different cell.

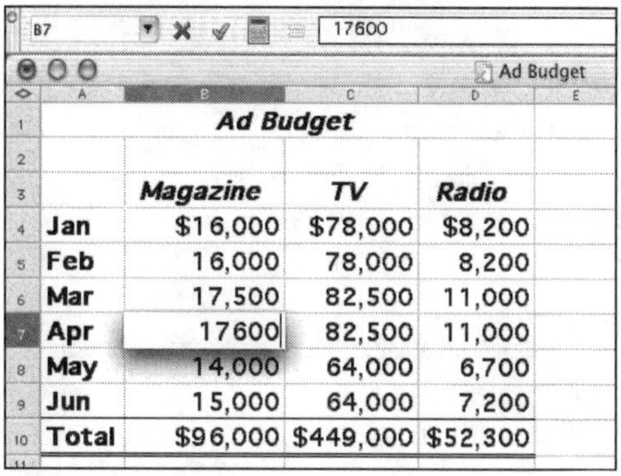
B7
17600
Ad Budget
Ad Budget
Magazine TV Radio
Jan $16,000 $78,000 $8,200
Feb 16,000 78,000 8,200
Mar 17,500 82,500 11,000
Apr 17600 82,500 11,000
May 14,000 64,000 6,700
Jun 15,000 64,000 7,200
Total $96,000 $449,000 $52,300

Figure 9.28 Click the cell and retype its contents.

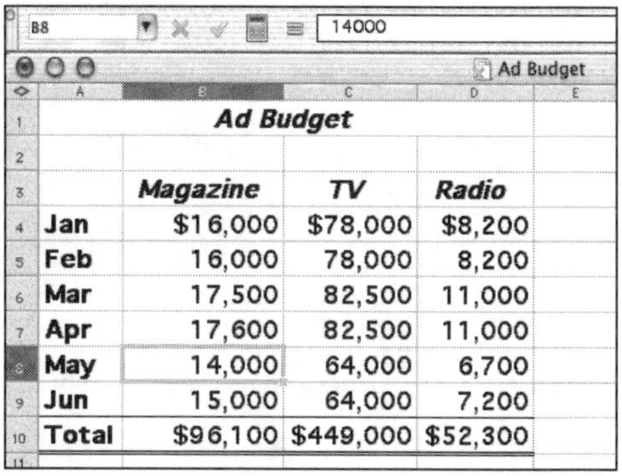
B8
14000
Ad Budget
Ad Budget
Magazine TV Radio
Jan $16,000 $78,000 $8,200
Feb 16,000 78,000 8,200
Mar 17,500 82,500 11,000
Apr 17,600 82,500 11,000
May 14,000 64,000 6,700
Jun 15,000 64,000 7,200
Total $96,100 $449,000 $52,300

Figure 9.29 Move to another cell to finish the revision.

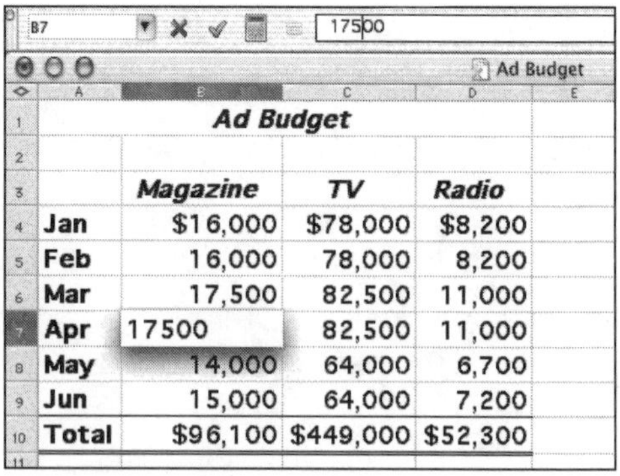
B7
17500
Ad Budget
Ad Budget
Magazine TV Radio
Jan $16,000 $78,000 $8,200
Feb 16,000 78,000 8,200
Mar 17,500 82,500 11,000
Apr 17500 82,500 11,000
May 14,000 64,000 6,700
Jun 15,000 64,000 7,200
Total $96,100 $449,000 $52,300

Figure 9.30 Edit a cell's contents in the Edit Line.

WORKING WITH LISTS

Microsoft discovered that a large portion of Excel users were setting up their worksheets to simply keep lists of information, so it added the new List Manager feature to Excel in Office 2001. This chapter shows how to use the List Manager to create and maintain simple lists that involve few calculations.

Creating a List

Getting started is easy. In fact, Excel may already have offered you the opportunity to use the List Manager.

To start a list:

1. Simply start entering your information into your Excel document. You may be presented with a query guessing that you're creating a list (**Figure 10.1**), along with an offer to invoke the List Manager. Click Yes to skip the List Wizard steps below.

   or

   Click the cell where you want the list to begin, and choose Insert > List to bring up the List Wizard (**Figure 10.2**).

2. In Step 1 of the List Wizard, tell Excel whether you want to start with a new list, an existing spreadsheet, or an external file (**Figure 10.3**). You can also tell it whether you want to open the list in a new worksheet or an existing one, and you can pick a particular starting cell. Click Next when you're ready.

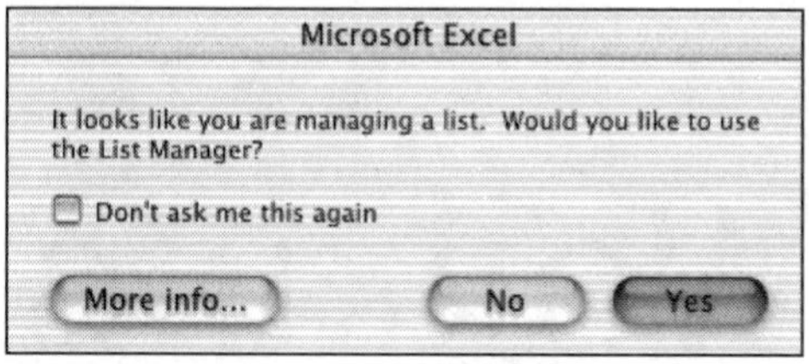

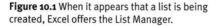

Figure 10.1 When it appears that a list is being created, Excel offers the List Manager.

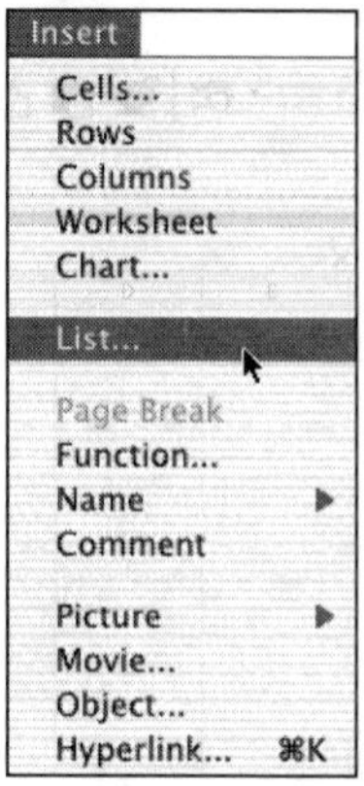

Figure 10.2 Choose Insert > List to bring up the List Wizard.

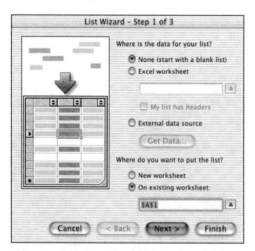

Figure 10.3 In the List Wizard, specify where the data is coming from and where you want to insert it.

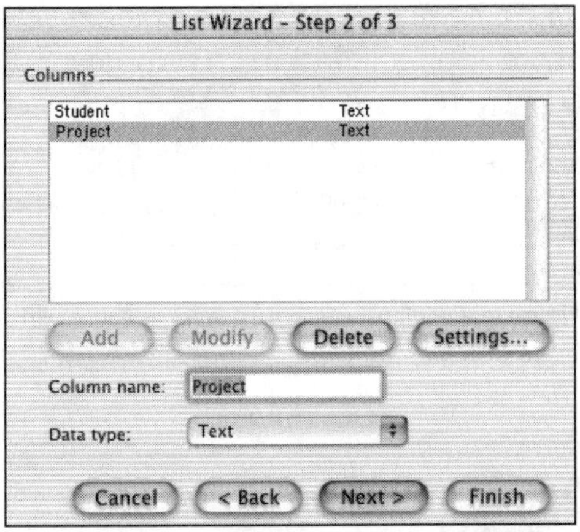

Figure 10.4 Specify column names and data types.

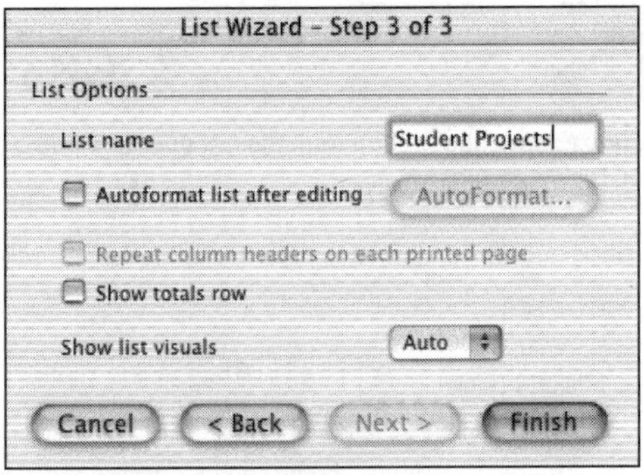

Figure 10.5 Name the list, and choose a totals row or AutoFormat style if you wish.

Figure 10.6 The list appears in the document in a list frame.

Figure 10.7 The List toolbar.

3. In Step 2 of the List Wizard (**Figure 10.4**), type in the name of each column for your list in order, and choose the data types from the pull-down list. Click Add after specifying each column. When you're finished, click Next.

4. In Step 3 of the List Wizard (**Figure 10.5**), give your list a name and indicate whether you want Excel to add a totals row for you. Here you may also choose an AutoFormat style. When you're done, click Finish.

The list appears where you specified, inside a special list frame (**Figure 10.6**).

✔ Tip

■ When your list appears, the List toolbar also appears (**Figure 10.7**); it offers the opportunity to redo any element of the list.

Editing a List

Any aspect of the list that you set up with the List Wizard can be easily modified later, through the List toolbar or menu selections. In the List toolbar you'll find all the editing tools for lists in one place.

To edit a list:

1. To add items to the list, simply type them into each cell as you would with any Excel worksheet (**Figure 10.8**). As you add each row, a new blank row appears in the list frame.

    or

    Click the List pop-up menu on the List toolbar and choose Form (**Figure 10.9**), and then use the Form dialog box (Sheet3) to enter items in the list (**Figure 10.10**).

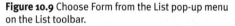

Figure 10.8 Adding items to a list that was set up with the List Wizard.

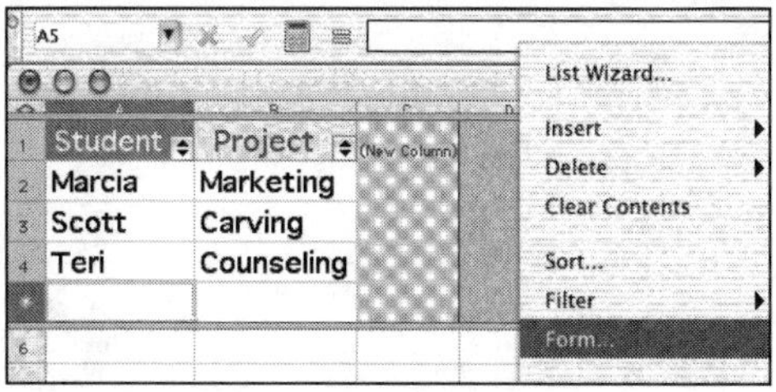

Figure 10.9 Choose Form from the List pop-up menu on the List toolbar.

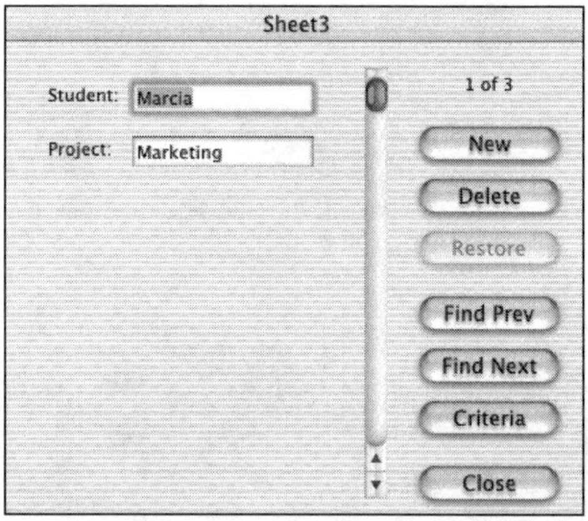

Figure 10.10 Enter list items in the Form dialog box.

EDITING A LIST

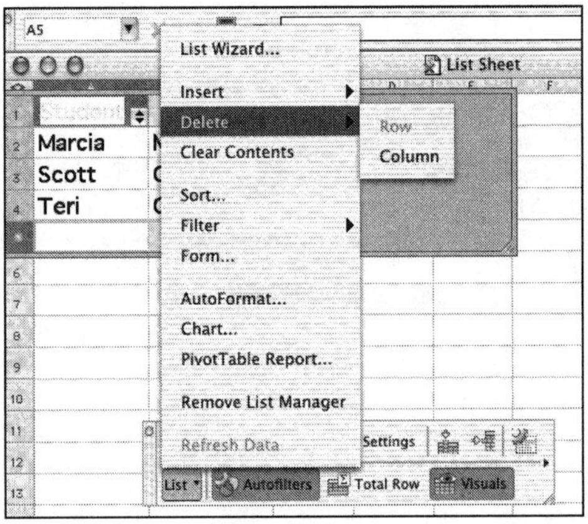

Figure 10.11 Delete a row.

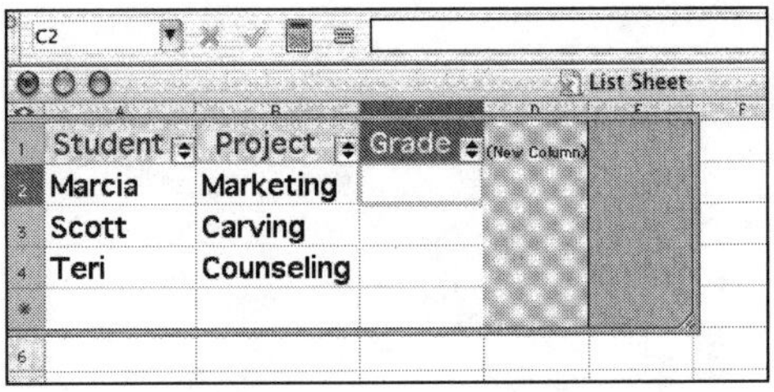

Figure 10.12 Click the New Column header to add a column.

2. To delete items from the list, click the row number to select the entire row, and choose List > Delete > Row from the List toolbar (**Figure 10.11**).

or

If you want to clear the contents of the selected row without deleting it, select List > Clear Contents.

3. To add a column, click the New Column header in the list frame and type the column name (**Figure 10.12**). Another New Column header appears.

✔ Tip

■ As you begin typing items, a list of previously typed contents of that column that start with the same characters appears; you may choose one item from the list as a shortcut. This is helpful when several rows in the list hold the same value; it saves you from typing all the characters in the repeated item every time you want to use it.

Formatting a List

Once you've created the list contents (or at least have a good start on them), you may want to change the format of the list. In addition to the standard capabilities you have when selecting a cell, group of cells, column(s), or row(s) (such as bold, italic, font, size, borders, and shading), you can also choose from a wide selection of list formats that Microsoft provides.

To format an entire list:

1. Pull up the List pop-up menu from the List toolbar and choose AutoFormat (**Figure 10.13**).

2. The AutoFormat dialog box appears (**Figure 10.14**). Click any of the Table format choices in the left pane to see a preview in the right pane of the format applied to your list.

3. When you have selected a format, click OK.

4. To get the full effect of your list's new appearance, click the Visuals button in the List toolbar to turn off the list frame graphics (**Figure 10.15**).

✔ Tips

■ In the AutoFormat dialog box, if you click the Options button, you can turn each of the AutoFormat elements, such as borders or shading, on or off individually (**Figure 10.16**).

■ Once you've formatted a list with AutoFormat, you can add any other formatting you'd like.

■ Clicking the Visuals button in the List toolbar a second time restores the list frame graphics.

■ To learn how to format a subset of the list (individual cells, ranges of cells, particular columns or rows), see Chapter 12.

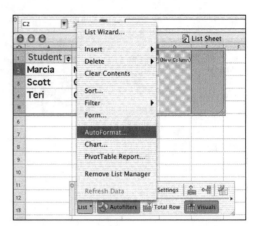

Figure 10.13 Choose AutoFormat from the List pop-up menu.

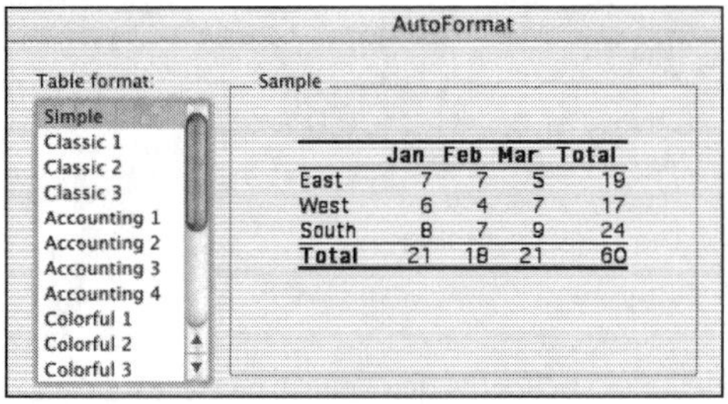

Figure 10.14 Select a format theme.

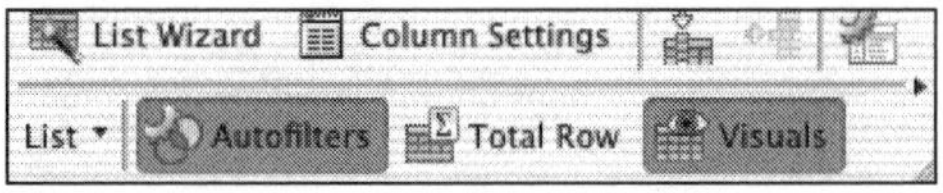

Figure 10.15 The Visuals button toggles the list frame graphics on and off.

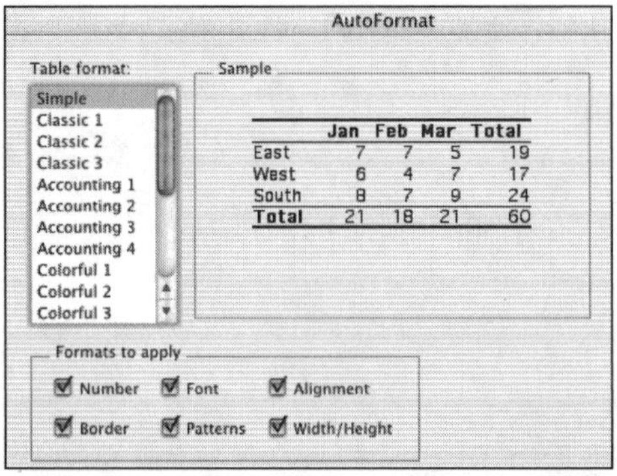

Figure 10.16 Select AutoFormat elements individually.

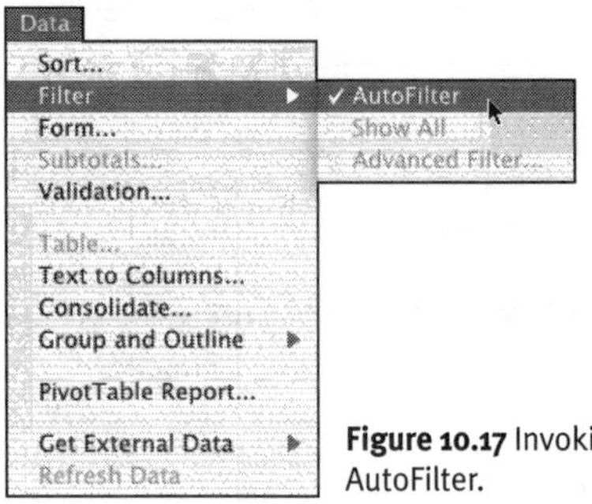

Figure 10.17 Invoking AutoFilter.

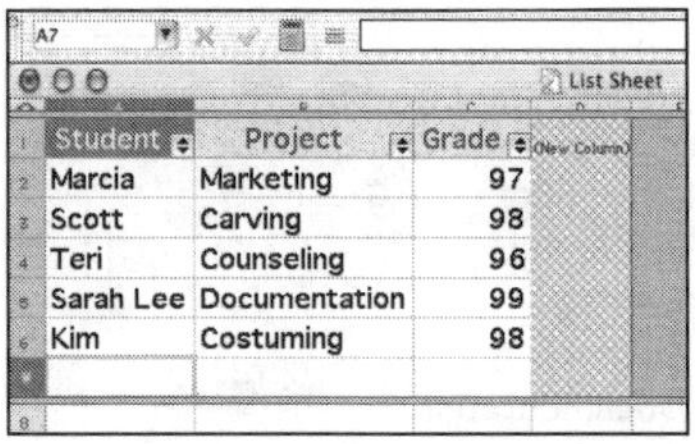

Figure 10.18 AutoFilter arrows appear next to column heads.

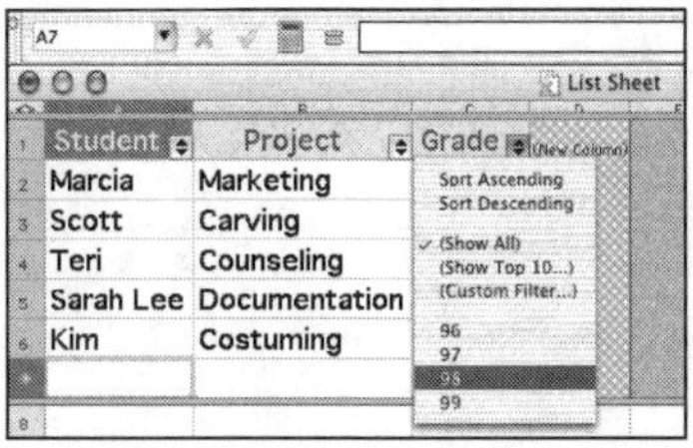

Figure 10.19 Choose a cell value.

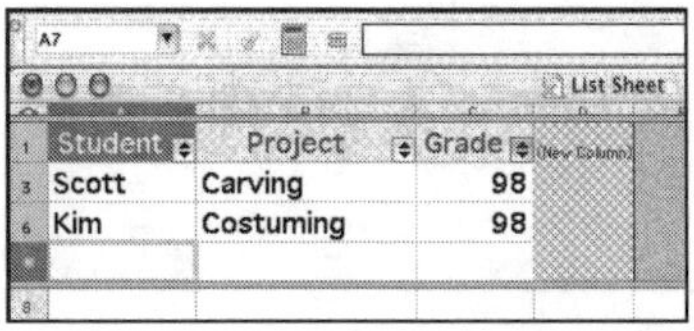

Figure 10.20 All rows with any other value are hidden.

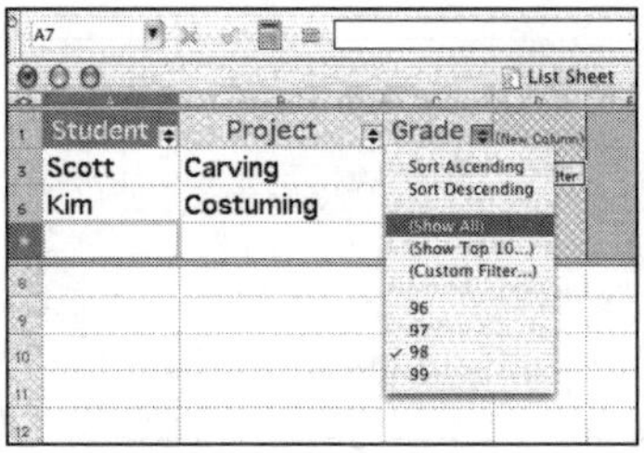

Figure 10.21 Show All reveals hidden rows.

Filtering a List

Once a list reaches a substantial length, you may want to selectively view rows that meet specific criteria. Excel allows this by temporarily hiding the rows that do not meet your criteria. Unfortunately, the method doesn't work while you're using the List Manager.

To find certain values in a list:

1. If you're using List Manager, copy the list to a new worksheet by selecting the entire list, then choosing Edit > Copy, File > New, and Edit > Paste.

   Leave at least one cell in the list selected. It's OK to leave the entire list selected, as it will be after the Paste operation.

2. Choose Data > Filter > AutoFilter (**Figure 10.17**). Arrows for criteria selection appear next to each column head (**Figure 10.18**).

3. Click and hold on the AutoFilter arrows next to the title of the column in which you want to apply a filter.

   You can hide rows of a column containing cell values that don't meet your selected criteria. Simply choose those values from the pop-up list (**Figures 10.19, 10.20**).

4. To show all the rows again, click and hold on the arrows again, and choose Show All (**Figure 10.21**).

   (continues on next page)

5. All the hidden rows are now visible again (**Figure 10.22**).

6. To select rows based on more complex criteria, click and hold on the arrows, and choose Custom Filter (**Figure 10.23**).

7. In the Custom AutoFilter dialog box (**Figure 10.24**), you can specify up to two criteria for that column, using value comparisons (for example, "greater than"), and connect them by And or Or. If you choose And, only rows that meet both criteria are shown (**Figure 10.25**). If you choose Or, rows that meet either criterion are shown.

✔ Tips

■ In the Custom Filter dialog box you can use wild-card characters to specify text values. Entering ? matches any one character ("s?nd" matches both "send" and "sand"); entering * matches any series of characters ("s*nd" matches "send," "sand," "sound," "strand," and so forth).

■ If you apply criteria to more than one column, each column's criteria operate only on the rows that show from the previous column's filtering.

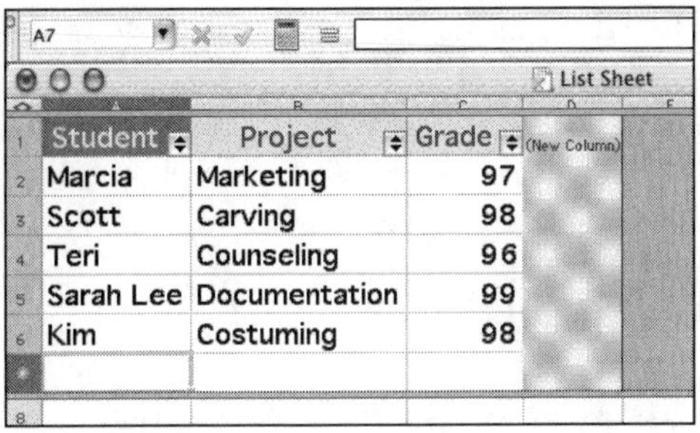

Figure 10.22 All rows are visible again.

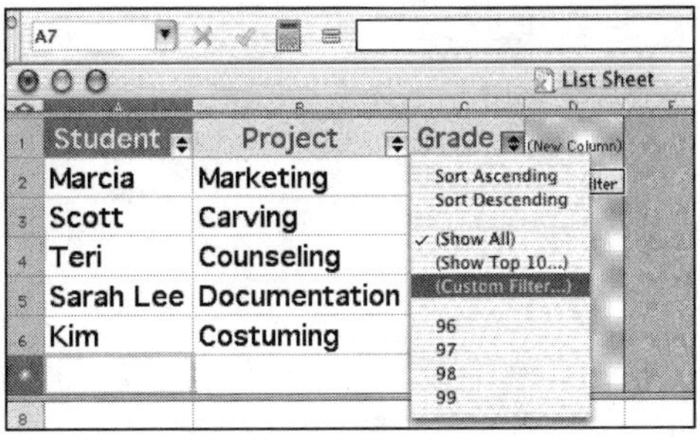

Figure 10.23 Invoke custom filtering for the column.

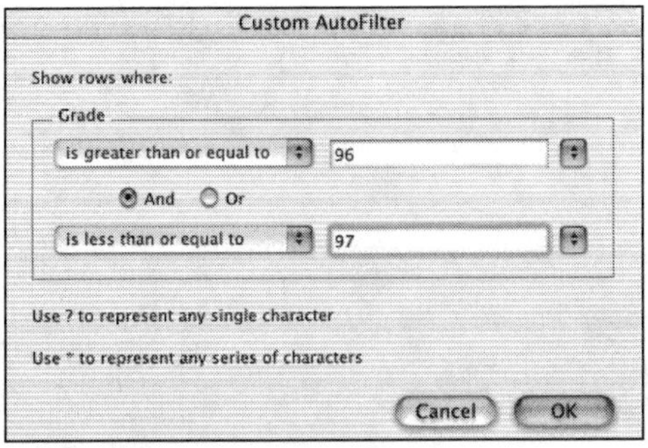

Figure 10.24 Choose criteria for filtering.

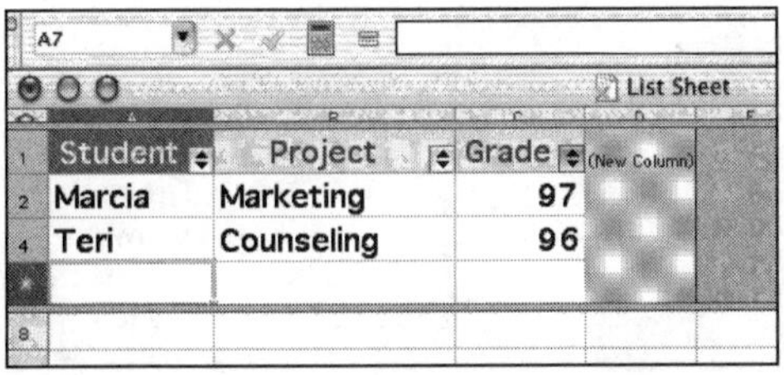

Figure 10.25 The list is filtered by the criteria chosen.

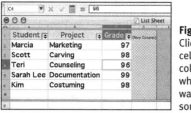

Figure 10.26
Click any cell in the column by which you want to sort.

Sort Ascending   *Sort Descending*

Figure 10.27
Choose a direction tool.

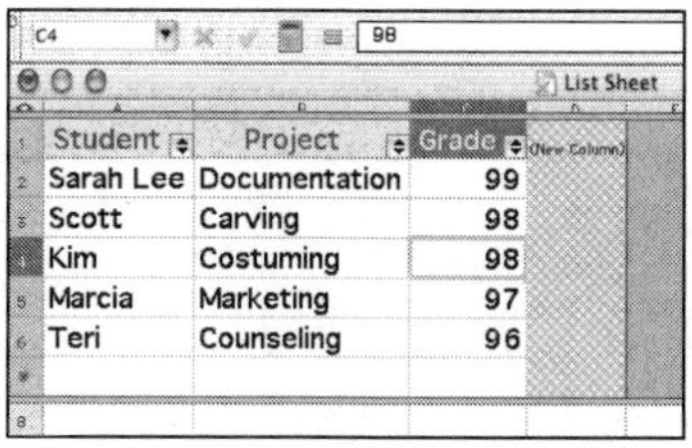

Figure 10.28
The sorted list.

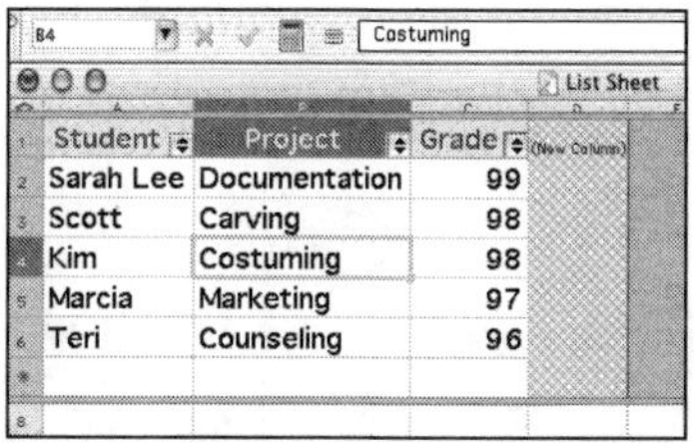

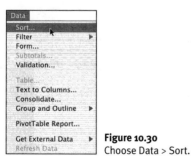

Figure 10.29
Click any cell in the list.

Figure 10.30
Choose Data > Sort.

Sorting a List

You can also sort a list by the values in one or more columns. Excel gives you tools to make this easy. To sort the most common way, you rearrange the rows based on the contents of the cells in one of the columns, and you can choose to sort in either ascending or descending order.

To perform a simple sort:

1. Click any cell in the column you're going to use to sort the rows (**Figure 10.26**).

2. Click either the Sort Ascending or the Sort Descending button in the toolbar (**Figure 10.27**).

   The rows of the list are rearranged (**Figure 10.28**).

✔ Tip

■ The ascending sort order begins with the digits 0 through 9, and then spaces, punctuation, and the letters A through Z. The descending sort order is the reverse.

You may want to do a more complex sort. Perhaps the primary sort column has the same value for several rows and you'd like those grouped together, but within that group you want to sort by the values in a different row. For example, say the list represents students' grades and several students have the same grade. You might want the rows sorted first by grade, with the highest grades at the top (descending order); and then, for the students with the same grade, you'd like those rows sorted by student name in ascending alphabetical order. You can achieve this using a complex sort.

To perform a complex sort:

1. Click any cell in the list (**Figure 10.29**).

2. Choose Data > Sort (**Figure 10.30**).

(continues on next page)

3. In the Sort dialog box, use the pull-down Sort by list to select the first column you'll use to sort, and choose Ascending or Descending (**Figure 10.31**).

4. Choose the second column to sort by in the Then by list, and choose Ascending or Descending. You can even choose a third sort column, if you wish. Click OK.

The list is sorted as you requested (**Figure 10.32**).

✔ Tips

■ If you want to sort by day or month, you'll probably prefer to sort in calendar order rather than alphabetically. To do that, in the Sort dialog box, click Options. The Sort Options dialog box appears. Choose the day or month format for the first sort column from the First key sort order list (**Figure 10.33**).

■ The Sort Options dialog box is also the place to tell Excel that instead of re-arranging rows based on the values of one or more columns, you want to rearrange the columns based on the values in one or more rows (you can pick any row, including the column headers). In the Orientation selections simply choose Sort left to right, and click OK (**Figure 10.34**). The pop-up Sort by and Then by lists in the Sort Options dialog box now contain row identifiers instead of column identifiers.

Figure 10.31
Select the sort criteria.

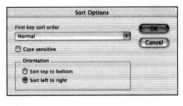

Figure 10.32
The sorted list.

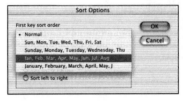

Figure 10.33
Choose calendar sort.

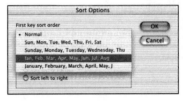

Figure 10.34
Choose to sort columns instead of rows.

SORTING A LIST

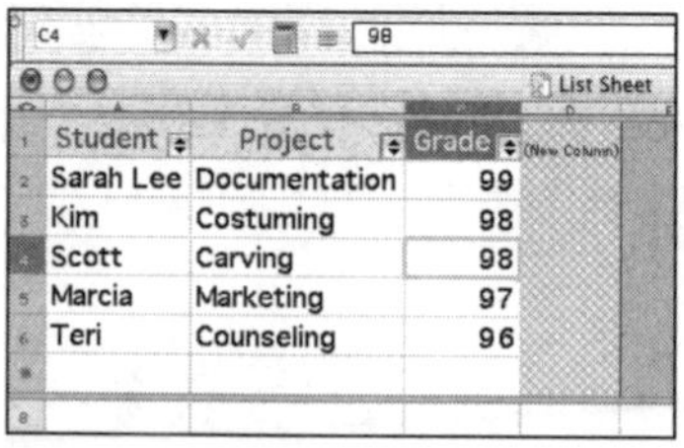

Figure 10.35
Click a cell in the column that you wish to validate.

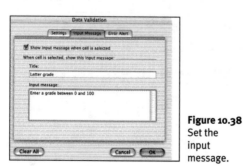

Figure 10.36 Invoke the Data Validation dialog box.

Validating Data in a List

You can enlist Excel's Office Assistant to help make sure the contents of a list meet your criteria for valid entries. For example, you may want to ensure that a zip code field contains only five digits. The validation tests are applied as you add items to your list.

To validate new entries in a list:

1. Click a cell in the column to which you'd like to apply validation criteria (**Figure 10.35**).

2. Choose Data > Validation (**Figure 10.36**).

3. In the Settings screen of the Data Validation dialog box, choose from the pop-up lists the criteria you wish to apply to the values entered in that column (**Figure 10.37**).

4. Click the Input Message tab, and enter the title and text of the message you want to pop up from the Assistant when a cell to be validated is selected (**Figure 10.38**).

(continues on next page)

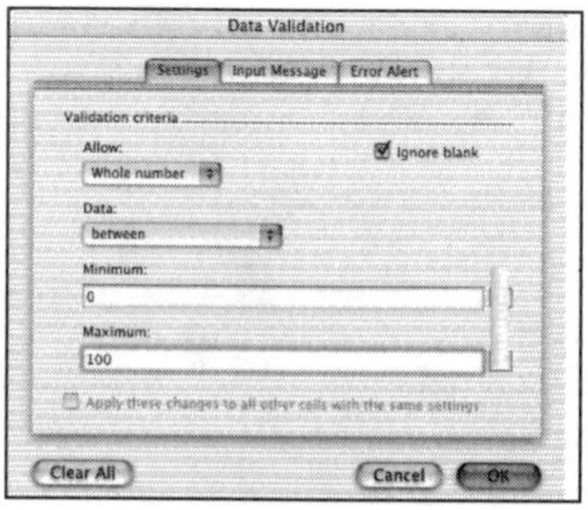

Figure 10.37
Set the validation criteria.

Figure 10.38
Set the input message.

5. Click the Error Alert tab. In this screen, you enter the title and text of the message you want to pop up if an incorrect value is entered.

You can choose whether you want a wrong value to prevent further work until corrected (Stop), provide a choice of whether or not to continue (Warning), or simply offer Information (**Figure 10.39**). Click OK when you're done.

When a new item is entered in the list and the appropriate cell is selected, the Input message pops up from the Assistant (**Figure 10.40**).

If an incorrect value is entered, the Assistant displays the Error message (**Figure 10.41**).

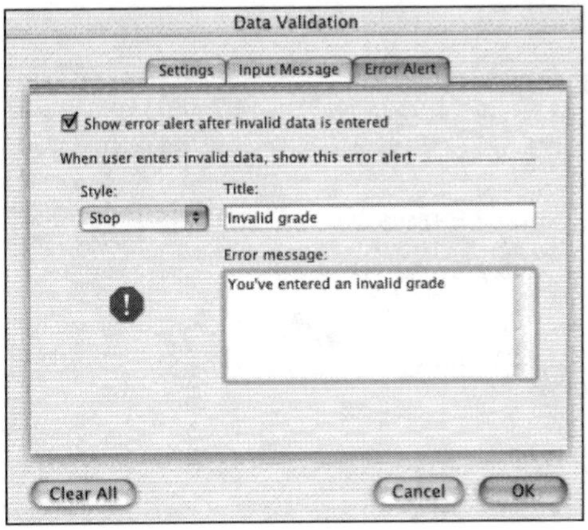

Figure 10.39 Set the error alert.

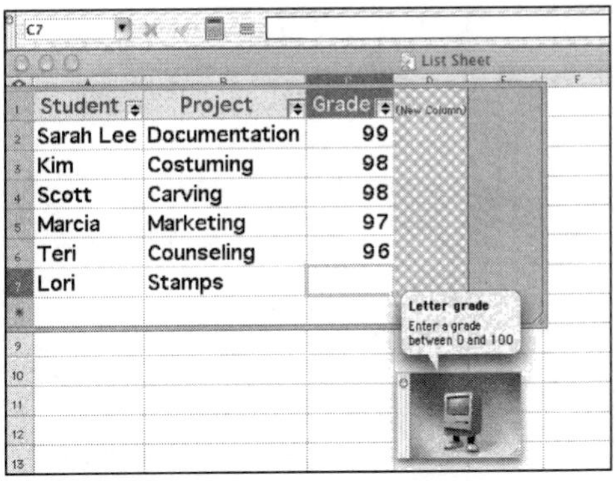

Figure 10.40 The Input message pops up.

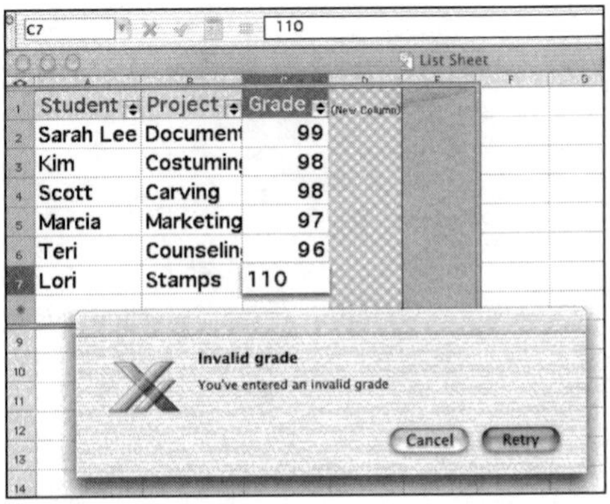

Figure 10.41 The Error message responds to an incorrect value.

ENTERING CALCULATIONS

Calculations are the way Excel "does the math." Even if you're only using Excel to keep a list, you may have a column of numbers in the list on which you would like to do some math (for example, adding up the number of boxes of cookies sold, or calculating batting averages). This is what Excel was created to do, so it has plenty of tools to save you time and effort.

Let's say you want the sum of a column of numbers to appear in the cell just below the last number in the column. Into that cell you type a *formula*, rather than text or a single number. How can Excel tell the difference between text or numbers and a formula? Formulas always begin with an equal sign (=). When you've finished entering the formula and move to another cell, what you see in the cell is no longer the formula itself but the result of the calculation you've asked it to do. Don't worry—you can still change the formula if you need to.

Formula Basics

To add two numbers in a cell, you could type =23+43, for example. To add the contents of two cells, you include their cell addresses in the formula, as in =B3+B4. The cell into which you type the formula displays the result of the calculation as soon as you move to a different cell (**Figure 11.1**).

If any numbers change in the cells that supply values to the formula, the result of the calculation changes immediately. This immediate recalculation lets you perform what-if analyses; you can see the change in the bottom line immediately when you change any of the contributing numbers.

To build a simple formula:

1. Click the destination cell for the formula (**Figure 11.2**).

2. Type an equal sign (=) (**Figure 11.3**).

3. Click the first cell you want to be in the calculation; its cell address appears in the formula (**Figure 11.4**).

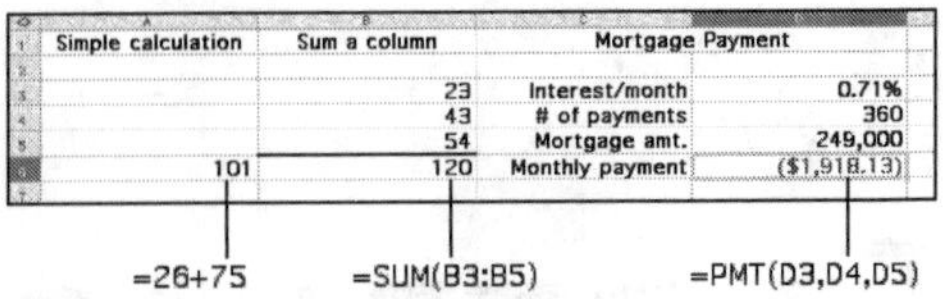

Figure 11.1 Some typical calculations.

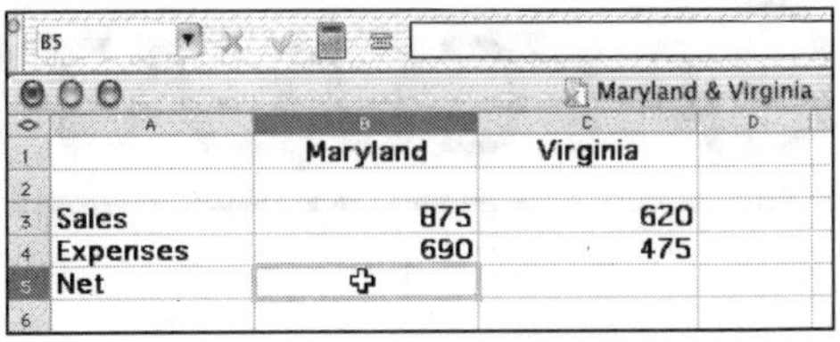

Figure 11.2 Click the cell where you want the formula.

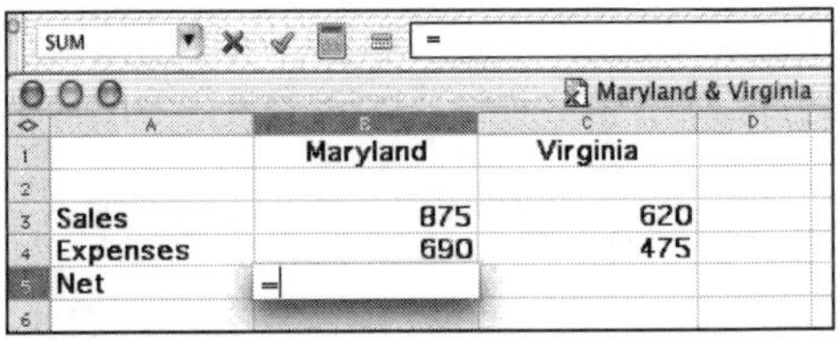

Figure 11.3 The formula is visible in the cell and in the Edit Line above the window.

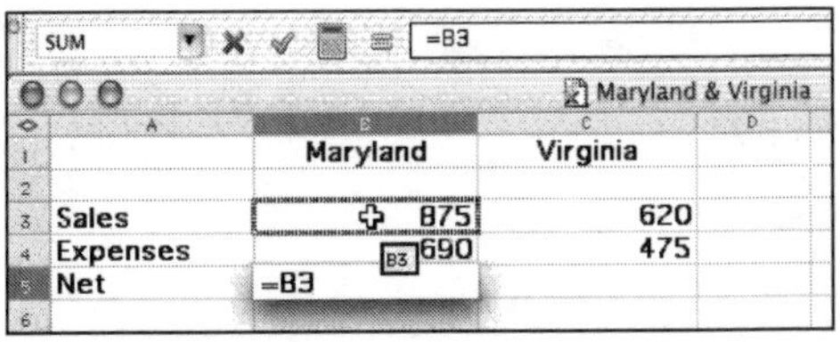

Figure 11.4 Click the cell containing the first value that's to appear in the formula.

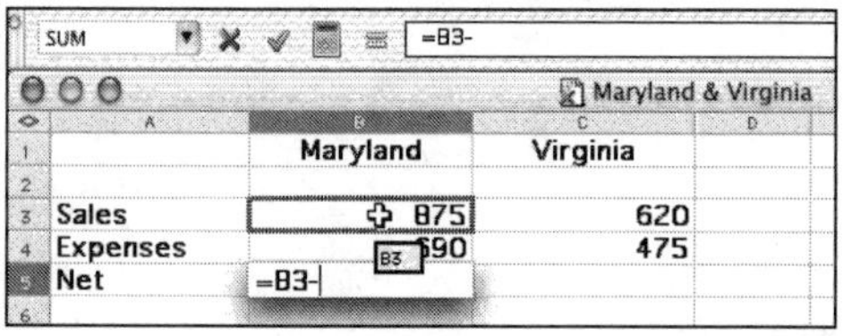

Figure 11.5 Type an operator.

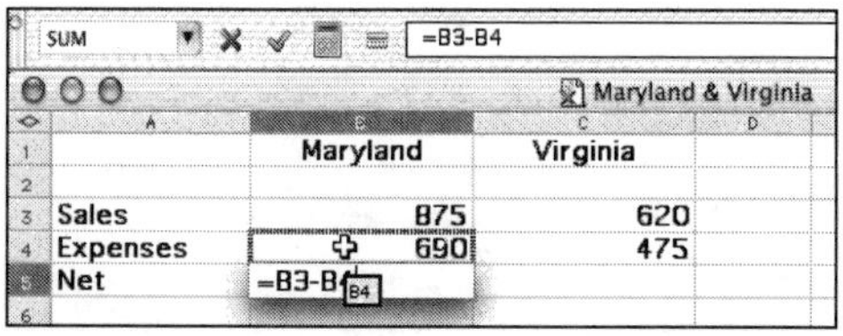

Figure 11.6 To include another cell reference in the formula, click the cell.

Table 11.1

Arithmetic Operators	
OPERATOR	ACTION
+	Add
–	Subtract
*	Multiply
/	Divide
%	Percent
^	Exponentiation

4. Type an operator (**Figure 11.5**). See **Table 11.1** for a list of arithmetic operators. There are other kinds as well.

5. Click the next cell whose address you want to appear in the formula (**Figure 11.6**).

6. If there's more to your formula, type the next operator.

or

Press [Enter] to enter the formula into the cell and display the result of the calculation.

✔ Tips

- If adjacent cells require a similar formula, you can copy the formula from cell to cell. See "Copying Formulas" below.

- You can enter a combination of typed numbers and cell addresses in formulas, such as =C2*2.5 (the contents of cell C2 multiplied by 2.5).

FORMULA BASICS

133

Using Common Functions

Functions are shortcuts for common calculations that would be difficult or impossible for you to create yourself with a basic formula. After you've had a chance to learn how they work, see **Table 11.2** at the end of this section for some common functions.

To total a column with the Sum function:

1. Click the cell in which you want the sum to appear (**Figure 11.7**).

2. Enter an equal sign (=) to start the formula (**Figure 11.8**).

3. Type the word sum (**Figure 11.9**).

4. Type an open parenthesis (Shift 9) (**Figure 11.10**).

5. Drag down the column of numbers to total (**Figure 11.11**).

6. Press Enter (**Figure 11.12**).

✔ Tips

■ You don't need to close the parentheses before pressing Enter. Excel will do it for you.

■ Excel provides hundreds of functions for common and uncommon calculations, including statistical, financial, date, time, and others (see Table 11.2 at the end of this section).

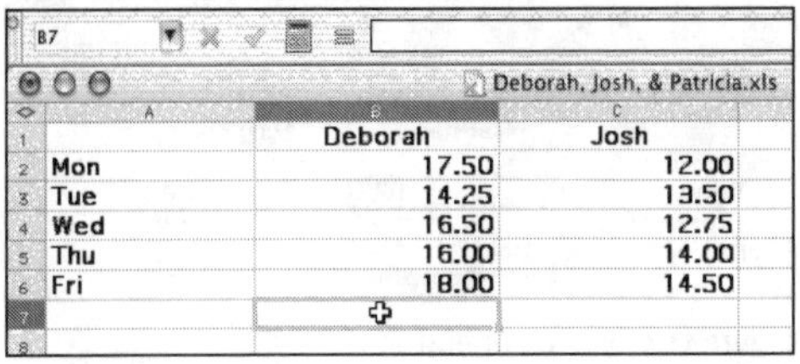

Figure 11.7 Click the cell in which you want the formula to appear.

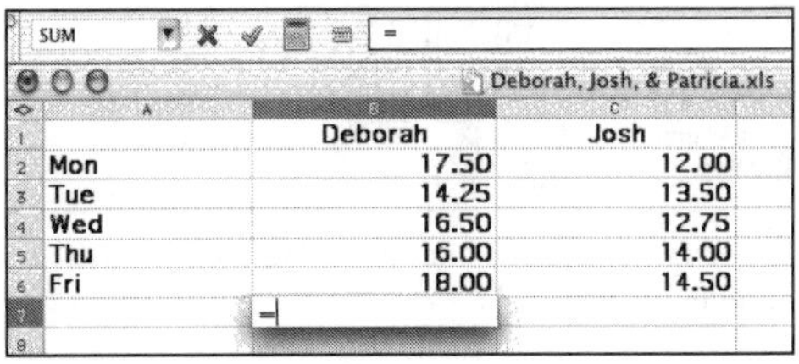

Figure 11.8 Start a formula with the equal sign.

Figure 11.9 Type sum.

Figure 11.10 Type an open parenthesis.

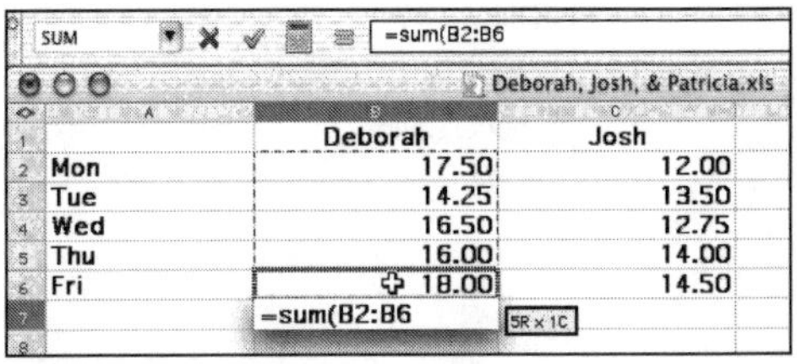

Figure 11.11 Drag across the range of summed cells, in this case B2 to B6.

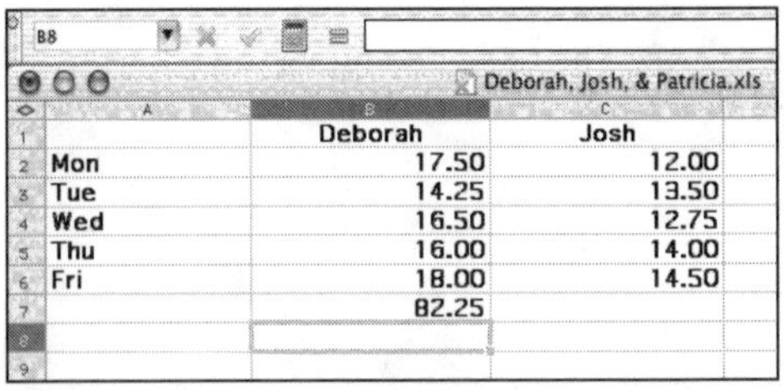

Figure 11.12 Press Enter to complete the formula.

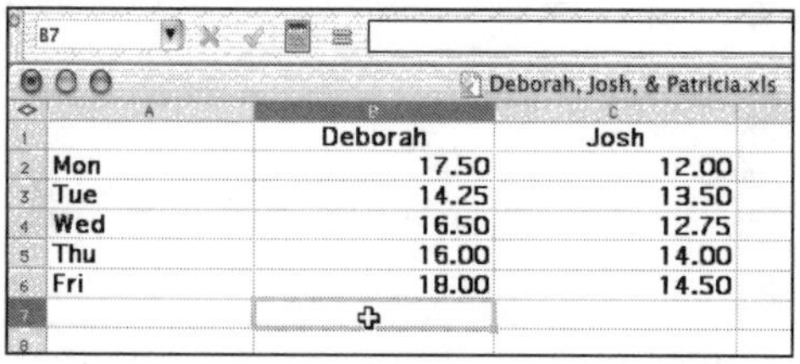

Figure 11.13 Click the cell in which you want the formula to appear.

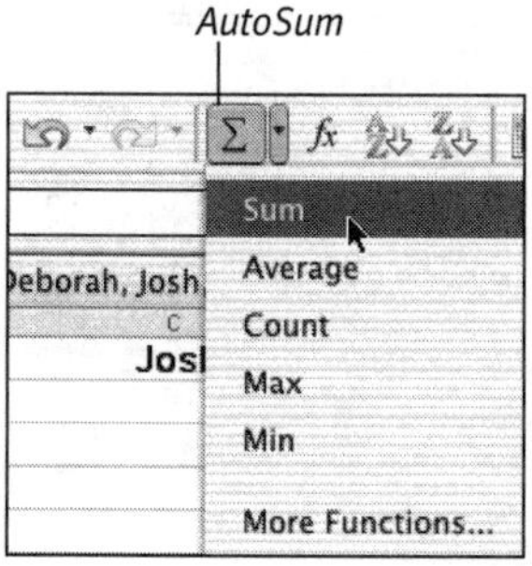

AutoSum

Figure 11.14 Click and hold the black triangle to the right of the AutoSum button to get the drop-down list; choose Sum.

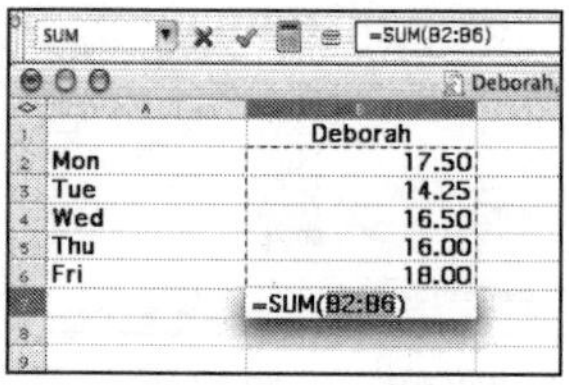

Figure 11.15 The completed formula.

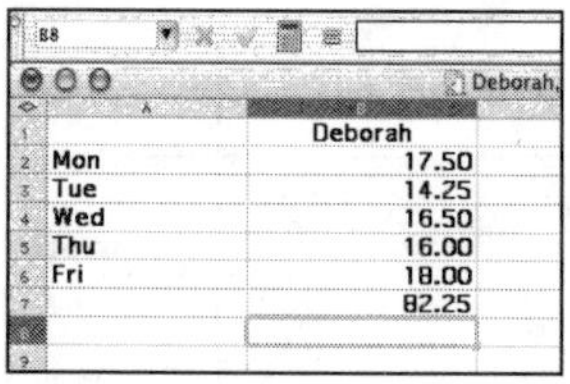

Figure 11.16 Press [Enter] to see the result of the calculation.

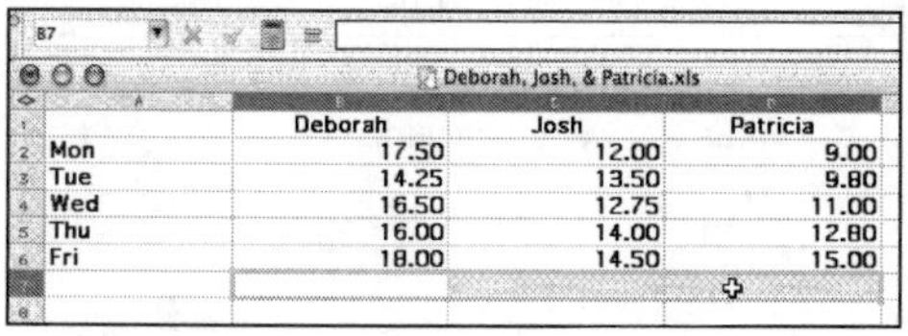

Figure 11.17 You can select the cells below any number of columns before invoking AutoSum.

To sum a column or row:

1. Click the empty cell below the last entry in the column or to the right of the last entry in the row (**Figure 11.13**). This is where the formula will go.

2. Click and hold the black triangle to the right of the AutoSum button on the toolbar; select Sum from the drop-down list of available functions (**Figure 11.14**).

3. The completed formula appears in the cell (**Figure 11.15**). Press [Enter] to see the result of the calculation (**Figure 11.16**).

✔ Tips

- Excel looks for a range of numbers to sum *above* the cell you've selected for the total. If it does not find a range of numbers, or if it finds text, it looks to the left for a range of numbers to sum.

- To calculate sums quickly for a number of adjacent columns, select the empty cells at the bottoms of all the columns before clicking the AutoSum button. Excel will insert a sum in each selected cell (**Figure 11.17**).

To calculate numbers in nonadjacent cells:

1. Click the cell where you want to enter the formula (**Figure 11.18**).

2. Start the formula as usual with an equal sign (=).

3. Enter a function followed by the open parenthesis (**Figure 11.19**).

4. Click the cell containing the first value you want to include (**Figure 11.20**).

5. Type a comma.

6. Click the next cell whose value you want to include (**Figure 11.21**).

7. Repeat steps 5 and 6 until you have included as many cells as necessary.

8. Press Enter to enter the formula.

✔ Tip

■ A formula can contain a combination of discrete cells and ranges, such as =SUM(B2,B4,B9:B11). This formula will add the contents of cells B2, B4, and B9 through B11.

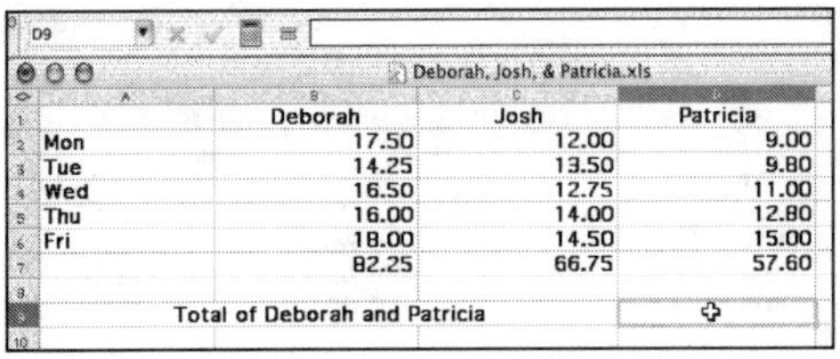

Figure 11.18 Click the cell in which you want the formula to appear.

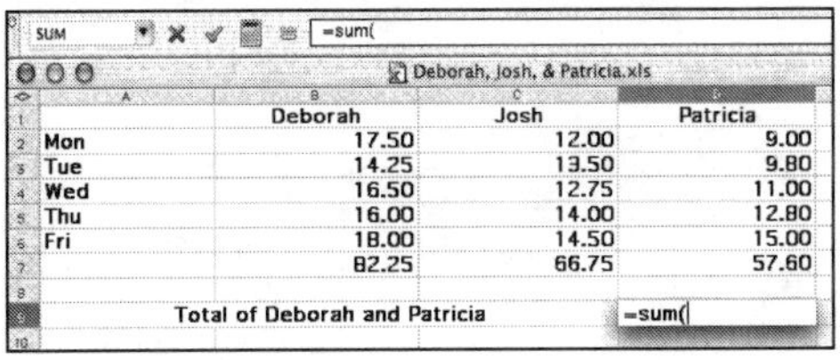

Figure 11.19 Enter the function.

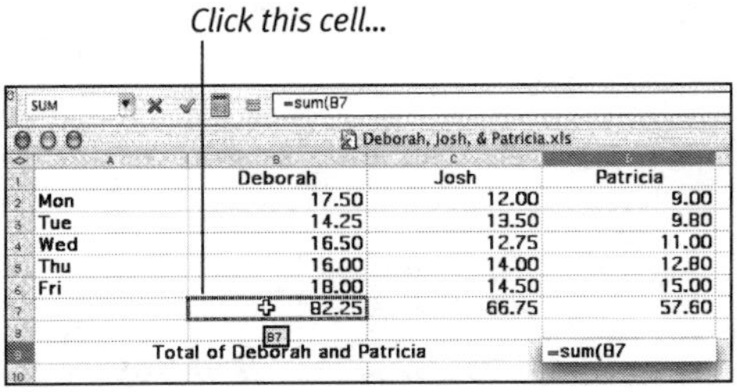

Click this cell...

Figure 11.20 Click a cell whose value you want to include.

...then type a comma and click this cell.

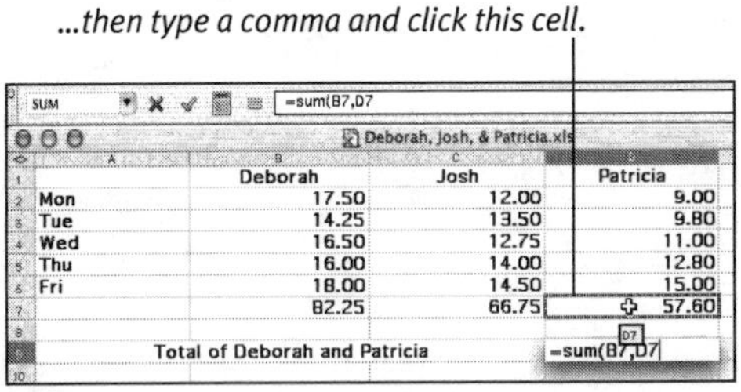

Figure 11.21 Type a comma and click the next cell whose value you want to include.

USING COMMON FUNCTIONS

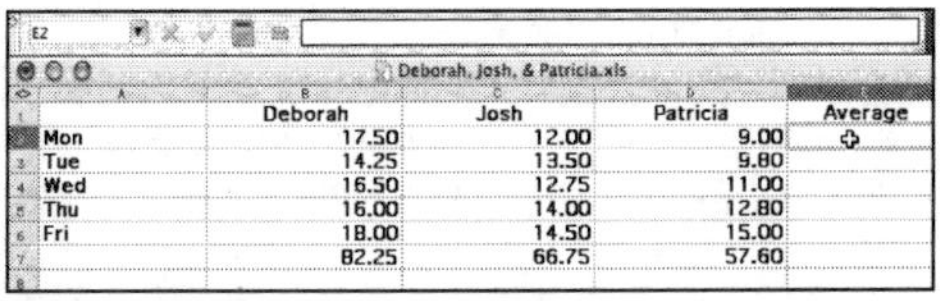

Figure 11.22 Click the cell in which you want the formula to appear.

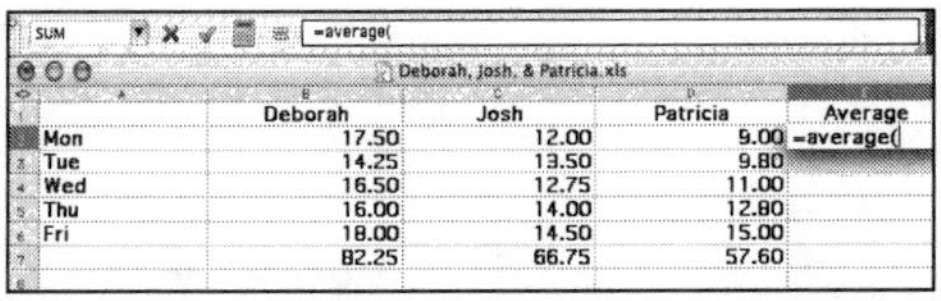

Figure 11.23 Type the equal sign, function name, and open parenthesis.

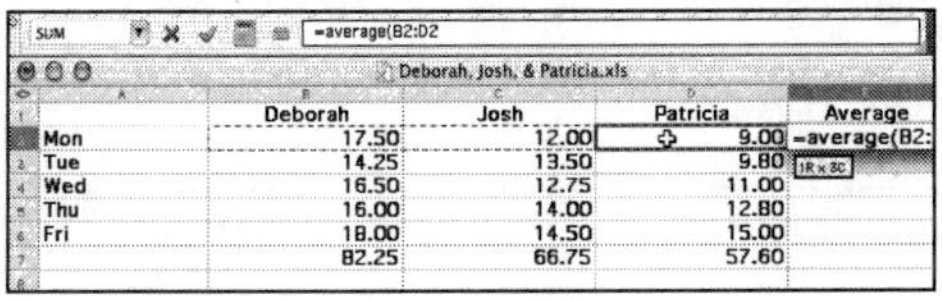

Figure 11.24 Drag across the cells whose values you are averaging.

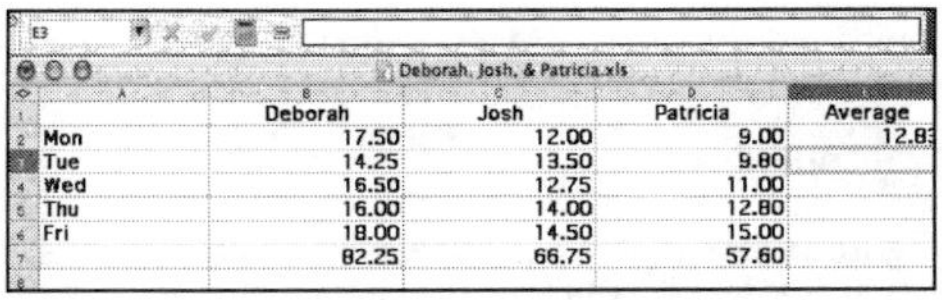

Figure 11.25 Press Enter .

To calculate the average of some numbers:

1. Click the cell where you want the average to appear (**Figure 11.22**).

2. Enter an equal sign (=).

3. Type the word *average* (**Figure 11.23**).

4. Enter an open parenthesis.

5. Drag across the cells you want to average (**Figure 11.24**).

6. Press Enter (**Figure 11.25**).

USING COMMON FUNCTIONS

137

To find and use any function:

◆ When you're entering a formula and you need a function, click the Paste Function tool in the toolbar (**Figure 11.26**).

The Paste Function tool takes you through the steps of building a formula (**Figures 11.27** to **11.30**).

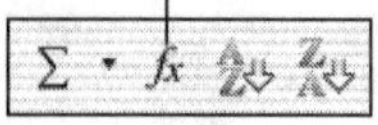

Paste Function

Figure 11.26 Click the Paste Function tool.

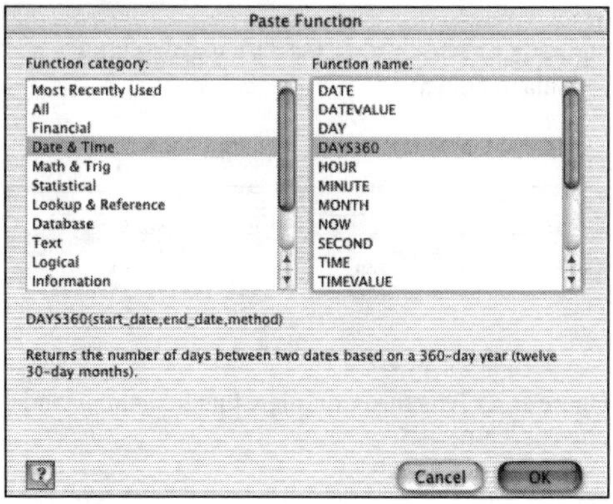

Figure 11.27 Select the desired function category on the left and the particular function you want on the right; click OK.

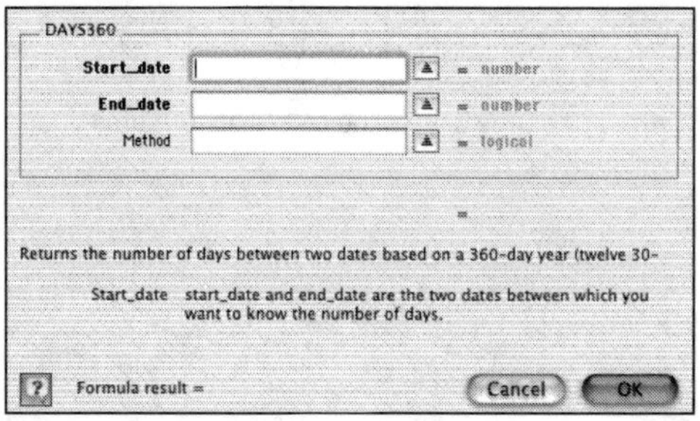

Figure 11.28 A dialog box appears in which you enter the arguments for the function you've chosen.

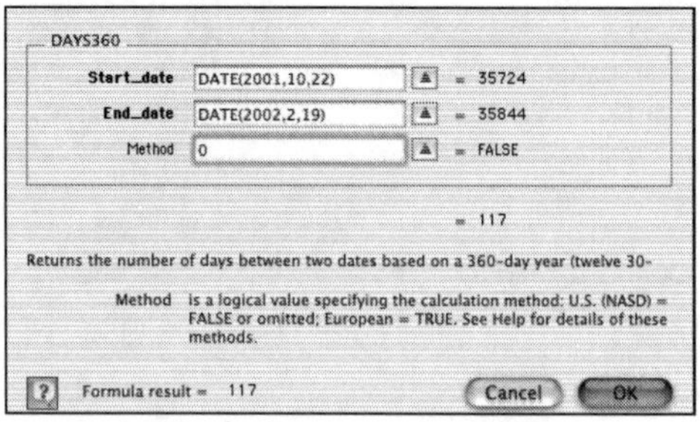

Figure 11.29 Enter the variables for the chosen function. You can enter other function calls as variables passed to a function. Click OK.

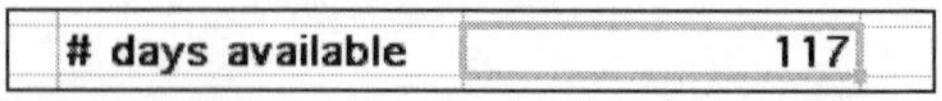

Figure 11.30 The result appears in the selected cell.

USING COMMON FUNCTIONS

Table 11.2

Some Useful Functions	
DATE(year, month, day)	Provides the serial number of a particular date.
DAYS360(start_date, end_date, method)	Calculates the number of days between two dates based on a 360-day year (used in some accounting functions).
TODAY()	Provides the serial number of today's date.
NOW()	Provides the serial number of the current date and time.
DDB(cost, salvage, life, period, factor)	Provides the depreciation of an asset for a specified period using the double-declining balance method or some other method you specify.
FV(rate, nper, pmt, pv, type)	Calculates the future value of an investment.
IRR(values, guess)	Provides the internal rate of return for a series of cash flows.
PV(rate, nper, pmt, fv, type)	Calculates the present value of an investment.
NPV(rate, value1, value2, ...)	Calculates the net present value of an investment based on a series of periodic cash flows and a discount rate.
PMT(rate, nper, pv, fv, type)	Calculates the periodic payment for an annuity or loan.
ROUND(number, num_digits)	Rounds a number to a specified number of digits.
SUM(number1, number2, ...)	Calculates the sum of all the numbers in the list of arguments.*
AVERAGE(number1, number2, ...)	Calculates the average (arithmetic mean) of the arguments.*
MAX(number1, number2, ...)	Calculates the maximum value in a list of arguments.*
MEDIAN(number1, number2, ...)	Calculates the median of the given numbers.*
MIN(number1, number2, ...)	Calculates the smallest number in the list of arguments.*
STDEV(number1, number2, ...)	Estimates standard deviation based on a sample.*
VAR(number1, number2, ...)	Estimates variance based on a sample.*
VALUE(text)	Converts text to a number.

*The expression (number1, number2, ...) can also be specified as a range (C25:C47).

USING COMMON FUNCTIONS

Using the Formula Calculator

Excel provides a handy graphical tool called the Calculator for entering formulas.

To build a formula with the Calculator:

1. Click the cell where you want the formula (**Figure 11.31**).

2. Choose Tools > Calculator.

   The Calculator appears, with the formula already started for you in its main window (**Figure 11.32**).

3. Click the buttons to build the formula.

   When the Calculator can evaluate the formula into a number, that number appears in the Answer box.

4. If the formula you want to create involves a sum, click the Sum button and the Calculator extends a pane to the right (**Figure 11.33**). Click and drag through the range of cells to sum, and click Insert to place the formula in the formula pane on the left. If that's all you want in your formula, click OK to place it in the selected cell (**Figure 11.34**).

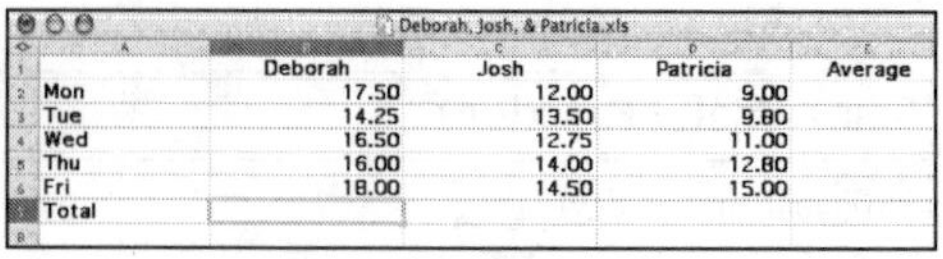

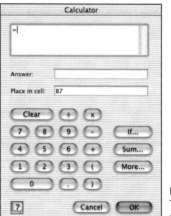

	Deborah	Josh	Patricia	Average
Mon	17.50	12.00	9.00	
Tue	14.25	13.50	9.80	
Wed	16.50	12.75	11.00	
Thu	16.00	14.00	12.80	
Fri	18.00	14.50	15.00	
Total				

Figure 11.31 Select the cell where you want the formula to appear.

Figure 11.32 The Calculator appears.

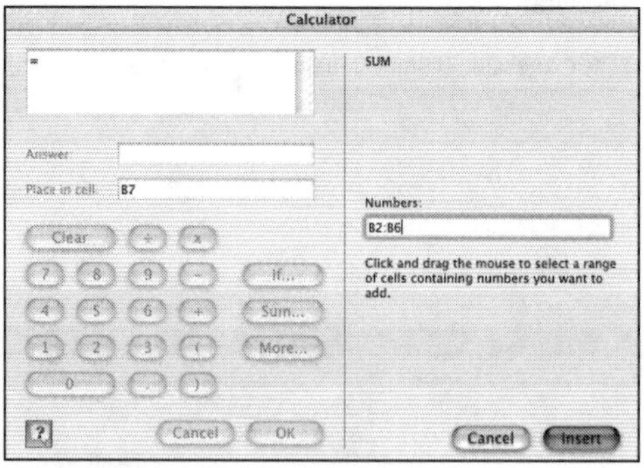

Figure 11.33 The pane for the Sum function appears.

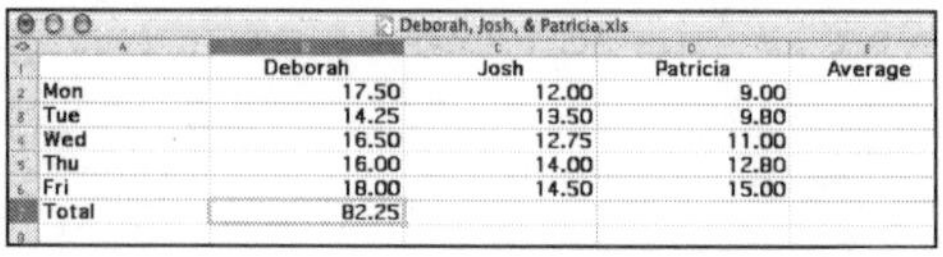

	Deborah	Josh	Patricia	Average
Mon	17.50	12.00	9.00	
Tue	14.25	13.50	9.80	
Wed	16.50	12.75	11.00	
Thu	16.00	14.00	12.80	
Fri	18.00	14.50	15.00	
Total	82.25			

Figure 11.34 The formula is calculated in the selected cell.

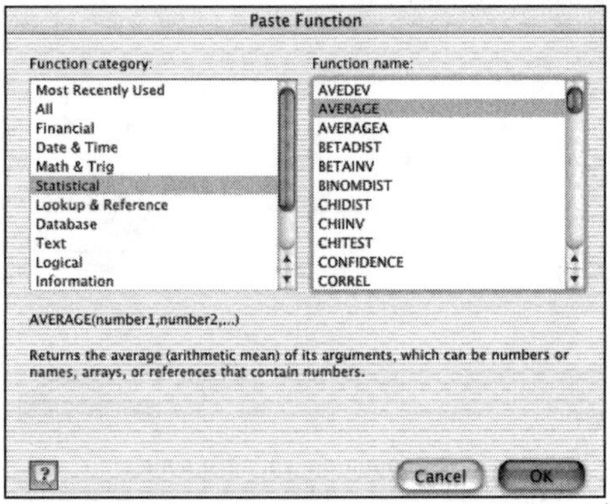

Figure 11.35 Function categories appear on the left; functions in the selected category appear on the right.

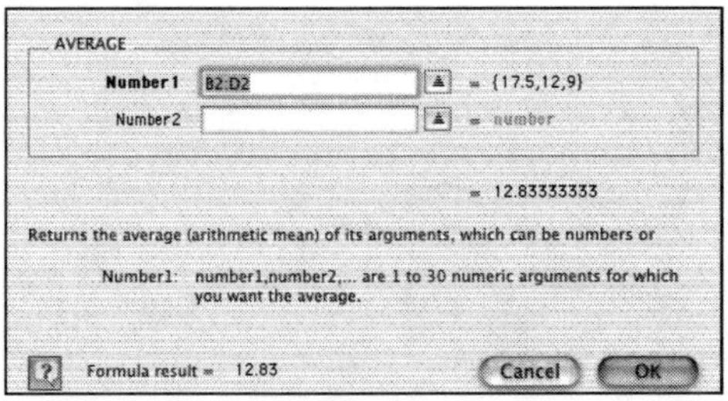

Figure 11.36 Enter the information that the function requires.

5. If you want to use a different function, click the More button. The Paste Function window appears with the complete list of available functions divided into categories on the left; clicking a category shows the list of functions available for that category (**Figure 11.35**). Choose the function you want and click OK.

6. Another window appears, prompting you for the appropriate function arguments (**Figure 11.36**). For many common functions, Excel will guess the cells you want to use as parameters. If it guesses wrong, you can click or click and drag through the correct cells, then click OK to include the function in the Calculator's formula pane.

(continues on next page)

USING THE FORMULA CALCULATOR

7. You can even set up a condition so that the formula varies depending on whether the condition is true or false. Click the If button to set it up; a pane extends to the right where you specify the condition and results (**Figure 11.37**). When you've defined the condition and results, click Insert and they appear in the Calculator's formula pane (**Figure 11.38**).

8. When the formula looks the way you want, click OK and it appears in the designated cell (**Figure 11.39**).

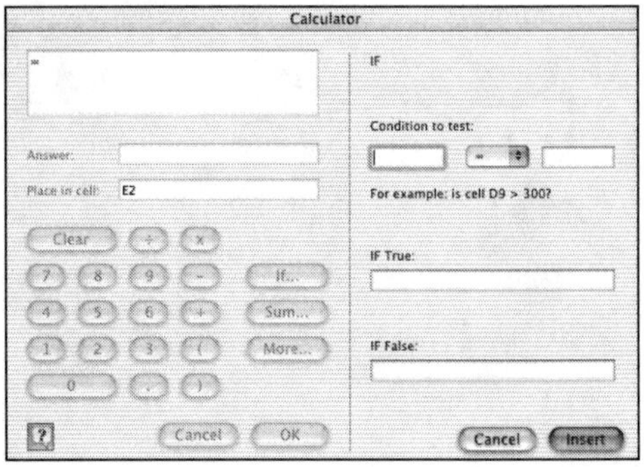

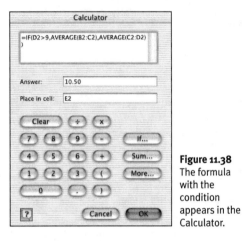

Figure 11.37 The conditional pane appears.

Figure 11.38 The formula with the condition appears in the Calculator.

	Deborah	Josh	Patricia	Average
Mon	17.50	12.00	9.00	10.50
Tue	14.25	13.50	9.80	
Wed	16.50	12.75	11.00	
Thu	16.00	14.00	12.80	
Fri	18.00	14.50	15.00	
Total	82.25			

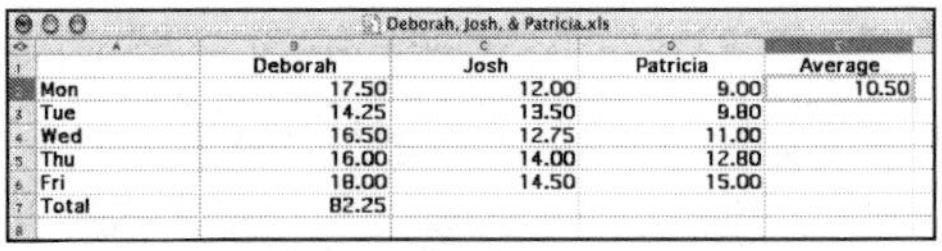

Figure 11.39 The formula appears in the selected cell.

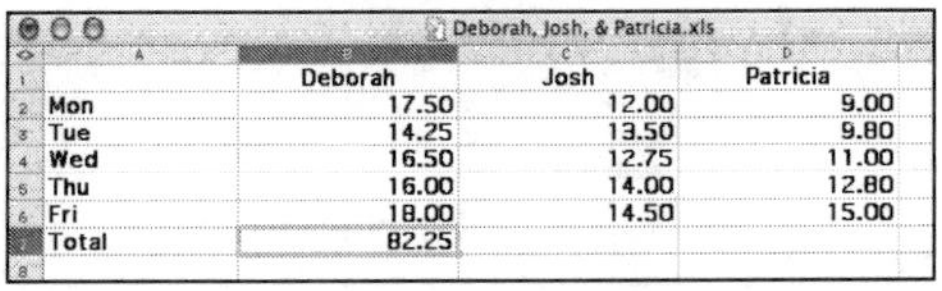

Figure 11.40 Click the cell that contains the formula.

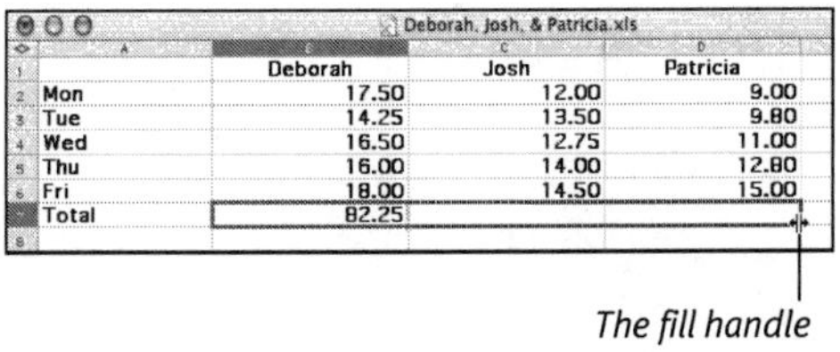

The fill handle

Figure 11.41 Drag the fill handle across adjacent cells.

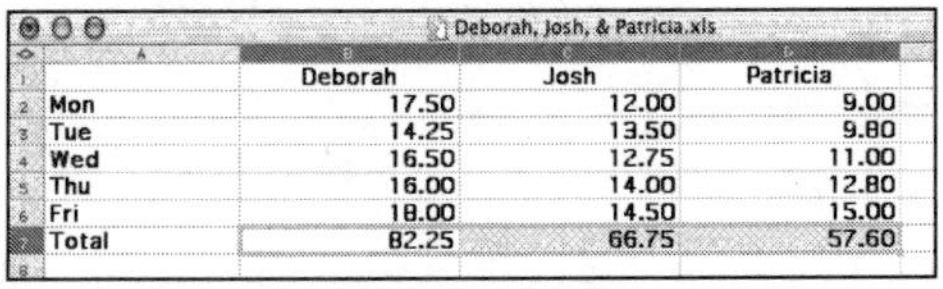

Figure 11.42 This copies the formula to the selected cells. Excel adjusts the formula while copying it across the columns so that the totals reflect the numbers in that column.

Copying Formulas

Sometimes you might want to do the same calculations for different columns or rows. Rather than rebuild the formula from scratch in each place, you can simply copy from one location to another. Excel is smart enough to change the formula automatically to refer to the new column or row.

To copy a formula to adjacent cells:

1. Click the cell containing the formula (**Figure 11.40**).

2. Drag the fill handle at the lower-right corner of the cell across the adjacent cells to which you want to copy the formula (**Figure 11.41**). The formula's results appear in each cell (**Figure 11.42**).

✔ Tip

■ Check copied formulas for accuracy if you refer in the formula to any cells in columns or rows other than the ones containing the formula. Excel sometimes guesses incorrectly about your intentions.

Auditing

To avoid bogus results from incorrect formulas, you can have Excel show you which cells have supplied data for a formula. If a formula uses a particular cell, the formula is said to *depend* on the cell, and the connection between them is a *dependency*.

To display formula dependencies:

1. Select the cell or cells that contain the formulas (**Figure 11.43**).

2. Choose Tools > Auditing > Trace Precedents (**Figure 11.44**).

   Arrows appear in the sheet, showing formula dependencies (**Figure 11.45**).

3. Choose Tools > Auditing > Trace Precedents again to see if an additional level of precedents exists.

4. To see which formulas depend upon a particular cell, click that cell and choose Tools > Auditing > Trace Dependents.

   Arrows point from the cell to the formulas that depend upon it (**Figure 11.46**).

✔ Tips

- To clear the arrows, choose Tools > Auditing > Remove All Arrows.

- The Auditing toolbar contains Trace Precedents and Trace Dependents buttons (**Figure 11.47**). To display the toolbar, choose Tools > Auditing > Show Auditing Toolbar. For some reason, Microsoft did not include the Auditing toolbar in the View > Toolbars list.

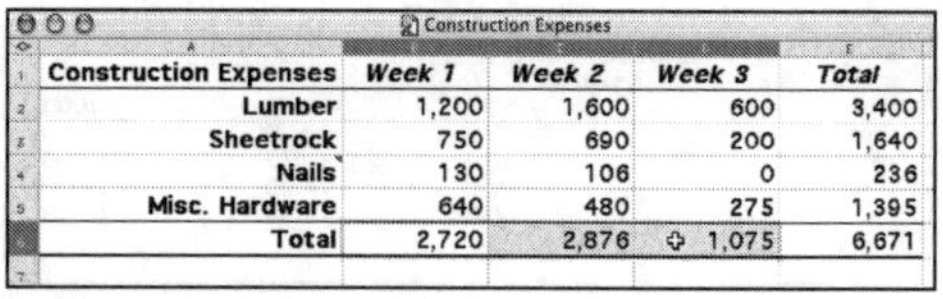

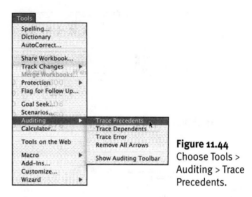

Figure 11.43 Select cells that contain formulas.

Figure 11.44 Choose Tools > Auditing > Trace Precedents.

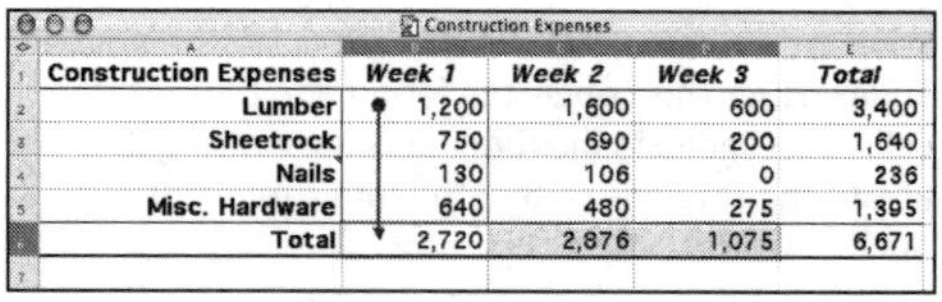

Figure 11.45 Arrows show formula dependencies.

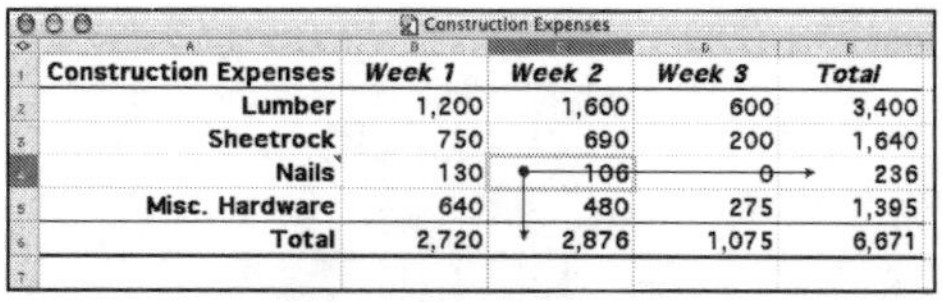

Figure 11.46 Dependence arrows appear.

Trace Precedents   *Trace Dependents*

Figure 11.47 Choose Tools > Auditing > Show Auditing Toolbar.

MAKING IT LOOK GOOD

At some point during the creation of your spreadsheet, you'll probably want to change the way the whole thing looks. Excel provides plenty of handy tools to control what's where on a spreadsheet and what it looks like.

Changing the Size of Columns and Rows

You can improve the organization of data in your spreadsheet by simply making a column or row wider or narrower. This technique is also useful if data in a certain column or row is causing the whole spreadsheet to look unbalanced, or you'd like to fit more columns or rows on a page. These are easy problems to fix.

To change the width of a column:

1. In the column you wish to change, place the mouse pointer on the right edge of the gray heading. The pointer changes to a horizontal double arrow (**Figure 12.1**).

2. Drag the double arrow right or left (**Figures 12.2**, **12.3**). While you're dragging, a yellow ScreenTip appears, containing the new width of the column, measured in characters.

To change the height of a row:

1. In the row you wish to change, place the pointer on the bottom edge of the gray heading. The pointer changes to a vertical double arrow (**Figure 12.4**).

2. Drag the double arrow up or down. The row height changes accordingly, and a yellow ScreenTip appears showing the new row height in points (one point is $1/72$ inch).

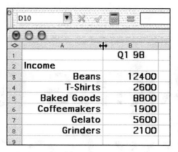

Figure 12.1 Point the mouse at the right edge of the column header; the pointer changes to a double arrow.

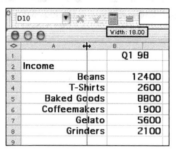

Figure 12.2 Drag right or left to change the column width.

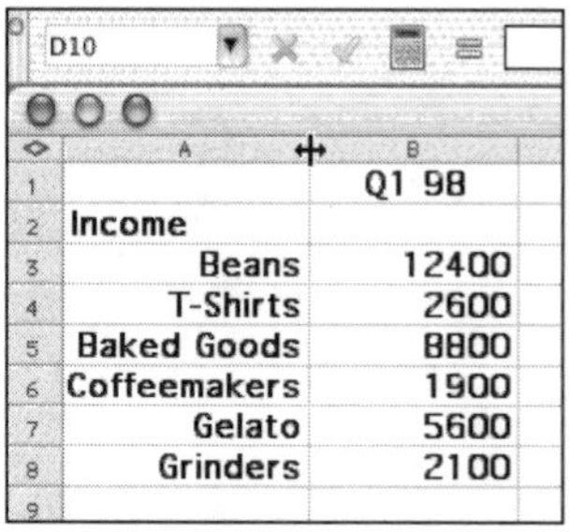

Figure 12.3 The column changes width.

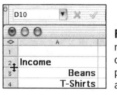

Figure 12.4 Point the mouse at the bottom edge of the row header; the pointer changes to a double arrow.

✔ Tips

- To adjust a column's width or a row's height automatically to accommodate its contents, double-click the column's right border or the row's bottom border when the pointer is a double arrow.

- To change the width of multiple columns or rows, select the columns or rows by dragging across their column-heading or row-heading buttons. Then drag the edge of any selected column-heading or row-heading button. All the selected columns or rows will change uniformly.

- You can also select Column or Row from the Format menu, then choose Width or Height from the submenu to get to the Column Width or Row Height dialog box. In these dialog boxes you can choose an exact setting.

CHANGING THE SIZE OF COLUMNS AND ROWS

Inserting and Deleting Columns and Rows

You can insert or delete as many rows or columns as you like in one operation.

To insert rows or columns:

1. Click any cell in the row or column where you'd like the new blank row or column (**Figure 12.5**). If you insert a row, it will appear above the selected cell; if you insert a column, it will appear to the left of the selected cell.

2. Choose Insert > Rows or Insert > Columns.

   The new row or column appears (**Figure 12.6**).

To delete rows or columns:

1. Select the cells, rows, or columns you want to delete.

2. Choose Edit > Delete.

   The Delete dialog box appears.

3. In the Delete dialog box, choose Shift cells left, Shift cells up, Entire row, or Entire column.

   If you choose Shift cells left or Shift cells up, the remaining cells will shift to the left or up, respectively. If you choose Entire row or Entire column, this will delete the entire row or column.

4. Click OK.

   The remaining cells adjust to compensate for the deleted cell, row, or column.

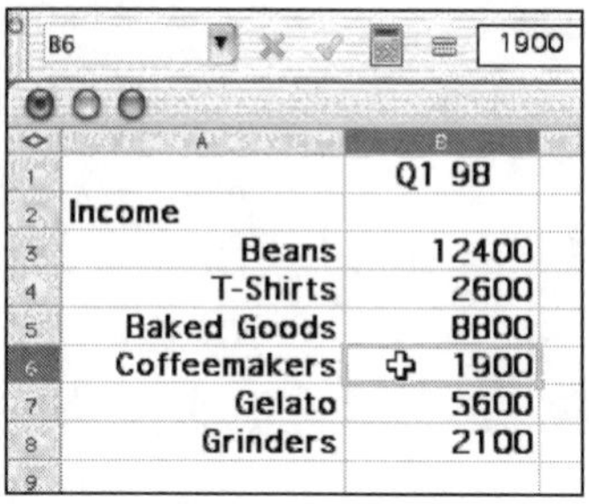

✔ Tips

■ To insert multiple rows, drag down the numbered row headings at the left to highlight the same number of rows you want to insert (**Figure 12.7**). To insert multiple columns, drag across multiple column-heading letters at the top.

Figure 12.5 Click a cell next to where you'd like a new row or column.

Figure 12.6 The new column or row appears to the left of or above the selection.

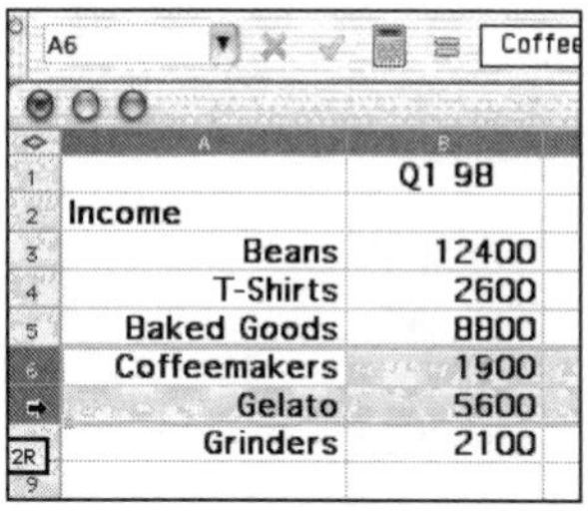

Figure 12.7 Drag across two row headings to specify two rows for insertion—here, rows 6 and 7.

■ You can also click a column or row heading and, while holding down Control, click the mouse button and choose Insert from the shortcut menu.

Inserting and Deleting Columns and Rows

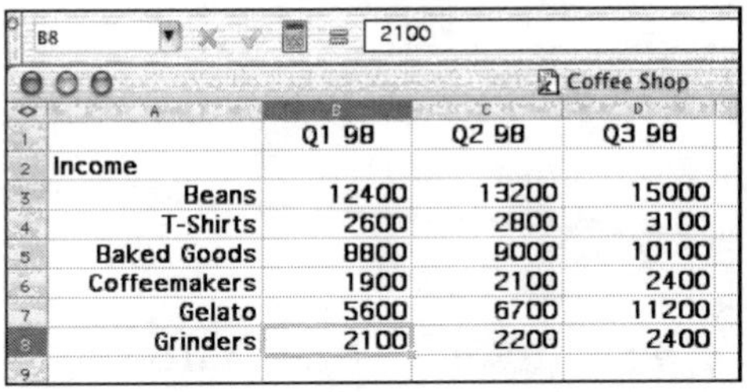

Figure 12.8 Click a cell to delete, or click the cell to the right of or below where you want a new one inserted.

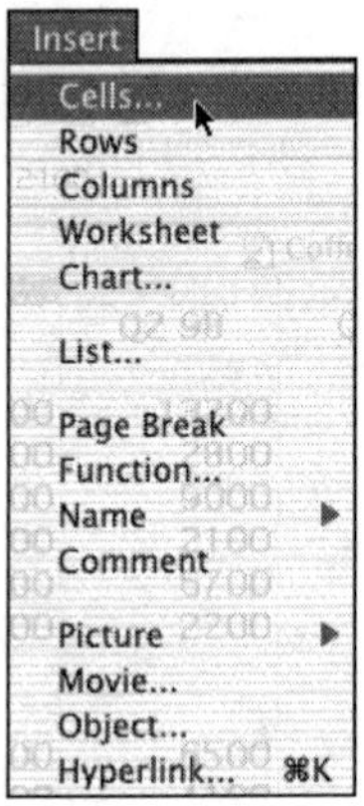

Figure 12.9 To insert a cell, choose Insert > Cells.

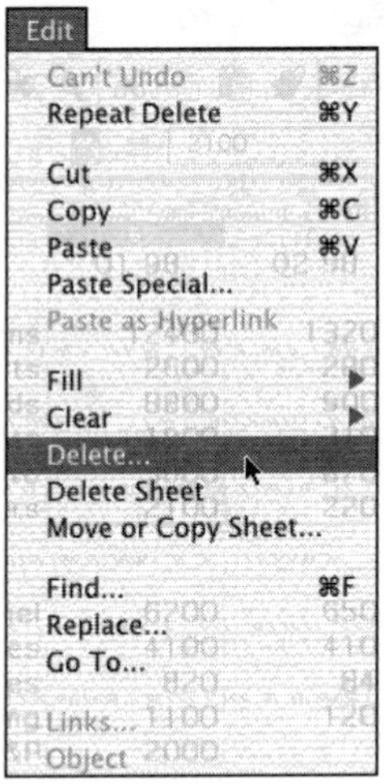

Figure 12.10 To delete a cell, choose Edit > Delete.

Inserting and Deleting Cells

When you tell Excel to insert or delete a cell within a range of data, Excel needs to know how to move the data that's located in adjacent cells. You specify your choice in either the Insert or Delete dialog box.

To insert or delete cells:

1. Click the cell below or to the right of where you want to add the new, blank cell (**Figure 12.8**).

   or

   Click the cell you want to delete.

2. To insert a cell, choose Insert > Cells (**Figure 12.9**), or click the mouse button while holding down (Control), and choose Insert from the shortcut menu. The Insert dialog box appears.

   or

   To delete a cell, choose Edit > Delete (**Figure 12.10**), or click the mouse button while holding down (Control), and choose Delete from the shortcut menu. The Delete dialog box appears.

   (continues on next page)

3. In the Insert dialog box, select either Shift cells right or Shift cells down (**Figure 12.11**).

or

In the Delete dialog box, select either Shift cells left or Shift cells up (**Figure 12.12**). The cells shift as specified (**Figure 12.13**).

✔ Tips

■ Pressing (Delete) clears the cell's contents, but it doesn't actually delete the cell from the spreadsheet.

■ To delete an entire row or column, select at least one cell in the row or column, choose Edit > Delete, and in the Delete dialog box choose either Entire Row or Entire Column.

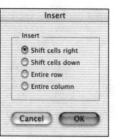

Figure 12.11 Choose Insert options.

Figure 12.12 Choose Delete options.

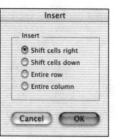

Figure 12.13 The inserted cell appears.

INSERTING AND DELETING CELLS

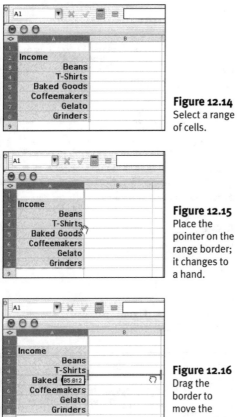

Figure 12.14
Select a range of cells.

Figure 12.15
Place the pointer on the range border; it changes to a hand.

Figure 12.16
Drag the border to move the range.

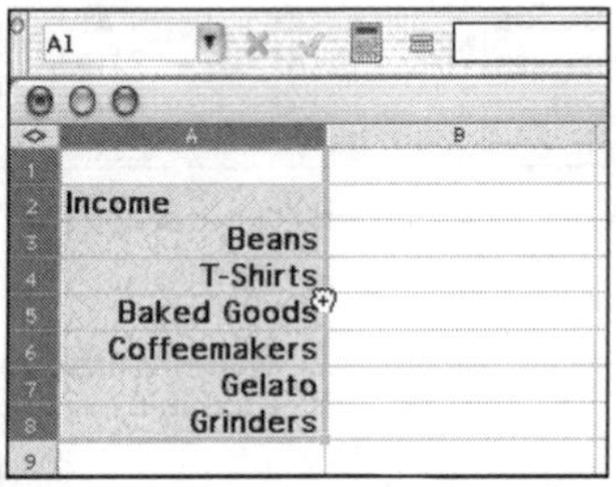

Figure 12.17
The plus sign appears in the hand to indicate that Excel is copying rather than moving the range.

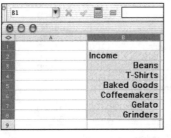

Figure 12.18
When you release the mouse button, Excel moves or copies the range.

Moving and Copying Data

Excel's drag-and-drop capability makes moving and copying data especially easy.

To move or copy a range of cells:

1. Select the range of cells to move or copy (**Figure 12.14**).

2. Place the pointer on the border of the range so that the pointer becomes a hand (**Figure 12.15**).

3. To move the cells, drag the border of the range to move the range to a new location (**Figure 12.16**). A yellow ScreenTip appears to indicate the destination.

   or

   To copy the cells, hold down (Option) while dragging the border of the range. A small plus sign (+) appears inside the pointer hand to indicate that you are copying rather than moving (**Figure 12.17**).

4. Release the mouse button to drop the range at the new location (**Figure 12.18**).

MOVING AND COPYING DATA

Working with Large Sheets

You can freeze the column and row headings to keep them from moving off the screen while you scroll through a large worksheet.

To freeze column and row headings:

1. Click the cell at the upper-left corner of the region that contains the data (**Figure 12.19**).

2. Choose Window > Freeze Panes (**Figure 12.20**).

   Lines appear in the spreadsheet to indicate which areas of the sheet you have frozen (**Figure 12.21**).

3. In a window that's too small to hold the entire spreadsheet, the row and column headings remain visible regardless of where you scroll horizontally or vertically (**Figure 12.22**).

✔ Tips

- After the headings are frozen, pressing (Control)(Home) moves the cell pointer to the upper-left corner of the data range instead of to cell A1.

- To unfreeze the panes, choose Window > Unfreeze Panes.

  Splitting a sheet lets you display and scroll through two or four different regions of the sheet independently. You can split the sheet horizontally, vertically, or both.

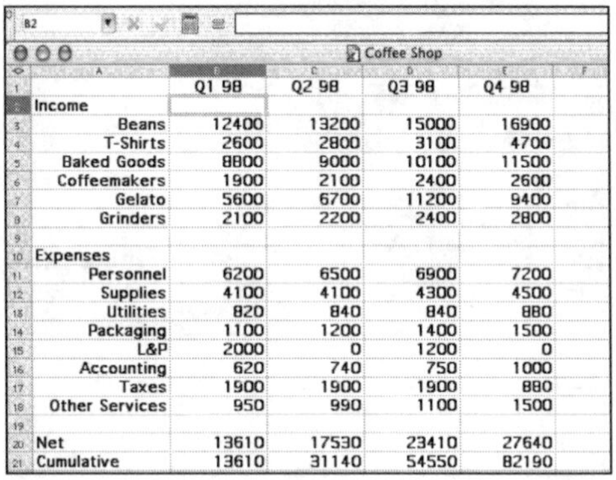

Figure 12.19 Click the upper-left cell in the data range.

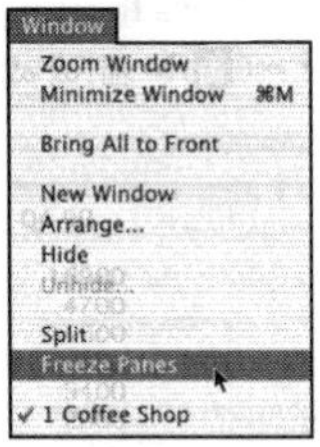

Figure 12.20 Choose Window > Freeze Panes.

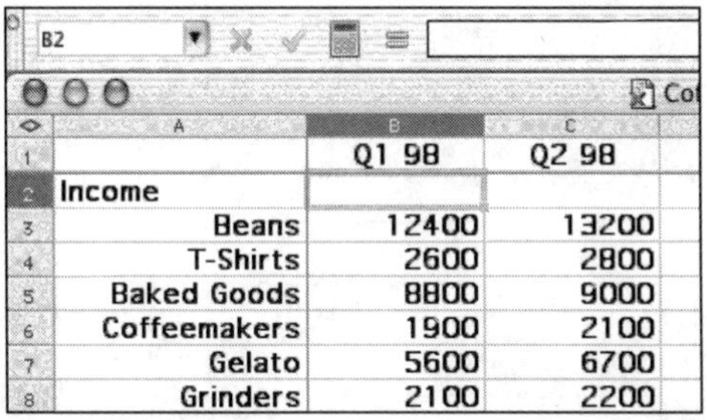

Figure 12.21 Vertical and horizontal lines set off the frozen headers.

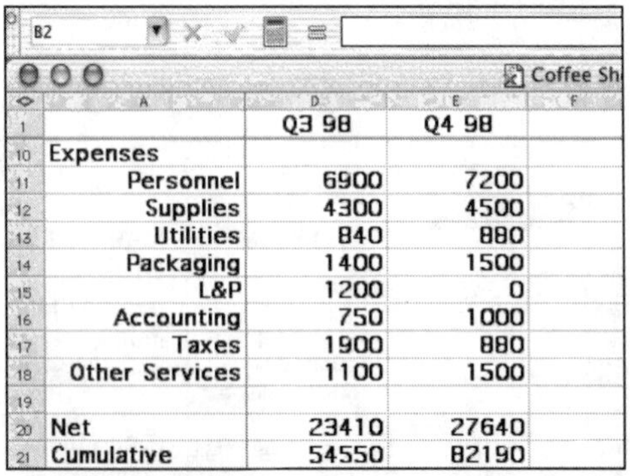

Figure 12.22 Headings stay visible when you scroll.

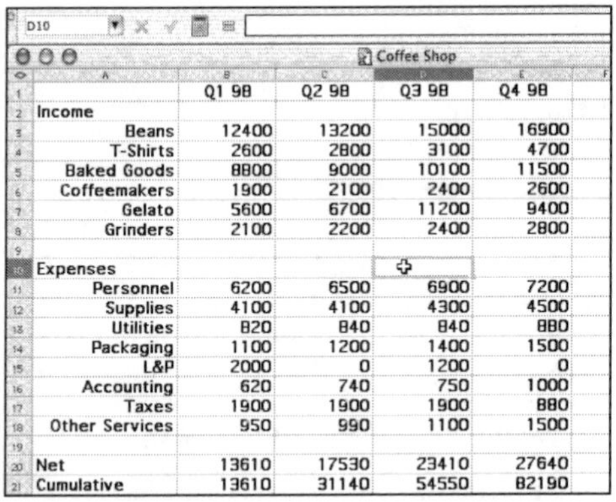

	Q1 98	Q2 98	Q3 98	Q4 98
Income				
Beans	12400	13200	15000	16900
T-Shirts	2600	2800	3100	4700
Baked Goods	8800	9000	10100	11500
Coffeemakers	1900	2100	2400	2600
Gelato	5600	6700	11200	9400
Grinders	2100	2200	2400	2800
Expenses				
Personnel	6200	6500	6900	7200
Supplies	4100	4100	4300	4500
Utilities	820	840	840	880
Packaging	1100	1200	1400	1500
L&P	2000	0	1200	0
Accounting	620	740	750	1000
Taxes	1900	1900	1900	880
Other Services	950	990	1100	1500
Net	13610	17530	23410	27640
Cumulative	13610	31140	54550	82190

Figure 12.23 To split a sheet, first click the cell at the intersection of the split.

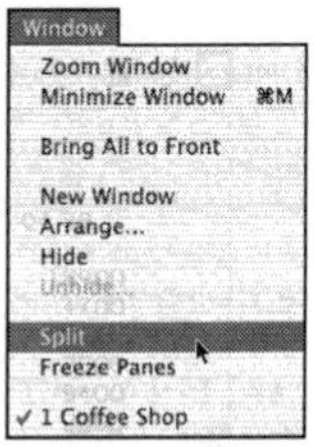

Figure 12.24 Choose Window > Split.

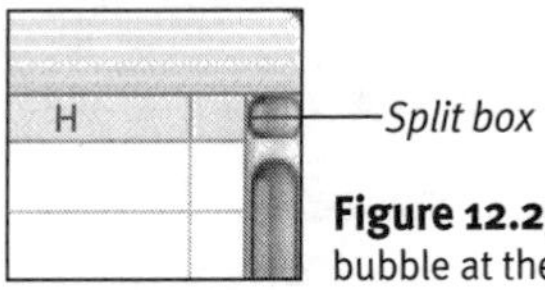

Split box

Figure 12.25 Find the Split bubble at the end of the scroll bar.

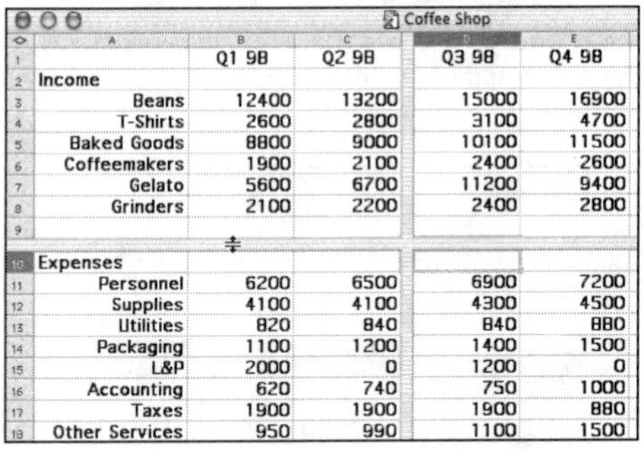

	Q1 98	Q2 98	Q3 98	Q4 98
Income				
Beans	12400	13200	15000	16900
T-Shirts	2600	2800	3100	4700
Baked Goods	8800	9000	10100	11500
Coffeemakers	1900	2100	2400	2600
Gelato	5600	6700	11200	9400
Grinders	2100	2200	2400	2800
Expenses				
Personnel	6200	6500	6900	7200
Supplies	4100	4100	4300	4500
Utilities	820	840	840	880
Packaging	1100	1200	1400	1500
L&P	2000	0	1200	0
Accounting	620	740	750	1000
Taxes	1900	1900	1900	880
Other Services	950	990	1100	1500

Figure 12.26 The pane splits where you drop the split bar.

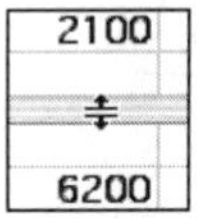

2100
6200

Figure 12.27 Drag the split bar to change the sizes of the panes.

To split a sheet into four panes:

1. Click the cell that you want to become the upper-left corner of the bottom-right pane (**Figure 12.23**).

2. Choose Window > Split (**Figure 12.24**).

To split a sheet into two panes:

1. Find the small split bubble at the top of the vertical scroll bar or the right end of the horizontal scroll bar (**Figure 12.25**).

2. Drag the split box down (on a vertical scroll bar) or to the left (on a horizontal scroll bar); a ghost of the split scroll bar appears in the spreadsheet as you move it.

3. Release the mouse button when the split bar is positioned where you want it (**Figure 12.26**).

✔ Tips

- To remove the split, choose Remove Split from the Window menu.

  or

  Drag the Split box back to its original position at the end of the scroll bar.

- You can drag the thick split lines to change the relative sizes of the panes (**Figure 12.27**).

Automatic Formatting

The fastest and easiest way to make a sheet presentable is to give it an AutoFormat. An AutoFormat creates a complete look for a range of cells by changing the font, text alignment, number formatting, borders, patterns, colors, column widths, and row heights. Excel provides a selection of AutoFormats, each with a different look.

To AutoFormat a range of cells:

1. Click any or all cells in the range you wish to format (**Figure 12.28**).

2. Choose Format > AutoFormat (**Figure 12.29**).

3. In the AutoFormat dialog box, select an AutoFormat from the list; a preview of that format appears to the right of the list (**Figure 12.30**). When you've made your final selection, click OK.

   This formats the range (**Figure 12.31**).

✔ Tips

- To remove an AutoFormat immediately after applying it, use Edit > Undo, or click the Undo button in the Standard toolbar.

- To remove an AutoFormat later, select the range, follow steps 2 and 3 above, and then choose None from the list of AutoFormats.

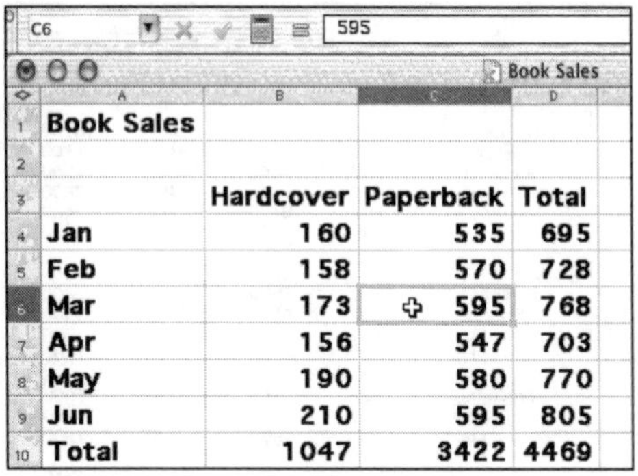

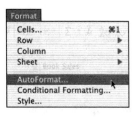

Figure 12.28 Click a cell in the range you're formatting.

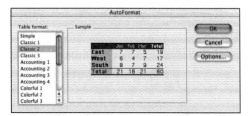

Figure 12.29 Choose Format > Autoformat.

Figure 12.30 Choose an AutoFormat from the list. A preview appears to the right.

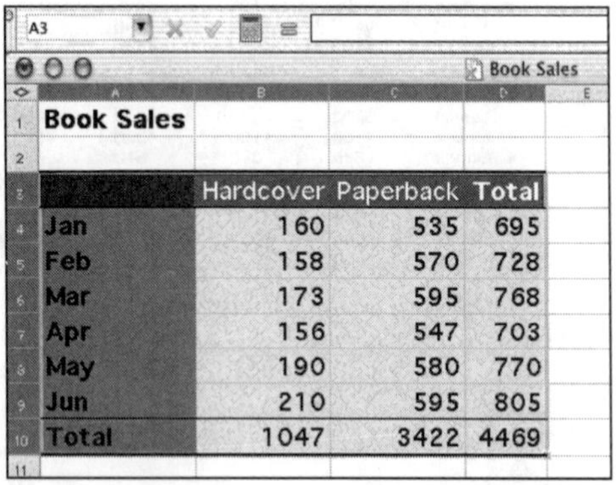

Figure 12.31 The AutoFormatted range.

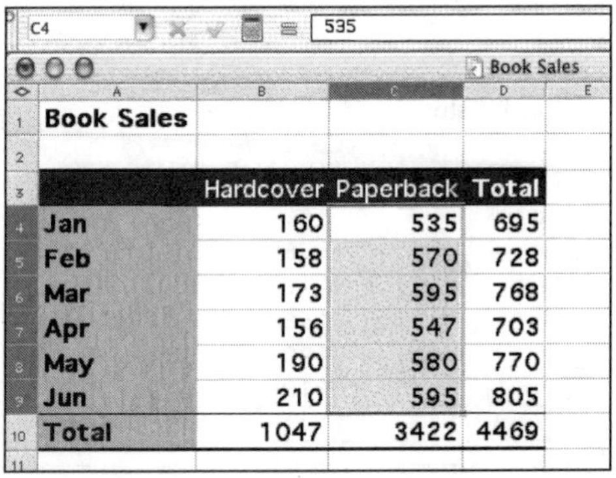

Figure 12.32 Select the cells to format.

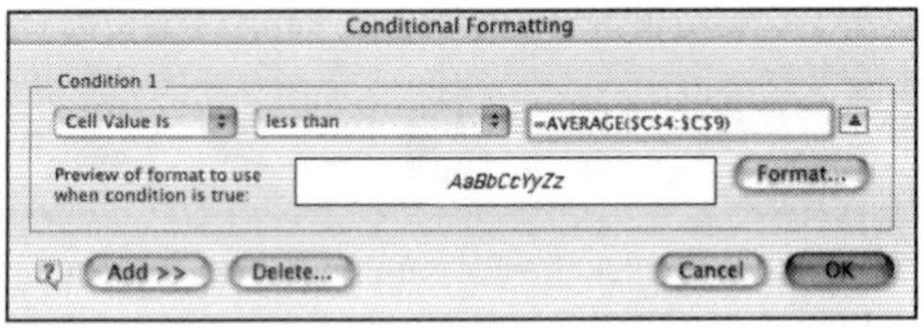

Figure 12.33 When you choose Format > Conditional Formatting, the Conditional Formatting dialog box appears. Choose your criteria and formats.

Conditional Formatting

You might want to apply different formats to different cells, depending on their value or whether they meet some other criteria. You can do this with Excel's conditional formatting feature.

To format cells based on conditions:

1. Select the cells you want to format (**Figure 12.32**).

2. Choose Format > Conditional Formatting.

3. In the Conditional Formatting dialog box, specify from the pull-down menus whether you want to apply the format based on the value of the cell or based on some formula (**Figure 12.33**). If you choose a formula, the formula must begin with an equal sign (=), and the formula must evaluate to either true or false instead of a number. In the language of mathematics, it must be a *Boolean expression*.

4. Click the Format button, and in the dialog box that appears, choose the font, border, and pattern formats you want to apply to the cells that meet the criteria.

5. If you have more than one criterion to apply, click Add in the Conditional Formatting dialog box, then define the second criterion. You may have up to three criteria, and the default format, applied to cells that meet none of the criteria, constitutes a fourth format possibility.

(continues on next page)

6. Click OK to apply the conditions. The cells are evaluated and formatted according to your criteria (**Figure 12.34**).

✔ Tips

■ You may copy conditional formats, like any other formats, to other cells, using the Format Painter tool in the Standard toolbar (**Figure 12.35**).

■ Among the available formats are colors: For example, you can designate numbers above a certain value as green, numbers below another value as red, and numbers in between the two as yellow. Spreadsheets color-coded this way are usually referred to in business graphics as *stoplight charts*.

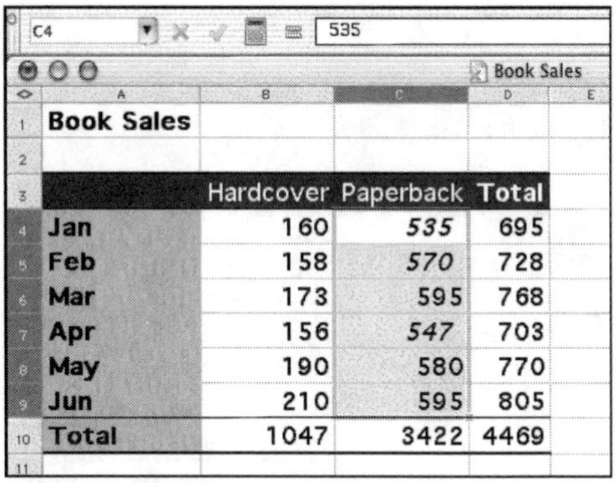

	A	B	C	D	E
1	Book Sales				
2					
3		Hardcover	Paperback	Total	
4	Jan	160	535	695	
5	Feb	158	570	728	
6	Mar	173	595	768	
7	Apr	156	547	703	
8	May	190	580	770	
9	Jun	210	595	805	
10	Total	1047	3422	4469	
11					

Figure 12.34 Excel formats the cells.

Format Painter

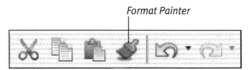

Figure 12.35 Click the Format Painter tool to copy formats.

Figure 12.36 Select the text cells to format.

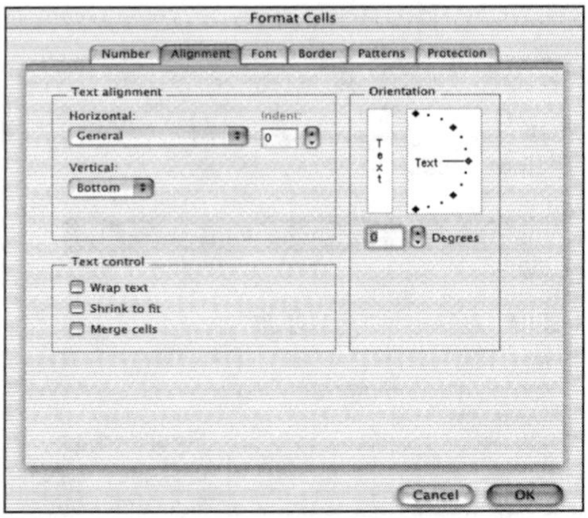

Figure 12.38 Choose alignment options in the Format Cells dialog box.

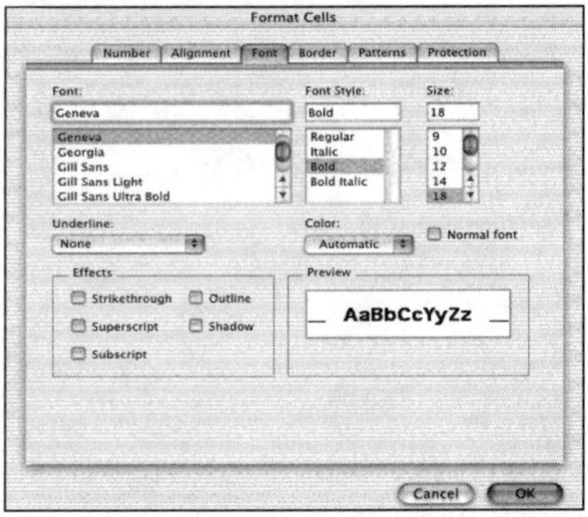

Figure 12.39 Choose font options.

Formatting Text

Excel offers a wide range of formatting selections for text. We'll get started with the dialog boxes and toolbar tools involved. Also, don't be shy about exploring the other tabs in the dialog boxes once you get the hang of the basics. If the Formatting toolbar isn't already visible, you can see it by choosing View > Toolbars > Formatting.

To format text:

1. Select the cell or cells that contain the text to format (**Figure 12.36**).

2. Choose formatting options by clicking the appropriate text-formatting buttons on the Formatting toolbar (**Figure 12.37**, below).

   or

1. Select the cell or cells that contain the text to format (Figure 12.36).

2. Choose Format > Cells, or [Control]-click the mouse button and choose Format Cells from the shortcut menu.

3. In the Format Cells dialog box, change options under the Alignment and Font tabs (**Figures 12.38**, **12.39**).

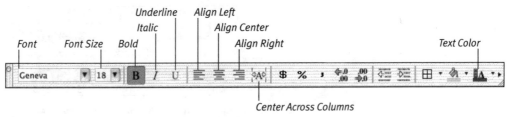

Figure 12.37 Text-formatting tools on the Formatting toolbar.

To center a title above a range:

1. Type the title into the leftmost cell above the range (**Figure 12.40**).

2. Select the cells above the range (**Figure 12.41**).

3. Click the Merge and Center button in the Formatting toolbar (**Figure 12.42**).

   or

   Choose Format > Cells. Then, in the Format Cells dialog box, click the Alignment tab. In the Horizontal pull-down menu of the Text alignment pane of the Alignment tab, choose Center. In the Text control pane, select Merge cells (**Figure 12.43**).

   This merges the cells over the range, centering the title within it (**Figure 12.44**).

✔ Tip

- Click the Merge and Center button again to return the text to left alignment.

Figure 12.40 Type the title.

Figure 12.41 Select the range.

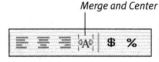

Merge and Center

Figure 12.42 Click the Merge and Center button.

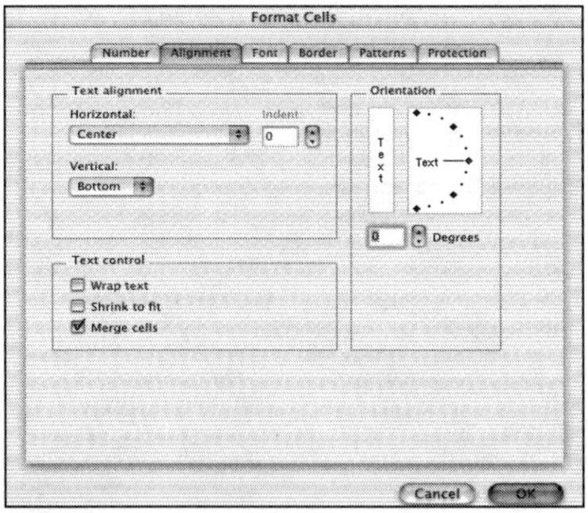

Figure 12.43 In Format Cells, choose Center and Merge cells under the Alignment tab.

Figure 12.44 The title appears centered over the range.

FORMATTING TEXT

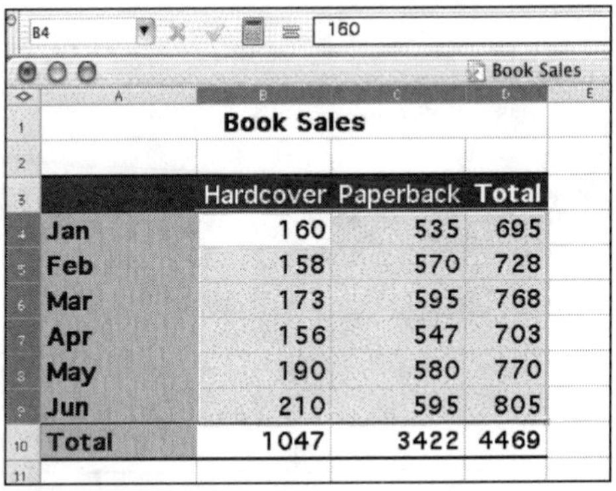

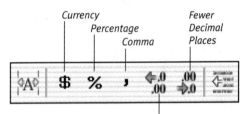

Figure 12.45 Select the numbers to format.

Currency
Percentage
Comma
Fewer Decimal Places

More Decimal Places

Figure 12.46 Choose a number tool from the Formatting toolbar.

Choose a category here ...
... and a format here.

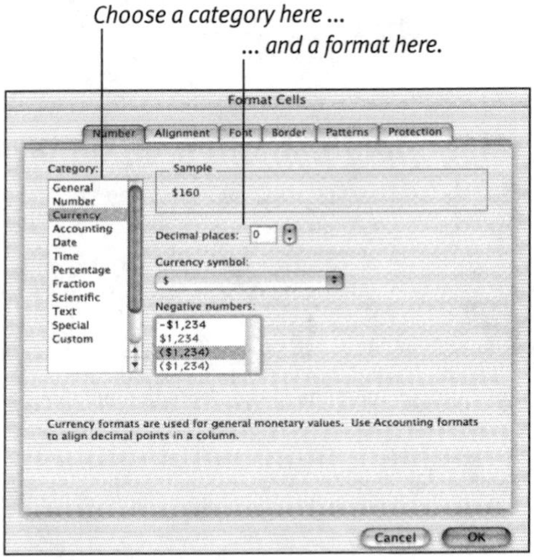

Figure 12.47 Choose a category and format options.

Formatting Numbers

As with text, Excel allows application of a wide variety of formats to numbers. If the Formatting toolbar isn't already visible, you can see it by choosing View > Toolbars > Formatting.

To format numbers:

1. Select the numbers to format (**Figure 12.45**).

2. Click the appropriate number-formatting button on the Formatting toolbar (**Figure 12.46**).

   or

   Choose Format > Cells. In the Number tab of the Format Cells dialog box, choose an item from the Category list and select the corresponding formatting options to its right (**Figure 12.47**).

✔ Tips

- Until you choose a special number format, Excel formats numbers with the General number format (right-aligned, up to 11 decimal places).

- If you enter numbers preceded by a dollar sign ($), Excel applies Currency formatting. If you enter numbers followed by a percent sign (%), Excel applies Percentage formatting.

- You can save number formatting as a style. See "To create a new style," later in this chapter.

FORMATTING NUMBERS

Borders and Shading

A border is a line or lines at the edge of a cell. You can use borders to divide the information on the sheet into logical regions. Borders appear on the screen and also print out when you print the sheet.

To apply a border:

1. Select the range to which you'd like to apply a border (**Figure 12.48**).

2. Click the pull-down button next to the Borders icon on the Formatting toolbar to see the full range of borders (**Figure 12.49**).

3. Select the pane on the display of borders that matches the border you want for the range (**Figures 12.50**, **12.51**).

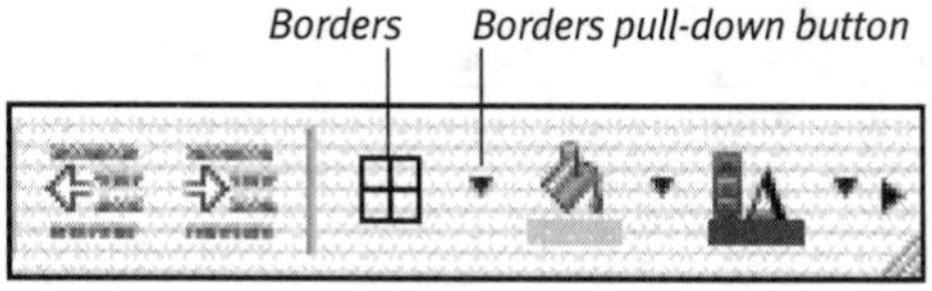

Figure 12.48 Select the cells to format.

Figure 12.49 Click the Borders pull-down button to see available borders.

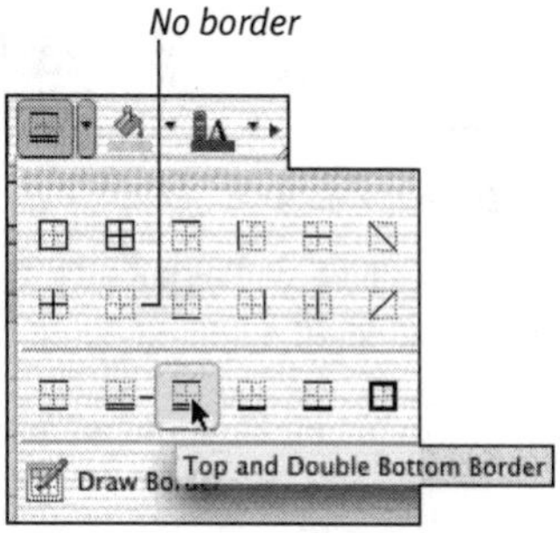

Figure 12.50 Select a border.

Figure 12.51 This adds the border to the range.

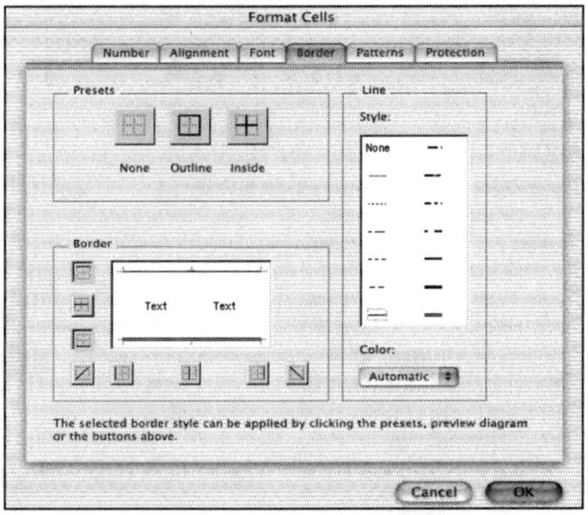

Figure 12.52 Choose a border, line style, and color.

or

1. Select the range to which you'd like to apply a border.

2. Choose Format > Cells, or [Control]-click and choose Format Cells from the shortcut menu.

3. Under the Border tab of the Format Cells dialog box, choose a border, a border style, and a color (**Figure 12.52**).

✔ Tips

- To choose the most recently used border, simply click the Borders icon in the Formatting toolbar rather than pull down the list of choices.

- To remove the borders around a range, select the range, click and hold the Borders pull-down button in the Formatting toolbar to open the display of border choices, and choose the No Border icon from that display.

BORDERS AND SHADING

Shading is a pattern or color that fills the cell or cells you choose.

To add shading to a range:

1. Select the range to which you'd like to add shading (**Figure 12.53**).

2. Choose Format > Cells, or Control-click and choose Format Cells from the shortcut menu.

3. Under the Patterns tab of the Format Cells dialog box, choose a color or shade of gray. To choose a monochrome pattern (in which all the pixels, or dots, are solid black or solid white), pull down the list of patterns and choose one at the top of the palette (**Figure 12.54**).

   This applies the pattern you choose to the selected range (**Figure 12.55**).

✔ Tips

■ Excel often applies shading automatically to parts of a range when you select an AutoFormat.

■ If the shading you apply makes it difficult to read the contents of the cell, try using the text-formatting options to change the color of the text to one that contrasts with the shading. Use the Color pull-down list in the Font tab of the Format Cells dialog box.

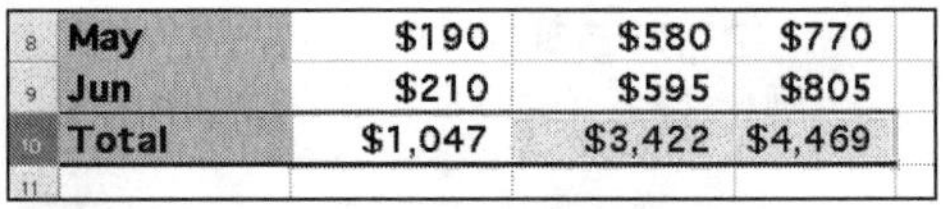

Figure 12.53 Select the cells to shade.

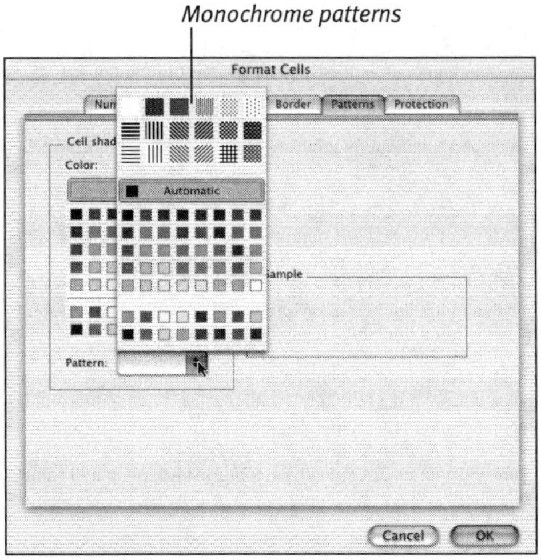

Figure 12.54 Choose a pattern.

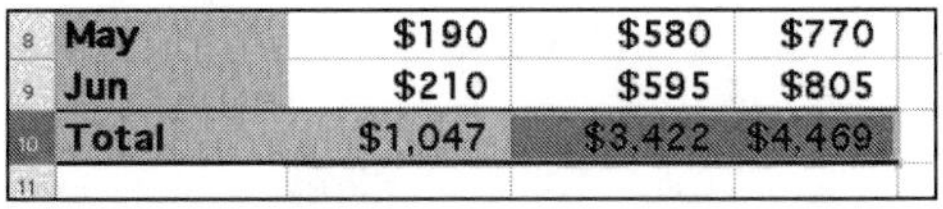

Figure 12.55 Excel applies the chosen pattern.

8	**May**	$190	$580	$770
9	**Jun**	$210	$595	$805
10	**Total**	$1,047	$3,422	$4,469
11				

Figure 12.56 Select the cells to format.

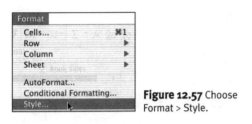

Figure 12.57 Choose Format > Style.

Choose a style here

Figure 12.58 Choose a style from the pull-down menu.

Using Styles

A style is a preset formatting combination. You can choose one of the existing styles or create your own.

To use existing styles:

1. Select the cells to format (**Figure 12.56**).

2. Choose Format > Style (**Figure 12.57**).

3. In the Style dialog box, choose a style from the pull-down Style name menu (**Figure 12.58**).

4. Make sure you've selected the checkboxes in the Style dialog box for the formatting aspects you'd like the style to apply.

✔ Tips

■ When [0] follows styles on the Style name pull-down menu, Excel formats them to zero decimal places.

■ Excel gives cells the Normal style unless you specify a different style.

■ To change the default cell formatting, modify the Normal style.

To create a new style:

1. Format a cell with all the formatting you want (**Figure 12.59**). See "Formatting Text" and "Formatting Numbers," above.

2. Choose Format > Style (**Figure 12.60**).

3. Type a new style name in the Style name field (**Figure 12.61**).

4. Click OK.

✔ Tip

- You can copy the styles from another open workbook by clicking the Merge button in the Style dialog box and selecting the other workbook.

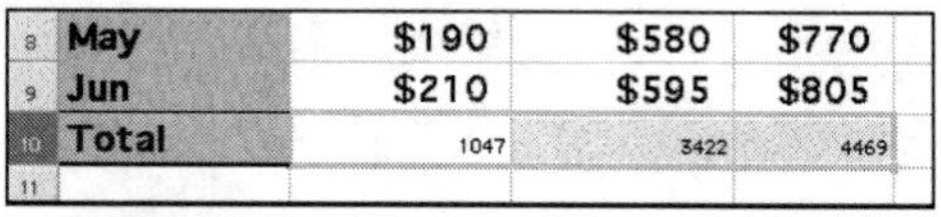

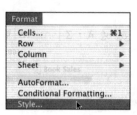

Figure 12.59 Format a cell.

Format		
Cells...	Σ · A	⌘1
Row		▶
Column		▶
Sheet		▶
AutoFormat...		
Conditional Formatting...		
Style...		

Figure 12.60 Choose Format > Style.

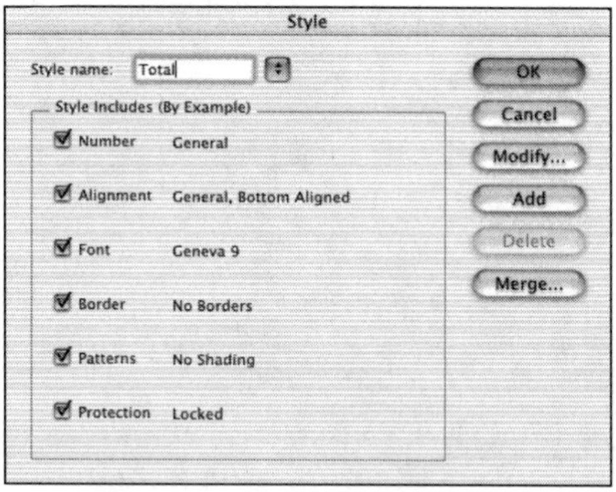

Figure 12.61 Type a new name in the Style name field.

USING STYLES

Using Multiple Worksheets

Each Excel workbook contains, by default, three worksheets (or simply sheets). If you only need one, you can easily ignore or delete the extras, and you can also add sheets if you need them. It may make sense to have a separate sheet for each of several entities, and another that consolidates the contents of all the others.

Switching Sheets

It's normally convenient to work with one sheet at a time, but if you're using multiple sheets in your workbook, you may want to switch between them occasionally.

To change the active sheet:

◆ Click the tab of the sheet you want to display (**Figure 13.1**).

The selected sheet replaces the previous one in the active window.

✔ Tips

■ If the tab you want is not visible, use the tab scrolling buttons to scroll through the tabs (**Figure 13.2**).

■ You can rearrange the order of sheets by dragging their tabs left or right.

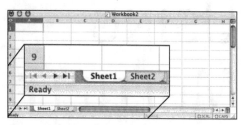

Figure 13.1 To change the active sheet, click the tab of the worksheet you want at the bottom left of the window.

First Sheet
Previous Sheet
Next Sheet
Last Sheet

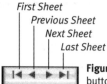

Figure 13.2 Use the tab scrolling buttons to scroll through sheets.

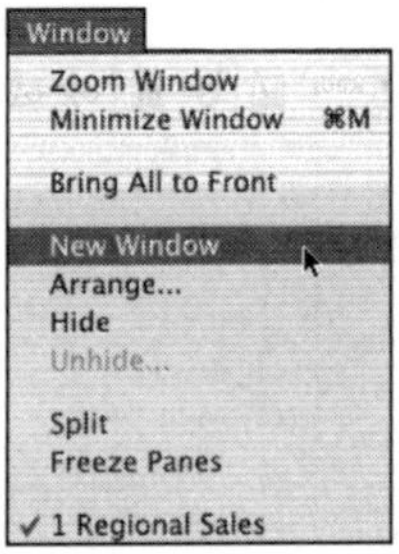

Viewing Multiple Sheets

Sometimes you may want to view the contents of multiple sheets at once. You do this by opening each sheet in a separate window and arranging the windows so you can see them all at once.

To view multiple sheets at once:

1. Choose Window > New Window (**Figure 13.3**).

2. When the window opens, click the tab of the sheet you want to open.

   The names of all open windows appear at the bottom of the Window menu. If you haven't renamed your sheets yet, they'll show up as Sheet1, Sheet2, Sheet3, and so on.

3. Choose Window > Arrange (**Figure 13.4**).

(continues on next page)

Figure 13.3 Choose Window > New Window.

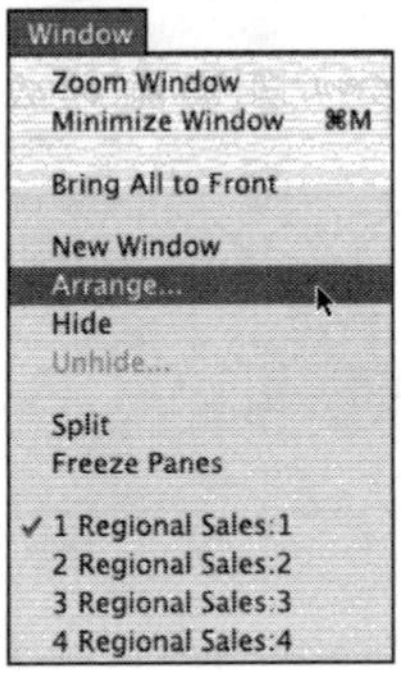

Figure 13.4 Choose Window > Arrange.

VIEWING MULTIPLE SHEETS

4. In the Arrange Windows dialog box, choose from the Arrange options (**Figure 13.5**).

Figure 13.6 shows the Tiled arrangement; **Figure 13.7** shows the Cascade arrangement.

✔ Tips

- The Tiled arrangement places the windows counterclockwise, starting from top left, in the order in which you opened the windows. If you want to arrange the windows differently, close them and reopen them with this arrangement in mind.

- To make one of the windows fill the screen, click the zoom box at the right end of its title bar; clicking the zoom box again returns the window to its arranged size and location.

- To hide one of the windows, click the Collapse box at the far right end of the window's title bar. That window then rolls up like a window shade into its title bar. Clicking the Collapse box again expands the window.

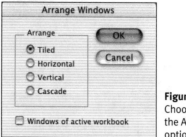

Figure 13.5
Choose from the Arrange options.

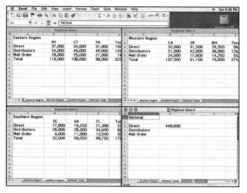

Figure 13.6 Tiled arrangement.

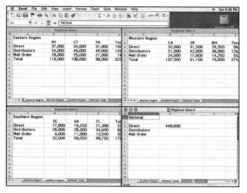

Figure 13.7 Cascade arrangement.

VIEWING MULTIPLE SHEETS

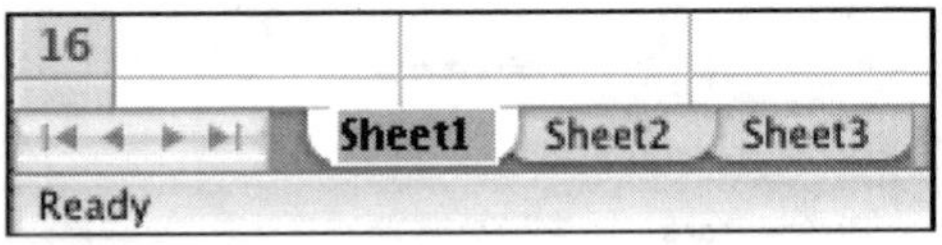

Figure 13.8 Double-click the tab of the sheet you want to rename.

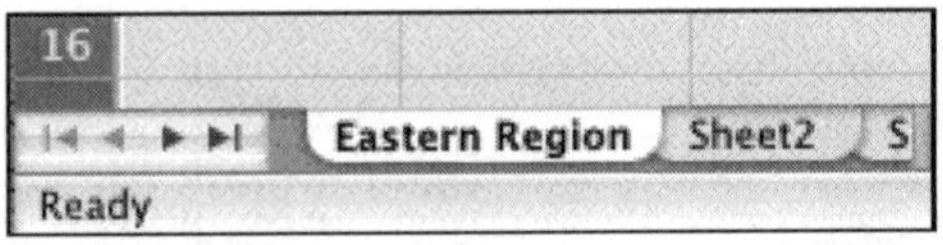

Figure 13.9 Type the new name.

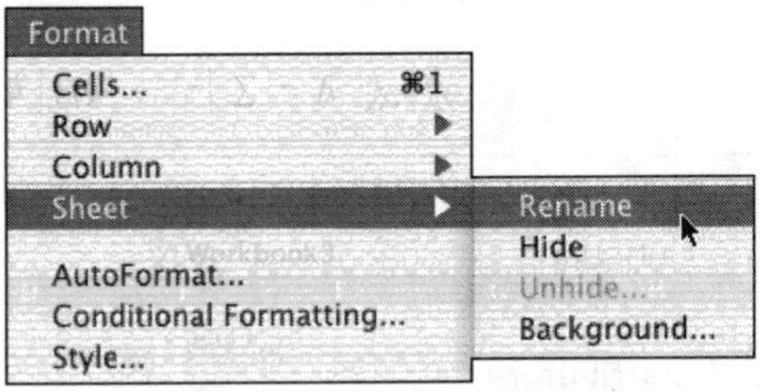

Figure 13.10 Choose Format > Sheet > Rename.

Naming Sheets

You can replace the default names for your sheets (Sheet1, Sheet2, and so on) with useful, informative names (for example, Marketing, Manufacturing, or Personnel).

To rename a sheet:

1. Double-click the tab of the sheet you want to rename (**Figure 13.8**).

2. Type the new name over the current name in the sheet tab (**Figure 13.9**).

✔ Tips

■ You can also choose Format > Sheet > Rename (**Figure 13.10**) to select the sheet name in the tab of the current sheet so it's ready for retyping.

■ Sheet names can be up to 31 characters long and can include spaces.

Referring to Data from Other Sheets

When building a formula, you can include data from another sheet.

To refer to another sheet:

1. Click the destination cell for the formula.

2. Start the formula as usual by entering an equal sign (=) in the cell (**Figure 13.11**).

3. Refer to cells on other sheets by switching to the sheets and then selecting the cell or cells (**Figure 13.12**). As you are building the formula, click a cell in another sheet; this adds a reference to that cell in the Edit Line of the sheet where you're building the formula. You can add an operator or function to the formula you're creating, then go to another sheet and click the next cell you need in the formula, and so on.

4. Press (Enter) when you finish building the formula. This returns you to the sheet where you built that formula (**Figure 13.13**).

   The formula (**Figure 13.14**) refers to the other sheets by name.

✔ Tip

- If you've named ranges in other sheets, you can enter the range names in the formula without worrying about which sheet the data is on. Excel will find the range on any sheet in the workbook. See "Naming Ranges of Cells" in Chapter 9.

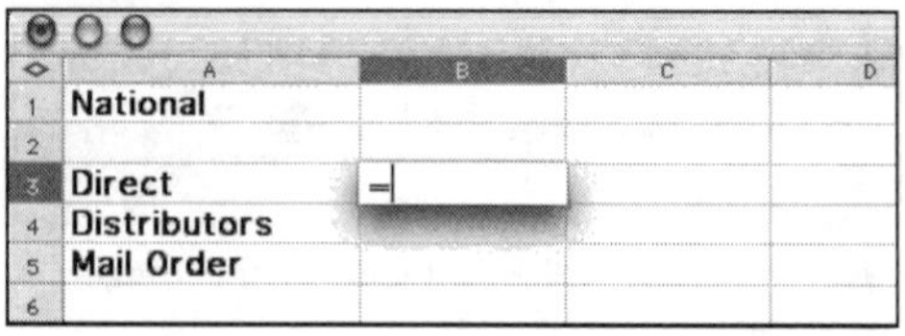

Figure 13.11 Start the formula with an equal sign.

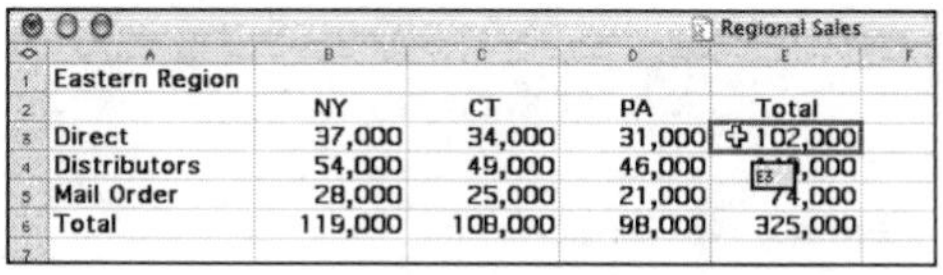

Figure 13.12 Switch to each sheet and select the cell(s) whose values you want to include in the formula.

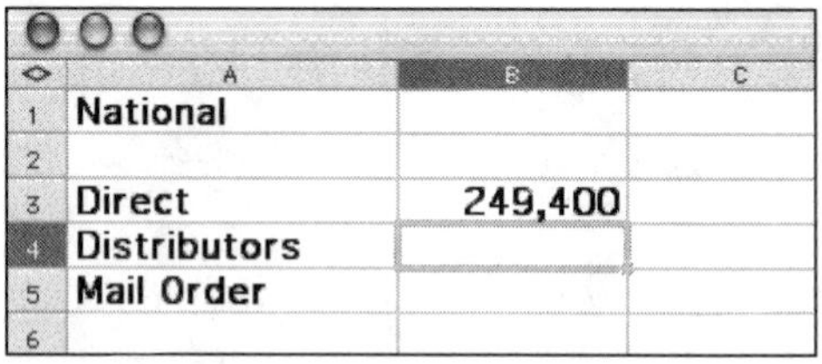

Figure 13.13 (Enter) returns you to the sheet where you built the formula.

=SUM('Eastern Region'!E3+'Western Region'!E3+'Southern Region'!E3)

Figure 13.14 The finished formula appears in the Edit Line.

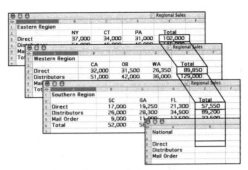

Figure 13.15 3D referencing combines the values in corresponding cells from different sheets into one consolidation sheet.

	A	B	C
1	**National**		
2			
3	**Direct**		
4	**Distributors**		
5	**Mail Order**		
6			

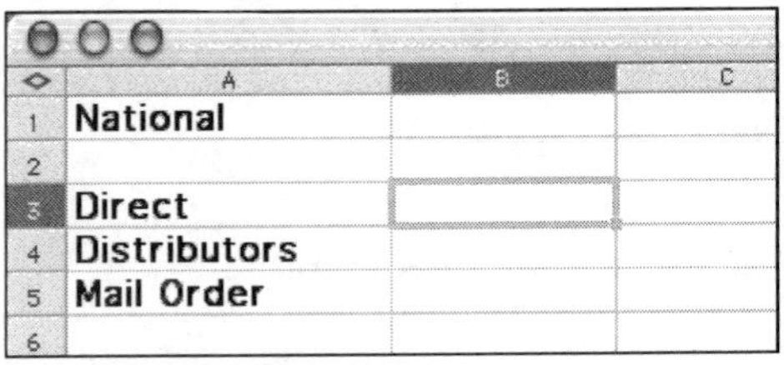

Figure 13.16 Click the destination cell on the consolidation sheet.

	A	B	C
1	**National**		
2			
3	**Direct**	=sum(	
4	**Distributors**		
5	**Mail Order**		
6			

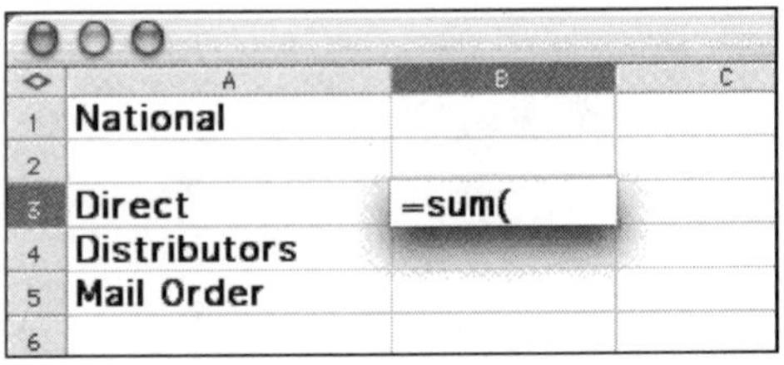

Figure 13.17 Start the formula.

Consolidating to a Sheet

When successive sheets of a workbook contain the same arrangement of data, you can sum ranges that extend *down* from sheet to sheet rather than across a single sheet. This is called *3D referencing* (**Figure 13.15**), and it's the preferred method of consolidation.

To consolidate using 3D referencing:

1. On the consolidation sheet, click the destination cell for the formula (**Figure 13.16**).

2. Start the formula by entering an equal sign followed by a function or operator, such as SUM, and an open parenthesis (**Figure 13.17**).

(continues on next page)

3. Select the cell or cells in the first sheet in the range of sheets (**Figure 13.18**).

4. Press and hold down (Shift).

Click the tab of the last sheet in the range (**Figure 13.19**).

5. Press (Enter) to complete the formula (don't click the tab for the consolidation sheet first). Click the formula cell in the consolidation sheet again to see the formula in the Edit Line (**Figure 13.20**).

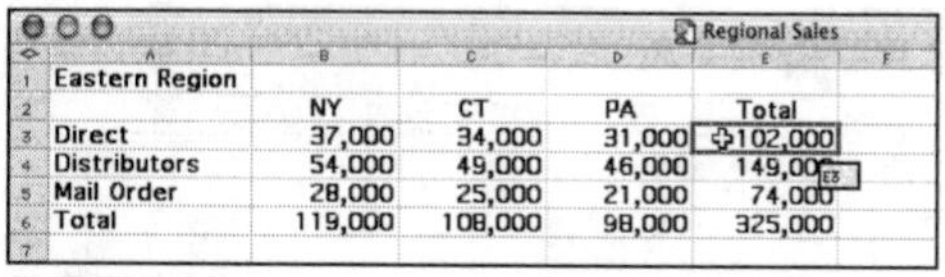

Figure 13.18 Select the cell(s) in the first sheet.

Figure 13.19 Holding down (Shift), click the tab for the last sheet in the range.

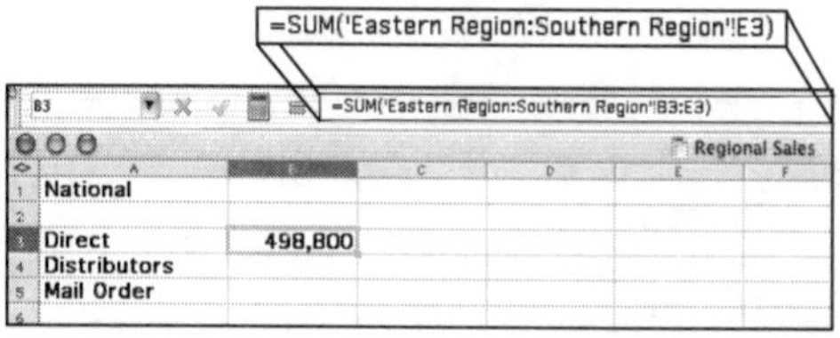

Figure 13.20 The completed formula.

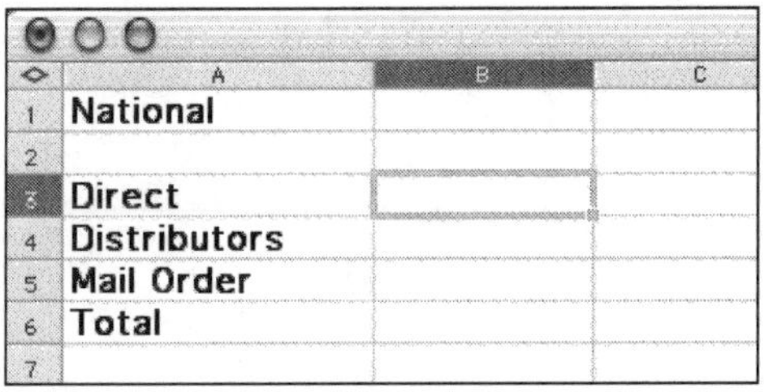

Figure 13.21 Click the upper-left cell of the destination range in the consolidation sheet.

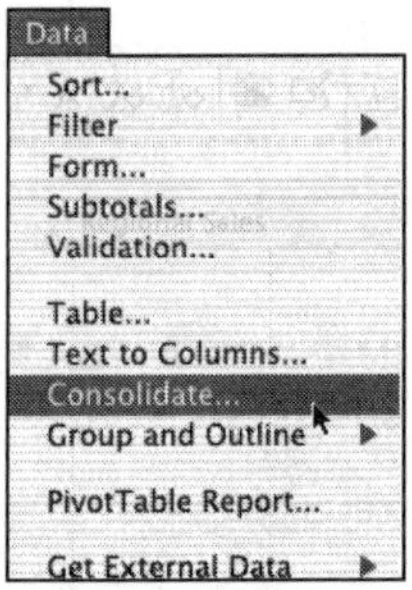

Figure 13.22 Choose Data > Consolidate.

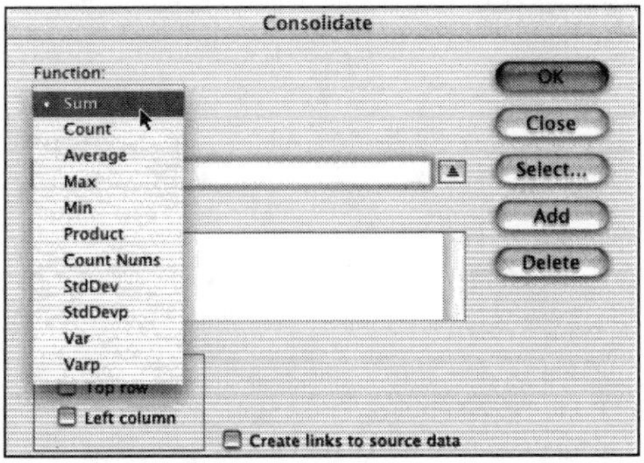

Figure 13.23 Choose a consolidation function.

You should be able to use 3D referencing pretty much regardless of your worksheets' organization, as long as you've organized them all in the same way. If you've taken the trouble to name the ranges of cells you want to consolidate, or if the corresponding columns have the same label in row 1 or the corresponding rows have the same label in column A in all the worksheets, you may find the Consolidate dialog box a little easier to use.

To use the Consolidate dialog box:

1. Click the upper-left cell of the range in the worksheet where you want to consolidate the data (**Figure 13.21**).

2. Choose Data > Consolidate (**Figure 13.22**).

3. In the Consolidate dialog box, choose from the drop-down Function list the function you want to apply to all the consolidated sheets (**Figure 13.23**). For example, you can add all the numbers, take the average, or find the maximum or minimum value.

(continues on next page)

4. For each sheet you want to include in the consolidation, enter a reference to the pertinent cells on that sheet in the Reference text box, then click Add (**Figure 13.24**). This is easiest if you've named the ranges of cells you want to use (as has been done in the example; see "Naming Ranges of Cells" in Chapter 9).

5. If you're identifying ranges by column or row headings, indicate which of these two options you want by clicking the appropriate radio button in the pane titled Use labels in.

6. Click OK. The consolidated data appears in the destination cell(s) of the consolidation sheet (**Figure 13.25**).

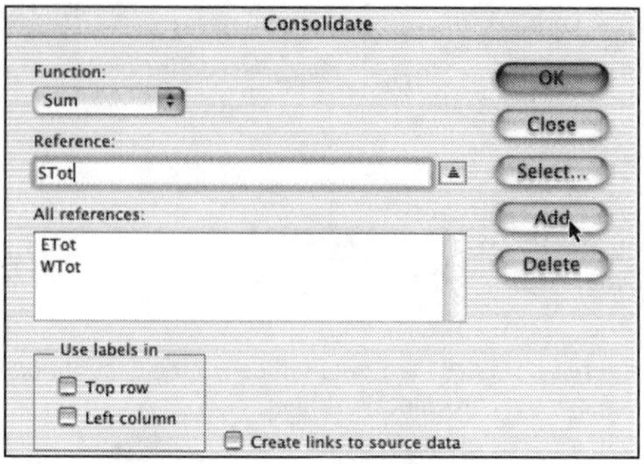

Figure 13.24 Enter references to the cell ranges you're consolidating.

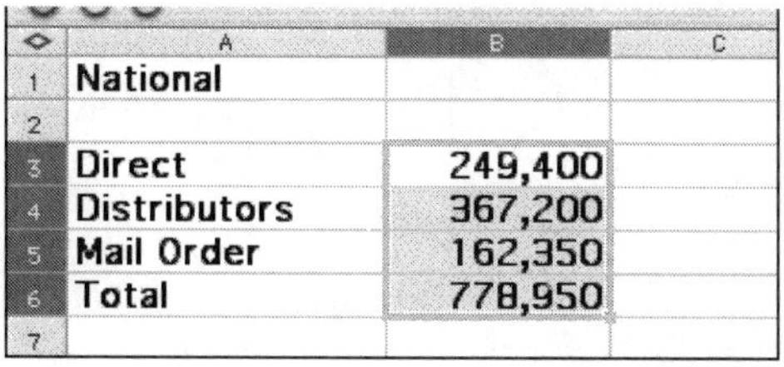

Figure 13.25 The consolidated data appears in the destination cells.

ANALYZING DATA

Excel offers several ways to analyze data while it is still in rows-and-columns format, including switching columns and rows with PivotTable techniques, finding values you don't have enough information to calculate directly, investigating the effects on the bottom line of changing the contributing factors, and solving for one value when you know all the others. Another way of analyzing data in Excel is to display it graphically in a chart; see Chapter 15, Charts, to get started using charts.

Reorganizing Data Using PivotTables

A PivotTable is an interactive table that summarizes and analyzes data from existing lists and tables. PivotTables are a convenient way to rearrange sheets in order to look at large amounts of data in different ways. Start with a long list or database, and create a PivotTable summary of the data. Then use the PivotTable features to quickly and easily change columns into rows, investigate details that make up the summary numbers, and find the presentation format that best reveals the information you want to know.

PivotTables are rich with functionality; a complete discussion of how to use all their features is beyond the scope of this book. We'll get you started creating PivotTables, and you can explore them from there.

To create a PivotTable:

1. Start with a database or list (**Figure 14.1**), and choose Data > PivotTable Report (**Figure 14.2**).
2. In the first screen of the PivotTable Wizard, specify the source of your data (**Figure 14.3**). Click Next.
3. In the second screen of the PivotTable Wizard, specify the cell range within the data source (**Figure 14.4**). Click Next.

Month	Rep	Product	Cases Opened	Cases Closed
Sep	Steve	EB	72	63
Sep	Steve	API	19	21
Oct	Steve	EB	74	76
Oct	Steve	API	17	16
Sep	Scott	EB	64	66
Sep	Scott	Reports	9	11
Oct	Scott	EB	67	68
Oct	Scott	Report	8	8
Sep	Brenda	IS	22	24
Sep	Brenda	DB	9	9
Oct	Brenda	IS	27	26
Oct	Brenda	DB	10	12
Sep	Gary	Reports	13	15
Sep	Gary	IS	4	7
Oct	Gary	Report	16	14
Oct	Gary	IS	8	6

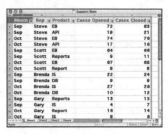

Figure 14.1 Start with a database or list.

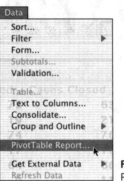

Figure 14.2 Choose Data > PivotTable Report.

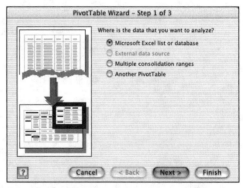

Figure 14.3 In the PivotTable Wizard, specify the source of your data.

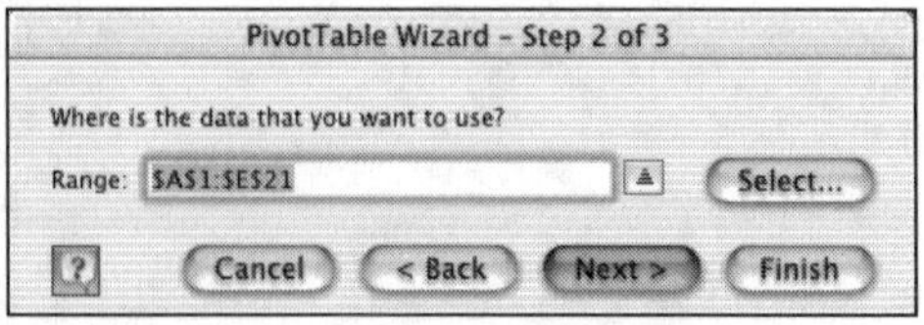

Figure 14.4 Specify the cell range within the data source.

Figure 14.5
Specify the report destination.

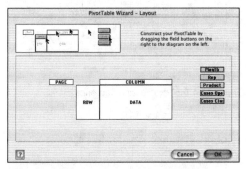

Figure 14.6 In the center of the PivotTable Wizard—Layout dialog box, specify the report layout.

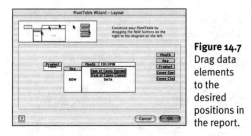

Figure 14.7 Drag data elements to the desired positions in the report.

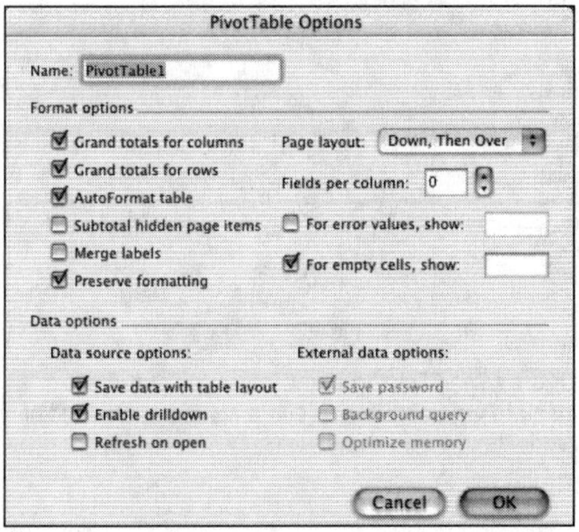

4. In the third screen of the PivotTable Wizard (**Figure 14.5**), specify whether you want the PivotTable report to appear in a new worksheet or in the current one.

5. Click the Layout button to get the PivotTable Wizard—Layout dialog box, a convenient place to specify the layout of the resulting PivotTable report (**Figure 14.6**). Here you can also drag the names of your data elements to any position in the layout (**Figure 14.7**). You'll probably want to drag the numeric items into the Data section. Click OK.

6. Clicking the Options button of the PivotTable Wizard's third screen brings up the PivotTable Options dialog box (**Figure 14.8**). Here you can specify a number of options for formatting and data. Click OK.

(continues on next page)

REORGANIZING DATA USING PIVOTTABLES

Figure 14.8 Specify data and formatting options.

7. Click Finish in the third Wizard screen. The PivotTable report appears (**Figure 14.9**).

   The floating PivotTable toolbar (**Figure 14.10**) also appears, containing the primary tools for manipulating a PivotTable report. Dragging the column data item (Month, in our example) to the row head and the row data item (Rep) to the column head instantly rearranges the data (**Figure 14.11**).

8. The PivotTable displayed is a summary of all items at the Page level (Product, in our example). Using the pull-down menu, you may choose to see the data for any individual product instead of the summary (**Figure 14.12**).

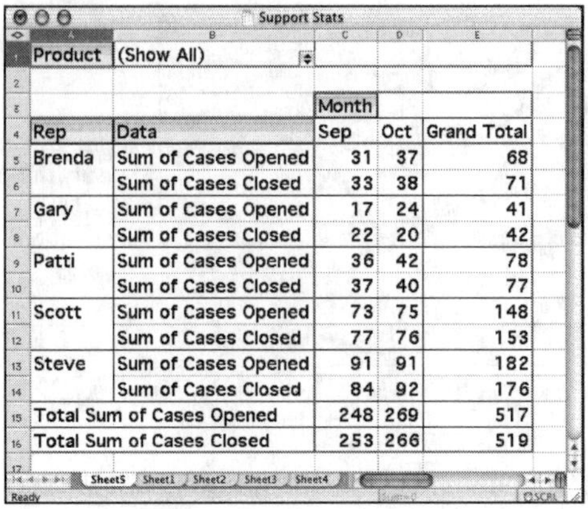

Product	(Show All)			
		Month		
Rep	Data	Sep	Oct	Grand Total
Brenda	Sum of Cases Opened	31	37	68
	Sum of Cases Closed	33	38	71
Gary	Sum of Cases Opened	17	24	41
	Sum of Cases Closed	22	20	42
Patti	Sum of Cases Opened	36	42	78
	Sum of Cases Closed	37	40	77
Scott	Sum of Cases Opened	73	75	148
	Sum of Cases Closed	77	76	153
Steve	Sum of Cases Opened	91	91	182
	Sum of Cases Closed	84	92	176
Total Sum of Cases Opened		248	269	517
Total Sum of Cases Closed		253	266	519

Figure 14.9 The PivotTable report appears.

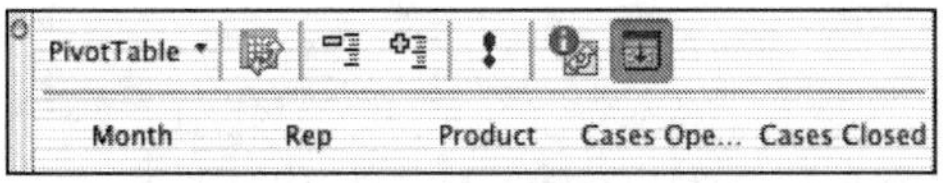

Figure 14.10 Use the PivotTable toolbar to manipulate the PivotTable.

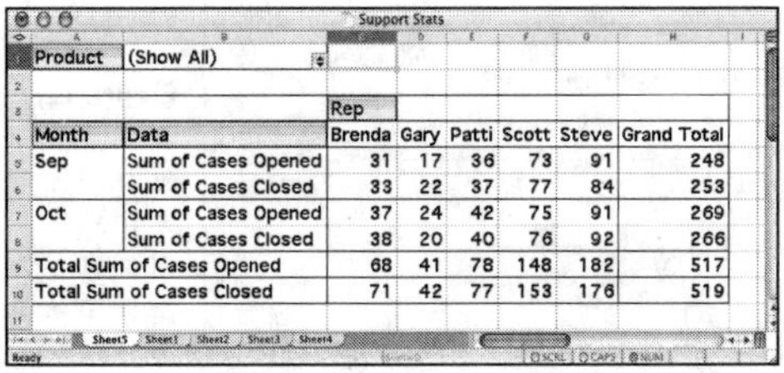

Product	(Show All)						
		Rep					
Month	Data	Brenda	Gary	Patti	Scott	Steve	Grand Total
Sep	Sum of Cases Opened	31	17	36	73	91	248
	Sum of Cases Closed	33	22	37	77	84	253
Oct	Sum of Cases Opened	37	24	42	75	91	269
	Sum of Cases Closed	38	20	40	76	92	266
Total Sum of Cases Opened		68	41	78	148	182	517
Total Sum of Cases Closed		71	42	77	153	176	519

Figure 14.11 Drag elements to row or column heads to change the layout.

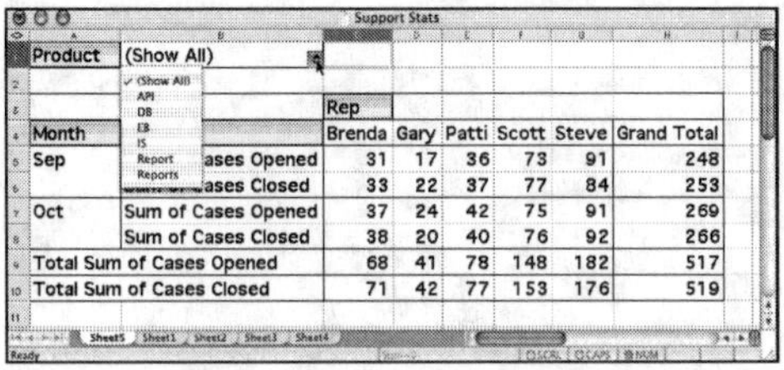

Product	(Show All)						
		Rep					
Month		Brenda	Gary	Patti	Scott	Steve	Grand Total
Sep	ases Opened	31	17	36	73	91	248
	ases Closed	33	22	37	77	84	253
Oct	Sum of Cases Opened	37	24	42	75	91	269
	Sum of Cases Closed	38	20	40	76	92	266
Total Sum of Cases Opened		68	41	78	148	182	517
Total Sum of Cases Closed		71	42	77	153	176	519

Figure 14.12 Click the arrow to use the pull-down menu to view details or a summary (here, it's a list of Products).

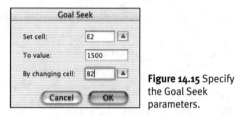

Purchase Price	Down Payment	Years	Interest	Monthly Payment
$247,000	$50,000	30	7.25%	$1,343.89

Figure 14.13 Make sure you include the value you want to find in the formula.

Tools

Spelling...
Dictionary
AutoCorrect...

Share Workbook...
Track Changes ▸
Merge Workbooks...
Protection ▸
Flag for Follow Up...

Goal Seek...
Scenarios...
Auditing ▸
Calculator...

Tools on the Web

Macro ▸
Add-Ins...
Customize...
Wizard ▸

Figure 14.14 Choose Tools > Goal Seek.

Goal Seek

Set cell: E2

To value: 1500

By changing cell: B2

Cancel   OK

Figure 14.15 Specify the Goal Seek parameters.

Goal Seek Status

Goal Seeking with Cell E2
found a solution.

Target value: 1500
Current value: $1,500.00

OK
Cancel
Step
Pause

Figure 14.16 The results appear in Goal Seek Status.

Purchase Price	Down Payment	Years	Interest	Monthly Payment
$247,000	$27,115	30	7.25%	$1,500.00

Figure 14.17 The cell in the sheet changes.

Goal Seeking

Use Goal Seeking to force a particular result in a calculation by changing one of its components. For example, if you know how much you can afford for a monthly payment on a loan, you can use Goal Seeking to find the down payment necessary to produce that monthly payment.

To set the result of a calculation and find a contributing value:

1. Confirm that the value you want to find is part of the formula that calculates the value you want to set (**Figure 14.13**).

2. Choose Tools > Goal Seek (**Figure 14.14**).

3. In the Goal Seek dialog box, specify the cell whose value you want to set (Monthly Payment, in our example), the value you want that cell to be, and the cell whose value can vary to make the result come out to the desired value (Down Payment) (**Figure 14.15**). Click OK.

4. If a solution is possible, the Goal Seek Status dialog box (**Figure 14.16**) will tell you, and the cell you selected to change will alter (**Figure 14.17**).

GOAL SEEKING

What-If Analysis

You may have calculations with some component variables you're not certain of, and perhaps you have several guesses as to what they might be. One way to handle the problem is to manually replace those numbers you're uncertain about with each of your guesses in turn, then let Excel recalculate the bottom line for each guess, one at a time. If you know you'd like to keep the sets of values for future use, Excel lets you do this with Scenarios. If you have no more than two variables that change between scenarios and you want to see the results for all your guessed values at once, you can use Excel's Data Tables.

To save your what-if scenarios:

1. Set up your spreadsheet with one of your guesses (**Figure 14.18**).

2. Choose Tools > Scenarios. The Scenario Manager dialog box appears (**Figure 14.19**).

3. Click Add. The Edit Scenario dialog box appears. Give this scenario a name, select the cells that change with each scenario, and add a comment if you like (**Figure 14.20**). Click OK.

4. The Scenario Values dialog box appears. Specify the values for the changing variables in this scenario (**Figure 14.21**). Click Add to add the next scenario to the list.

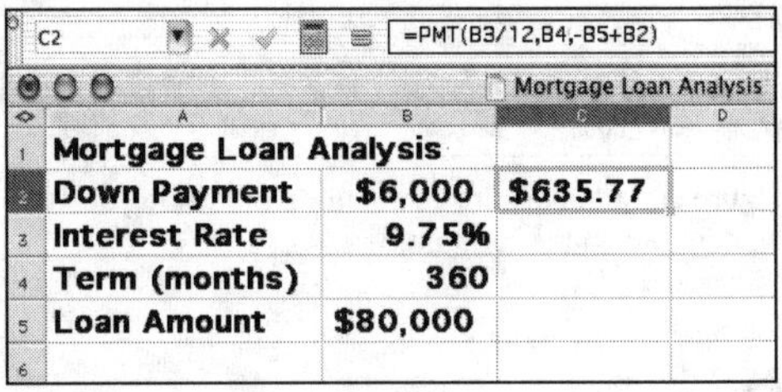

Figure 14.18 Set up the spreadsheet.

Figure 14.19 Choose Tools > Scenarios to get the Scenario Manager dialog box.

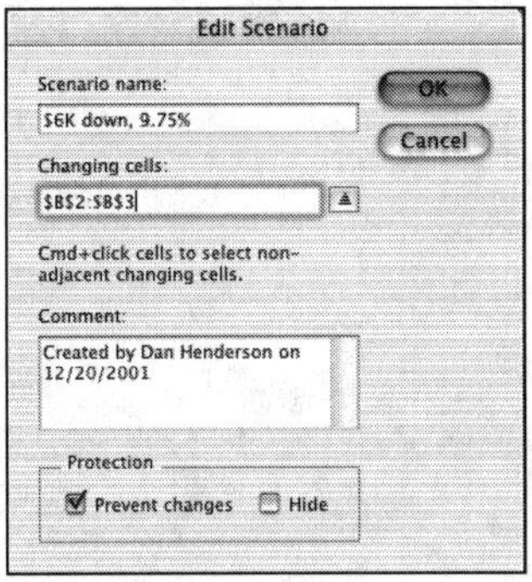

Figure 14.20 Add your scenarios.

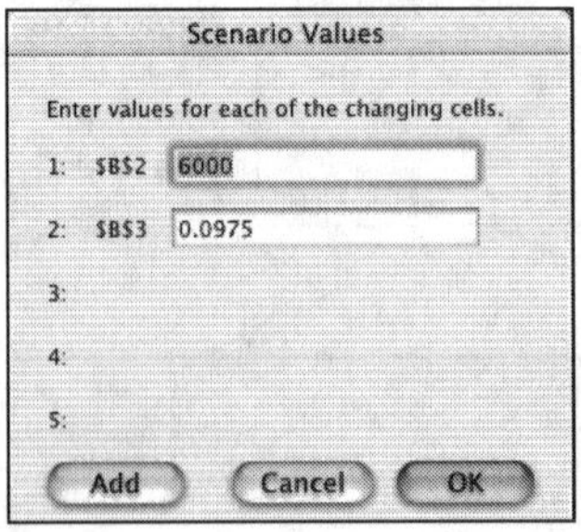

Figure 14.21 Specify the values for each scenario.

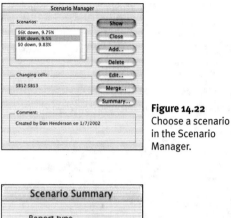

Figure 14.22
Choose a scenario in the Scenario Manager.

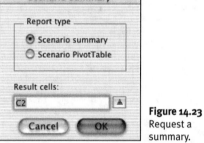

Figure 14.23
Request a summary.

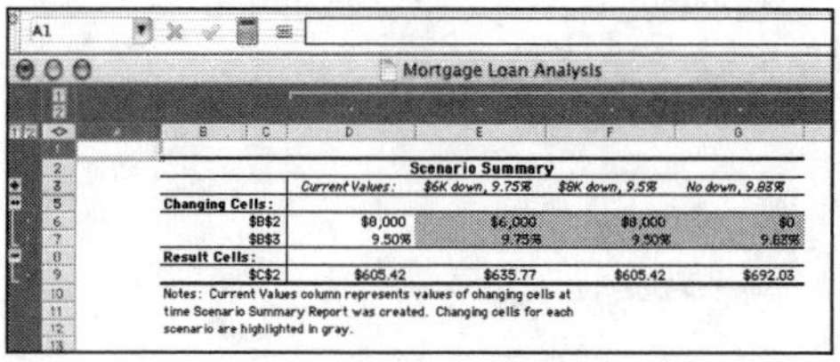

5. Repeat Steps 3 and 4 until you have all your scenarios entered, and then click OK. The Scenario Manager dialog box appears (**Figure 14.22**), with all your saved scenarios listed in the pane on the left. To see the results of any one of them, click it in the left pane, and then click the Show button. Excel substitutes those values for the variables in your spreadsheet and calculates the results.

6. To see a summary of all the scenarios in one new sheet, click Summary in the Scenario Manager dialog box. The Scenario Summary dialog box appears (**Figure 14.23**), giving you the chance to choose between a Scenario summary format and a Scenario PivotTable report. You can also specify which results cell you want reported, in case you have more than one.

The report you choose appears in a new sheet in the same workbook (**Figure 14.24**).

Figure 14.24 The scenario summary appears in a new sheet.

If the summary is really what you're interested in, and you'd like to see all your results in one sheet, you can get there directly with Data Tables, as long as you don't have more than two numbers that change between scenarios.

To see all your results at once:

1. Set up your spreadsheet as in the example (**Figure 14.25**), with your set of values for one of the variables (in this example, the interest rate) extending down the column below the cell that contains the formula, and your set of values for the other variable (in this example, the number of months of the loan) extending to the right of the formula cell on the same row.

2. Select the range of cells spanned by the formula and your values (**Figure 14.26**).

3. Choose Data > Table (**Figure 14.27**). The Table dialog box appears (**Figure 14.28**).

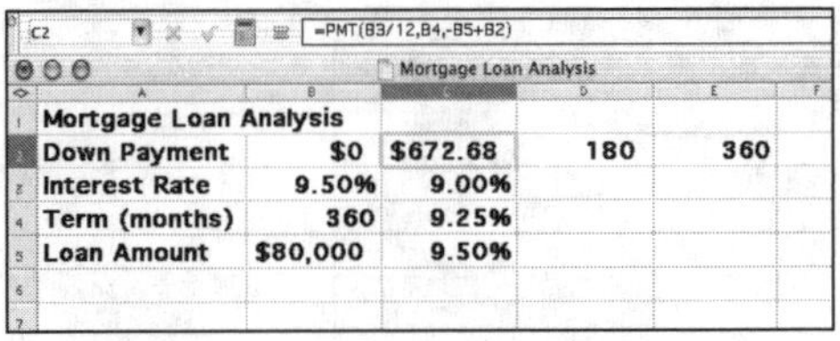

Figure 14.25 Set up your spreadsheet.

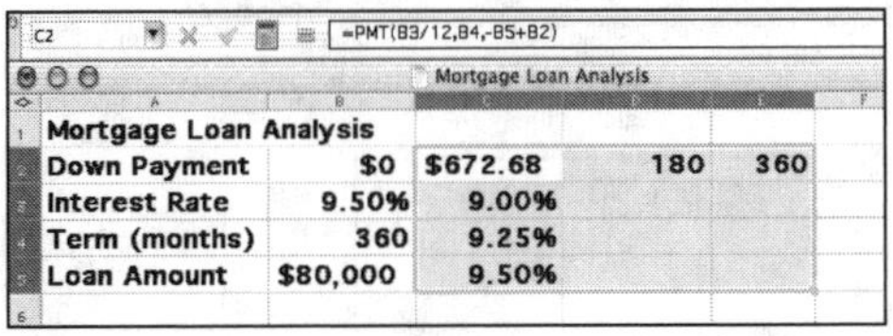

Figure 14.26 Select the range of cells spanned by your formula and variables.

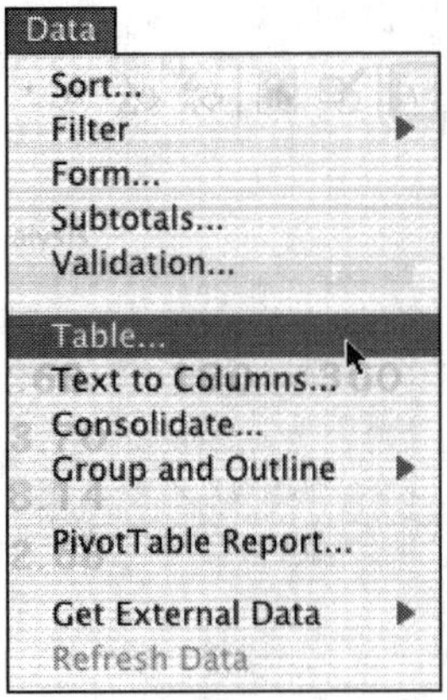

Figure 14.27 Choose Data > Table.

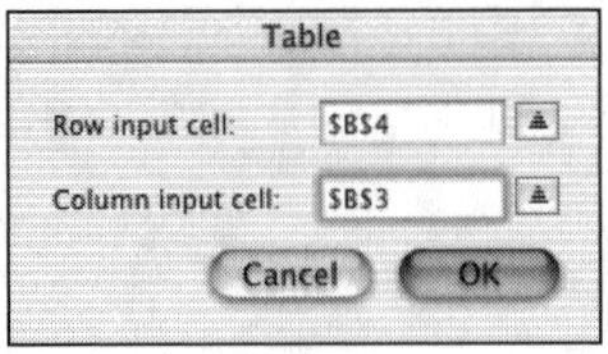

Figure 14.28 Fill in the Table dialog box.

WHAT-IF ANALYSIS

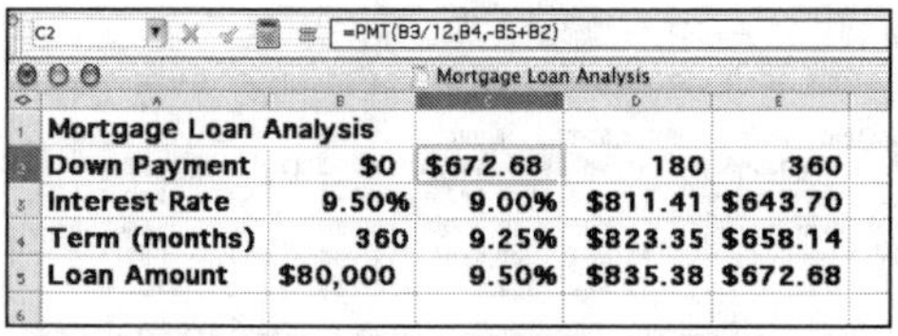

Figure 14.29 The table range is filled.

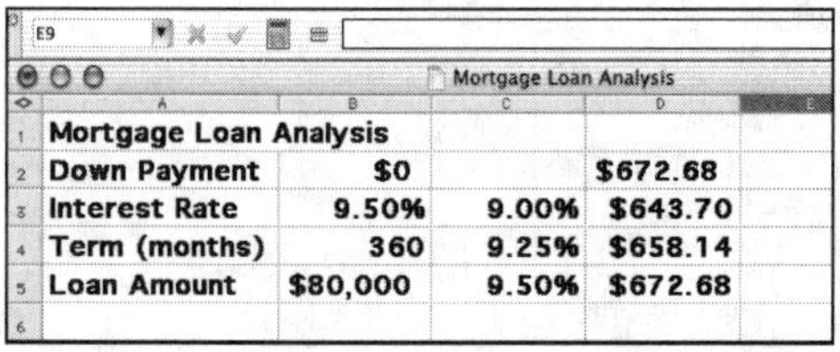

Figure 14.30 Use either a column or a row for a single variable.

4. For the Row input cell box, click the cell containing the variable for which you've provided values in the row to the right of the formula (B4 in our example, since the row values are the term of the loan). For the Column input cell box, click the cell containing the variable for which you've provided values in the column under the formula (B3 in our example, since the column values are the interest rate). Click OK.

The cells in the table range are filled with the results of the formula using the corresponding pairs of variable values (**Figure 14.29**).

✔ Tip

■ If you have only one variable that's changing, arrange its values in either a row or column, with the formula cell at the end of the blank row or column to be filled in by the Data Table operation (**Figure 14.30**). In our example, we've put the values for the one variable that's changing (interest rate) in a column (C3 through C5), and then put the formula in D2. Excel puts formula results for the different interest rates in D3 through D5.

Answering Complex Questions with Solver

If you have a more complex situation where you need to maximize a value (such as total profits), minimize a value (such as total expenses), or arrive at a particular value by changing one or more variables that contribute to the calculation, you can do it with Solver. In our example, we'll attempt to maximize profits by varying advertising expenses.

To maximize or minimize a value using Solver:

1. Look for Tools > Solver. If it isn't there, install it from the Value Pack, under the Excel Add-Ins section.
2. Set up your spreadsheet including any formulas (in our example, the formulas are for Profit in row 7 and Totals in column F) (**Figure 14.31**).
3. Choose Tools > Solver (**Figure 14.32**).
4. The Solver Parameters dialog box appears (**Figure 14.33**). Set the target cell you want Solver to focus on, and then choose whether you want to maximize, minimize, or arrive at a particular value. To tell Solver which cells to change in order to arrive at the desired value, enter references to them in the By Changing Cells text box. You may also set constraints on cells; in our example, we know we want to spend at least $25,000 on advertising over the year, so we've constrained total advertising to greater than or equal to that value.
5. Click Solve. Excel tries different values for the changing cells until it finds a combination that meets the target criteria and constraints. It puts the answers in the spreadsheet (**Figure 14.34**) and presents you with options for whether to keep them there or restore the original values (**Figure 14.35**).

	Q1	Q2	Q3	Q4	Totals
Units Sold	3,592	4,390	3,192	4,789	15,963
Sales Revenue	$143,662	$175,587	$127,700	$191,549	$638,498
Cost of Sales	89,789	109,742	79,812	119,718	399,061
Advertising	10,000	10,000	10,000	10,000	40,000
Overhead	21,549	26,338	19,155	28,732	95,774
Profit	$22,324	$29,507	$18,733	$33,099	$103,663

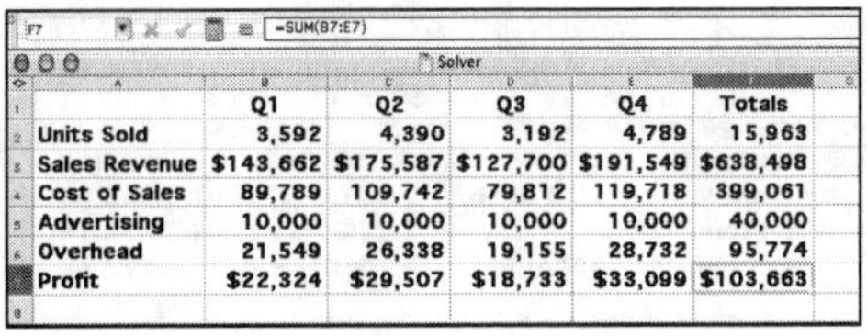

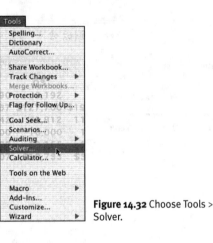

Figure 14.31 Set up your spreadsheet.

Figure 14.32 Choose Tools > Solver.

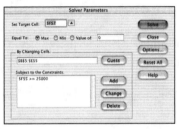

Figure 14.33 Set the Solver parameters.

	Q1	Q2	Q3	Q4	Totals
Units Sold	3,592	4,390	3,192	4,789	15,963
Sales Revenue	$143,662	$175,587	$127,700	$191,549	$638,498
Cost of Sales	89,789	109,742	79,812	119,718	399,061
Advertising	6,250	6,250	6,250	6,250	25,000
Overhead	21,549	26,338	19,155	28,732	95,774
Profit	$26,074	$33,257	$22,483	$36,849	$118,663

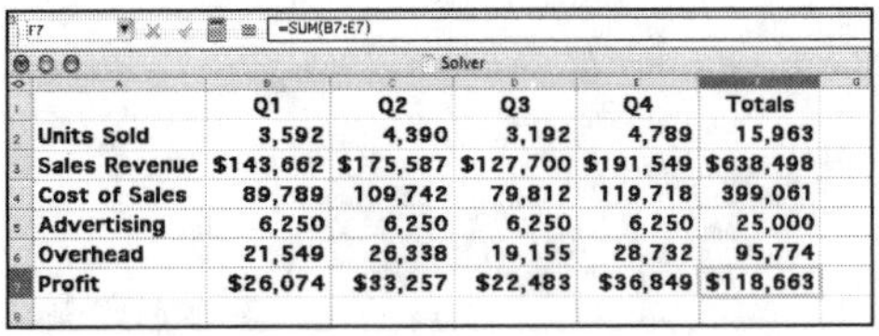

Figure 14.34 The answer appears in the spreadsheet.

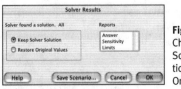

Figure 14.35 Choose Keep Solver Solution or Restore Original Values.

CHARTS

Numeric information is often easiest to understand when presented graphically. In Excel you can make a default chart with a single keystroke. Once Excel has created the chart, you can tailor it to your needs by clicking any element and using Excel's tools to edit that element. You can add, change, or delete titles, labels, legends, and gridlines. You can choose from nearly two dozen different chart styles, including bar, column, line, area, pie, scatter, bubble, and radar charts, and you can add 3D effects to many of them. You can easily add, change, or remove color, patterns, and shading, and you can change the scale, labeling, and look of the axes. If you go back and edit the data used to create the chart, the chart changes on the fly to reflect the new values. Don't be afraid to experiment with options you don't completely understand; you can easily undo almost any change by using Edit > Undo or the Undo button on the Standard toolbar.

Creating Charts

Curious about how to create a chart with one keyboard stroke? It's preceded by a mouse operation, but it's still just one keyboard stroke, and it creates a chart invoking all the defaults.

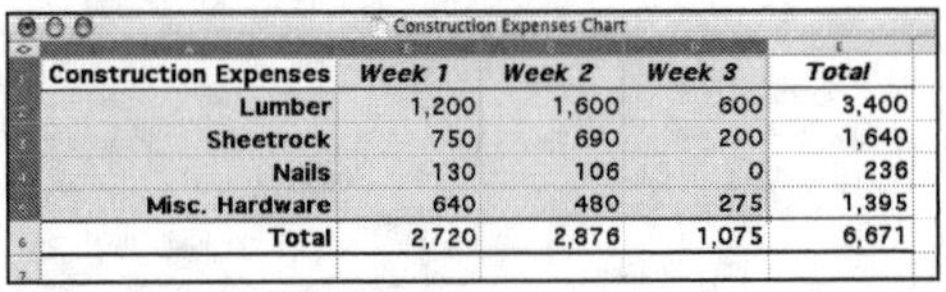

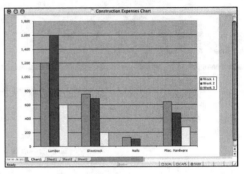

Construction Expenses	Week 1	Week 2	Week 3	Total
Lumber	1,200	1,600	600	3,400
Sheetrock	750	690	200	1,640
Nails	130	106	0	236
Misc. Hardware	640	480	275	1,395
Total	2,720	2,876	1,075	6,671

Figure 15.1 Select the data to chart.

To create a chart most quickly:

1. Select the data to chart (**Figure 15.1**).

2. Press F11 to get a chart with all the default settings. If you haven't changed the default chart type, you get a column chart of the selected data, and it appears in a new worksheet (**Figure 15.2**).

Excel also has a Chart Wizard to give you more control of the process, letting you choose options along the way. For most charts, you'll probably want to use the Chart Wizard.

Figure 15.2 The default chart appears on a new sheet.

Chart Wizard

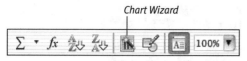

Figure 15.3 Click the Chart Wizard button.

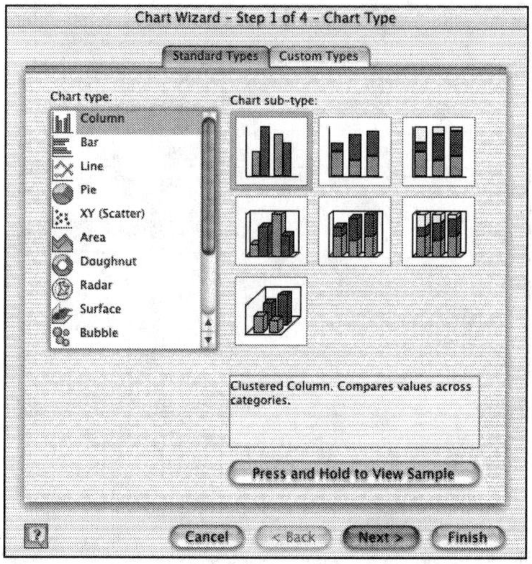

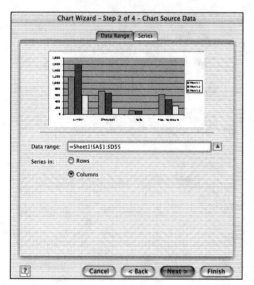

Figure 15.4 Select a chart type on the left.

To create a chart with the Chart Wizard:

1. Click the Chart Wizard button on the Standard toolbar (**Figure 15.3**).

2. In Chart Wizard Step 1, select a chart type (**Figure 15.4**). Click Next.

3. In Chart Wizard Step 2, confirm the data (**Figure 15.5**). Click Next.

(continues on next page)

Figure 15.5 Confirm the data range.

4. In Chart Wizard Step 3, add titles; change gridlines; and place the legend, data labels, and data table where you want them to go (**Figure 15.6**). Click Next.

5. In Chart Wizard Step 4, choose whether to embed the chart in an existing worksheet or create it in a separate sheet, and then click Finish (**Figure 15.7**).

The completed chart is displayed (**Figure 15.8**).

✔ Tips

■ To chart nonadjacent data, press ⌘ while dragging over the selected cells.

■ You can change the default chart type from a column chart to any other type you use frequently. Click a chart and choose Chart > Chart Type. In the Chart Type dialog box, select a chart type to use, and then click the Set as Default Chart button (**Figure 15.9**).

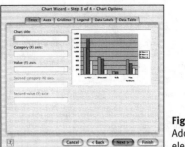

Figure 15.6 Add the text elements.

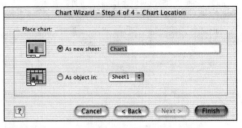

Figure 15.7 Choose the chart destination.

Figure 15.8 The completed chart appears.

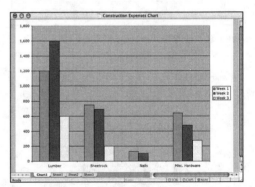

Figure 15.9 Select a chart type and click the Set as Default Chart button.

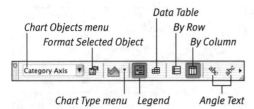

Figure 15.10 The Chart toolbar.

Figure 15.11 Choose Format > Selected Chart Area, and in the dialog box that appears, select the format item for the selected object.

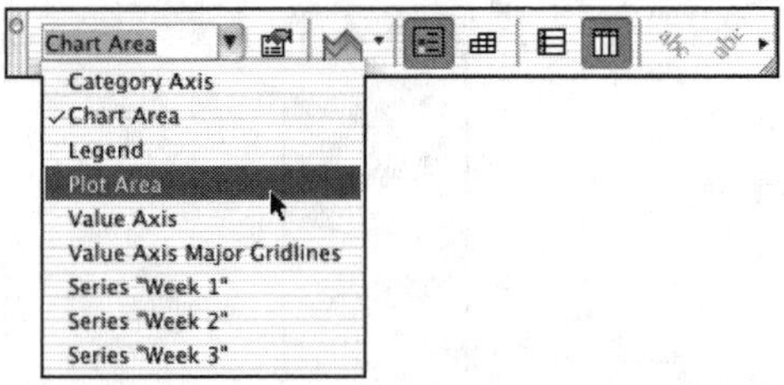

Figure 15.12 Pull down the Chart Objects menu in the Chart toolbar.

Modifying Charts

There are several ways to get to the dialog box you need to change any element of your chart.

To modify a chart element:

1. Double-click a chart object to bring up the formatting dialog box appropriate for that object.

    or

    Click a chart object, and use the Chart toolbar's Format Selected Object button to bring up the appropriate formatting dialog box (**Figure 15.10**).

    or

    Click a chart object, pull down the Format menu, and choose the first selection (the name of the first selection will reflect the type of object selected) to bring up the appropriate dialog box (**Figure 15.11**).

    or

    Pull down the Chart Objects menu in the Chart toolbar, choose the object you want to modify, and click the Chart toolbar's Format Selected Object button (the tool tip you see when you pause the pointer over the button reflects the kind of object you've chosen from the Chart Objects menu) to bring up the appropriate dialog box (**Figure 15.12**).

2. Change the options you want to change, and click OK to apply the changes.

✔ Tips

■ While a chart is active, you can click any part once to select it, or double-click the part to obtain a dialog box where you can specify or change the formatting for that part.

■ Drag the chart to move it on the sheet, or drag the handles of its window to resize the chart.

Now that you know generally how to get to the appropriate dialog box to edit any element of the chart you choose, we'll delve a little deeper into the specifics of the different elements.

To modify the chart type and data series:

1. Click the chart to make it active and make the Chart menu available, if it isn't already.

2. Choose Chart > Chart Type to bring up the Chart Type dialog box, and choose from the Chart type menu (**Figure 15.13**).

   or

   Pull down the Chart Type menu in the Chart toolbar to select one of the available types from that menu (**Figure 15.14**).

3. Click a data series in the chart. References to the cells that contain data for that series appear in the Formula Bar above the chart, and a tip window appears, defining any data point you pause the mouse over (**Figure 15.15**). If you wish to change which cells define that series, you can edit the references in the Formula Bar.

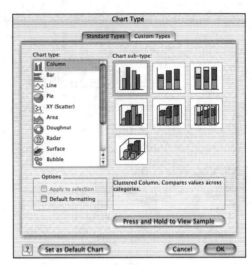

Figure 15.13 Choose a chart type.

Figure 15.14 Pull down the Chart Type menu from the Chart toolbar.

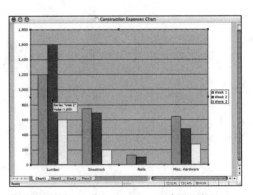

Figure 15.15 Pause the mouse over a data point to reveal its details; click a data point to see its series cell references in the Formula Bar.

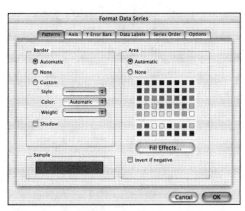

Figure 15.16 Choose the data-series formatting options.

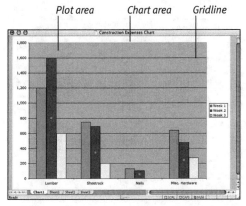

Plot area   Chart area   Gridline

Figure 15.17 Note the chart and plot areas and the gridlines.

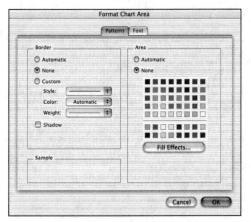

Figure 15.18 Select chart-area options.

4. Double-click a data series to bring up the Format Data Series dialog box (**Figure 15.16**).

5. Use the Patterns, Axis, Y Error Bars, Data Labels, Series Order, and Options tabs to change virtually any aspect of the data series.

6. Click either the By Row or the By Column button on the Chart toolbar to specify whether each series is a row or a column of data in the sheet containing the data cells.

✔ Tip

■ Chart > Chart Type offers more options than the Chart Type menu on the Chart toolbar.

The *chart area* is the background of the sheet in which you draw the chart. The *plot area* is the background of the chart itself, inside the axes. The *gridlines* are lines in the plot area denoting major values in the axes (**Figure 15.17**).

To modify the chart area, plot area, and gridlines:

1. Double-click the chart area to bring up the Format Chart Area dialog box (**Figure 15.18**). Under the Patterns tab, change the border surrounding the chart area, its color, and any fill effects, such as gradient or texture or even using a picture for the chart area. Click the Font tab to set the font characteristics of the axis labels, legend, and chart title.

(continues on next page)

2. Double-click the plot area to bring up the Format Plot Area dialog box (**Figure 15.19**). Use the options under the Patterns tab to change the border surrounding the plot area, its color, and any fill effects, such as using a gradient, texture, or even a picture for the plot area.

3. Double-click a gridline to open the Format Gridlines dialog box (**Figure 15.20**). Use the options under the Patterns tab to change the style, color, and weight of the gridlines. Use the options under the Scale tab to change the scale of the axis connected to these gridlines and the crossing point of the other axis.

✔ Tip

■ Format the most general elements of the chart (such as the chart area) first, and then format individual elements within that area (such as axis labels).

The title, axes, and legend are the text identifiers you use to label aspects of the chart.

To modify the title, axes, and legend:

1. Double-click the chart title to bring up the Format Chart Title dialog box (**Figure 15.21**). You cannot resize the title text box using the handles.

2. Double-click an axis to bring up the Format Axis dialog box (**Figure 15.22**). Use the Patterns, Scale, Font, Number, and Alignment tabs to format those aspects of the axis.

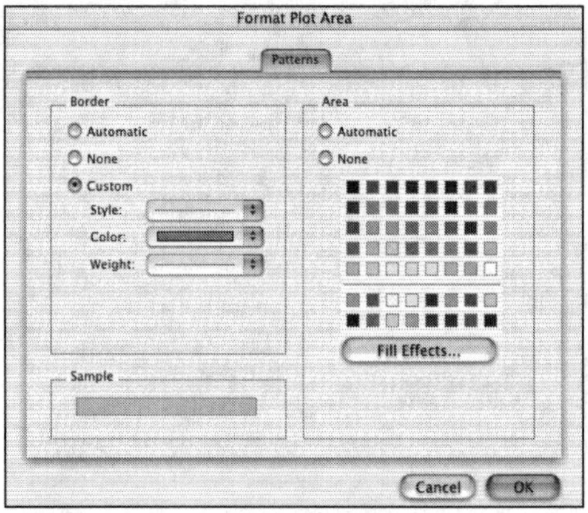

Figure 15.19 Select plot-area options.

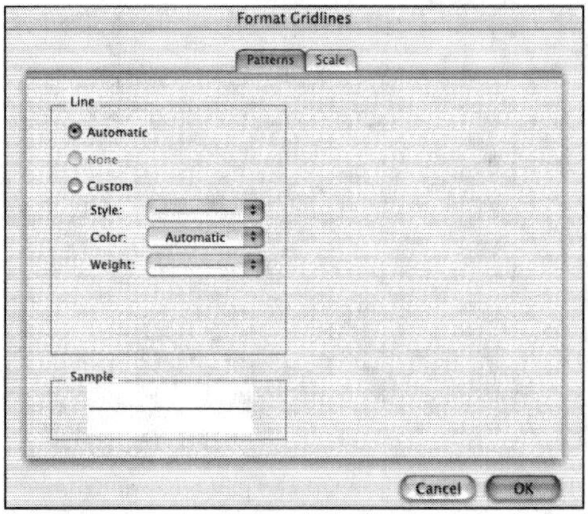

Figure 15.20 Select gridline options.

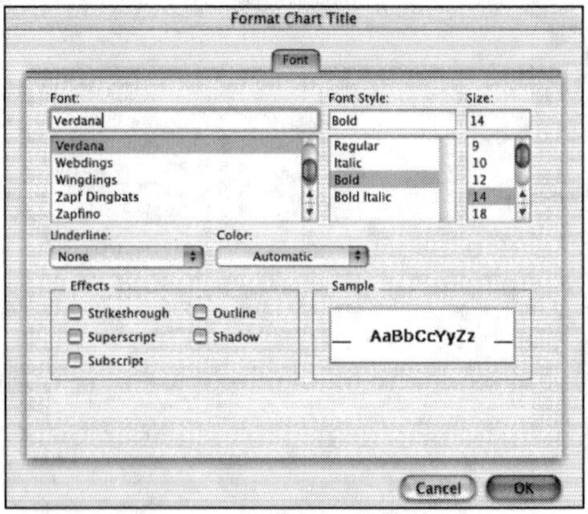

Figure 15.21 Select chart-title options.

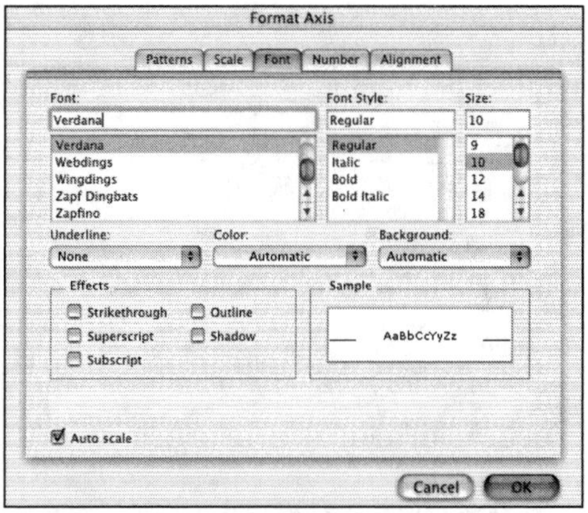

Figure 15.22 Select axis options.

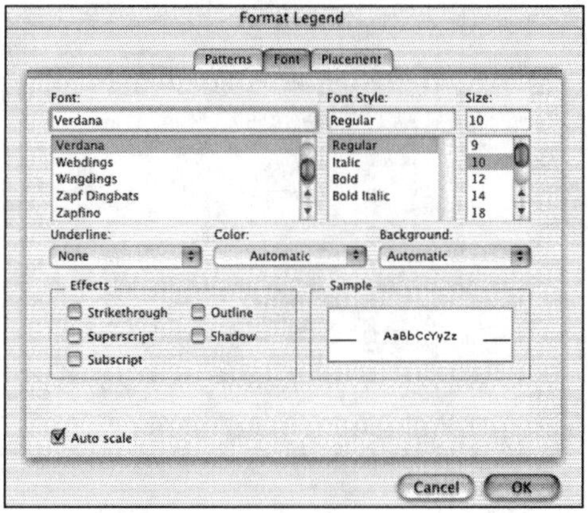

Figure 15.23 Select legend options.

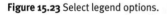

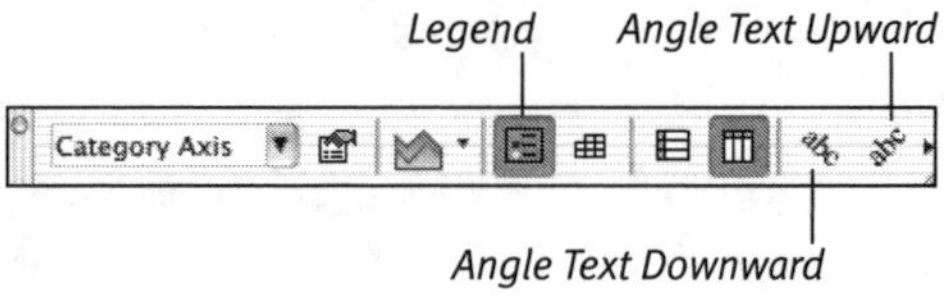

Figure 15.24 Select chart options.

3. Double-click the legend to bring up the Format Legend dialog box (**Figure 15.23**). Use the Patterns, Font, and Placement tabs to change any of those aspects of the legend. The Placement tab contains the controls for the placement of the legend in the chart area. If you wish to format only one of the legend entries, double-click it, or choose Format > Selected Legend Entry (⌘ 1) to format it.

✔ Tips

■ To delete elements such as the title or legend, click the element's border and press Delete .

■ You can also use buttons on the Chart toolbar to add or delete a legend, or to angle axis text upward or downward (**Figure 15.24**).

Adding Error Bars

Error bars are lines drawn through data points to indicate the possible range of uncertain values (the "plus or minus" uncertainty).

To add error bars to a chart:

1. Select a data series to which you want to add error bars, and bring up the Format Data Series dialog box by double-clicking the data series (see "To modify the chart type and data series," earlier in this chapter).

2. Under the Y Error Bars or X Error Bars tab of the dialog box, set the options you want (**Figure 15.25**). X Error Bars are available only for scatter or bubble charts.

3. Click OK; the error bars appear (**Figure 15.26**).

✔ Tip

■ Chart types that accept only Y error bars include 2D area, bar, column, and line. Chart types that accept either X or Y error bars or both include x-y (scatter) and bubble charts.

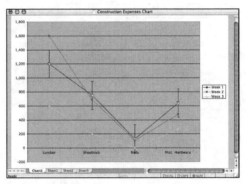

Figure 15.25 Select error-bar options.

Figure 15.26 The error bars appear.

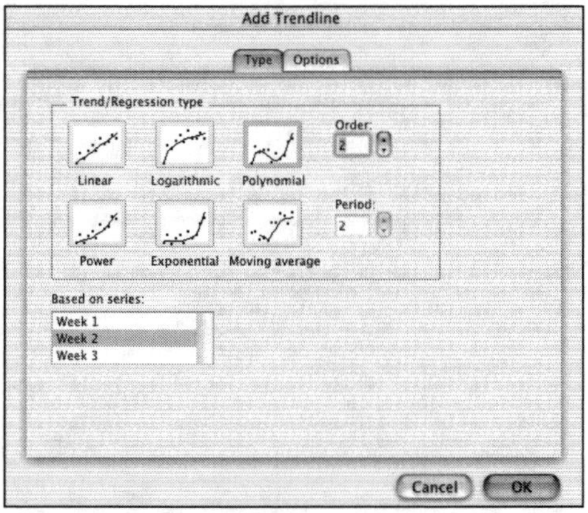

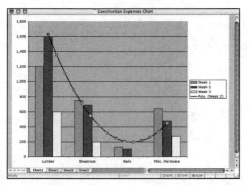

Figure 15.27 Select trendline options.

Figure 15.28 The trendline appears.

Adding Trendlines

A *trendline* is a smooth line or curve drawn through the points of a data series that indicates the general trend of the series of values.

To add a trendline to a chart:

1. Click a data series for which you want to add a trendline. From the Chart menu, choose Add Trendline to bring up the Add Trendline dialog box (**Figure 15.27**). Use the options in the dialog box to define the kind of trendline you want.

2. Click OK; the trendline appears (**Figure 15.28**).

DATABASE TECHNIQUES

	A	B	C	D	E	F
			Employee		Total vacation	Vacation
1	Fname	Lname	no.	Status	days	days used
2	Deborah	Hannon	2176	Permanent	25	5
3	Teri	Harget	1744	Permanent	15	4
4	Vickie	Wilson	3244	Temporary	0	0
5	Chip	August	2044	Permanent	10	1
6	Susan	Verhoek	3105	Temporary	0	0
7	Jeffrey	Brewer	1126	Permanent	25	2
8	Katherine	Howard	2986	Permanent	15	9
9						

Figure 16.1 Records appear in rows; fields appear in columns.

Sheet1

Fname:	Deborah		1 of 7
Lname:	Hannon		New
Employee no.:	2176		Delete
Status:	Permanent		Restore
Total vacation days:	25		Find Prev
Vacation days used:	5		Find Next
			Criteria
			Close

Figure 16.2 Use the data form to add records.

Unless you work with extremely large databases containing thousands of sets of data or need a complex database structure, Excel can provide all the database power you require.

In Excel, you enter data in rows. Each row is a *record* (one complete set of information). Each column is a *field*, and each field contains one particular type of information in the record (**Figure 16.1**). Rather than enter information directly into the cells of a sheet, you can create a fill-in-the-blanks data form to make it easier to enter, edit, delete, and search through information (**Figure 16.2**). You can also import databases created elsewhere, in programs such as FileMaker Pro or Microsoft SQL Server.

After you enter the data, you can search through it, sort it, and pull out only the information that matches particular criteria.

Setting Up a Database

Setting up a database is a lot like setting up a list, and you can use the List Manager to do so if you prefer. The following instructions don't rely on the List Manager. See Chapter 10, Working with Lists, for more information about using the List Manager.

To create a database in Excel:

1. In either a new or an existing worksheet, enter the field names at the tops of a group of adjacent columns (**Figure 16.3**).

2. Enter the data into the rows below the field names (**Figure 16.4**).

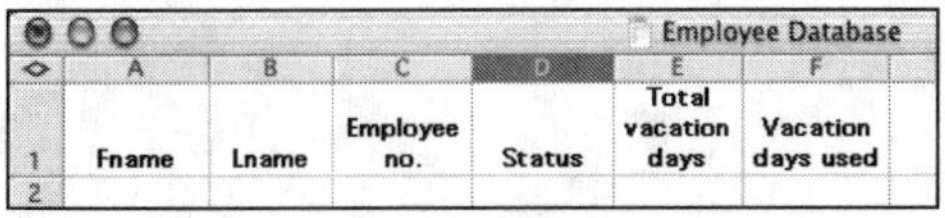

✔ Tips

■ Press Tab when you complete a cell to move to the next cell to the right.

■ Press Enter when you complete a cell to move to the next cell below.

Figure 16.3 Set up your field names.

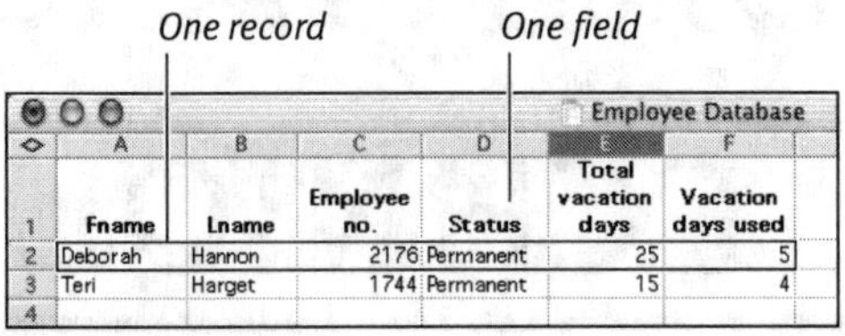

Figure 16.4 Enter records (your data).

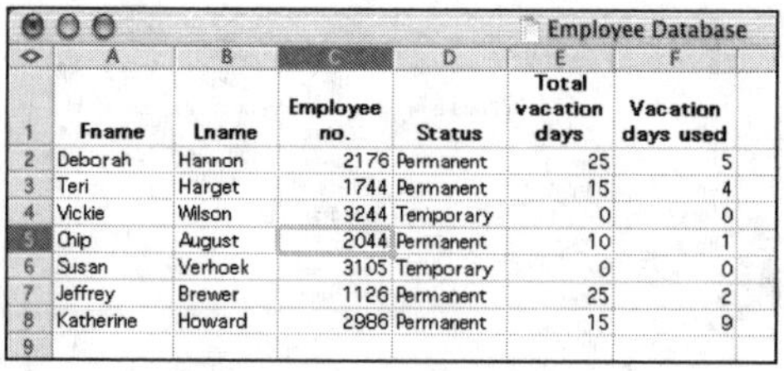

Figure 16.5 Click any cell in the database.

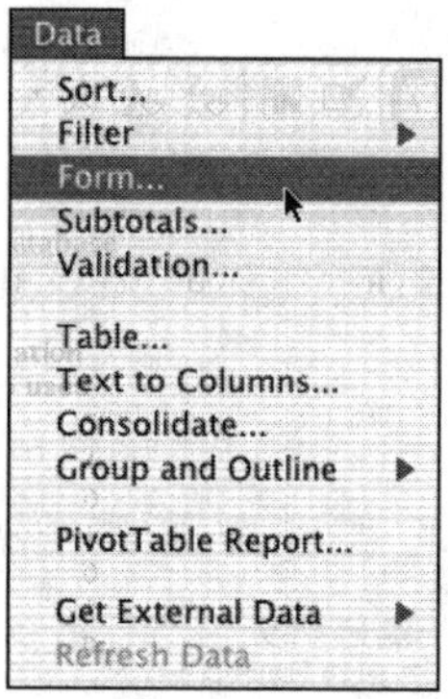

Figure 16.6
Choose Data > Form.

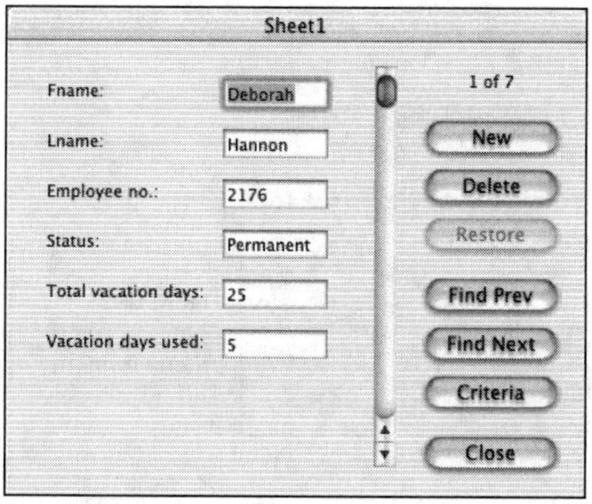

Figure 16.7 Fill in the form for each new record.

Filling In the Form

Just as you can use a form to create lists, you may use a form to create database entries.

To use a form for data entry:

1. Click any cell that contains data (**Figure 16.5**).

2. Choose Data > Form (**Figures 16.6, 16.7**).

3. Click the New button in the dialog box to add a new record to the database, and fill in the form fields appropriately.

✔ Tips

- The form always opens with the text fields populated by the first record in the database.

- To put away the form, click Close.

- Press (Tab) to move from field to field in a form.

- Press (Shift)(Tab) to return to the previous field in a form.

Sorting and Filtering

Sorting and filtering work the same way with a database as with a list.

To sort a database:

1. Click any cell in the database (**Figure 16.8**).
2. Choose Data > Sort (**Figure 16.9**).
3. In the Sort dialog box, choose a field name from the Sort by pull-down menu (**Figure 16.10**).
4. To perform secondary and tertiary sorts on the data, choose additional fields from the two Then by pull-down menus, also in the Sort dialog box.
5. To sort from smallest to largest or earliest to latest, choose Ascending. To sort from largest to smallest or latest to earliest, choose Descending.
6. Click OK. The data in the database is sorted (**Figure 16.11**).

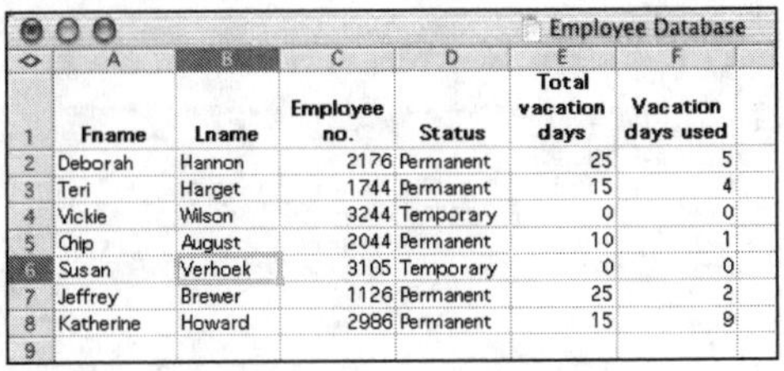
Employee Database

	A	B	C	D	E	F
1	Fname	Lname	Employee no.	Status	Total vacation days	Vacation days used
2	Deborah	Hannon	2176	Permanent	25	5
3	Teri	Harget	1744	Permanent	15	4
4	Vickie	Wilson	3244	Temporary	0	0
5	Chip	August	2044	Permanent	10	1
6	Susan	Verhoek	3105	Temporary	0	0
7	Jeffrey	Brewer	1126	Permanent	25	2
8	Katherine	Howard	2986	Permanent	15	9
9						

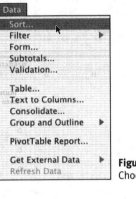

Figure 16.8 Click any cell in the database.

Figure 16.9 Choose Data > Sort.

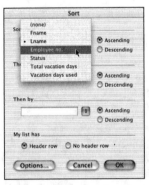

Figure 16.10 Choose the sort criteria from the Sort by pull-down menu.

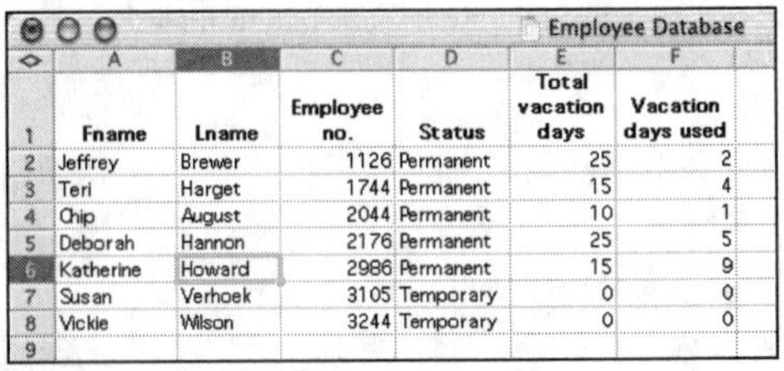
Employee Database

	A	B	C	D	E	F
1	Fname	Lname	Employee no.	Status	Total vacation days	Vacation days used
2	Jeffrey	Brewer	1126	Permanent	25	2
3	Teri	Harget	1744	Permanent	15	4
4	Chip	August	2044	Permanent	10	1
5	Deborah	Hannon	2176	Permanent	25	5
6	Katherine	Howard	2986	Permanent	15	9
7	Susan	Verhoek	3105	Temporary	0	0
8	Vickie	Wilson	3244	Temporary	0	0
9						

Figure 16.11 The database is sorted.

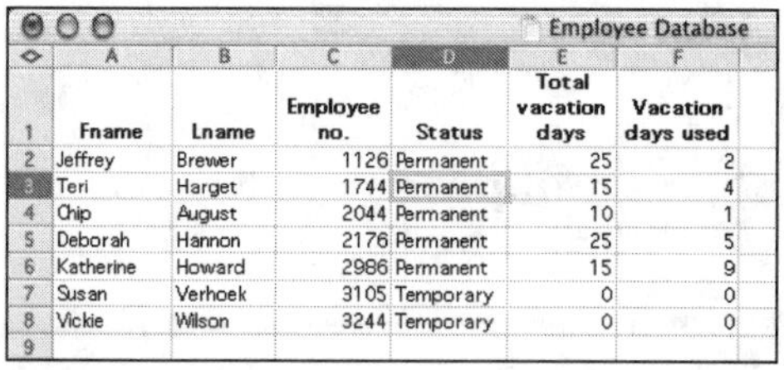

Figure 16.12 Click any cell in the database.

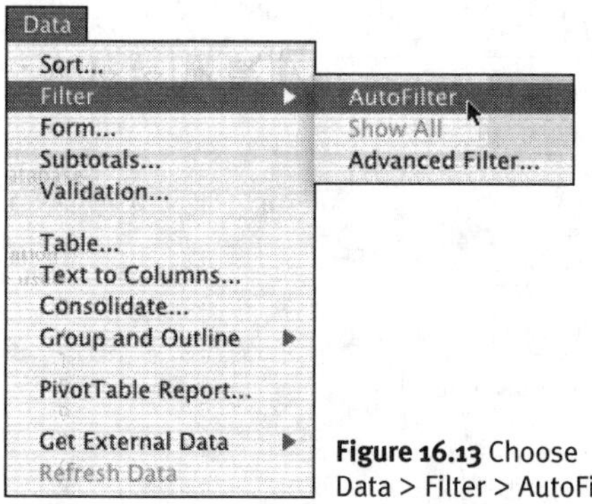

Figure 16.13 Choose Data > Filter > AutoFilter.

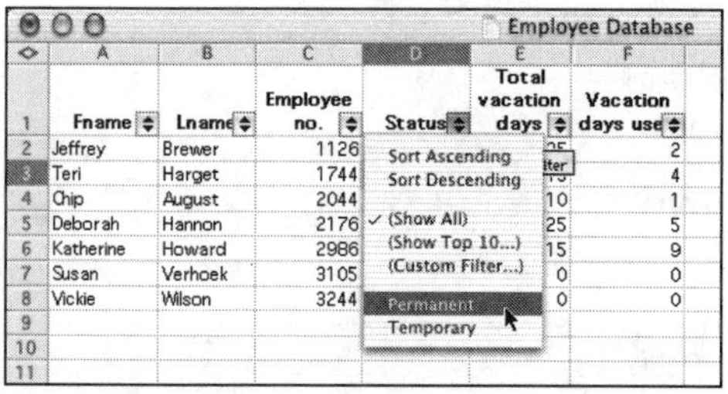

Figure 16.14 Select the filter criterion from a pull-down menu.

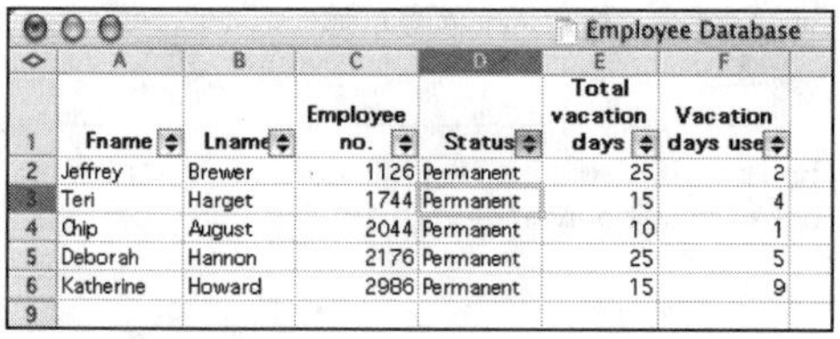

Figure 16.15 Only the data that match the filter criteria appear.

Filtering a database also works the same way as with a list.

To filter a database:

1. Click any cell in the database (**Figure 16.12**).

2. Choose Data > Filter > AutoFilter (**Figure 16.13**).

3. Click any of the pull-down buttons next to the field names to see a menu of the filter criteria for that field (**Figure 16.14**).

4. Choose a criterion on the menu to view only those records that match that criterion (**Figure 16.15**).

✔ Tips

- To stop filtering, choose Data > Filter > AutoFilter again.

- When the database is filtered, the row numbers of the extracted data appear in blue.

- The field upon which you filter the database shows a blue pull-down button.

- The data that don't meet the criteria aren't deleted, only hidden temporarily.

SORTING AND FILTERING

To create subtotals:

1. Select any cell in the database.

2. Choose Data > Subtotals (**Figure 16.16**).

3. In the Subtotal dialog box, select a field from the pull-down menu labeled At each change in (**Figure 16.17**). A subtotal appears each time this field changes value. A grand total appears at the bottom of the list (**Figure 16.18**).

✔ Tip

■ Use the controls to the left of the database to show only the subtotals (Figure 16.18).

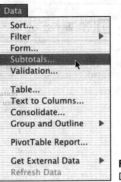

Figure 16.16 Choose Data > Subtotals.

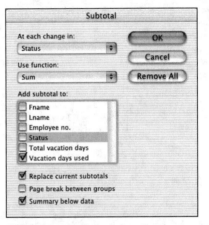

Figure 16.17 Specify the subtotal options.

Figure 16.18 Use the slide indicators on the far left to control the display of detail.

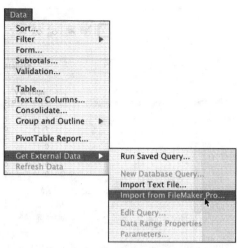

Figure 16.19 Choose Data > Get External Data > Import from FileMaker Pro.

Using Databases from Outside Excel

You can import the contents of text files into Excel (see "Bringing In Data from Outside Excel" in Chapter 9). Since FileMaker Pro is the most common database on the Mac, Excel has special provisions for easily importing FileMaker Pro databases.

To import a FileMaker Pro database:

1. Drag and drop a FileMaker Pro file onto the Excel icon.

    or

    Choose Data > Get External Data > Import from FileMaker Pro (**Figure 16.19**), and open the database file in the standard Open dialog box that appears.

2. Work with the FileMaker Pro database as you would any other.

You can copy and paste information from a page opened in a Web browser, or open an HTML file directly into Excel (you may lose some of the information in the process). It is also fairly easy to retrieve data from the Web using HTML forms. Microsoft provides several sample queries, which you may edit, or you can create your own. We'll show a sample retrieval from one of the queries supplied with Office v. X in the Microsoft Office X > Office > Queries folder.

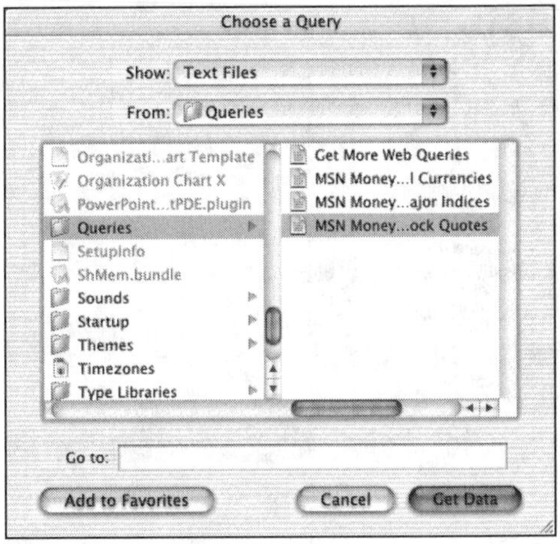

To retrieve data from the Web into Excel:

1. Choose Data > Get External Data > Run Saved Query.

2. The Choose a Query dialog box appears. Select the saved query and click Get Data (**Figure 16.20**).

3. The Returning External Data to Microsoft Excel dialog box appears. Specify the destination for the query results (**Figure 16.21**), and click the Properties or Parameters button to open a dialog box that gives you more control over the results.

4. Our example requests a stock ticker symbol to retrieve a stock quote. Click the Parameters button to enter the stock symbol in the dialog box that appears (**Figure 16.22**), then click OK. Enter the requested parameter, and click OK.

5. The query report appears in the worksheet (**Figure 16.23**).

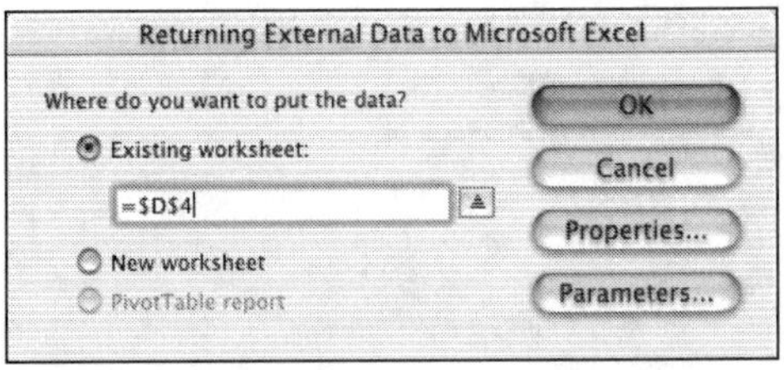

✔ Tips

- To create your own database query, choose Data > Get External Data > New Database Query.

- Office 2001 provided support for retrieval from SQL databases via ODBC, but that feature has been removed in Office v. X.

Figure 16.20 Select the saved query, and click Get Data.

Figure 16.21 Specify the destination for the report.

Figure 16.22 Click Parameters, and in the Enter Parameter Value dialog box specify any requested parameters.

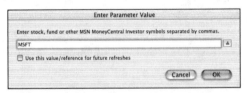

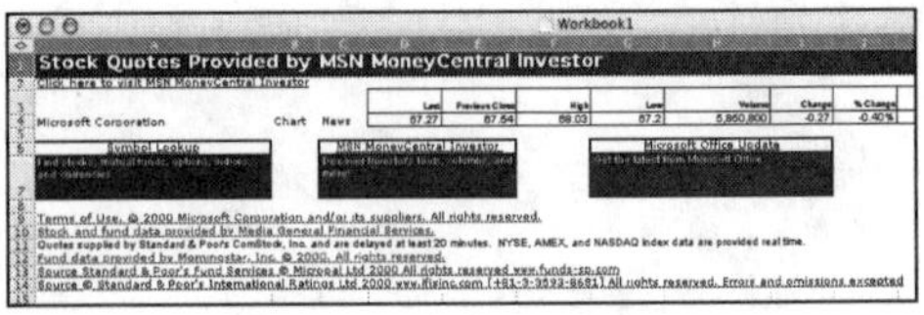

Figure 16.23 The query report appears.

SHARING
WORKBOOKS

You may find yourself in a work group in which several people need to edit or update the same Excel workbooks. Excel gives you some tools to distribute workbooks on the Web or over an internal network, protect areas of workbooks that should not be changed, and track and review the changes made.

Publishing Workbooks on the Web

Excel makes it easy to save workbooks or worksheets on the Web. One advantage of publishing this way is that people who need to see the contents don't need to have Excel installed in order to open the file; all they need is a Web browser. You can also preview what the file will look like when opened in a Web browser.

To preview the file's Web appearance:

1. Start with a workbook open in Excel (**Figure 17.1**).

2. Choose File > Web Page Preview (**Figure 17.2**).

   If your Web browser isn't already open, Excel will launch it, and the active worksheet will appear in your Web browser as it will appear on the Web (**Figure 17.3**).

✔ Tip

■ Comment indicators appear as outlined numbers (Figure 17.3) and work the same way as they do in Excel. Pausing the pointer over an indicator makes the comment box appear (**Figure 17.4**).

Figure 17.1 Create or open a workbook.

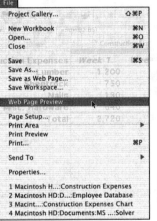

Figure 17.2 Choose File > Web Page Preview.

Comment indicator

Figure 17.3 The worksheet appears in your Web browser.

Construction Expenses	Week 1	Week 2	Week 3	Total
Lumber	1,200	1,600	600	3,400
Sheetrock	750	690	200	1,640
Nails	130	106	0	236
Misc. Hardware	640	480	275	1,395
Total	2,720	2,876	1,075	6,671

Construction Expenses	Week 1	Week 2	Week 3	Total
Lumber	1,200	1,600	600	3,400
Sheetrock	750	690	200	1,640
Nails	130	106	0	236
Misc. Hardware	640	480	275	1,395
Total	2,720	2,876	1,075	6,671

Dan Henderson:
All unused nails may be returned for refund.

Figure 17.4 Pause the pointer over the comment indicator to make the comment box appear.

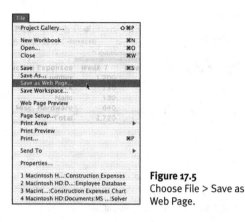

Figure 17.5
Choose File > Save as
Web Page.

Once the workbook looks the way you want
it to in Web Page Preview, you can save it as
a Web page.

To save a file as a Web page:

1. Choose File > Save as Web Page
   (**Figure 17.5**).

2. In the Save dialog box that appears
   (**Figure 17.6**), the Web Page file format
   is automatically chosen, and the custom-
   ary PC file-name extension (.htm) is
   added to the file name. Here you also
   have the option to save the entire workbook, the currently active worksheet, or
   just the currently selected cells.

3. If this is a workbook or sheet you update
   regularly and you want to schedule future
   automatic saves, click the Automate button to call up the Automate dialog box
   (**Figure 17.7**). Here you may choose to
   save the Excel document automatically as
   a Web document every time you save it or
   on a set schedule.

4. Back in the Save dialog box (Figure 17.6),
   clicking Web Options gives you the
   opportunity to specify Web-specific
   settings, such as the page title and keywords that a search engine would pick
   up (**Figure 17.8**).

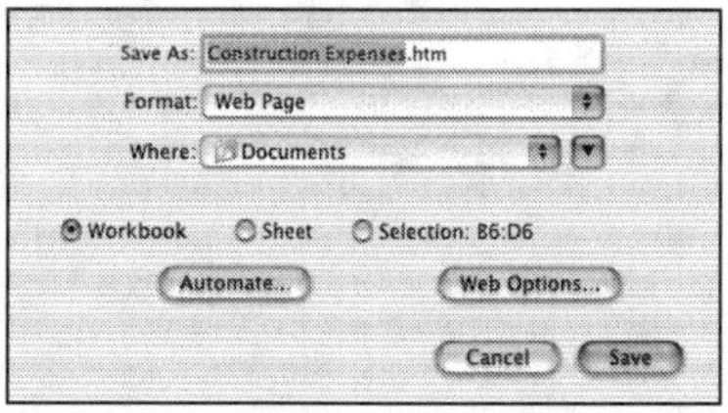

Figure 17.6 Choose the file destination and
options.

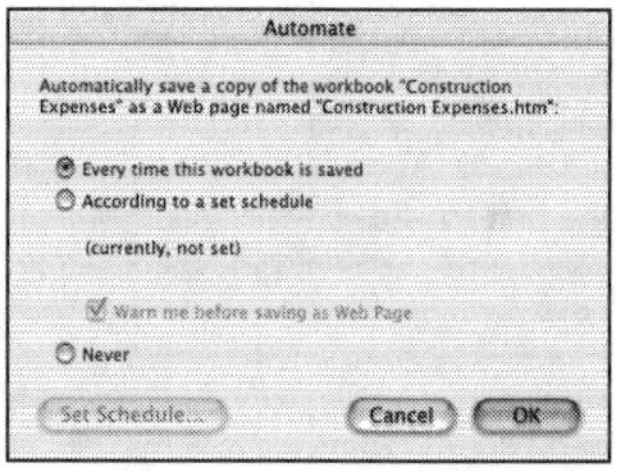

Figure 17.7
Choose
automation
options.

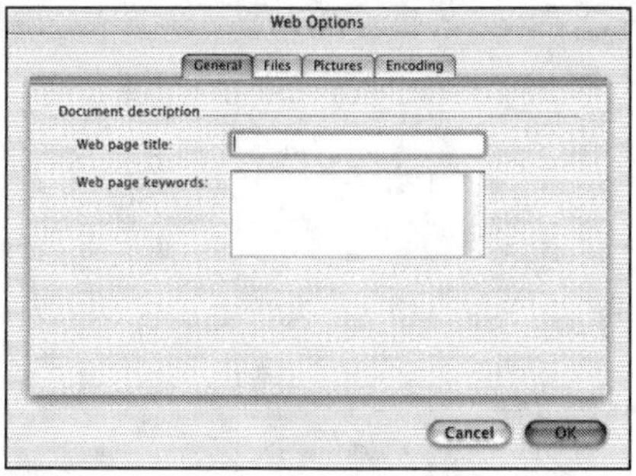

Figure 17.8 Choose Web options.

PUBLISHING WORKBOOKS ON THE WEB

Sharing Workbooks on a Network

If you have a network available, your network administrator should be able to tell you how to access the file servers for the purpose of saving shared documents. In this section we'll cover the steps necessary to allow multiple people to edit the same workbook, regardless of where it's stored.

To set up a workbook for multiple users:

1. Choose Tools > Share Workbook (**Figure 17.9**).

2. In the Share Workbook dialog box, under the Editing tab, check the box to select Allow changes by more than one user at the same time (**Figure 17.10**).

3. Under the Advanced tab (**Figure 17.11**) you can set options for managing the changes made by multiple users.

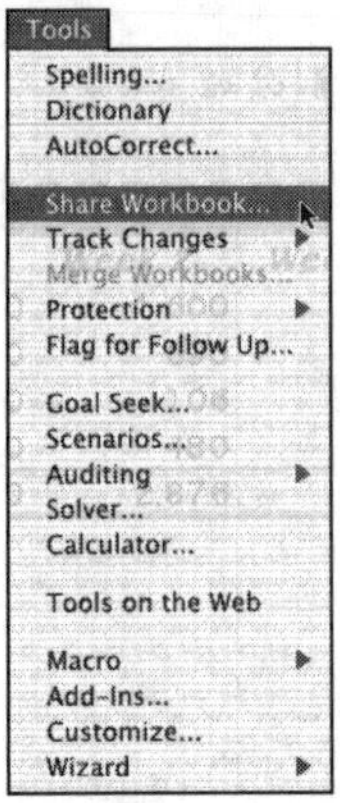

Figure 17.9 Choose Tools > Share Workbook.

Figure 17.10 Check the box to allow changes.

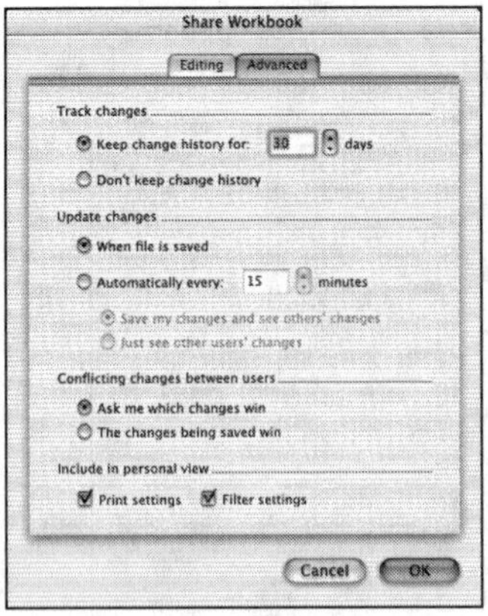

Figure 17.11 Set options for managing the changes.

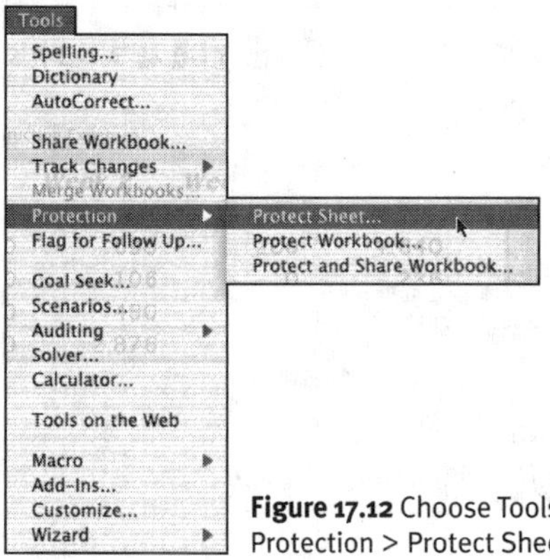

Figure 17.12 Choose Tools > Protection > Protect Sheet.

Figure 17.13 Choose what you want to protect.

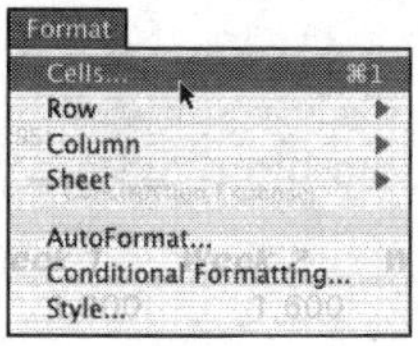

Figure 17.14 Choose Format > Cells.

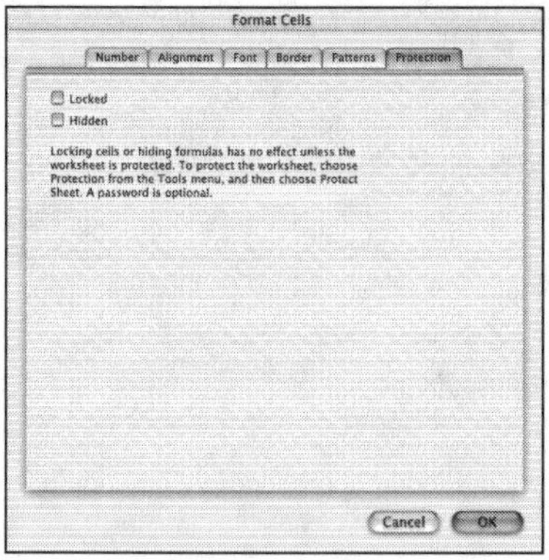

Figure 17.15 Unlock cells you want others to be able to edit.

Protecting Workbooks

You can protect selected aspects of workbooks or worksheets from changes, which may be useful in a sharing environment.

To protect a worksheet:

1. Choose Tools > Protection > Protect Sheet (**Figure 17.12**).

2. In the Protect Sheet dialog box (**Figure 17.13**), you can choose to protect the contents and other elements of cells. If you want users to be able to change specific cells, select those cells and choose Format > Cells (**Figure 17.14**). In the Format Cells dialog box, click the Protection tab (**Figure 17.15**), and remove the checkmark from the Locked box.

3. In the Protect Sheet dialog box, checking the box next to Objects protects items such as charts, graphics, and buttons from change or deletion.

(continues on next page)

PROTECTING WORKBOOKS

4. If you choose to protect Scenarios, then any scenarios not hidden are protected from change.

5. In the Protect Sheet dialog box, you have the opportunity to enter a password, and after clicking OK you are asked to confirm it (**Figure 17.16**).

6. To unprotect a sheet after protecting it, choose Tools > Protection > Unprotect Sheet (**Figure 17.17**). You'll be prompted for the password (**Figure 17.18**).

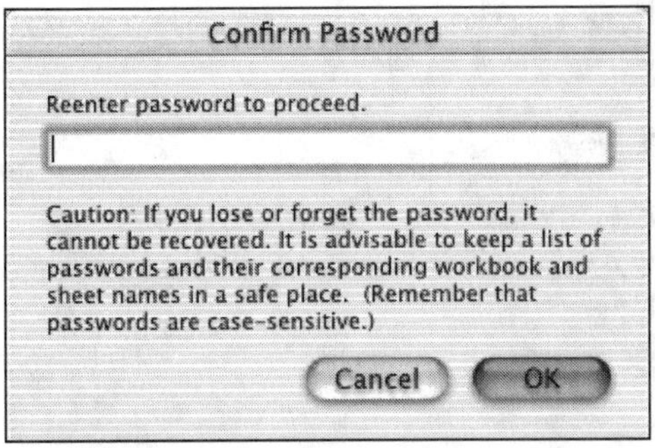

Confirm Password

Reenter password to proceed.

Caution: If you lose or forget the password, it cannot be recovered. It is advisable to keep a list of passwords and their corresponding workbook and sheet names in a safe place. (Remember that passwords are case-sensitive.)

Cancel   OK

Figure 17.16 Confirm your password.

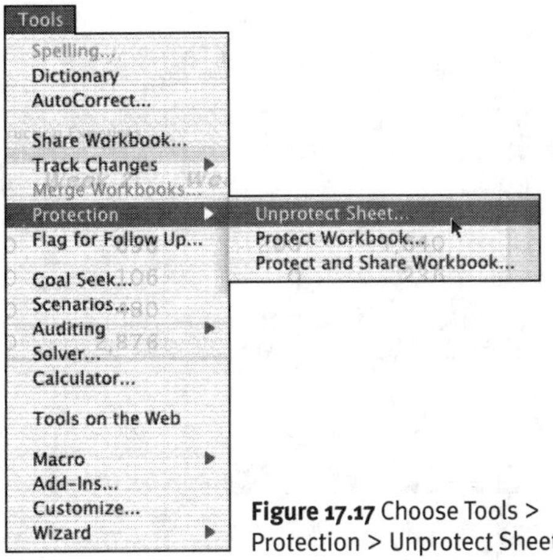

Tools
Spelling...
Dictionary
AutoCorrect...

Share Workbook...
Track Changes   ▶
Merge Workbooks...
Protection   ▶   Unprotect Sheet...
Flag for Follow Up...   Protect Workbook...
                            Protect and Share Workbook...
Goal Seek...
Scenarios...
Auditing   ▶
Solver...
Calculator...

Tools on the Web

Macro   ▶
Add-Ins...
Customize...
Wizard   ▶

Figure 17.17 Choose Tools > Protection > Unprotect Sheet.

Unprotect Sheet

Password:

Cancel   OK

Figure 17.18 Enter your password to unprotect the sheet.

PROTECTING WORKBOOKS

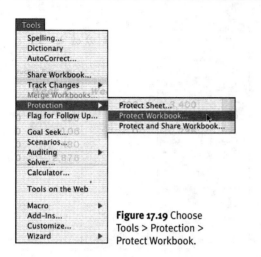

Figure 17.19 Choose Tools > Protection > Protect Workbook.

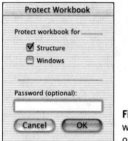

Figure 17.20 Choose workbook-protection options.

You may also protect aspects of an entire workbook, in addition to aspects of individual worksheets.

To protect an entire workbook:

◆ Choose Tools > Protection > Protect Workbook (**Figure 17.19**). The Protect Workbook dialog box appears (**Figure 17.20**).

If you choose to protect Structure, users can't rename, move, add, or delete sheets in the workbook.

If you choose to protect Windows, users can't move or resize the windows associated with a workbook. They may, however, hide them.

Passwords work as they do for sheet protection.

Unless you take precautions, another user may turn change tracking off in a shared workbook that tracks changes.

To protect change tracking:

1. Choose Tools > Protection > Protect and Share Workbook (**Figure 17.21**).

2. The Protect Shared Workbook dialog box appears (**Figure 17.22**). Check the box to select Sharing with track changes.

3. Protect Shared Workbook passwords work similarly to passwords in the sheet-protection feature explained above.

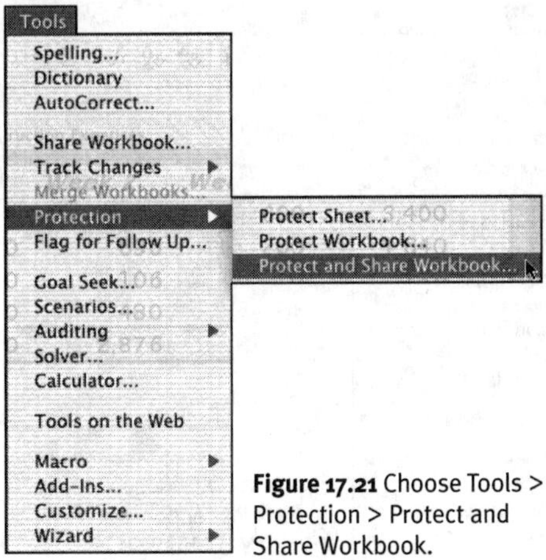

Figure 17.21 Choose Tools > Protection > Protect and Share Workbook.

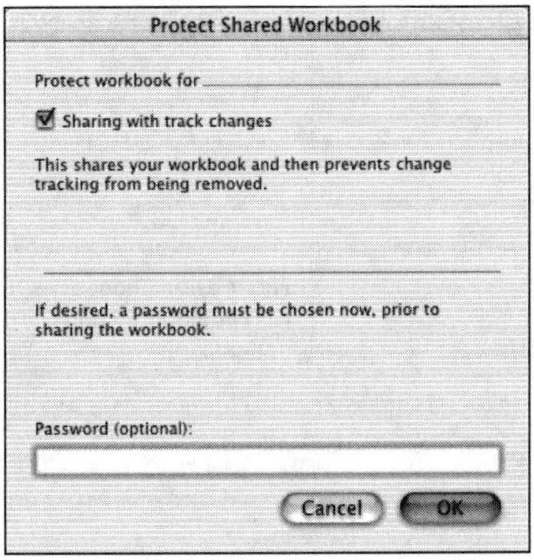

Figure 17.22 Select Sharing with track changes.

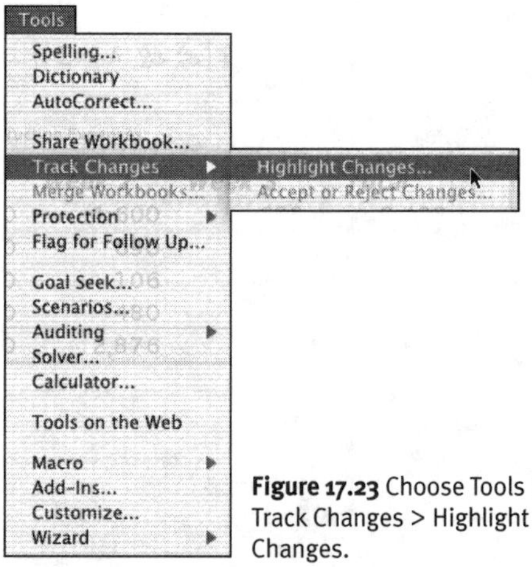

Figure 17.23 Choose Tools > Track Changes > Highlight Changes.

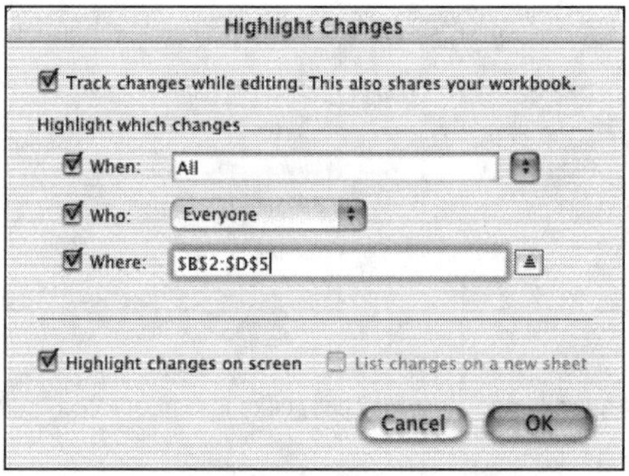

Figure 17.24 Choose which changes to track.

Tracking and Reviewing Changes

You can share Excel workbooks with others and automatically track their changes. This makes managerial review especially convenient.

To set up change tracking:

1. Choose Tools > Track Changes > Highlight Changes (**Figure 17.23**).

2. In the Highlight Changes dialog box that appears, use the selections to determine which changes to highlight. To fill in the Where field, simply drag through the appropriate cells (**Figure 17.24**).

3. Tracked cells display a colored triangle in the upper-left corner. To see a change notation, move the pointer onto the cell (**Figure 17.25**).

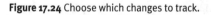

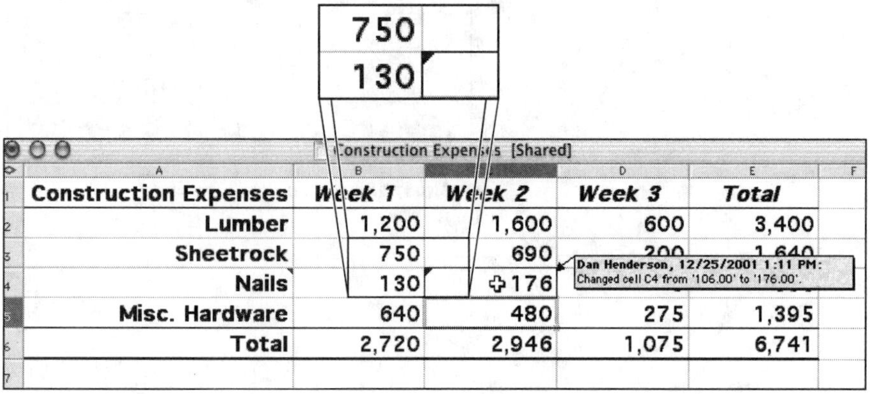

Construction Expenses	Week 1	Week 2	Week 3	Total	
Lumber	1,200	1,600	600	3,400	
Sheetrock	750	690	200	1,640	
Nails	130	⊕176			
Misc. Hardware	640	480	275	1,395	
Total	2,720	2,946	1,075	6,741	

Dan Henderson, 12/25/2001 1:11 PM: Changed cell C4 from '106.00' to '176.00'.

Figure 17.25 Move the pointer over a changed cell to see details.

When someone else has changed cells that have been set up for tracking changes, you may accept or reject the changes.

To review changes:

1. Choose Tools > Track Changes > Accept or Reject Changes (**Figure 17.26**).

2. In the Select Changes to Accept or Reject dialog box that appears, use the three areas to determine which changes to review. To fill in the Where field, you can drag through the appropriate cells (**Figure 17.27**).

3. Click a cell that matches the criteria set up in Step 2 to bring up the Accept or Reject Changes dialog box (**Figure 17.28**).

4. In the dialog box, use the buttons (Accept, Reject, Accept All, Reject All) to exercise your choices.

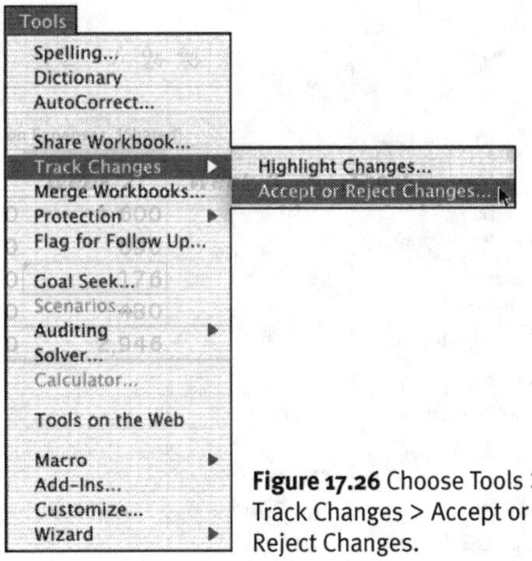

Figure 17.26 Choose Tools > Track Changes > Accept or Reject Changes.

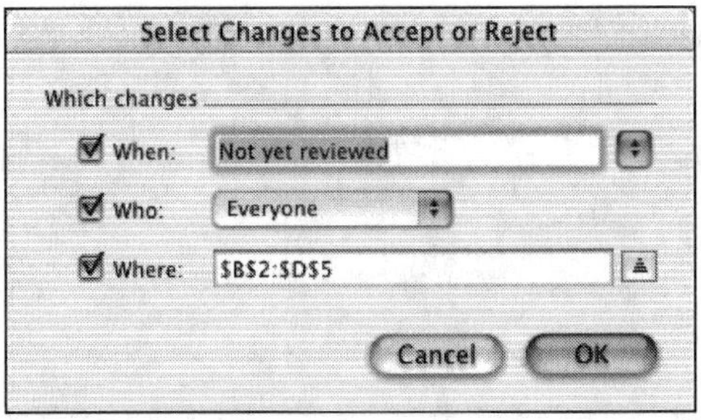

Figure 17.27 Select the changes to accept or reject.

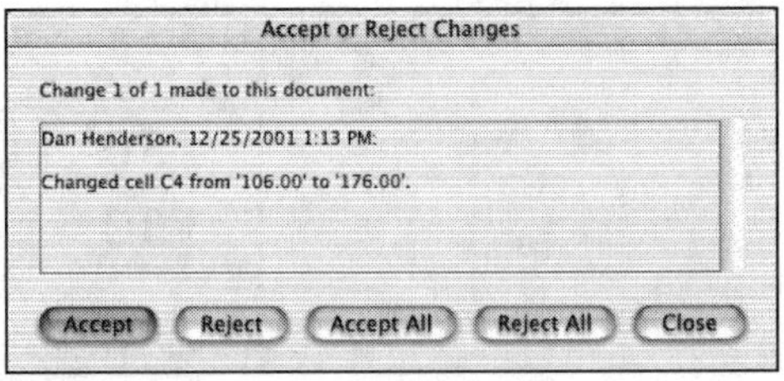

Figure 17.28 Accept or reject changes.

Part IV: Microsoft PowerPoint

GETTING STARTED

PowerPoint provides you with all the tools necessary to create impressive onscreen, Web-based, and traditional slide presentations. You can choose from a variety of templates designed to help you create a presentation with a compelling visual message.

Creating New Presentations

As in Word and Excel, the Project Gallery serves as the starting point for a PowerPoint presentation. You can design a presentation completely from scratch, or you can base it on a template.

To create a new presentation:

1. Double-click the Microsoft PowerPoint icon in the Microsoft Office X folder.

   PowerPoint launches and the Project Gallery window opens.

2. To create a presentation from scratch, click the PowerPoint Presentation icon (**Figure 18.1**).

   or

   To use a template, choose Presentations from the Category menu in the left panel of the Project Gallery window, and choose a template from either the Content or Designs categories that best matches the type of presentation you want to create (**Figure 18.2**).

3. Click OK.

PowerPoint Presentation icon

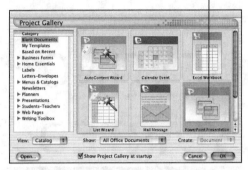

Figure 18.1 Click the PowerPoint Presentation icon to create a new presentation from scratch (without a template).

Presentations categories Templates

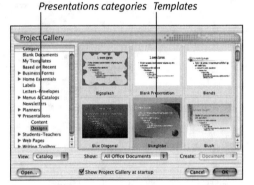

Figure 18.2 To create a presentation from a template, choose a Presentations category from the list on the left and a template from those shown on the right.

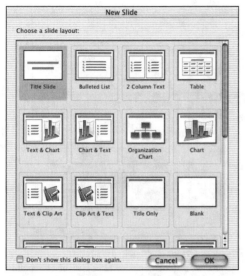

Figure 18.3 Choose a layout for the first slide from the New Slide dialog box.

4. If you're creating a presentation based on a Content template, the presentation appears immediately.

or

If you're creating a blank presentation or one based on a Designs template, the New Slide dialog box appears (**Figure 18.3**). Choose a layout for the first slide, and then click OK. A new presentation opens (**Figure 18.4**).

✔ Tips

■ You can also start a new presentation by choosing File > New Presentation (⌘N).

■ The difference between Content and Designs templates is that the former category provides an entire set of suggested slides and topics.

Figure 18.4 The new presentation appears. (In this example, it's based on a template.)

Using the AutoContent Wizard

Alternatively, you can turn to the AutoContent Wizard to walk you through the process of creating a presentation. The AutoContent Wizard offers a variety of presentation outlines in which you can replace the sample text with your own. Each outline generates a presentation with a particular look. You can change the look by choosing a different template.

To use the AutoContent Wizard:

1. Open the Project Gallery window by choosing File > Project Gallery (Shift ⌘ P).

2. In the Category list, choose Blank Documents, click the AutoContent Wizard, and click OK.

 The AutoContent Wizard appears (**Figure 18.5**).

3. Choose a category from the pop-up menu, and then choose a presentation type and format from the list presented. Click Next to continue.

4. Choose an output option for your presentation and indicate whether you will need to create handouts (**Figure 18.6**). Click Next to continue.

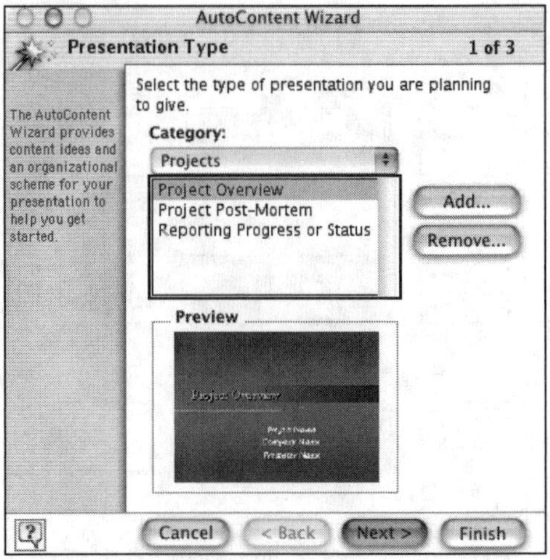

Figure 18.5 The AutoContent Wizard steps you through the process of generating the framework of a template-based presentation.

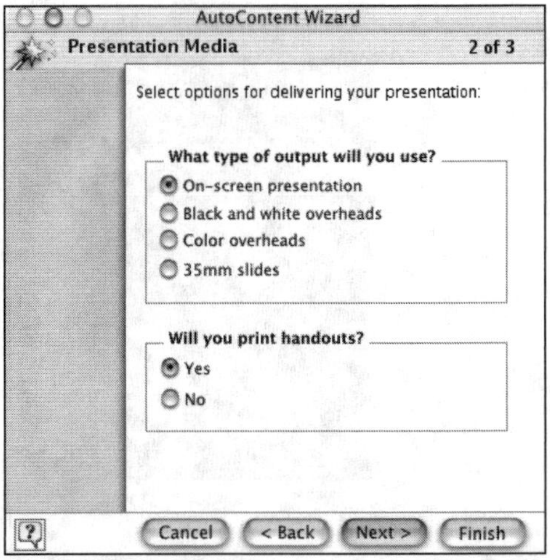

Figure 18.6 On the second screen of the AutoContent Wizard, choose output options.

Figure 18.7 Enter title information and specify footer contents on the final screen of the AutoContent Wizard.

Figure 18.8 The result is a complete presentation, including suggested slides and text.

5. Enter the text for the title slide (**Figure 18.7**). You can also specify information to print in the footer of each slide. Click Finish.

The structure of your chosen presentation appears (**Figure 18.8**).

✔ Tips

- To return to a previous step, you can click Back in any Wizard dialog box.

- To skip the remaining steps and accept the default choices, you can click Finish at any time.

Changing Views

Changing views is like getting a different perspective on your presentation. You can change your view to focus on specific elements of your work. For instance, if you need to rearrange slides, you can use the Slide Sorter view. Each view shows a different aspect of the presentation. You can switch views at any time.

◆ *Normal view* displays the text, slide, and notes so you can work on all parts of your presentation in one window (Figure 18.4).

◆ *Outline view* displays only the text of the presentation in outline form (**Figure 18.9**).

◆ *Slide view* displays one slide at a time so you can concentrate on modifying the text and graphics of each slide (**Figure 18.10**).

Figure 18.9 Outline view.

Figure 18.10 Slide view.

CHANGING VIEWS

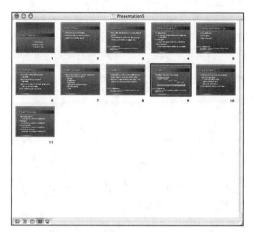

Figure 18.11 Slide Sorter view.

Notes go here

Figure 18.12 Notes Page view.

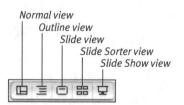

Normal view
  Outline view
    Slide view
      Slide Sorter view
        Slide Show view

Figure 18.13 To change views, click one of the icons in the bottom-left corner of the presentation window.

◆ *Slide Sorter view* displays miniatures, or thumbnails, of all slides. You can reorganize them by clicking and dragging or go directly to any slide by double-clicking it. You can also add and edit the transition effects within and between slides (**Figure 18.11**).

◆ *Notes Page view* lets you enter and edit the speaker's notes that accompany the slides (**Figure 18.12**).

◆ *Slide Show view* displays the presentation as an onscreen slide show.

To change views:

◆ Click the appropriate icon in the lower-left corner of the presentation window (**Figure 18.13**) or choose a view from the View menu.

✔ Tip

■ Outline view is only accessible from the icons, while Notes view is only provided as a View menu command. You can access all other views in either manner.

Adding and Deleting Slides

Designing presentations is seldom a linear process. Along the way, you'll have many occasions where you will need to add or delete slides. You can do so in any view other than Slide Show. The following procedures explain how to accomplish this in Outline view.

To add a slide:

1. A new slide is always inserted *after* the currently active slide. Click anywhere in a slide's title or text to make it the current slide.

   A thumbnail of the selected slide appears in the right side of the presentation window.

2. Click the New Slide icon on the Standard toolbar (**Figure 18.14**). You can also choose Insert > New Slide or press ⌃Control M.

3. Select a layout for the new slide from the New Slide dialog box (**Figure 18.15**).

   The new slide is added to the presentation. The insertion point is automatically positioned in the outline so you can give the slide a title (**Figure 18.16**).

New Slide icon

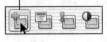

Figure 18.14 You can insert a slide into the presentation by clicking the New Slide icon on the Standard toolbar.

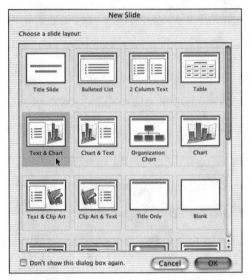

Figure 18.15 Select a layout for the new slide.

New slide

Figure 18.16 A space is inserted into your presentation for the newly created slide.

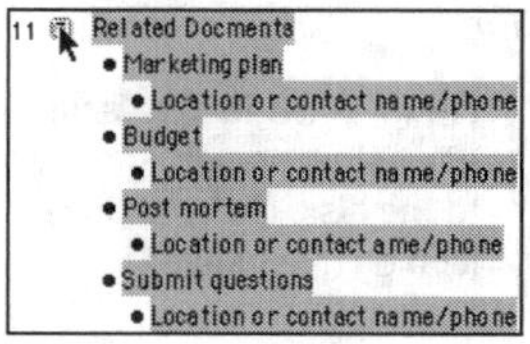

Figure 18.17 To select a slide for deletion in Outline View, click the icon beside the slide's number.

To delete a slide:

1. Click the slide icon to the right of the slide number (**Figure 18.17**). This selects all outline text for the slide.

2. Choose Edit > Delete Slide or press ⌊Delete⌋. The active slide is immediately deleted.

✔ Tips

■ When using the Edit > Delete Slide command, it's sufficient to place the insertion marker in *any* part of the slide's outline text.

■ To recover a slide you mistakenly deleted, choose Edit > Undo Clear or press ⌘Z.

Saving Presentations

Don't forget to save a presentation you're working on, especially if you need to use it again or share it with others. PowerPoint allows you to save presentations in a variety of formats that can be used in different ways. For example, you can save a presentation in HTML format for viewing on the Web in any browser, save it as a slide show, or save it as a QuickTime movie. **Table 18.1** lists some of the supported save formats.

To save a presentation:

1. Choose File > Save or press ⌘S. You can also click the Save icon in the Standard toolbar (**Figure 18.18**).

2. If you've previously saved the presentation, the new version overwrites the old one and you can continue working.

    or

    If this is the first time you've saved the presentation, the Save As dialog box appears (**Figure 18.19**). Enter a name for the presentation, choose the format in which you'd like to save it, choose a destination location on the disk, and click the Save icon.

✔ Tips

- If you want to save a previously saved presentation with a new name, in a different format, or in another location on the disk, use the File > Save As command rather than File > Save.

- Another way to save a presentation as a Web page is to choose File > Save as Web Page

Save button

Figure 18.18 To save a new or existing presentation to the disk, click the Save icon on the Standard toolbar.

Figure 18.19 In the Save As dialog box, enter a name for the presentation, choose a format and location, specify options, and click Save.

Table 18.1

PowerPoint File Formats

FILENAME EXTENSION	FORMAT
.ppt	PowerPoint presentation
.pps	PowerPoint slide show
(no extension)	PowerPoint package
.mov	PowerPoint movie
.pot	Design template
.htm	Web page

SAVING PRESENTATIONS

CREATING YOUR PRESENTATION

Customizing presentations in PowerPoint X is as straightforward as it's always been. The first part of this chapter explains the basics of working with text and graphics within individual text blocks and slides. The second part shows how to use different style masters to add design and color to portions of your presentation or to the entire thing.

Adding Text to Slides

Many slides have specific areas where you can type the title and other text.

To create a text slide:

1. On the Standard toolbar, click the New Slide icon (**Figure 19.1**). You can also choose Insert > New Slide.

2. In the New Slide dialog box (**Figure 19.2**), select any style of slide that contains text and then click OK.

   The new slide appears (**Figure 19.3**).

3. Click the "Click to add title" or "Click to add text" placeholder and type the text.

4. Click the next placeholder and continue typing text (**Figure 19.4**).

✔ Tips

- When you finish typing text in a placeholder, you can press Option Return to jump to the next placeholder.

- When you finish typing the text in the bottommost placeholder on any slide, you can press Option Return to automatically create another slide of the same type.

- To format text, set paragraph alignment, or create additional bullet or number lists, you can choose commands from the Format menu, the Formatting toolbar, or the Formatting Palette.

New Slide icon

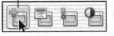

Figure 19.1 You can create a new slide by clicking the New Slide icon on the Standard toolbar.

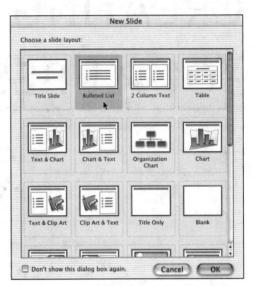

Figure 19.2 Select a layout for the slide from the New Slide dialog box.

Figure 19.3 The new slide appears, ready for you to add text and embellish it.

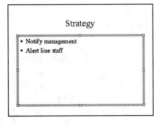

Figure 19.4 Click the next placeholder and type your text.

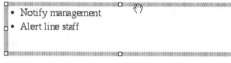

Figure 19.5 When a text block is selected, handles and a frame appear around it.

Figure 19.6 To reposition a text block, drag it by its border.

Working with Text Blocks

You can select characters, words, or paragraphs within a text block the same way you do in a Word document (see "Using Text," Chapter 1). However, PowerPoint differs a bit in the manner in which you move and format text blocks.

To select a text block:

◆ Click anywhere in a text block. The selected text block is surrounded by a border and handles (**Figure 19.5**), enabling you to move and resize it as necessary.

To move or resize a text block:

◆ To move a selected text block, move the cursor over the border until it changes to an open hand (**Figure 19.6**), and then drag the block to a new position on the slide.

◆ To resize a selected text block, click any handle and drag.

✔ Tips

■ To resize a text block proportionally, hold down Shift as you drag any corner handle.

■ To resize a text block from its center, hold down Option as you drag any corner handle. (If the block was originally centered on the slide, this procedure will keep it centered.)

■ Once a text block is selected, you can select text within it using normal editing procedures.

■ Text inside a resized text block automatically rewraps to fit the new size of the block.

WORKING WITH TEXT BLOCKS

Adding Graphics to Slides

You can embellish slides by adding images from the Clip Gallery or other image files that are stored on your hard disk. (The Value Pack, included on the Office v. X CD-ROM, contains additional clip art.)

To add clip art to a slide:

1. Create a new slide, choosing Text & Clip Art or Clip Art & Text as the format.

    The new slide appears (**Figure 19.7**).

2. Double-click the clip-art placeholder.

    The Clip Gallery: PowerPoint window appears (**Figure 19.8**).

3. Select a category from the list on the left, or perform a search by entering keywords in the Search field.

    The selected clip art appears in the panel on the right.

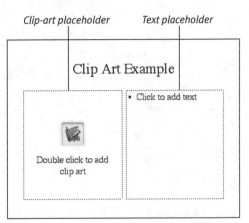

Clip-art placeholder   Text placeholder

Figure 19.7 This slide layout is intended for a combination of clip art and text.

Figure 19.8 Choose a clip-art image from the Clip Gallery.

Inserted clip art   *Picture toolbar*

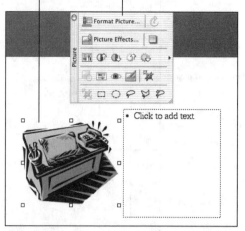

Figure 19.9 The chosen clip-art image appears in the placeholder, and the Picture toolbar opens.

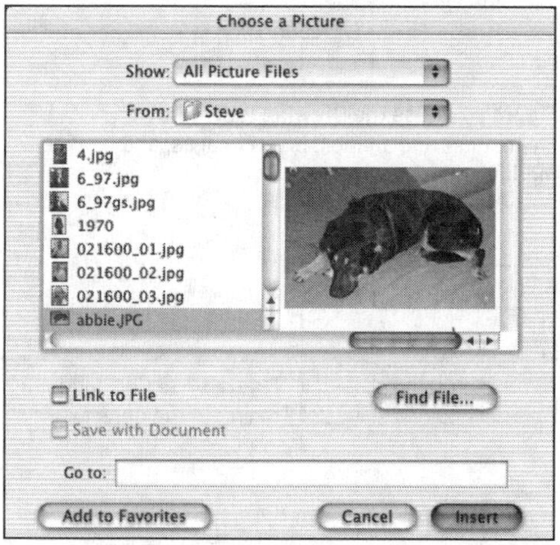

Figure 19.10 You can insert an image file from the disk by selecting it in the Choose a Picture dialog box.

4. Select an image and click Insert.

The picture is inserted into the placeholder and the Picture toolbar appears (**Figure 19.9**). (Note that if the Formatting Palette is open, the Picture toolbar will *not* appear.)

✔ Tips

■ To insert a *different* type of image (such as a photo), follow the same procedure but create a new slide that contains a Picture placeholder. When you double-click the placeholder, the Choose a Picture dialog box opens (**Figure 19.10**), allowing you to select a picture from your hard disk.

■ Even if you haven't created a slide with a placeholder for clip art, you can manually insert clip art into *any* slide by choosing Insert > Picture > Clip Art.

■ Click the Format Picture icon on the Picture toolbar to open the Format Picture dialog box and access more tools you can use to control the look and location of clip art.

ADDING GRAPHICS TO SLIDES

Drawing Objects

If you can't find clip art you like or if you want to create your own artwork, you can use the drawing tools to create objects for your slides.

To draw an object:

1. If the Drawing toolbar isn't visible, display it by choosing View > Toolbars > Drawing (**Figure 19.11**).

2. Switch to a view that clearly displays the slide, and then select a drawing tool.

3. Click and drag to create the object (**Figure 19.12**). The outline appears as you drag.

   Depending on the tool selected, you can draw basic shapes (such as rectangles, lines, and ovals) or special shapes (such as smiley faces, banners, and flowchart objects).

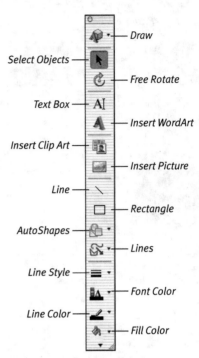

Figure 19.11 Use the Drawing toolbar to create lines and shapes, insert images, and modify graphics.

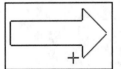

Figure 19.12 Click and drag to create the object.

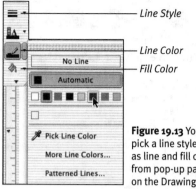

Line Style

Line Color
Fill Color

Figure 19.13 You can pick a line style, as well as line and fill colors, from pop-up palettes on the Drawing toolbar.

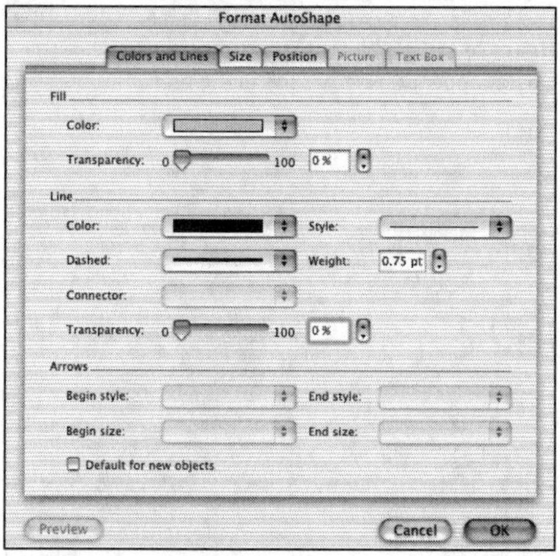

Figure 19.14 If you have elaborate object-formatting requirements, you may wish to use the Format AutoShape dialog box.

4. To format the object, select it and do one of the following:

   ◆ Select options from the Line Style, Line Color, and Fill Color pop-up palettes on the Drawing toolbar (**Figure 19.13**).

   ◆ Double-click the object or choose Format > AutoShape, and then select options in the Format AutoShape dialog box (**Figure 19.14**).

✔ Tips

■ To add text to a drawn object, select the Text Box tool, click inside the object, and type. (Some objects, such as the Callouts in the AutoShapes menu, are automatically enclosed in a text box.)

■ To group shapes, hold down ⸢Shift⸥ as you click each object for the group, click the Draw button on the Drawing toolbar, and choose Group from the pop-up menu.

■ To change object layering, select an object, click the Draw tool's pop-up menu, and choose Arrange > Send to Back or another layering command.

DRAWING OBJECTS

233

Creating a Common Graphic Background

You can create a presentation with a consistent theme by adding graphics to the background. An image placed on a slide master will appear in the background of every slide in the presentation. You can choose graphics from the art collections included with Office or use your own images.

To add graphics to the background:

1. Choose View > Master > Slide Master or press [Shift] as you click the Slide View icon in the bottom-left corner of the document window.

   The Slide Master window appears (**Figure 19.15**).

2. Choose > Insert > Picture > From File.

   The Choose a Picture dialog box appears (**Figure 19.16**).

3. Select a picture file and click Insert.

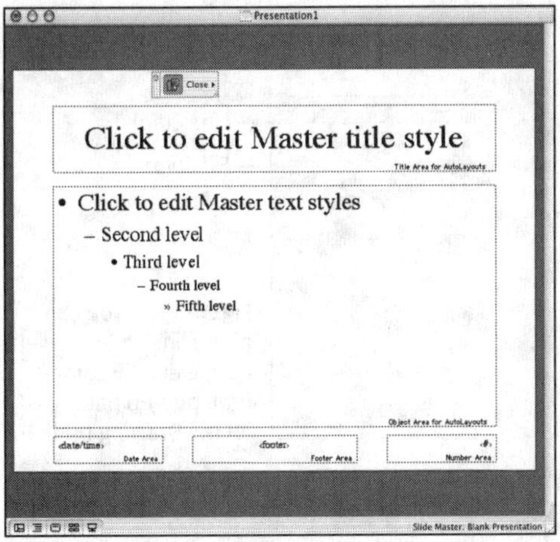

Figure 19.15 Graphics and text added to the slide master appear on every slide in the presentation.

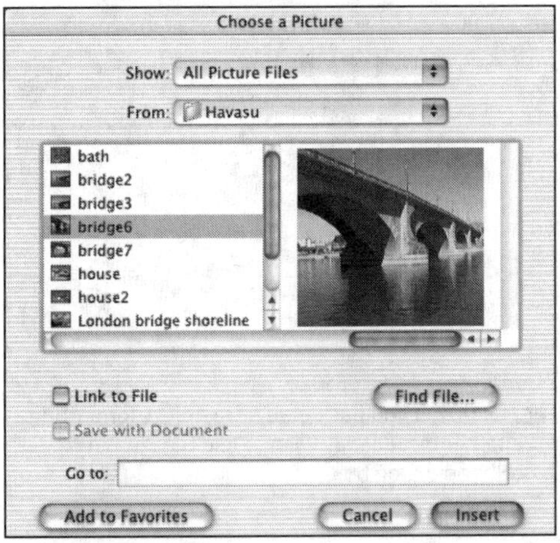

Figure 19.16 Select a graphic to add to the slide master and click Insert.

Preview using currently active slide

Figure 19.17 If you wish, you can resize a placed image so it completely covers the slide master (as shown here).

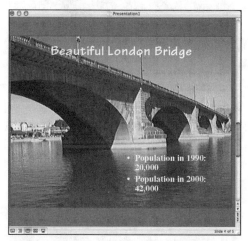

Figure 19.18 The graphic is now visible in the background of every slide in the presentation.

4. Modify the graphic background object, if needed, using the tools on the Drawing toolbar. Resize or move the image if necessary (**Figure 19.17**).

5. Click a View icon (or choose a command from the View menu) to leave Slide Master view and see the effect of your changes (**Figure 19.18**).

✔ Tips

- You can copy and paste a graphic image from another program onto the slide master, or copy and paste graphics from the slide master of another presentation onto the slide master of the current one.

- Any graphics that are already on the slide master as part of the template background must be ungrouped before you can modify them.

Applying Background Color and Fill Effects

You can add color to the background of your presentation to make it more appealing or compelling. Partner the color with a fill technique (such as a gradient) to create depth and a polished, professional look. (Background color and fill effects can vary from slide to slide or can be applied to all the slides in the presentation.)

To change the background color or fill effects:

1. If you intend to apply a background color or fill effect to only a specific slide in the presentation, display or select that slide. When you're applying the color or fill effect to all slides in the presentation, the specific slide displayed doesn't matter.

2. Choose Format > Slide Background.
   The Background dialog box appears.

3. Select a color from the ones displayed in the pull-down menu (**Figure 19.19**), or choose More Colors to select a color from a color picker (**Figure 19.20**).
   Any fill effects you specify in the next step will be applied to the selected color.

4. *Optional:* Choose Fill Effects from the pull-down menu. Select the desired features from the Fill Effects dialog box (**Figure 19.21**). Click OK when you're done.

5. *Optional:* To preview the chosen color and effects in the current slide, click the Preview button.

6. Click Apply to apply the color and effects to only the displayed slide. Click Apply to All to affect all slides.

✔ Tip

■ Another way to apply a background color and fill effects to all slides in a presentation is to add them to the slide master.

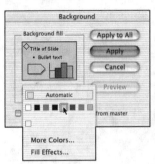

Figure 19.19 You can choose a solid fill color from the Background dialog box's pull-down menu.

Select a color picker

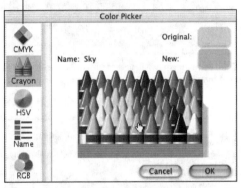

Figure 19.20 If you choose More Colors from the pull-down menu, you can select from additional colors or—depending on the color picker you use—generate a custom color.

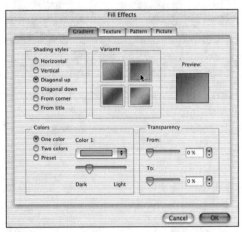

Figure 19.21 Select settings for the background fill effect from the options presented in the Fill Effects dialog box.

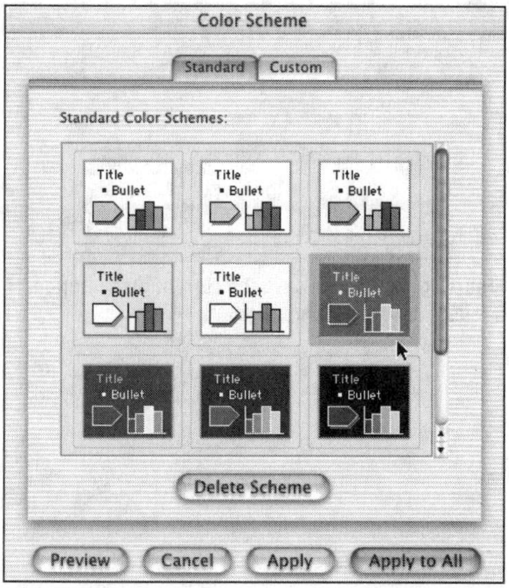

Figure 19.22 To use a predefined color scheme, select one from the Standard tab of the Color Scheme dialog box.

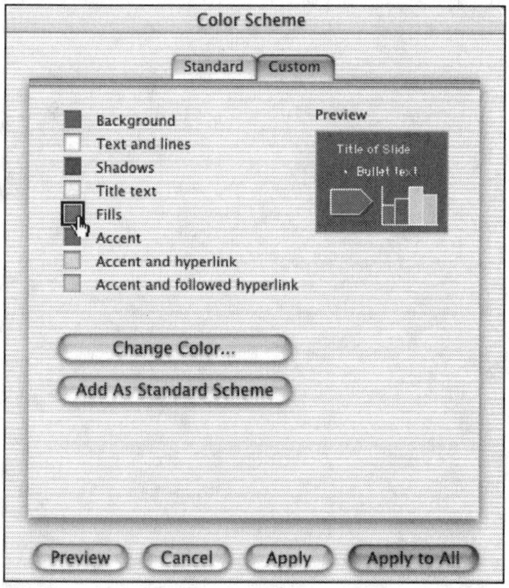

Figure 19.23 To create your own color scheme, specify colors for the eight types of effects shown on the Custom tab of the Color Scheme dialog box.

Changing the Color Scheme

You can also add consistency to your presentation by selecting a color scheme for it. The eight colors of the color scheme are applied to all the elements on the current slide or all the slides in the presentation—unless you change the color of a specific element. You can select predefined color schemes or create your own.

To specify a color scheme:

1. If you intend to apply the color scheme to only a specific slide in the presentation, display or select that slide. When you're applying the color scheme to all the slides in the presentation, the specific slide displayed doesn't matter.

2. Choose Format > Slide Color Scheme. The Color Scheme dialog box appears.

3. To specify a predefined color scheme, select one on the Standard tab of the Color Scheme dialog box (**Figure 19.22**).

   or

   To create a custom color scheme, click the Custom tab (**Figure 19.23**). Specify new colors by selecting an element's color box and then clicking the Change Color button.

4. *Optional:* To preview the chosen color scheme in the current slide, click the Preview button.

5. To apply the color scheme to only the displayed slide, click Apply. To apply it to all slides, click Apply to All.

✔ Tip

■ The color scheme is stored in a template, so if you switch templates, you'll switch color schemes, too.

Saving and Reusing a Custom Design

After spending many hours modifying a PowerPoint template or creating an impressive presentation from scratch, you can optionally save its design elements as a custom template that you can use as the basis for future presentations.

1. Choose File > Save As.

2. On the Save dialog box that appears, choose Design Template from the Format pull-down menu (**Figure 19.24**).

3. Name the template and click Save.

By default, the template is stored in the My Templates folder, making it available to you as a choice in the Project Gallery window.

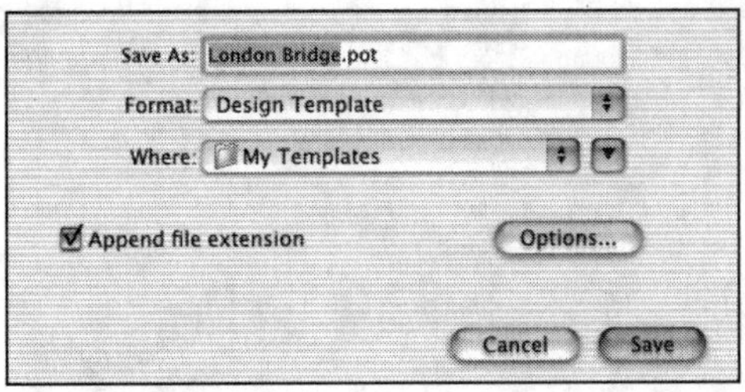

Figure 19.24 You can save the current presentation as a reusable Design Template.

WORKING WITH CHARTS AND GRAPHS

A chart or graph can make complex numerical information easier to interpret by expressing it visually.

To create or edit a chart, PowerPoint uses Microsoft Graph, the same charting module Excel uses. When you create a chart in Graph, Graph's menus and toolbars replace those of PowerPoint.

The following instructions will help you add and modify charts and graphs for use in a presentation. Note that the terms *chart* and *graph* are used interchangeably throughout this chapter. It's also important to note that all editing of the chart type and its elements are done from within Graph, *not* in PowerPoint.

Starting a Chart

You can use either of the following procedures to add a chart to a slide.

To add a chart to a chart layout:

1. Click the New Slide icon on the Standard toolbar. You can also choose Insert > New Slide or press Control M.

   The New Slide dialog box appears (**Figure 20.1**).

2. Select one of the three layouts that includes a chart placeholder: Chart, Text & Chart, or Chart & Text.

3. Click OK.

   The chart-layout slide appears (**Figure 20.2**).

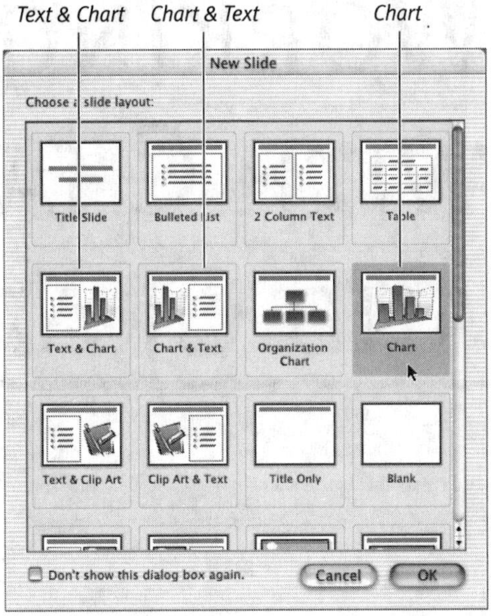

Figure 20.1 In the New Slide dialog box, choose a layout that includes a chart placeholder.

Figure 20.2 Double-click the chart placeholder on the slide.

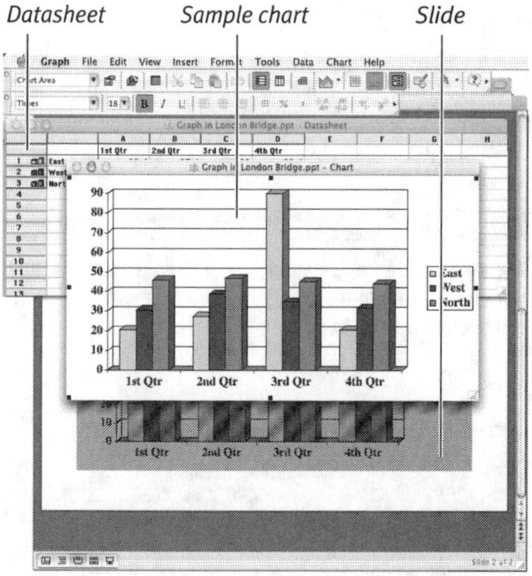

Datasheet   Sample chart   Slide

Figure 20.3 A sample chart and datasheet appear in Graph.

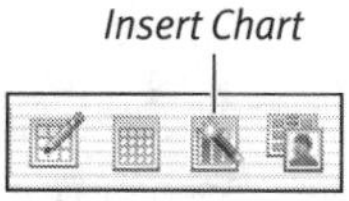

Insert Chart

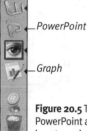

Figure 20.4 Click the Insert Chart icon on the Standard toolbar.

PowerPoint

Graph

Figure 20.5 The Dock has icons for both PowerPoint and Graph. Click the appropriate icon to make one of these programs active.

4. To add a chart to the new slide, double-click where you see the "Double click to add chart" text.

Graph launches, and a sample chart and datasheet appear (**Figure 20.3**).

To add a chart to a nonchart layout:

1. Select the slide to which you'd like to add the chart.

The particular layout of the current slide is unimportant; layout elements are merely guidelines you can use or ignore as you see fit.

2. Choose Insert > Chart, or click the Insert Chart icon on the Standard toolbar (**Figure 20.4**).

Graph launches, and a sample chart and datasheet appear.

✔ Tips

■ You can add a chart from any view (see "Changing Views" in Chapter 18, Getting Started).

■ While working on a chart, Graph adds its icon to the Dock (**Figure 20.5**). To switch between PowerPoint and Graph, click the appropriate icon in the Dock.

STARTING A CHART

Entering Your Own Data

Now that you have a chart started, you can replace the sample data in the datasheet with your own data (**Figure 20.6**).

To enter your data:

1. Click any cell in the Excel-like datasheet, and then replace its contents. As you make new entries, the chart automatically changes to reflect the new data.

   or

   Drag from the top left to the bottom right to select the range of cells that will contain your data (**Figure 20.7**). Complete each cell entry by pressing Enter or Tab. The former will move the cursor down the columns in the selected range, while the latter will move the cursor across the rows in the range. When the cursor reaches the bottom of a column or the end of a row, it will jump to the top of the next column or the beginning of the next row, respectively.

2. To send the datasheet to the background and view the graph, click the View Datasheet icon on the Standard toolbar (**Figure 20.8**) or click any visible part of the graph.

✔ Tips

■ Rather than typing your data, you may want to import existing data into the datasheet using the File > Import File command. Graph understands a variety of common data formats, such as Excel worksheets and tab-delimited text files.

■ To exclude a row or column of data from the graph (effectively hiding that row or column), double-click the row or column heading (**Figure 20.9**). Double-click the heading again to include the row or column data in the graph.

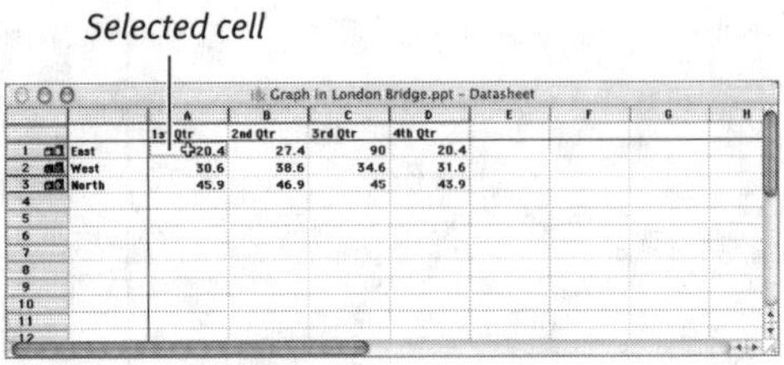

Selected cell

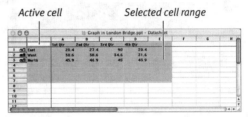

Figure 20.6 On the datasheet, you'll replace the sample data, column headers, and row headers with your own data. Click any cell and begin typing.

Active cell   Selected cell range

Figure 20.7 To enter data by rows or columns, begin by selecting all the cells necessary to contain your data.

Figure 20.8 Click the View Datasheet icon on the Standard toolbar to switch between the graph and datasheet views.

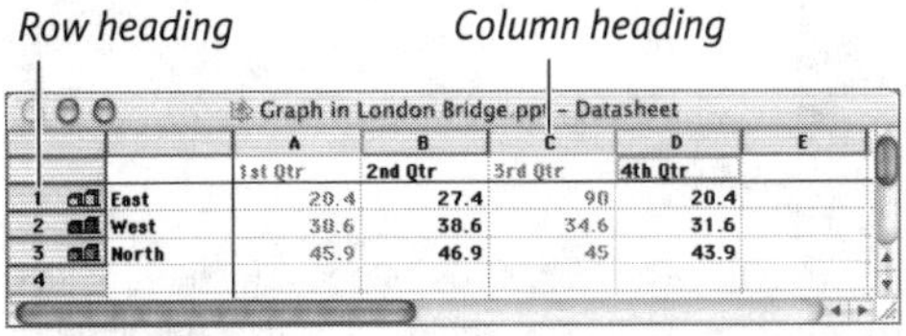

Row heading   Column heading

Figure 20.9 Double-click a row or column heading to exclude that row or column. Excluded data is colored gray. In this example, columns A and C are excluded.

Handle

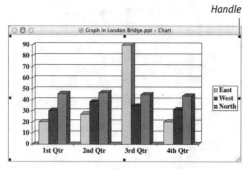

Figure 20.11 Handles appear when the chart is selected.

Chart Type icon

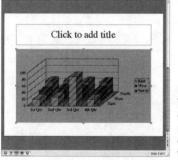

Figure 20.12 Click the Chart Type icon on the Standard toolbar and select a chart type.

Changing the Chart Type

After creating a chart in Graph, you're free to change its type or modify its appearance by choosing commands and options from the Standard toolbar as shown in **Figure 20.10** at the bottom of this page.

To change a chart's type:

1. In Graph, switch to the datasheet window or select the chart (handles appear around it, as shown in **Figure 20.11**).

2. Click the down arrow beside the Chart Type icon on the Standard toolbar, and then select another style of chart (**Figure 20.12**).

   The revised chart appears in the Graph window and on the PowerPoint slide (**Figure 20.13**).

(continues on next page)

Figure 20.13 The new chart type replaces the old one on the slide.

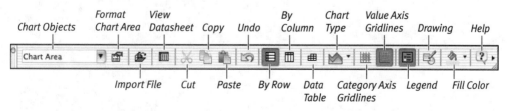

Figure 20.10 You can format a chart in Graph using the commands available on the Standard toolbar.

CHANGING THE CHART TYPE

✔ Tips

■ Choose Chart > Chart Type to select from additional chart styles (**Figure 20.14**).

■ If you want to experiment with several chart styles, you can turn the Chart Type drop-down list in Step 2 into a floating palette. Open the Chart Type list and click the double line at its top. You can then drag the palette to any point on the screen. When you're ready to dismiss the palette, click its close button.

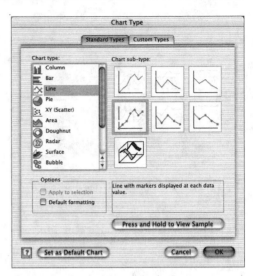

Figure 20.14 The Chart Type dialog box presents several additional chart types that are not available from the Standard toolbar's Chart Type palette.

Legend icon

Figure 20.15 You can show or hide the legend by clicking the Legend icon on the Standard toolbar.

Legend

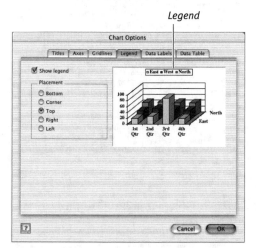

Figure 20.16 You can show or hide the legend, as well as specify its placement, on the Legend tab of the Chart Options dialog box.

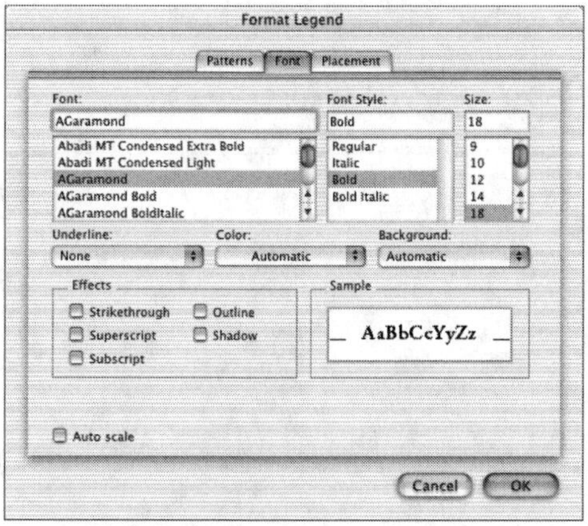

Figure 20.17 Use the Format Legend dialog box to specify formatting options for the legend.

Adding Legends to a Chart

A *legend* graphically explains the meaning of the various data series on a chart or graph.

To show or hide the legend:

◆ Switch to Graph and click the Legend icon on the Standard toolbar (**Figure 20.15**).

The Legend icon works as a toggle, hiding or displaying the chart's legend with each click. When the legend is active, the icon is darkened.

✔ Tips

■ You can also add a legend and specify its position by choosing Chart > Chart Options. In the Chart Options dialog box, switch to the Legend tab (**Figure 20.16**), choose settings, and click OK.

■ As is the case with other objects in Office, after selecting the legend you can modify it in many ways:

▲ To move the legend, click in its center and then drag it to a new position.

▲ To change the legend size, drag any handle.

▲ To change the legend text, edit it in the datasheet.

▲ To change the font, size, or style of the legend text, you can either double-click the legend, choose Format > Selected Legend, or (Control)-click the legend and choose Format > Legend from the pop-up menu that appears. In the Format Legend dialog box, select options from the Font tab (**Figure 20.17**).

Displaying Gridlines

You can elect to display or hide gridlines on any chart. Gridlines can help viewers interpret the data, since they make it easier to see the approximate size or value of each data point. You can add gridlines to any chart other than pie and doughnut charts.

To use a gridline:

◆ Switch to Graph, and click the Category Axis Gridlines (vertical) and/or the Value Axis Gridlines (horizontal) icon on the Standard toolbar (**Figure 20.18**).

The Gridlines icons work as toggles, hiding or displaying the gridlines with each click. When a gridline option is active, its icon is darkened.

✔ Tips

■ You can also add gridlines by choosing Chart > Chart Options. On the Gridlines tab of the Chart Options dialog box (**Figure 20.19**), you can specify Major Gridlines or Minor Gridlines for each axis.

■ To format a set of gridlines (changing their style, color, or weight), select a Category Axis or Value Axis gridline on the chart, double-click the gridline (or choose Format > Selected Gridlines), and then set options in the Format Gridlines dialog box that appears (**Figure 20.20**).

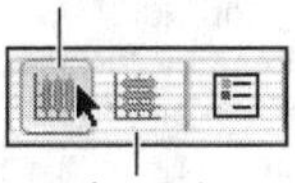

Category Axis Gridlines

Value Axis Gridlines

Figure 20.18 Click the Category Axis Gridlines or the Value Axis Gridlines icon on the Standard toolbar to activate or deactivate a particular set of gridlines. When a class of gridlines is active, its toolbar icon is darkened.

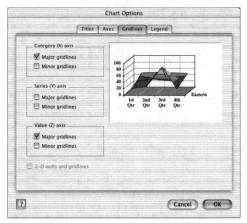

Figure 20.19 You can specify Major and Minor gridlines for each axis in the Gridlines tab of the Chart Options dialog box.

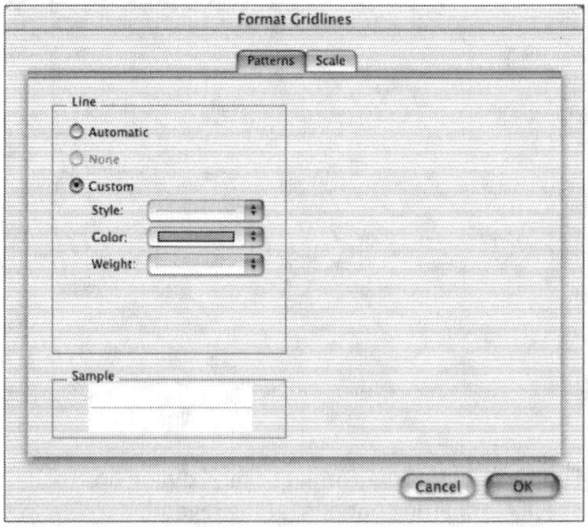

Figure 20.20 You can accept the default gridline style or specify custom formatting in the Format Gridlines dialog box.

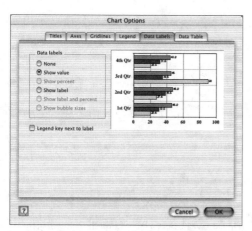

Figure 20.21 Click the Data Labels tab in the Chart Options dialog box and select a label option to enable labeling for all data points.

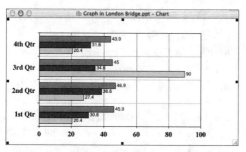

Figure 20.22 The chart with data labels applied.

Labeling Data Points

You can label the data values in your chart to highlight the differences between them or to make it simpler for readers to interpret the chart.

To add a label for every data point:

1. Choose Chart > Chart Options.

2. In the Chart Options dialog box, click the Data Labels tab, select the desired labeling option (**Figure 20.21**), and click OK.

   The chart is redrawn with labels (**Figure 20.22**).

To add labels for a single data series:

1. In Graph, select a data series on the chart. (In a bar or column chart, for example, you'd click any colored bar to select all members of that data series.)

2. Choose Format > Selected Data Series. The Format Data Series dialog box appears (**Figure 20.23**).

3. On the Data Labels tab, select an option and click OK.

   The chart is redrawn as specified.

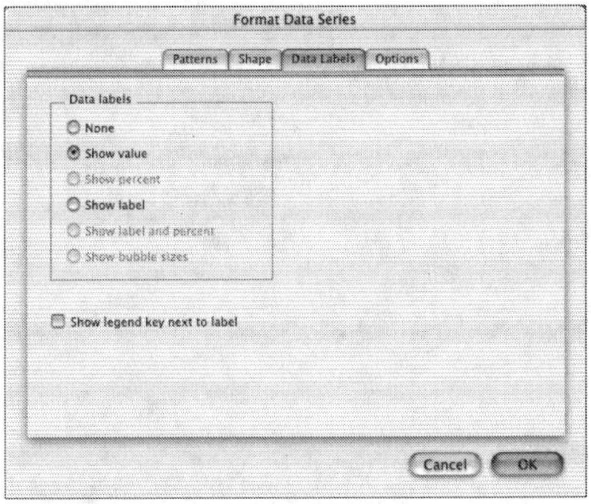

✔ Tips

■ You can also specify a separate data label for an individual data point, enabling you to label only the highest and lowest values on a chart, for example. Click to select a single data value on the chart and then choose Format > Selected Data Point.

■ To remove all data labels from a chart, choose None on the Data Labels tab of the Chart Options dialog box (Figure 20.21). To remove data labels from only a selected series, choose None on the Data Labels tab of the Format Data Series dialog box.

Figure 20.23 Select a label-formatting option in the Data Labels tab of the Format Data Series dialog box and click OK.

Formatting Data Labels

You can format the data labels (changing the font, number format, or alignment) for each data series. Open the Format Data Labels dialog box (**Figure 20.24**) using any of these methods: double-click a data label, select a data label and choose Format > Selected Data Labels, or [Control]-click a data label and choose Format Data Labels. Make the desired formatting changes and click OK. Repeat the process for each data series.

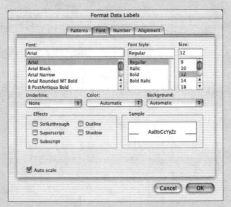

Figure 20.24 You can adjust the placement, number format, or font used for the labels in the Format Data Labels dialog box.

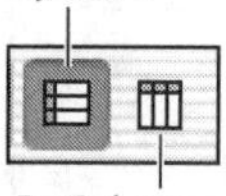

By Rows

By Columns

Figure 20.25 Click the By Row or By Column icon on the Standard toolbar to specify the arrangement of your data series in the datasheet.

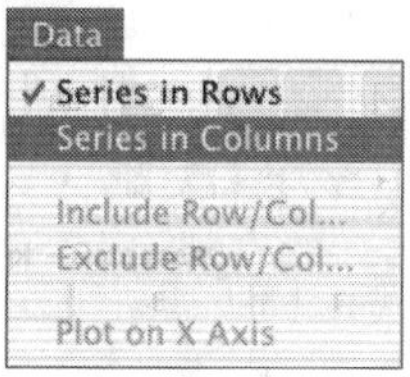

Data

✓ Series in Rows
Series in Columns

Include Row/Col...
Exclude Row/Col...

Plot on X Axis

Figure 20.26 You can also specify the arrangement of your data in the datasheet by choosing Data > Series in Rows or Data > Series in Columns.

Specifying the Data Arrangement

You can arrange the data in your datasheet by rows or by columns. To specify whether each row or each column is a data series, do one of the following:

◆ Click the By Row or By Column icon on the Standard toolbar (**Figure 20.25**).

◆ Choose Data > Series in Rows or Data > Series in Columns (**Figure 20.26**). The checked command represents the current choice.

Formatting a Chart Element

You can format the appearance of any element on a chart, such as one set of bars, one line, or an axis. You can also change the style of any data series in the chart by formatting the series.

To format a chart element:

1. In Graph, click the chart to make it active, if necessary.

2. Click to select the chart element that you want to format and then double-click it.

   The appropriate dialog box for the chosen element appears, such as Format Chart Area (with the entire chart selected), Format Axis, Format Data Labels, Format Data Series, or Format Legend.

3. Choose formatting options and click OK.

✔ Tip

- To avoid opening the *wrong* dialog box, you can [Control]-click an element and choose the command from the pop-up menu that appears (**Figure 20.27**). Alternatively, you can simply select a chart element and then choose the relevant command from the Format menu.

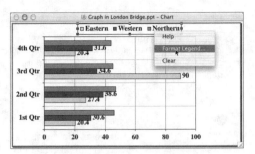
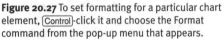

Figure 20.27 To set formatting for a particular chart element, [Control]-click it and choose the Format command from the pop-up menu that appears.

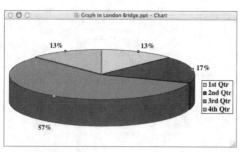

Figure 20.28 Click the pie chart to select it. Handles appear around it.

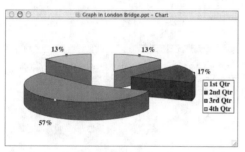

Figure 20.29 Drag outward to explode the entire pie.

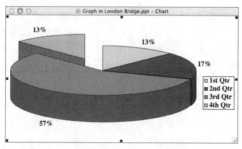

Figure 20.30 If you select a single slice and drag it, you can separate that slice from the rest of the pie.

Cutting a Pie Chart

If you've created a pie chart in Graph, you can *explode* the chart (pull all the pieces out from the center to make it more visually interesting) or pull out an individual piece (to emphasize a particular data value).

To explode or cut a pie chart:

1. In Graph, click the chart to make it active, if necessary.

2. To explode the pie chart, click once to select the entire pie (**Figure 20.28**) and then drag outward (**Figure 20.29**).

3. To pull a selected slice away from the pie, click once to select the entire pie, and then click a second time to select only the slice you want to cut. Then drag that particular slice outward (**Figure 20.30**).

✔ Tip

■ To rejoin a cut slice with the pie, drag that slice back to the center of the pie. To rejoin an exploded pie, drag *any* slice back to the center of the pie.

Creating Stock Charts

Stock charts (also known as *high-low-close charts*) can present the daily prices and, optionally, the opening price and daily volume for a given stock. Stock charts can also be used to present other types of numeric data, such as daily temperatures or barometric-pressure readings.

To create a high-low-close stock chart:

1. In Graph, switch to the datasheet and arrange the data in columns.

   Depending on the type of chart you intend to create, you should arrange the columns in one of the following manners:

   ◆ Date, High, Low, Close (**Figure 20.31**).

   ◆ Date, Open, High, Low, Close.

   ◆ Date, Volume, High, Low, Close.

   ◆ Date, Volume, Open, High, Low, Close.

2. Choose Data > Series in Columns (if it isn't already chosen).

3. Choose Chart > Chart Type.

	Date	High	Low	Close	D
1	9/28	15.91	15.39	15.51	
2	10/1	15.99	15.23	15.54	
3	10/2	15.83	14.88	15.05	
4	10/3	15.36	14.83	14.98	
5	10/4	16.25	14.99	15.88	
6	10/5	16.15	14.99	16.14	
7	10/8	16.35	15.5	16.2	
8	10/9	16.2	15.63	16	
9	10/10	16.85	15.95	16.82	
10	10/11	17.74	16.85	17.74	
11	10/12	18.08	16.86	18.01	
12	10/15	18.38	17.95	17.99	
13	10/16	18.2	17.77	18.01	
14	10/17	18.41	16.96	16.99	
15	10/18	18.23	17.29	18	
16	10/19	18.4	17.88	18.3	
17	10/22	19.07	18.09	19.02	
18	10/23	19.42	17.87	18.14	
19	10/24	19.09	17.75	18.95	
20	10/25	19.25	18.16	19.19	
21	10/26	19.25	18.62	18.67	
22	10/29	18.67	17.6	17.63	
23	10/30	18	17.06	17.6	

Figure 20.31 This datasheet contains the daily prices from September 28 to December 28, 2001, for Apple Computer's stock.

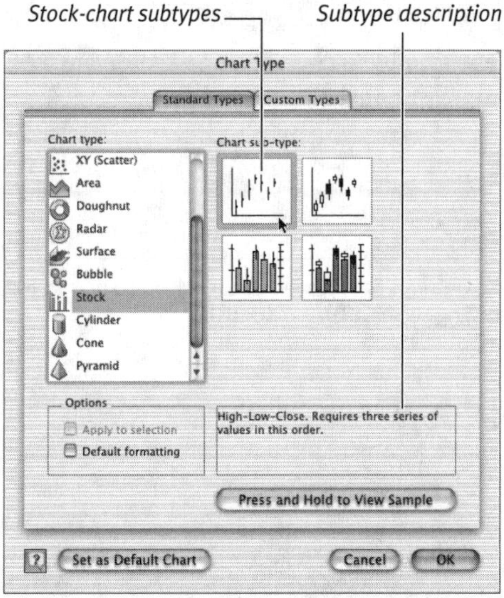

Stock-chart subtypes — Subtype description

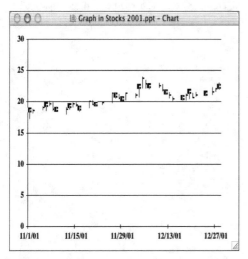

Figure 20.32 Select Stock as the chart type and select one of the four subtypes. (As you click each subtype, a description of its data requirements appears in the text box below.)

Figure 20.33 This is the high-low-close chart for the Apple stock data.

4. In the Chart Type dialog box (**Figure 20.32**), click the Standard Types tab, select Stock from the Chart type list, and select the type of stock chart that matches your datasheet. Click OK.

The graph appears (**Figure 20.33**).

✔ Tips

■ You can download trading data for a stock over a range of dates at `http://chart.yahoo.com/d`. After the data appear, click the Download Spreadsheet Format link to generate an Excel worksheet that you can rearrange to match Graph's requirements. Copy and paste the data into your Graph datasheet.

■ You can add a variety of trendlines to the chart by choosing Chart > Add Trendline.

CREATING STOCK CHARTS

Working with 3D Charts

In modern graph programs, the most impressive charts are three-dimensional—adding depth and perspective to an otherwise flat-looking image.

1. In Graph, click the chart to make it active, if necessary.

2. Choose Chart > 3-D View.

   The 3-D View dialog box appears (**Figure 20.34**).

3. Click the large arrows to raise or lower the elevation. Click the rotation axes to change the angle on the horizontal plane.

   You can see the effect of the elevation and rotation changes in the preview window.

4. *Optional:* To change the perspective, remove the checkmark from the Right angle axes check box and click the perspective arrows that appear.

5. *Optional:* To alter the height of the chart and the chart elements, remove the checkmark from the Auto scaling check box and enter a percentage (such as 40 or 120) in the Height text box.

6. To view the effect of your settings on the graph, click the Apply button. When you are satisfied with the settings, click OK.

   The graph is reformatted to match the 3-D View settings (**Figure 20.35**).

✔ Tip

■ For greater precision, you can enter specific numeric values in any of the text fields.

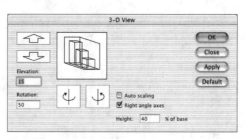

Figure 20.34 Specify elevation, rotation, and perspective settings in the 3-D View dialog box.

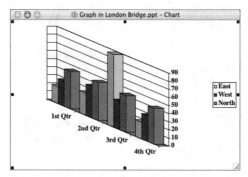

Figure 20.35 Here's a bar chart with 3D settings applied.

ORGANIZATION CHARTS AND TABLES

Figure 21.1. Organization Chart is an associated program that you launch from within PowerPoint.

Organization charts (or *org charts*) can be a very useful part of a business presentation. Org charts are actually created not within PowerPoint but in a separate application called Organization Chart. You access this application through PowerPoint, and then build the chart (**Figure 21.1**) in the Organization Chart window.

Adding an Organization Chart to a Slide

To make it easy to add an organization chart to a slide, PowerPoint provides an org-chart layout. All you have to do is select this layout and create the chart.

To add an org chart to a slide with an Org Chart layout:

1. To create a new slide, click the New Slide icon on the Standard toolbar, choose Insert > New Slide, or press Control M.

   The New Slide dialog box appears (**Figure 21.2**).

2. Select the Organization Chart layout, and click OK.

3. On the new slide, double-click the "Double click to add org chart" place-holder (**Figure 21.3**).

   Organization Chart launches (**Figure 21.4**).

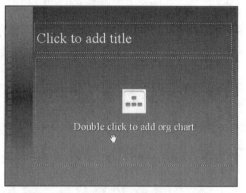

Figure 21.2 Create a new slide that uses the Organization Chart layout.

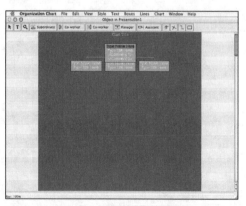

Figure 21.3 To launch Organization Chart, double-click the org-chart placeholder in the new slide.

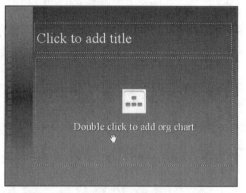

Figure 21.4 Organization Chart launches and displays the framework of a new org chart.

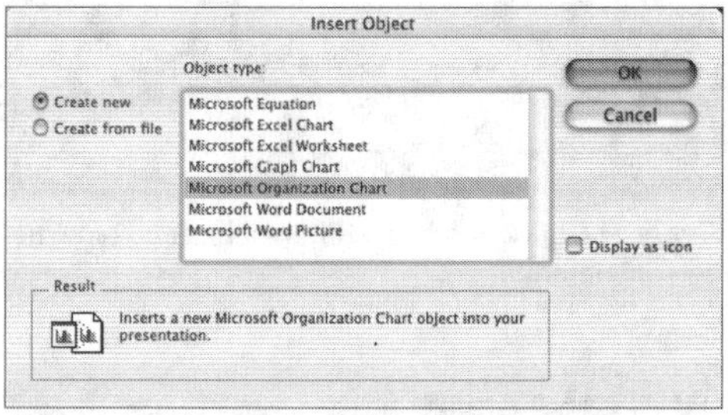

Figure 21.5 Select Create new and Microsoft Organization Chart in the Insert Object dialog box.

To add an org chart to a slide with a different layout:

1. Select the slide on which you'd like to add the org chart.

2. Choose Insert > Object.

   The Insert Object dialog box appears (**Figure 21.5**).

3. Click the Create new radio button, select Microsoft Organization Chart as the Object type, and click OK.

   Organization Chart launches.

✔ Tip

- While you're working on an org chart, Organization Chart adds its icon to the Dock. To switch between PowerPoint and Organization Chart, click the appropriate icon in the Dock.

ADDING AN ORGANIZATION CHART TO A SLIDE

Adding People

Adding people's names to an organization chart is straightforward. Each person's name and title appear in his or her own box. A person's placement in the org chart depends on his or her position in the organization's hierarchy.

To add people:

1. Type the name of the organization's head in the text box that is preselected when Organization Chart launches.

2. Press Tab to highlight the next line within the same box, and then type the person's title or position.

3. Click a different box and enter the person's name and title (**Figure 21.6**).

   or

   Press ⌘↓, ⌘→, or ⌘← to move to the box below, to the right, or to the left, respectively, and enter the person's name and title.

✔ Tips

■ When you are finished entering the names and titles for these initial positions, you may want to transfer the information to your PowerPoint slide by choosing one of the File > Update commands (or by pressing Option ⌘ S). Unlike Microsoft Graph (see Chapter 20, Working with Charts and Graphs), Organization Chart doesn't update slides automatically—you must do so manually (**Figure 21.7**).

■ To edit the information in a box, click the box, pause briefly, and then click again to place the insertion pointer in the text. If you double-click too quickly, the program may think you want to select the current box and all others at the same level.

Figure 21.6 Click or tab to a different box and type the person's information.

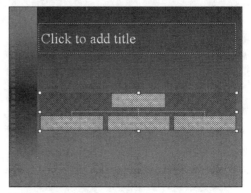

Figure 21.7 To transfer the org chart to your slide (as shown here), choose one of Organization Chart's File > Update commands.

New subordinate

Figure 21.9 A new subordinate box appears.

New subordinates

Marcia Smith
Director of Development

Figure 21.10 By clicking the Subordinate icon three times and then clicking Marcia Smith's box, you can simultaneously create three new subordinate boxes.

Adding Subordinates

The initial org-chart structure contains only a manager and three *subordinates*, but you can add more subordinates.

To add a subordinate:

1. Click the Subordinate icon on the Icon bar as shown in **Figure 21.8** at the bottom of this page.

2. Click the box of the position that requires a new subordinate.

   A subordinate box appears (**Figure 21.9**).

✔ Tips

- To add multiple subordinates beneath a position, click the Subordinate icon once for each subordinate, and then click the box of the position to which you are adding the subordinates (**Figure 21.10**).

- To add a coworker box beside a box, click one of the Co-worker icons on the Icon bar (depending on whether you want to display the coworker to the left or right), and then click the box of the position to which the coworker will be added.

- To move a subordinate box beneath another member's box, drag the subordinate box on top of the other member's box, and then release the mouse button.

  Whether a moved person will be added as a subordinate, left coworker, or right coworker depends on which *edge* of the box you drag him or her onto. Drag onto the left edge of the box to add the person as a left coworker, onto the right edge to add the person as a right coworker, or onto the bottom edge to add the person as a subordinate.

| ▲ | T | 🔍 | ⊥ Subordinate | ⊢ Co-worker | ⊣ Co-worker | ⊤ Manager | ⊐ Assistant | ╫ | ✕ | ⌐. | ▢ |

Figure 21.8 To create a new subordinate, coworker, manager, or assistant, click the relevant icon on the Icon bar and then click the box associated with that person.

ADDING SUBORDINATES

Adding Assistants

Adding assistants is like adding subordinates. There is no limit to the number of assistants you can add.

To add an assistant:

1. Click the Assistant icon on the Icon bar.

2. Click the box of the member who is to receive the assistant.

   An assistant box appears (**Figure 21.11**).

✔ Tips

■ You can add several assistants to a single organization member by clicking the Assistant icon once for every assistant you want to add before clicking the box of the member who will receive the assistants.

■ To delete an assistant box (or any other box on the org chart), click the box and then press ⌈Delete⌉.

   Note that if you delete the box of someone who is not one of the lowest members in a group (a supervisor, for example), Organization Chart will do its best to reorganize the remaining boxes. You may have to make some corrections.

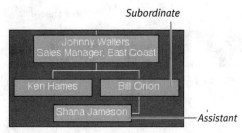

Figure 21.11 Note the difference in the connecting lines used to display subordinates and assistants.

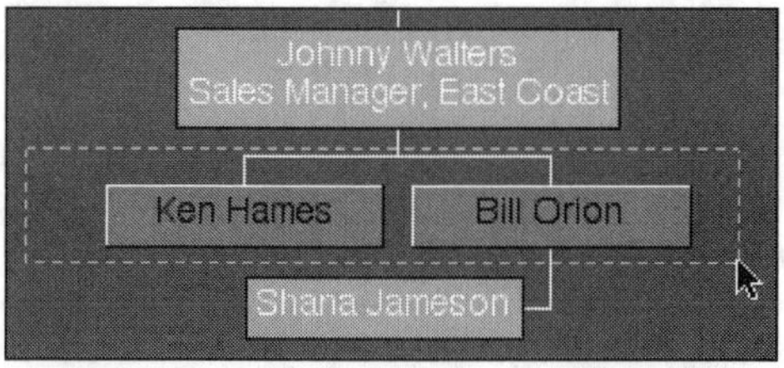

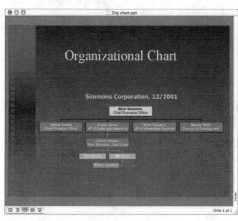

Figure 21.12 If you want to format several boxes simultaneously, click and drag a selection rectangle around them.

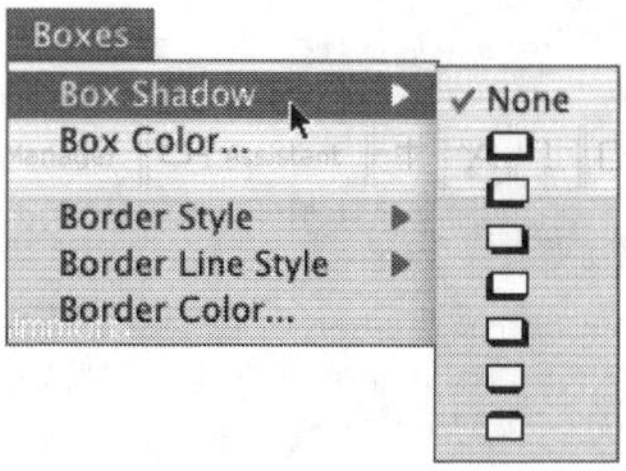

Figure 21.13 Choose commands from the Boxes menu to format a box's shadow, fill color, and border characteristics.

——Bold

Figure 21.14 You can apply formatting uniformly to all the text in a box or selectively to certain text.

Figure 21.15 As you create and edit the org chart, you can transfer it to your slide at any time. Once you've transferred it, you can freely move and resize it as needed.

Formatting an Org Chart

You can change the look of an organization chart to suit your taste. If the org chart will be an important part of your presentation, you may want to spend some extra time formatting its boxes, lines, and text.

To format selected boxes:

1. Click to select a box.

   or

   (Shift)-click to select multiple boxes.

   or

   Drag a selection rectangle to enclose multiple boxes (**Figure 21.12**).

2. Choose formatting commands from the Boxes menu (**Figure 20.13**).

To format selected text:

1. Select the text you want to format.

2. Choose formatting commands from the Text menu.

   The new formatting is applied to the selected text.

To format connecting lines:

◆ Select one or more connecting lines, and then choose options from the Lines menu.

✔ Tips

■ To apply the same formatting to all the text in a box, simply select the box and then choose the formatting commands. You can also apply text formatting to selected text within a box, such as a person's name (**Figure 21.14**) or title.

■ To select multiple line segments, draw a selection rectangle around them or (Shift)-click the segments.

■ To save the formatted org chart and transfer it to the slide (**Figure 21.15**), choose one of the File > Update commands.

More Org Chart Tips

Organization Chart has many capabilities the preceding pages don't touch on. Here are some additional tips and areas you may want to explore:

◆ You can add text anywhere on the org chart—to include comments, titles, and so forth. Select the Text tool on the Icon bar, click any empty space on the chart, and begin typing. The resulting text is an object that you can format and move as you wish.

◆ The right end of the icon bar contains a set of drawing tools you can use to embellish your org chart (**Figure 21.16**). In order, they are the Horizontal/Vertical Line tool, the Diagonal Line tool, the Connecting Line tool, and the Rectangle tool.

All but the Connecting Line tool are for drawing additional objects on the org chart. The Connecting Line tool is used to draw additional connections between member boxes (showing shared subordinates, for example). To use it, click one box and then drag to the second box.

◆ You can change the chart's background color by choosing Chart > Background Color.

◆ You might also want to experiment with different chart styles using options in the Style menu. For example, you can select the boxes of several people in a department and display them using one of the alternate "group" styles, such as Style > Stacked Group No Boxes (**Figure 21.17**).

◆ In addition to Shift-clicking or dragging a selection rectangle to select multiple boxes, you can select specific classes of boxes and objects by choosing commands from the Edit > Select submenu (**Figure 21.18**).

◆ You can launch Organization Chart at any time by double-clicking the org chart on your slide.

Horizontal/Vertical
  Connecting Line tool

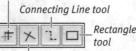

Rectangle tool

Diagonal Line tool

Figure 21.16 The Icon bar also contains several useful drawing tools.

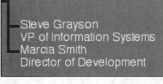

Figure 21.17 You can choose alternate ways of displaying groups in your org chart, such as Stacked Group No Boxes (shown here).

Edit	
Undo Draw Operation	⌘Z
Cut	⌘X
Copy	⌘C
Copy Setup	⇧⌘C
Paste	⌘V
Clear	
Select ▶	All ⌘A
Select Levels...	All Assistants
	All Co-Managers
	All Managers
	All Non-Managers
	Group ⌘G
	Branch ⌘B
	Lowest Level
	Connecting Lines
	Background Objects

Figure 21.18 Another way to select objects for simultaneous formatting is to choose a command from the Edit >Select submenu.

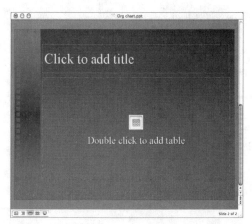

Figure 21.19 To begin creating a table, double-click the table placeholder on the new slide.

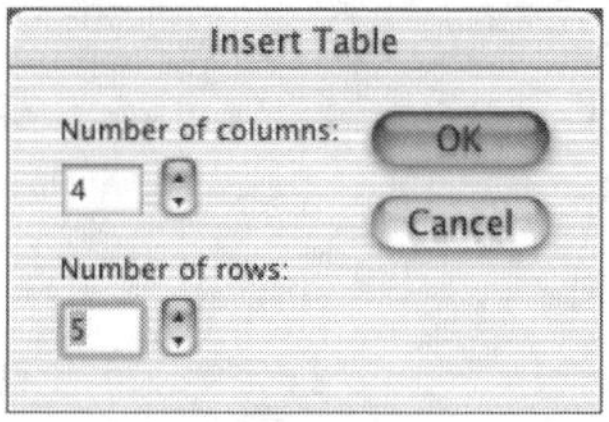

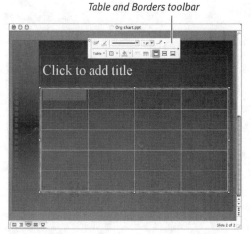

Figure 21.20 Specify the number of columns and rows for the new table in the Insert Table dialog box.

Table and Borders toolbar

Figure 21.21 A blank table with the specified number of columns and rows appears on the slide. Use the Table and Borders toolbar to format the cells and modify the table.

Adding a Table to a Slide

Tables can help present information efficiently. Creating and formatting a table in PowerPoint is similar to performing the same tasks in Word. See Chapter 7, Creating Tables, for more details.

To add a table to a slide:

1. Click the New Slide icon on the Standard toolbar.

2. In the New Slide dialog box, select the Table layout and click OK.

   The new slide appears (**Figure 21.19**).

3. Double-click the "Double click to add table" placeholder on the new slide.

   The Insert Table dialog box appears (**Figure 21.20**).

4. Specify the number of columns and rows, and then click OK.

   The table is added to the slide, and the Tables and Borders toolbar appears (**Figure 21.21**).

5. Enter the table's text. Format it as desired by selecting cells and choosing commands from the Tables and Borders toolbar.

To add a table to an existing slide:

1. Decide which slide you want to add the table to, and then make that slide active.

2. Click the Insert Table icon on the Standard toolbar, and then drag to select the desired number of rows and columns (**Figure 21.22**).

   or

   Choose Insert Table, specify the number of columns and rows in the Insert Table dialog box (Figure 21.20), and click OK.

✔ Tip

■ You can also format selected table cells by choosing the Format > Table command.

Insert Table icon

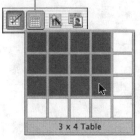

Figure 21.22 You can add a table to *any* slide by clicking the Insert Table icon on the Standard toolbar, and then dragging to set the number of rows and columns.

PREPARING THE PRESENTATION FOR VIEWING

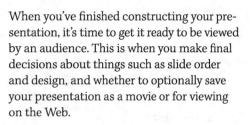

When you've finished constructing your presentation, it's time to get it ready to be viewed by an audience. This is when you make final decisions about things such as slide order and design, and whether to optionally save your presentation as a movie or for viewing on the Web.

The first part of this chapter covers the preparation of your presentation; the second part discusses options for presenting it.

Using the Slide Sorter

Use Slide Sorter View to get an overview of your presentation. It's similar to viewing 35mm slides on a light table. You can reorder slides, switch templates to change the look of the presentation, and delete or duplicate slides.

To switch to Slide Sorter View:

◆ Click the Slide Sorter View icon in the bottom-left corner of the PowerPoint document window (**Figure 22.1**).

 or

 Choose View > Slide Sorter.

✔ Tip

■ To switch to viewing a single slide, double-click the slide, or select the slide and then click the Slide View icon.

To reorder slides:

1. Click the slide you want to move, and then drag it to a new position.

2. A vertical line appears, indicating where the slide will be inserted when you release the mouse button (**Figure 22.2**).

3. Release the mouse button to drop the slide into its new position.

✔ Tips

■ To move a contiguous group of slides, click and drag the mouse across the slides to select them (**Figure 22.3**), and then drag the group to the new position.

■ To move a noncontiguous group (**Figure 22.4**), Shift-click to select each slide, and then drag the group to the new position. All selected slides will appear in sequence and in the same relative order.

Figure 22.1 One way to switch to Slide Sorter View is by clicking the appropriate icon at the bottom of the PowerPoint window.

Current destination *Selected slide*

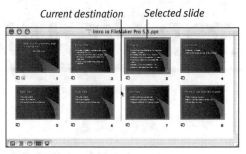

Figure 22.2 When you're rearranging slides, a line indicates where the slide will be moved if you release the mouse button.

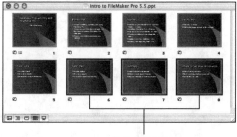

Selected slides

Figure 22.3 You can click and drag the mouse across multiple slides to move them as a group. In this example, slides 6 to 8 are selected.

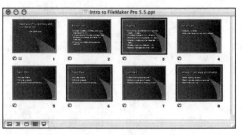

Figure 22.4 You can also move a group of noncontiguous slides by Shift-clicking to select them. In this example, slides 3, 6, and 8 are selected.

Figure 22.5 Click the Slide Design icon on the Standard toolbar to apply a different template to the current presentation.

Figure 22.6 Pick the design you want from the Choose a Slide Design dialog box.

Figure 22.7 The new design is applied to the slides.

To delete or duplicate slides:

1. Select the slide(s) you want to delete or duplicate.

2. Do one of the following:

◆ To delete the slide(s), choose Edit > Delete Slide or press ⌐Delete⌐.

◆ To duplicate the slide(s), choose Edit > Duplicate or press ⌘ D.

✔ Tip

■ You can reverse the effects of a duplication or deletion if you immediately choose the Edit > Undo command (or press ⌘ Z).

To change the design of your slides:

1. Click the Slide Design icon on the Standard toolbar (**Figure 22.5**) or choose Format > Slide Design.

2. In the Choose a Slide Design dialog box (**Figure 22.6**), select one of the designs from the Designs folder.

3. Click Apply.

The slides change to the new design (**Figure 22.7**).

✔ Tips

■ If you prefer, you can alter the slide design of only *selected* slides. Select the slides before issuing the Format > Slide Design command. In the Choose a Slide Design dialog box, click the Apply to selected slides radio button.

■ Another way to change the appearance of part of a presentation is to select slides, choose Format > Slide Color Scheme or Format > Slide Background, and select a different color scheme or background color for the slides.

USING THE SLIDE SORTER

Adding Transition Effects

Transition effects are optional visual effects, such as dissolves, splits, and wipes, used for transitions between slides. You can choose either PowerPoint or QuickTime transitions, and apply different transitions to different slides.

1. In Slide Sorter view, select the slide for which you want to specify a transition.

2. To apply a PowerPoint transition to the selected slide, do one of the following:

   Choose a transition from the Slide Transition Effects pull-down menu on the Slide Sorter toolbar (**Figure 22.8**). A preview of the effect appears on the selected slide.

   or

   Click the Slide Transition button on the Slide Sorter toolbar or choose Slide Show > Slide Transition. In the Slide Transition dialog box (**Figure 22.9**), set Effect, Sound, and Advance slide options, and then click Apply.

Figure 22.8 Choose a transition from the Slide Transition Effects list on the Slide Sorter toolbar.

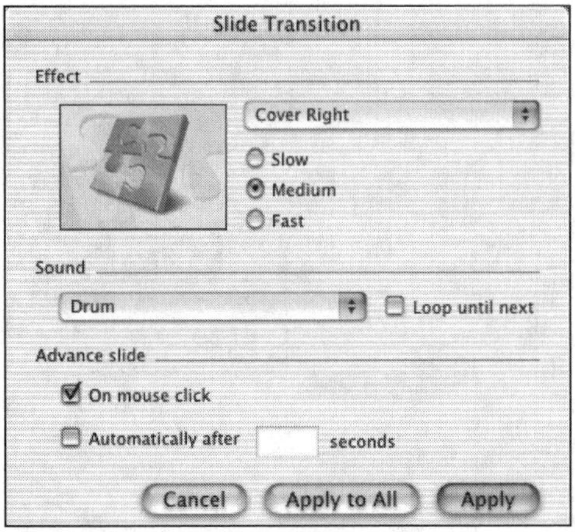

Figure 22.9 To set the options for a PowerPoint transition, select a transition effect from the Slide Transition dialog box.

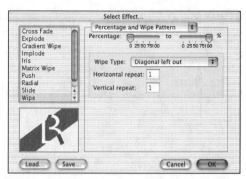

Figure 22.10 Choose QuickTime transition effects in this dialog box.

Figure 22.11 A clickable Transition Effect icon appears beneath any slide that has a transition specified for it.

Transition Effect icon

3. To apply a QuickTime transition, choose QuickTime Transition or Select QuickTime Transition from the Slide Transition Effects pull-down menu. In the Select Effect dialog box (**Figure 22.10**), select a transition, specify options, and click OK.

✔ Tips

■ To apply the same transition to multiple slides, Shift-click to select the slides, and then choose a transition effect.

■ To preview a slide's transition, click the Transition Effect icon beneath any slide in Slide Sorter View (**Figure 22.11**).

■ If you base the presentation on a template, you may find that many slides already have transitions. To remove transitions from selected slides, choose No Transition from the Slide Transition Effects pull-down menu.

■ If you will be saving the presentation as a movie, restrict yourself to QuickTime transitions; they're optimized for QuickTime playback.

Adding Animation Within Slides

Motion within slides is referred to as *animation*. You can add a variety of animation effects to slides to grab your audience's attention.

To add text animation:

1. In Slide Sorter View, click the slide to which you want to add text animation.

2. Choose Slide Show > Animations, and select an effect from the submenu (**Figure 22.12**).

✔ Tips

- To use the same text animation for multiple slides, [Shift]-click the slides to select them, and then choose an effect.

- In Slide Sorter View, a slide that contains an animation has a bulleted text icon beneath it (**Figure 22.13**). To preview the effect, click the icon or choose Slide Show > Animation Preview.

- You can also animate graphics. To do so, switch to Slide, Normal, or Outline View, select the graphic, and then choose an animation from the Slide Show > Animations submenu.

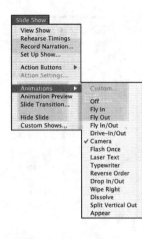

Figure 22.12 Select an animation effect from the Animations submenu.

Figure 22.13 A clickable Animation icon appears beneath any slide that has an animation specified for it.

Animation icon

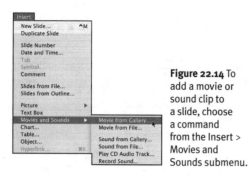

Figure 22.14 To add a movie or sound clip to a slide, choose a command from the Insert > Movies and Sounds submenu.

Movie frame   *Sound icon*

Figure 22.15 The movie frame or sound icon appears on the slide.

Start options

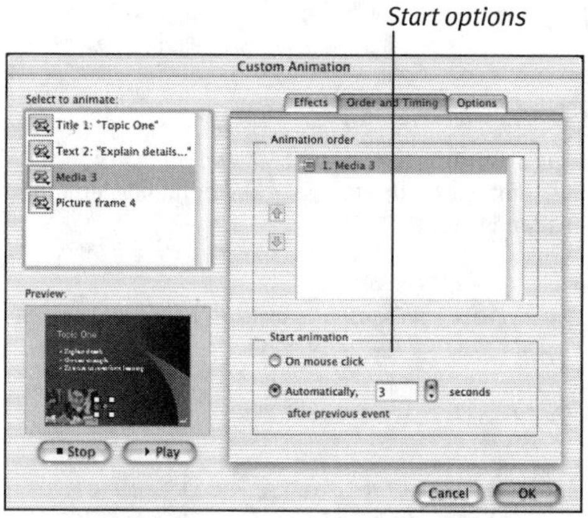

Figure 22.16 On the Order and Timing tab of the Custom Animation dialog box, you can specify when a movie or sound clip will play.

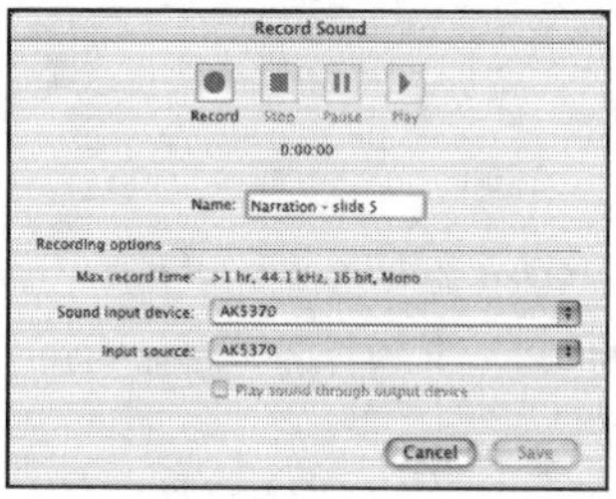

Figure 22.17 You can record your own audio clips or narration in the Record Sound dialog box.

Adding Sound and Movies

To enliven a presentation, you can add sound and movies to selected slides.

To add sound or a movie:

1. In Normal, Slide, or Outline View, select the slide to which you would like to add a movie or sound clip.

2. Choose a command from the Insert > Movies and Sounds submenu (**Figure 22.14**).

3. If you choose Movie from Gallery or Sound from Gallery, the appropriate Clip Gallery window opens.

   or

   If you choose Movie from File or Sound from File, the Insert Movie or Insert Sound dialog box appears.

4. Select the movie or sound clip you want to add to the slide.

5. Click the Insert or Choose button.

   A movie frame or sound icon appears on the slide (**Figure 22.15**).

✔ Tips

■ You can determine when a movie or sound clip starts playing. Select the item on the slide, and then choose Slide Show > Animations > Custom. In the Custom Animation dialog box (**Figure 22.16**), you can specify whether the clip plays as soon as the slide opens, so many seconds after the previous event, or on a mouse click.

■ Another way you can add sound to a presentation is by specifying between-slide transitions and within-slide animations.

■ You can also create your own sound clips. Choose Insert > Movies and Sounds > Record Sound (**Figure 22.17**). To record slide narration in the same manner, choose Slide Show > Record Narration.

Creating Handouts and Speaker Notes

From within PowerPoint, you can prepare *handouts* (printouts of the slides to give to the audience) or notes to assist you during the presentation.

To create handouts:

1. Choose View > Master > Handout Master. The Handout Master appears (**Figure 22.18**).

2. Click one of the icons on the Handout Master toolbar to indicate the number of slides you want displayed per page.

3. *Optional:* Edit the header or footer text.

4. Click the Close icon on the toolbar.

5. Choose File > Print.

6. In the Print dialog box, choose Microsoft PowerPoint from the pop-up menu (**Figure 22.19**).

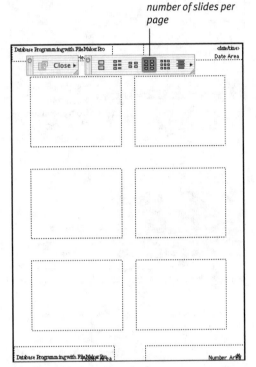

Click to specify the number of slides per page

Figure 22.18 On the Handout Master, you can specify the number of slides per page and optionally edit the header and footer.

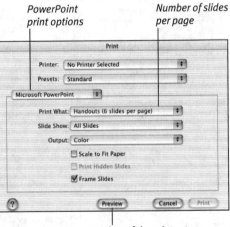

PowerPoint print options

Number of slides per page

Generate a preview of the printout

Figure 22.19 To print handouts, specify the appropriate options in the Print dialog box.

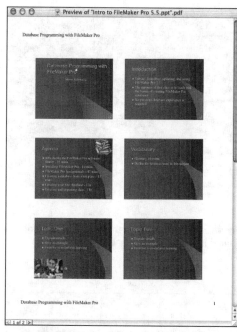

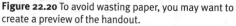

Figure 22.20 To avoid wasting paper, you may want to create a preview of the handout.

Notes area

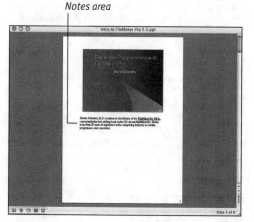

Figure 22.21 If they are present, notes appear beneath each slide when you're in Notes Page View.

7. Choose Handout (*x* slides per page) from the Print What pop-up menu. Review the remaining settings.

8. Click Print to print the handouts, or click Preview to create an Adobe Acrobat file that you can view in Apple's Preview program (**Figure 22.20**).

To create speaker notes:

◆ Choose View > Notes Page. Click the notes placeholder to type speaker notes for a particular slide (**Figure 22.21**).

or

Switch to Normal View and enter notes in the text window beneath each slide.

✔ Tip

■ Your notes will *not* appear on the slides during the presentation.

Rehearsing a Presentation

It's always a good idea to rehearse your presentation, especially if there's a time limit. When you've finished assembling the presentation, you can rehearse it and time how long each slide must remain onscreen.

To rehearse the presentation:

1. Choose Slide Show > Rehearse Timings. The first slide in the presentation appears. A timer is in the bottom-right corner (**Figure 22.22**).

2. Perform the presentation exactly as you would in front of an audience.

3. Click the mouse, press ⊡, or press ⎵Spacebar⎵ to advance from one action to the next within a slide, as well as to move from slide to slide.

4. At the end of the slide show, a dialog box appears, showing the total time the presentation took (**Figure 22.23**). Click Yes or No to indicate whether you want to record the time for each slide (for later use in playing the slide show on automatic).

5. If you click Yes, a second dialog box appears (**Figure 22.24**). Click Yes again if you'd like to switch to Slide Sorter View and review the slide timings.

✔ Tips

- You can immediately stop a rehearsal or slide show by pressing ⎵Esc⎵.

- You can also halt a show by moving the cursor to the lower-left corner of the screen, clicking the icons that appear, and choosing End Show from the pop-up menu (**Figure 22.25**). There are other useful options in the menu, including a pen cursor you can use to write or draw onscreen during the presentation.

Timer

Figure 22.22 When you're rehearsing a presentation, a timer is displayed in the bottom-right corner of the slide.

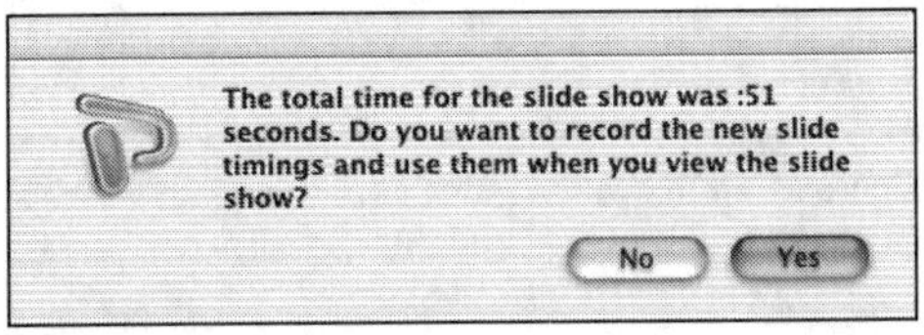

The total time for the slide show was :51 seconds. Do you want to record the new slide timings and use them when you view the slide show?

No   Yes

Figure 22.23 Choose whether to record the presentation time for use in future viewings of the slide show.

Do you want to review timings in slide sorter view?

No   Yes

Figure 22.24 You can switch to Slide Sorter View to review the individual slide timings.

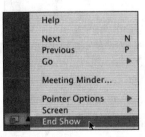

Figure 22.25 This pop-up menu of useful presentation options is available in the bottom-left corner of every slide.

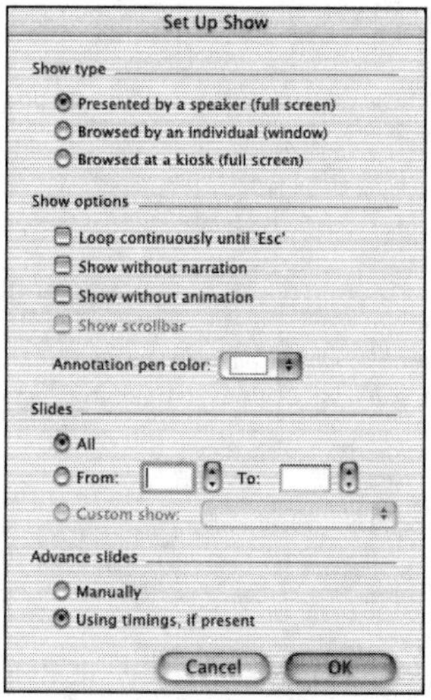

Figure 22.26 In the Set Up Show dialog box, you can set play options for your slide show.

Running a Slide Show

You can view your show at any time to get an idea of how it will look to an audience. Before finalizing it, however, you should consider the available play options. For example, you can opt to control when slides change or to let the show run automatically.

To set options for a slide show:

1. Choose Slide Show > Set Up Show.

   The Set Up Show dialog box appears (**Figure 22.26**).

2. Specify the type of show, the display options, which slides will be shown, and the method used to advance slides.

   This is where you can elect to advance each slide manually by clicking the mouse. Or you can display each slide for a specific amount of time before advancing to the next one (using the timings you set in the rehearsal).

3. Click OK.

To view the slide show:

◆ To view the show from the beginning, choose Slide Show > View Show or View > Slide Show.

   or

   To view the slide show but start with some slide other than the first one, switch to Slide Sorter View. Click the first slide to view, and then click the Slide Show View icon in the bottom-left corner of the window.

✔ Tip

■ Windows users who don't own Power-Point can use PowerPoint Viewer 97 (available for download from Microsoft's Web site, www.microsoft.com) to view presentations.

Publishing a Presentation on the Web

One way to share your presentation with a large audience is to publish it in HTML (HyperText Markup Language) format, enabling it to be viewed with any current Web browser, such as Internet Explorer or Netscape Navigator.

To create a presentation for the Web:

1. Choose File > Save As Web Page.

   A Save As dialog box appears (**Figure 22.27**).

2. Select a folder in which to save the presentation, and name the resulting file.

3. Click the Web Options button.

   The Web Options dialog box appears (**Figure 22.28**).

4. On the General tab, type a title for the Web page. (This title will appear in the upper-left corner of the browser window.) You may also wish to enter a series of keywords for the page, enabling Internet search engines to index and find it.

5. Click the Appearance tab and choose settings from the pull-down menus (**Figure 22.29**).

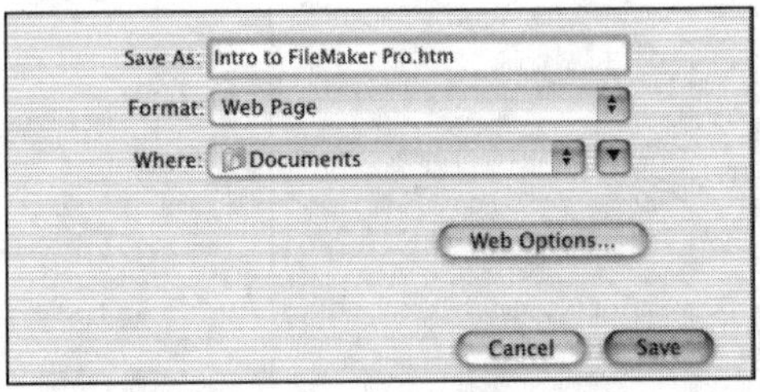

Figure 22.27 When you're saving a presentation for display on the Web, you'll set options in this Save As dialog box.

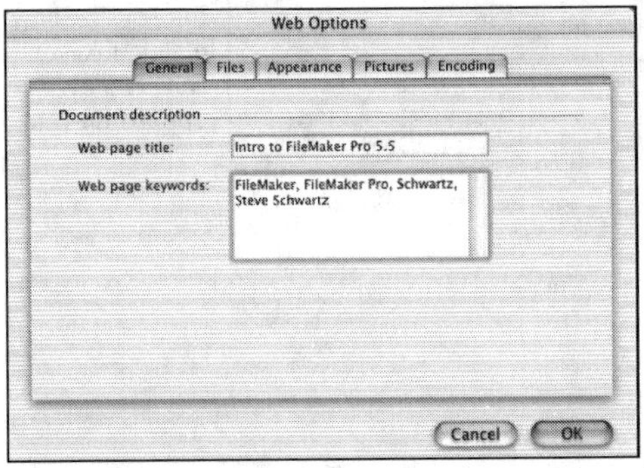

Figure 22.28 Enter a title for your Web presentation on the General tab of the Web Options dialog box.

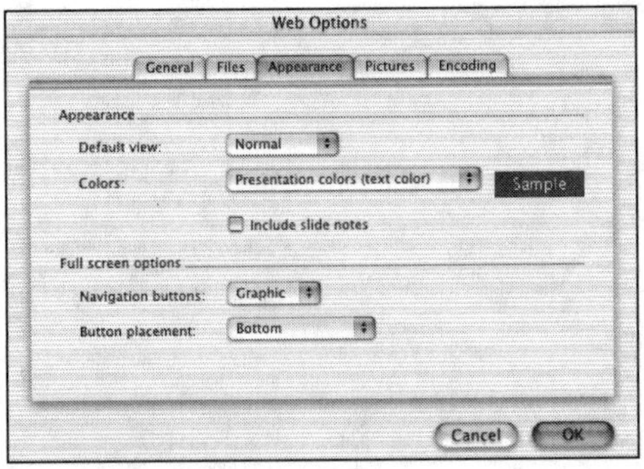

Figure 22.29 Set Appearance options, such as the color of text, the style of navigation buttons, and whether your notes will be displayed.

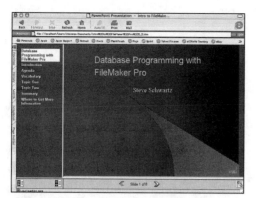

Figure 22.30 The presentation can be viewed and navigated in any current Web browser.

6. On the Pictures tab, choose a target monitor size.

7. When you are done changing settings, click OK to close the Web Options dialog box.

    The Save As dialog box reappears.

8. Click Save.

    The presentation is saved as an HTML file (with the extension .htm), along with a folder containing the graphics and additional pages.

9. Navigate to the location where you saved the .htm file, and double-click it to view the presentation in your browser (**Figure 22.30**).

✔ Tips

■ As you can see, you can view a Web-based presentation directly from your hard disk. This means if you want *others* to view it, all you have to do is send them the .htm file and the accompanying folder.

■ Of course, the *real* destination of a Web presentation is typically the Internet or a company intranet. For instructions on publishing your presentation to the Web or to an intranet, ask your Internet Service Provider or your network administrator, respectively.

Part V: Microsoft Entourage

EMAIL

Since electronic mail first became available, it has been the centerpiece of most people's Internet use. Entourage is the program in Microsoft Office v. X that handles it. Using Entourage, you can send and receive messages to and from anyone else who has an email address, attach files to outgoing messages, organize incoming and outgoing mail, and link email to other items.

In addition to email, Entourage lets you manage your contacts (Chapter 24), schedule (Chapter 25), to-do list (Chapter 26), notes (Chapter 27), and newsgroups (Chapter 28).

Setting Up Your Account

In order to use email, you need an account with an Internet Service Provider (ISP). If your account is with America Online (or any other proprietary service), you won't be able to use Entourage for email. The literature you got with your ISP account or the ISP's tech-support staff can tell you whether the service uses Post Office Protocol (POP) or Internet Message Access Protocol (IMAP) for email. These are the "languages" Entourage speaks.

When you first run Entourage, the Assistant pops up to ask if you want Entourage as your default email program. If you choose it as the default, anytime you do something that requires an email program (such as clicking an email link in a Web site), Entourage opens.

To set up your account:

1. Choose Tools > Accounts (**Figure 23.1**).

2. In the Accounts dialog box (**Figure 23.2**), click New.

3. In the first screen of the Account Setup Assistant (**Figure 23.3**), enter your name as you would like it to appear. Click the right-arrow icon to continue.

Figure 23.1 Choose Tools > Accounts.

Figure 23.2 Click New to add an account.

Figure 23.3 Enter your name.

Figure 23.4 Enter your email address or sign up for a Hotmail account.

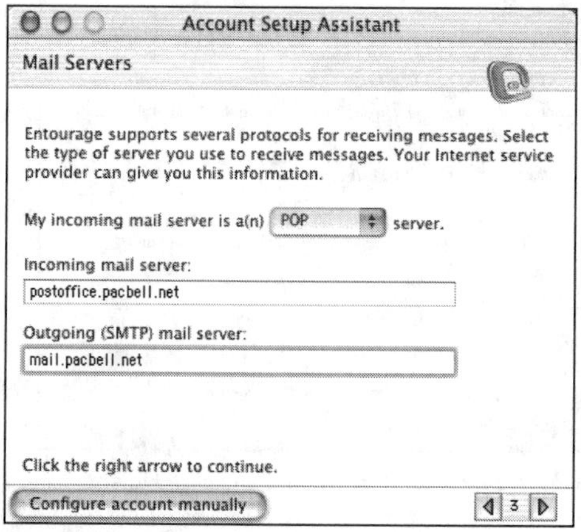

Figure 23.5 Select the type of server and enter the server names.

4. In the second screen (**Figure 23.4**), enter your email address or, if you prefer, click the second button to sign up for a Hotmail account. Hotmail is a free, Web-based email service that Microsoft provides. Click the right-arrow icon to continue.

   If you choose to set up a Hotmail account, the next screen of the Assistant offers a Hotmail sign-up button. Click it to open your Web browser and go to the Hotmail home page. Click the New user? Sign up now! link and fill out the forms. When you're done, return to Entourage.

5. In the third screen (**Figure 23.5**), specify which protocol your ISP uses (POP or IMAP; if you're not sure, it's probably POP), and enter the names of the incoming and outgoing email servers your ISP provides. Click the right-arrow icon to continue.

   (continues on next page)

6. In the fourth screen (**Figure 23.6**), enter your ISP account name (typically the part of your email address to the left of the @) and your password, and choose whether you want your password saved. If you do not choose to save your password, the system will prompt you for it every time you connect to your ISP's email server. Click the right-arrow icon to continue.

7. In the final screen (**Figure 23.7**), enter a name for this account, and click Finish.

8. The account appears in the list (**Figure 23.8**). From here you can edit or delete it. If you have more than one account defined, make one of them the default account.

9. Close the Accounts window.

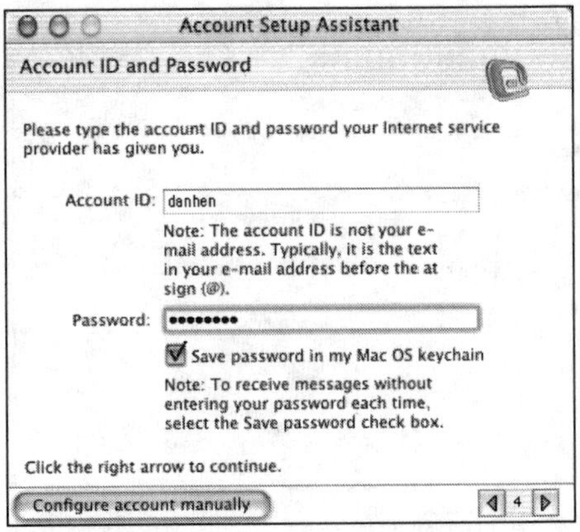

Figure 23.6 Enter your account ID and password.

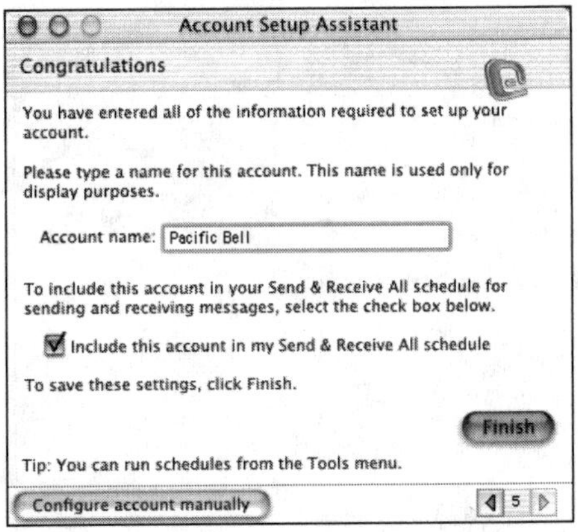

Figure 23.7 Name the account and click Finish.

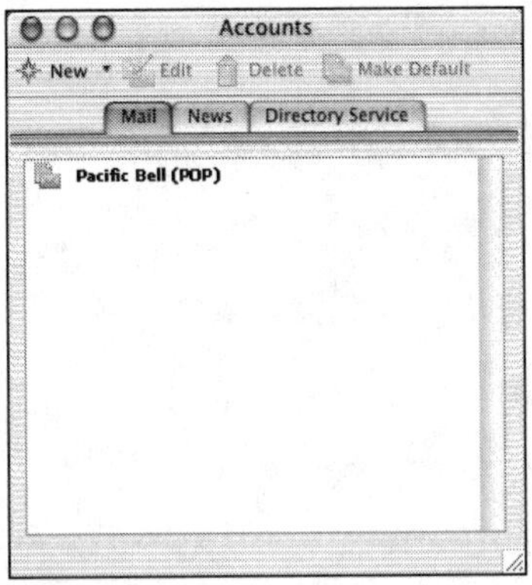

Figure 23.8 The account appears in the Accounts list.

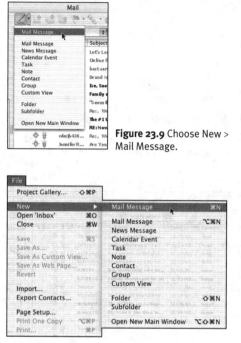

Figure 23.9 Choose New > Mail Message.

Figure 23.10 Choose File > New > Mail Message.

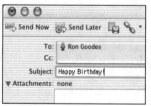

Figure 23.11 Enter the address(es) of your recipient(s).

Figure 23.12 Enter the subject of the message.

Sending Mail and Files

One of the most basic functions of email is sending messages. You can send text messages with attached files, which your recipients can download to their computers.

To send email:

1. Click the Mail button in the upper-left corner of the main window, and then click the New tool in the toolbar. If you click and hold down the New tool, a menu of different kinds of Entourage documents appears, from which you may choose an option (**Figure 23.9**). If you simply click the New tool once, you'll get a new email-message form.

   or

   Choose File > New > Mail Message ($\mathcal{H}$$\boxed{N}$) (**Figure 23.10**).

2. A new email-message form appears with the address window on top (**Figure 23.11**). You can type the email address(es) to which you want to send your message. If the recipients' contact information is in your address book, start typing their names. As you type, Entourage presents a list of possibilities from the address book, based on what you've typed so far, and you can choose from the list.

3. When you finish entering addresses and press Return, the message window appears with the address(es) entered and the pointer poised in the Subject field. Type the subject (**Figure 23.12**).

(continues on next page)

4. Press Return again, and the pointer appears in the body of the message, ready for you to type (**Figure 23.13**).

5. When you've finished typing the message, click one of these buttons at the top left of the message window: Send Now (if you're currently connected to your ISP and want to send the message immediately), Send Later (you can write several email messages, choose Send Later, and connect to your ISP later to send them all at once), or Save as Draft (if you want to edit the message before sending it) (**Figure 23.14**).

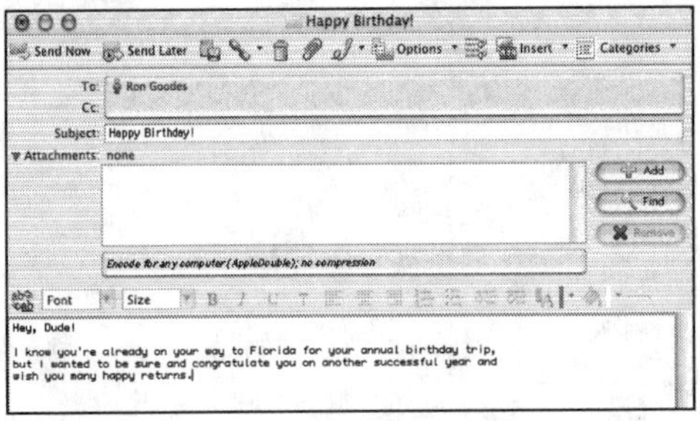

Figure 23.13 Enter the text of your message.

Figure 23.14 Click Save as Draft if you want to edit the message later before sending it.

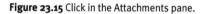

Figure 23.15 Click in the Attachments pane.

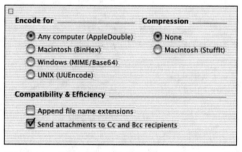

Figure 23.16 Click Add to attach a file if you know where it is, or Find if you want Find File to locate it.

Figure 23.17 Choose the attachment options.

You may want to send a file with your message. It's polite to make sure that your recipient(s) can open and use the file, and that it's free of viruses. You should also make sure the attachment is small enough for the recipient's computer to handle easily. If the recipient has a slow Internet connection, a large attachment will tie up his or her system while it downloads.

To attach a file to an email message:

1. While the message-composition window is open, click in the Attachments pane between the Subject field and the message body (**Figure 23.15**).

2. Click one of the buttons to the right of the Attachments pane (**Figure 23.16**): Add, to bring up the standard Get File dialog box, or Find, to switch to the Finder's file finder.

   or

   Drag the file's icon into the Attachments pane. You can also drag files here from the Finder's Find File results.

3. To remove a file from the list of attachments, click to select it, and click the Remove button.

4. Click the field immediately below the Attachments pane to open the Attachments options dialog box (**Figure 23.17**). Leave the Encode for setting option at Any computer (AppleDouble), unless you're sure the recipient needs another choice. If you choose to compress the files (usually a good idea—it can dramatically reduce send and receive times), make sure the recipient has the StuffIt Expander program to decompress them. It's available free for both Mac and Windows from www.aladdinsys.com.

5. Send the message.

Reading Mail

Entourage gives you several options for reading mail and downloading attached files.

To retrieve waiting mail manually from a POP account:

1. Click the Send & Receive button at the top of the main window (**Figure 23.18**).

   or

   Choose Tools > Send & Receive > Send & Receive All (⌘K) (**Figure 23.19**).

2. You may also send and receive mail from just one account by choosing that account when you click and hold the Send & Receive button, or choosing it from the Tools > Send & Receive submenu.

3. If you haven't set up your account to save your password, enter it when prompted.

4. The waiting mail arrives in your in-box. With Inbox selected in the Folder List, a one-line summary of each incoming message appears in the upper-right (Message List) pane (**Figure 23.20**).

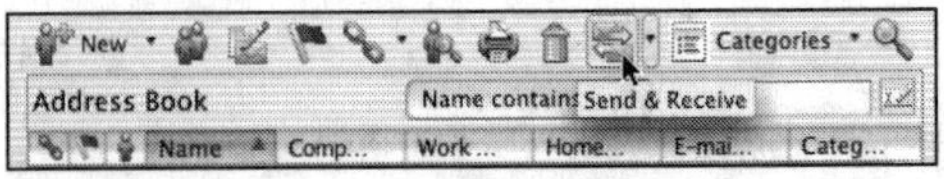

Figure 23.18 Click Send & Receive to retrieve mail.

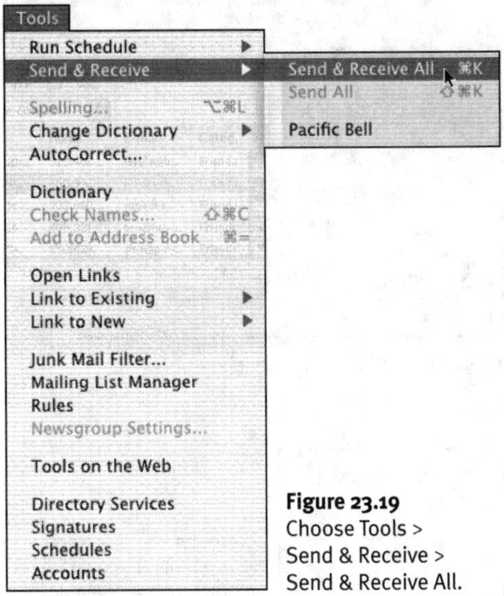

Figure 23.19 Choose Tools > Send & Receive > Send & Receive All.

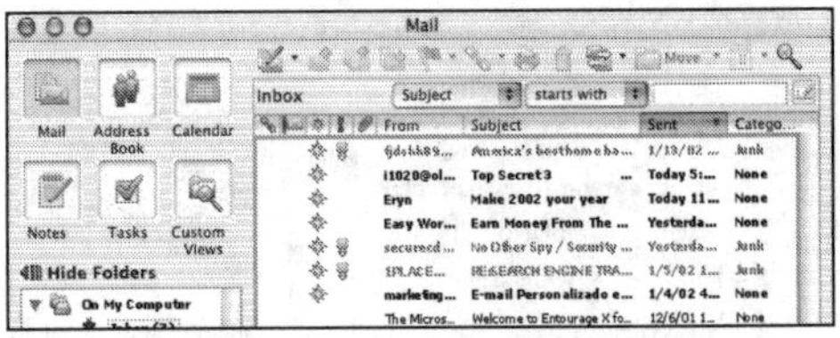

Figure 23.20 The Inbox shows your new messages in bold.

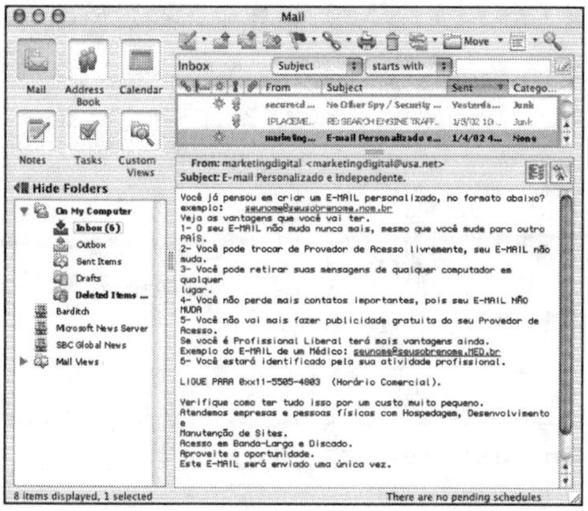

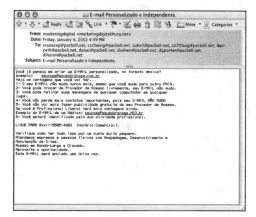

Figure 23.21 Click a message in the Message List to see its contents in the Preview pane.

Figure 23.22 The message opens in a separate window.

To retrieve waiting mail manually from a Hotmail or IMAP account:

1. Click the Hotmail or IMAP account item in the Folder List.

2. Click the triangle next to the item to expand the Folder List.

3. Click the folder containing the messages you want to read.

4. If you haven't set up your account to save the password, enter it when prompted.

5. A one-line summary of each message in the folder appears in the upper-right (Message List) pane of the window.

To read a newly received message:

1. Click a message summary in the Message List, and the message appears below in the Preview pane (**Figure 23.21**). If you don't see the Preview pane, you can show it by choosing View > Preview Pane.

2. Double-click a message summary in the Message List, and the message opens in a new window (**Figure 23.22**), with buttons across the top for the various message-handling options.

To manage attachments to received email:

1. When you click a message in the Message List that contains an attachment, an Attachments pane opens between the Message List and the Preview pane (**Figure 23.23**).

2. Click an attachment and select one of the three buttons on the right, which allow you to open the file, save it to disk, or remove it (**Figure 23.24**). It's a good idea to save attachments to disk and let your virus-protection software scan them before you open them. Be sure to keep your virus definitions up to date.

3. If a message has multiple attachments and you want to either remove them all or save them all to the same place, you can choose Message > Remove All Attachments or Message > Save All Attachments (**Figure 23.25**). If you want to remove some but not all of the attachments, click a single attachment, (Shift)-click to extend the selection to a range of attachments, or (Control)-click to add individual attachments to the selection. When you've selected the attachments you want to remove, click the Remove button to the right of the Attachments window.

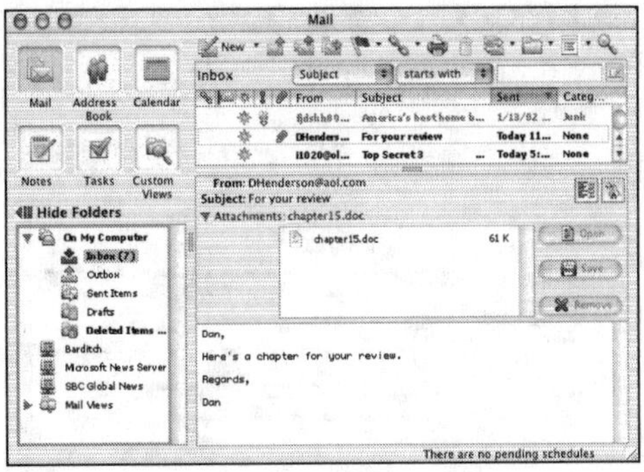

Figure 23.23 The Attachments pane opens.

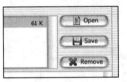

Figure 23.24 Select an attachment and click Open, Save, or Remove.

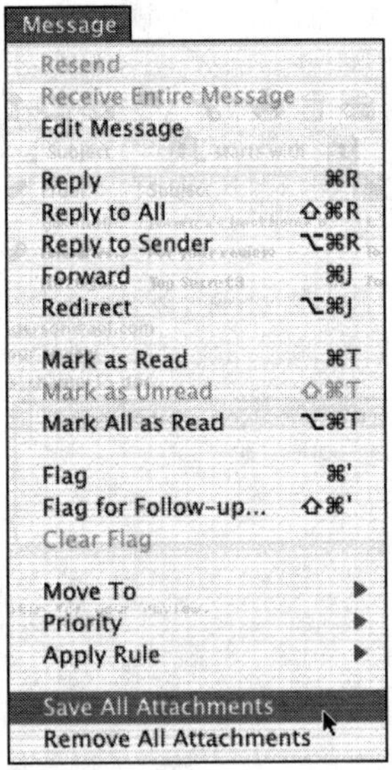

Figure 23.25 Choose Message > Save All Attachments.

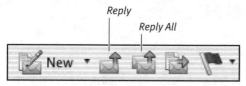

Figure 23.26 Click to reply to the sender or to all recipients (from the main window).

Figure 23.27 Click to reply to the sender or to all recipients (from the message's own window).

Replying to Mail

There are several ways to reply to email you have received. We'll discuss the options and make a recommendation.

To reply to a message:

1. It's polite, especially when replying to someone who gets and sends a lot of email, to quote in your reply only the relevant parts of the message sent to you. By default (you can change the option), the entire original message is quoted, but this is usually too much. Select a subset of the text before replying, and only that subset will be quoted. There's no way to quote discontinuous blocks of text, so just select from the beginning to the end of your quotes, and delete unwanted parts from the reply.

2. If you're replying from the main window with the Message List and Preview pane, click the Reply or Reply All button at the top of the main window (**Figure 23.26**). Reply sends the reply only to the person who sent you the message; Reply All sends it to the message's other recipients as well.

3. If you've opened the message in its own window, the Reply and Reply All buttons also appear at the top of that window (**Figure 23.27**).

(continues on next page)

REPLYING TO MAIL

4. You may also choose Message >
Reply (⌘R) or Message > Reply to
All (⌘Shift R) (**Figure 23.28**). Use
Message > Reply to Sender (⌘Option R)
to reply to a message you received from
a mailing list, unless you are certain
you want everyone on the list to see
your reply.

5. If the original message text you're quoting is difficult to read because of odd line
lengths or lots of previous quoting,
Entourage gives you an easy way to clean
that up. Choose Edit > Auto Text Cleanup
(**Figure 23.29**).

   or

   Hold down (Control), click in the message
   body, choose Auto Text Cleanup from the
   pop-up menu, and choose a submenu
   option.

✔ Tip

■ Text underlined with a red squiggly line
  has been flagged by the spelling checker.
  (Control)-click flagged words to get the
  spelling checker's options, including suggested corrections.

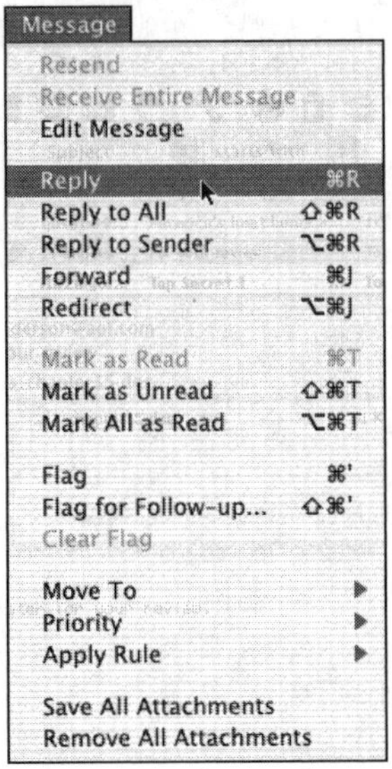

Figure 23.28
Choose Message >
Reply, Reply to All,
or Reply to Sender.

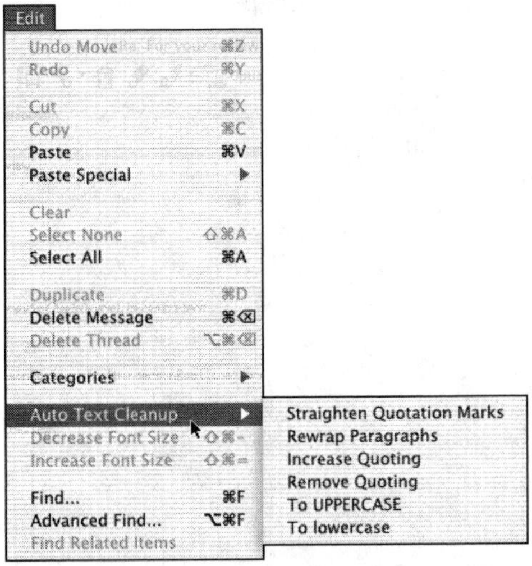

Figure 23.29 Choose Edit > Auto Text Cleanup.

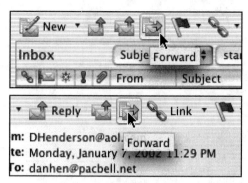

Figure 23.30 Click the Forward button at the top of the main window (top) or the message's own window (bottom).

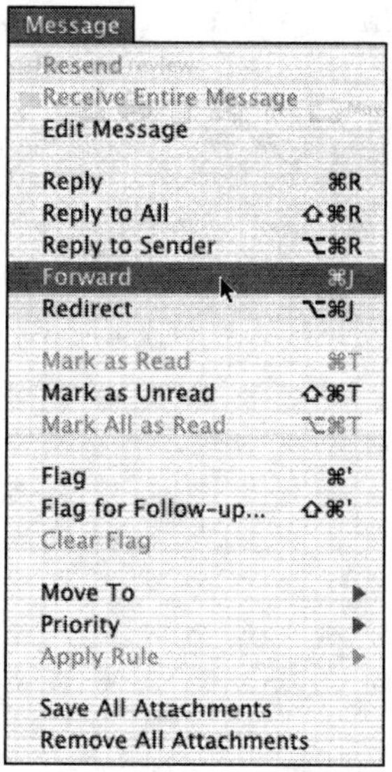

Message
Resend
Receive Entire Message
Edit Message

Reply   ⌘R
Reply to All   ⇧⌘R
Reply to Sender ⌥⌘R
Forward   ⌘J
Redirect   ⌥⌘J

Mark as Read   ⌘T
Mark as Unread ⇧⌘T
Mark All as Read ⌥⌘T

Flag   ⌘'
Flag for Follow-up... ⇧⌘'
Clear Flag

Move To   ▶
Priority   ▶
Apply Rule   ▶

Save All Attachments
Remove All Attachments

Figure 23.31
Choose Message >
Forward.

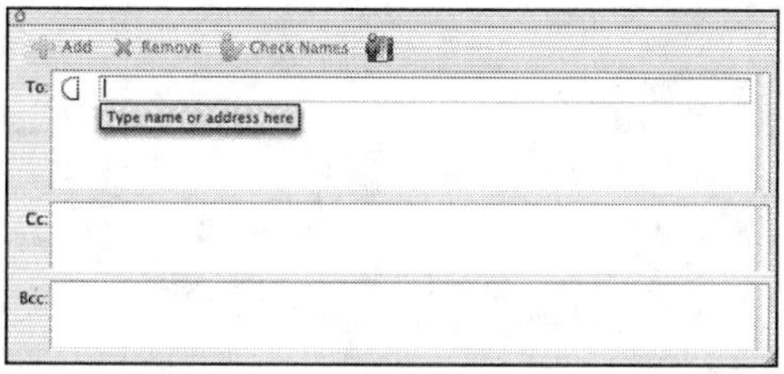

Figure 23.32 Enter the address(es) of the recipient(s).

Forwarding and Redirecting Mail

If you receive mail that you want to send to others, you can choose to either forward or redirect it. When you forward mail, you can add your own comments, and the recipients see a message that came from you; any replies go to you. If you redirect it, on the other hand, you cannot alter or add to it, and the message appears to have come from the original sender; any replies go to that sender.

To forward mail:

1. With the message selected in the Message List or opened in its own window, click the Forward button at the top of the window (**Figure 23.30**).

   or

   Choose Message > Forward (⌘J) (**Figure 23.31**).

2. In the address boxes, enter the address(es) to which you wish to forward the message (**Figure 23.32**), and press Return.

3. The message's subject is selected, and by default it is the original subject preceded by FW. You may change it if you wish. Press Return again.

4. The pointer is placed at the top line of the message body. You can add an introductory note to the message's body or edit it however you wish.

5. You can also add attachments to forwarded mail.

6. Send it just as you would send original mail.

To redirect mail:

1. With the message selected in the Message List or opened in its own window, choose Message > Redirect (⌘ Option J) (**Figure 23.33**).

2. In the address window that appears (**Figure 23.34**), enter the addresses to which you wish to redirect the email.

3. With redirected mail you may not edit the subject or message body, or add attachments.

4. Send the message just as you would send original mail.

Figure 23.33
Choose Message >
Redirect.

Figure 23.34 Enter the address(es) of the recipient(s).

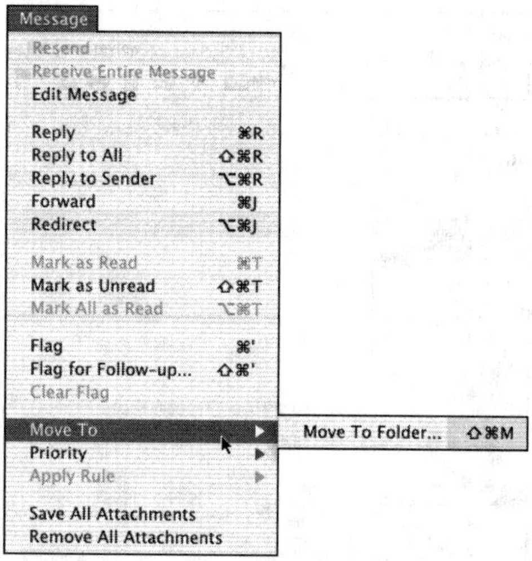

Figure 23.35 Choose Message > Move To > Move To Folder.

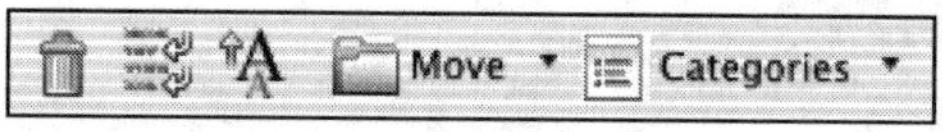

Figure 23.36 Click the Move button.

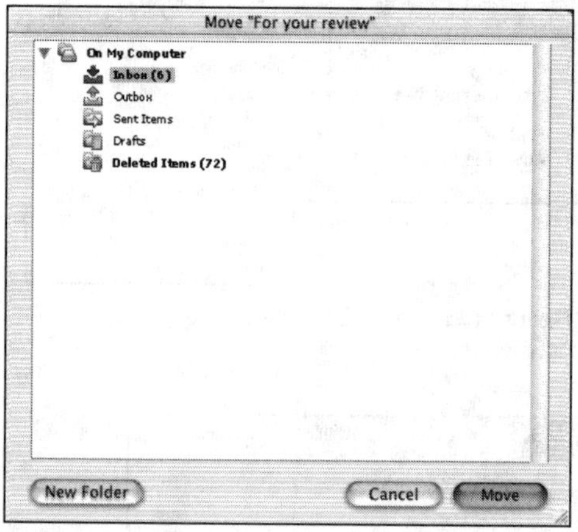

Figure 23.37 Click New Folder to add a new folder.

Figure 23.38 Name the new folder.

Organizing Mail

Once you start getting a significant volume of email, you'll need to organize it. Entourage gives you several tools for the purpose. You can save mail in folders you create (to create a folder, choose File > New > Folder, or press ⌘ Shift N), and then sort and filter the messages you see in the Message Lists into those folders. You can also assign various attributes, such as Categories, by which you can sort or filter messages. Finally, you can define Rules, which take particular actions upon receipt of messages that match your criteria.

To save mail in folders:

1. Drag a message from the Message List to a folder in the Folder List.

   or

   Select one or more messages in the Message List, or open one in its own window.

2. Choose Message > Move To> Move To Folder (⌘ Shift M) (**Figure 23.35**).

   or

   Click the Move button (**Figure 23.36**) at the top of the window.

3. In the dialog box that appears (**Figure 23.37**), create a new folder, or choose to move the message to an existing folder.

4. If you create a new folder (**Figure 23.38**), you have the option to create the folder as a subfolder of the folder selected in the previous dialog box.

To assign categories to messages:

1. To set up your list of available categories, click and hold the Categories button at the top of the window (**Figure 23.39**), and choose Edit Categories (**Figure 23.40**).

   or

   Choose Edit > Categories > Edit Categories (**Figure 23.41**).

2. In the dialog box that appears (**Figure 23.42**), edit the list of categories. You can assign names and associated colors.

3. To assign a category to a message, select the message in the Message List, click and hold the Categories button at the top of the window, and select a category. The list name changes to the category you've chosen.

Figure 23.39 Click and hold down the Categories button.

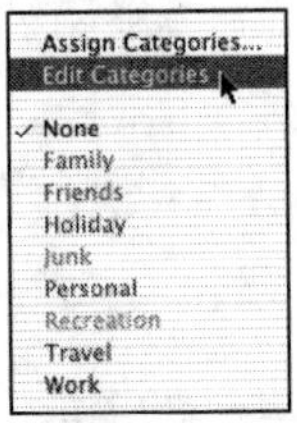

Figure 23.40 Choose Edit Categories from the pop-up menu.

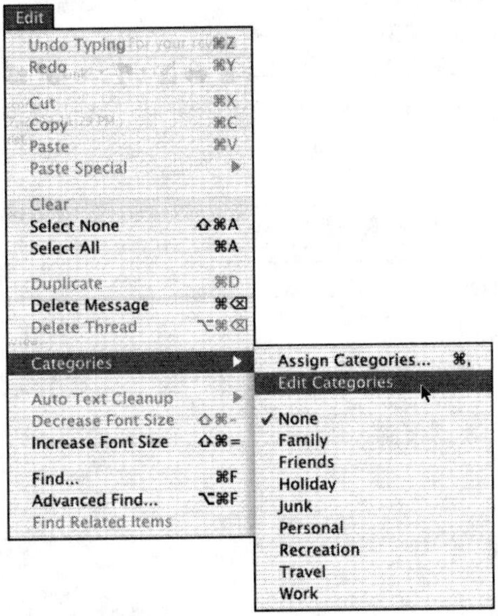

Figure 23.41 Choose Edit > Categories > Edit Categories.

Figure 23.42 Click New to add a category.

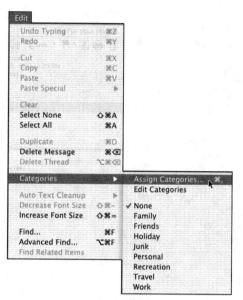

Figure 23.43 Click Edit > Categories > Assign Categories.

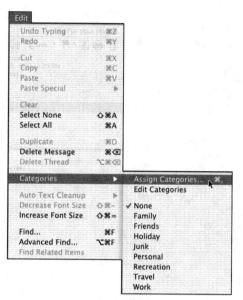

Figure 23.44 Choose the categories to assign, and set one as Primary.

4. To assign multiple categories to a single message, select the message in the Message List, click and hold the Categories button at the top of the window, and choose Assign Categories.

   or

   Choose Edit > Categories > Assign Categories (⌘⎡,⎤) (**Figure 23.43**).

5. In the dialog box that appears (**Figure 23.44**), click the check boxes next to the categories you wish to assign. Although it is possible to assign multiple categories to a single message, there's room to show only one of these categories. This is the message's *primary* category. If you wish to change the primary category for an item, click to select it, and then click the Set Primary button.

✔ Tip

■ If you assign a category to a contact in your Address Book, future email from that contact will have that category as its primary one.

To sort the mail in a folder:

1. Select a folder in the Folder List.

2. Click one of the column headings in the Message List to sort by that column (**Figure 23.45**). To toggle between ascending and descending values, click the column heading again.

Message contains links to other items?

Message completely downloaded? Copy still on server?

Message already read or previewed?

Priority

Message contains attachments?

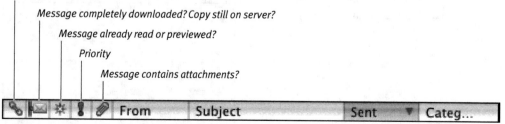

Figure 23.45 Click any column head to sort messages in that column.

To filter the mail in a folder:

1. Select the folder in the Folder List.

2. In the bar between the toolbar and the column heads (**Figure 23.46**), use the pull-down menus to choose the filtering field (the left menu) and whether to match the beginning of the field or a substring of it (the right menu, which offers the options Starts With and Contains). In the text box, type the filter value. The button on the far right clears the filter.

3. Press [Return], and all the messages in the Message List that do not match the filter criterion are hidden.

To use Rules for processing mail:

1. Choose Tools > Rules (**Figure 23.47**). The Rules dialog box appears (**Figure 23.48**).

2. Choose the appropriate tab for the mail type to which you want the rule to apply, and click New. The Edit Rule dialog box appears (**Figure 23.49**).

3. Give the rule a name, specify the criteria that trigger the rule, and choose the actions to take.

4. Click OK.

✔ Tip

■ Use the buttons in the Edit Rule dialog box to edit or delete rules, or to move them up or down in the processing order.

Figure 23.46 Specify Filter settings.

Figure 23.47 Choose Tools > Rules.

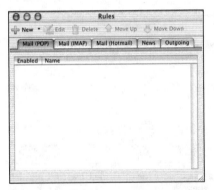

Figure 23.48 Click New to create a new rule.

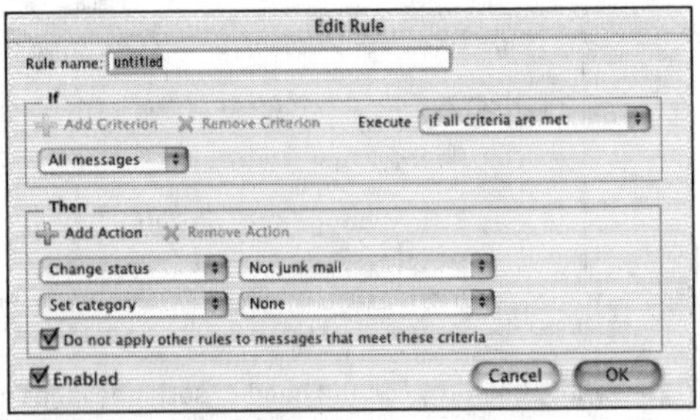

Figure 23.49 Name the rule; specify criteria and actions.

ORGANIZING MAIL

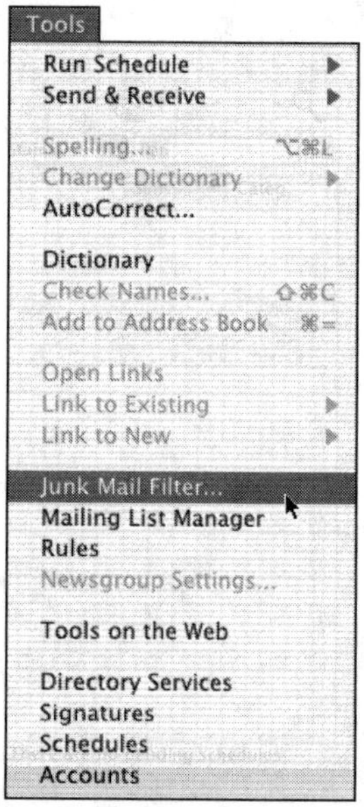

Tools

Run Schedule ▶
Send & Receive ▶

Spelling... ⌥⌘L
Change Dictionary ▶
AutoCorrect...

Dictionary
Check Names... ⇧⌘C
Add to Address Book ⌘=

Open Links
Link to Existing ▶
Link to New ▶

Junk Mail Filter...
Mailing List Manager
Rules
Newsgroup Settings...

Tools on the Web

Directory Services
Signatures
Schedules
Accounts

Figure 23.50
Choose Tools >
Junk Mail Filter.

Dealing with Junk Mail

Anyone who has an email account will get junk mail, and it will increase in volume as you send messages to corporations, newsgroups, and mailing lists and through Web sites. Entourage provides a special case of its Rules capability to help you deal with junk mail.

To filter junk mail:

1. Choose Tools > Junk Mail Filter (**Figure 23.50**).

2. In the dialog box that appears (**Figure 23.51**), check the box next to Enable Junk Mail Filter if it isn't already checked. Use the slider to set the sensitivity of the filter lower (it marks fewer messages as junk) or higher (it marks more messages as junk). The formula Entourage uses to identify junk mail is complex; adjust the sensitivity by trial and error if you notice too many or too few messages getting marked as junk.

3. When the Junk Mail Filter is enabled, it assigns the Junk Mail category to any message it deems to be junk mail. In the Junk Mail Filter dialog box, you can also choose to mark junk mail as read, or to run an AppleScript to do anything else you like with junk mail. You may also choose Tools > Rules and set up any actions you like for junk mail.

(continues on next page)

Junk Mail Filter

☑ Enable Junk Mail Filter

Sensitivity

Drag left to classify fewer messages as junk, or drag right to classify more messages as junk. To ensure that messages from someone are not classified as junk, add the sender to your Address Book.

Low   Average   High

Do not apply to messages from these domains

Type the domain, the part of an e-mail address that follows "@". For example, type "CompanyName.com" to prevent applying the Junk Mail Filter to messages from that company. Type a comma between domains.

Perform additional actions on junk mail

☐ Mark as read

☐ Run AppleScript: <none selected>   Select...

Cancel   OK

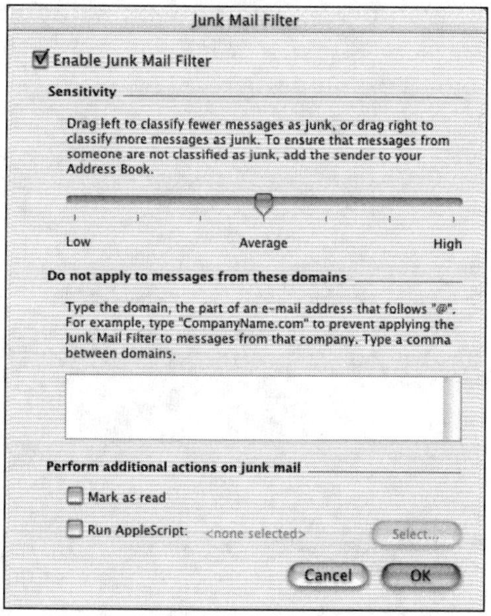

Figure 23.51 In this dialog box you can enable the Junk Mail Filter, specify its sensitivity, and take other actions.

4. In the Junk Mail Filter dialog box, you can enter a list of *domains* (the part of an email address after the @ sign) never to classify as junk mail. If you don't want Entourage to classify mail from certain individuals as junk, enter them as contacts in your address book; Entourage never classifies as junk mail from anyone in your address book.

5. Don't simply delete all messages that wind up in the Junk Mail category; Entourage's filter isn't perfect, and you may lose messages you wanted to keep. You can usually tell what's really junk in the Message List by the sender or subject; if in doubt, read the message.

6. When you're satisfied that all the messages in your Inbox that carry the Junk Mail category are really junk, you can filter on that category, choose Edit > Select All (⌘A), and drag all the Junk messages from the Message List to Deleted Items, to some other folder, or to the Trash on the desktop.

Run Schedule ▶
Send & Receive ▶

Spelling... ⌥⌘L
Change Dictionary ▶
AutoCorrect...

Dictionary
Check Names... ⇧⌘C
Add to Address Book ⌘=

Open Links
Link to Existing ▶
Link to New ▶

Junk Mail Filter...
Mailing List Manager
Rules
Newsgroup Settings...

Tools on the Web

Directory Services
Signatures
Schedules
Accounts

Figure 23.52 Choose Tools > Mailing List Manager.

Mailing List Manager

＋ New ✎ Edit 🗑 Delete

Enabled	Name

Figure 23.53 Click New to specify settings for a mailing list.

Edit Mailing List Rule

Name: Untitled

Mailing List | Advanced

List address:

☑ Move messages to folder: Inbox
☐ Also move messages that I send to the list to this folder
☐ Set category: None

Notes:

Cancel | OK

Figure 23.54 Specify the list address and actions to take on mailing-list messages.

Managing Mailing Lists

It's common to subscribe to mailing lists designed to connect people with common interests. When you're a member of a mailing list, you get a copy of all messages sent to that list, and when you post a message (if the moderator allows posting), everyone who subscribes will get a copy of your message. Entourage gives you a special case of its Rules function to handle mailing-list messages.

To manage mailing-list subscriptions:

1. Choose Tools > Mailing List Manager (**Figure 23.52**).

2. In the dialog box that appears (**Figure 23.53**), add a rule for each mailing list to which you belong.

3. In the Edit Mailing List Rule dialog box (**Figure 23.54**), specify the list address and desired disposition of messages from and to each list. Make sure the box next to Enabled in the Mailing List Manager is checked, and click OK.

Address Book

The Office Address Book is the repository of your contact information for people, companies, and organizations. In addition to the standard information normally stored in an address book (such as names, home and work addresses, phone numbers, and email addresses), any Address Book record can also store a birth date, picture, anniversary date, spouse's name, children's names, and notes. You can even define custom fields if you feel that an important bit of information is missing.

✔ Tips

- Like Office 2001, Office X supports multiple users (referred to as *identities*). In addition to having separate email, each user who shares a copy of Office on a single Macintosh also has a separate Address Book. To learn how to switch from one user to another, see the tip at the end of "Email" in Chapter 2, Office v. X and the Internet.

- While you will probably create and edit most of your contact records from within Entourage, the contact information is also available to you from Word's Contact toolbar. Using the toolbar, you can create new records, insert contact data into your documents (to address letters, for example), and perform mail merges. For additional information, see "Using the Contact Toolbar" and "Using the Data Merge Manager" in Chapter 8, Creating Newsletters, Labels, and More.

Adding Contacts

You may have been using a different program to manage your address book until now. Entourage can help you import that information from several of the most popular programs, as well as from a text file. And you can add contact records manually or create them from received email messages, too.

Importing an address book

There's nothing more painful than having to re-create an address book simply because you've changed programs or upgraded to a new version. Happily, Entourage can import contact data from many programs.

To import an existing address book:

1. Choose File > Import.

   The Import wizard appears, displaying the Begin Import screen (**Figure 24.1**).

2. Select the Import information from a program option, and then click the right-arrow icon to continue.

   The Choose a Program screen appears (**Figure 24.2**).

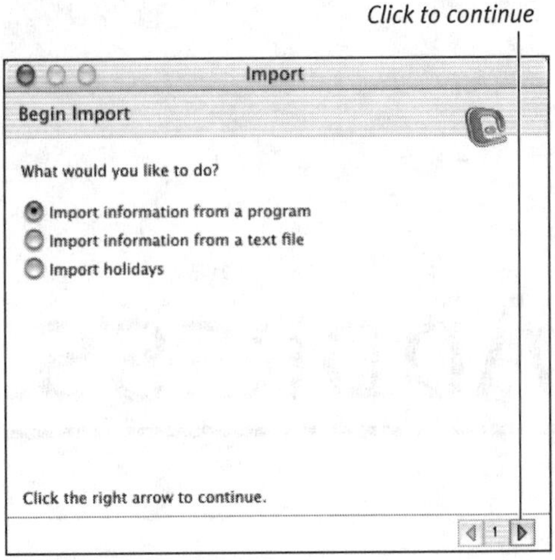

Click to continue

Figure 24.1 In the Import wizard's first screen, select Import information from a program and click the right arrow.

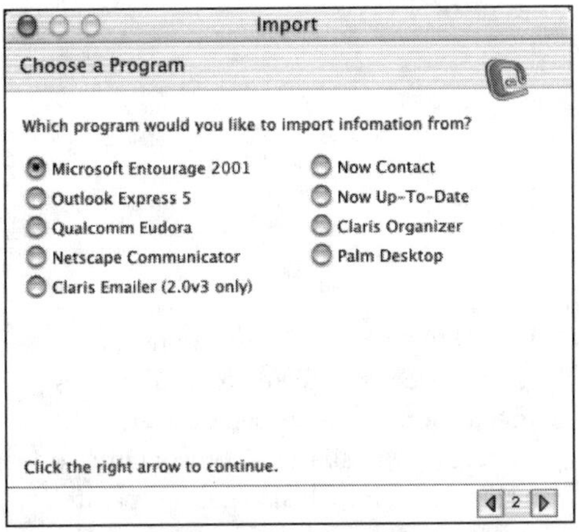

Figure 24.2 Select the program in which your address data is currently stored.

Figure 24.3 Select Contacts and any other data you wish to import. (The choices vary from program to program.)

3. If your address data is stored in one of the listed programs, select the program and click the right arrow to continue.

   The Ready to Import screen appears (**Figure 24.3**).

4. From the list of options, make sure Contacts is checked—this represents your address data. Depending on the program selected, you may also be able to import other Entourage-compatible data, such as calendar events. After making your selections, click the right arrow and follow the remaining instructions.

✔ Tip

■ If your current address book program *isn't* listed in step 3, open the program and export its data as a tab- or comma-delimited text file, if possible. Then return to the Import wizard, select Import information from a text file, and select Import contacts from a tab- or comma-delimited text file.

Creating contact records from email messages

You can extract email addresses from received messages and use them as the basis for new contact records.

To create a contact record from a received email message:

1. Do one of the following:

   ◆ Select the message header in the message list, and choose Tools > Add to Address Book or press ⌘=.

   ◆ Control-click the message header in the message list, and choose Add Sender To Address Book from the pop-up menu that appears (**Figure 24.4**).

   ◆ Select the message header in the message list, and Control-click any email address in the header section of the message above the Preview pane. Choose Add to Address Book from the pop-up menu that appears (**Figure 24.5**). (This also allows you to select other recipients, not just the sender.)

   The contact record for the new address-book entry appears (**Figure 24.6**).

2. Fill in as much additional contact information for the person, company, or organization as you like. Click the tabs to move from section to section of the record. If you make additions or changes, click the Save toolbar icon when you are finished.

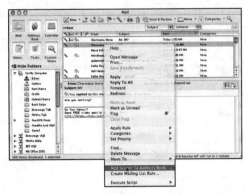

Figure 24.4 You can Control-click a message header in the message list and choose Add Sender To Address Book.

Figure 24.5 You can also Control-click an email address above the Preview Pane and choose Add to Address Book from the pop-up menu.

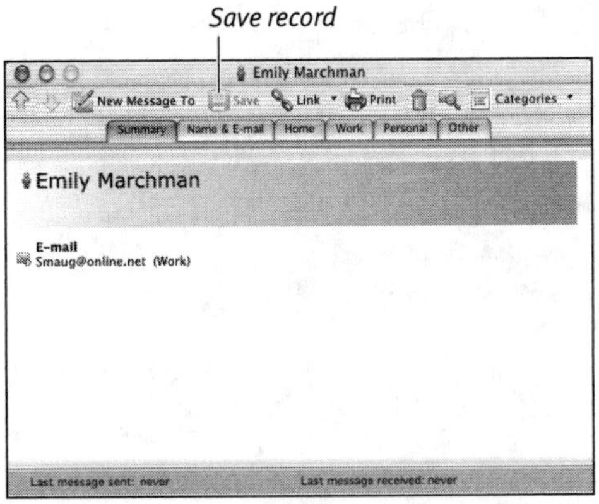

Figure 24.6 Complete the rest of the information for the contact, and then save the record.

Click here to view menu

Figure 24.7 You can create a new contact record by clicking the down arrow beside the New icon and choosing Contact.

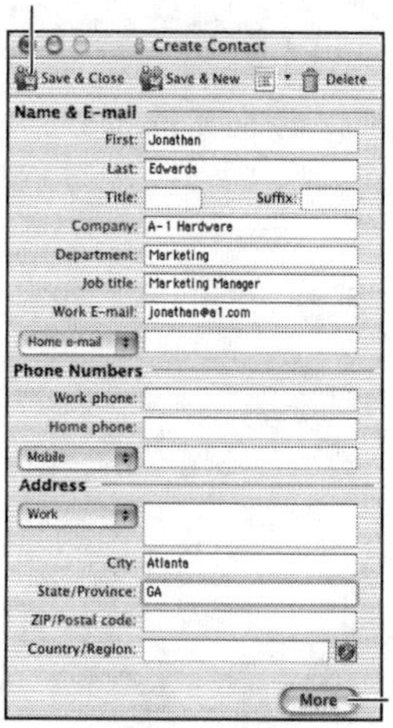

Save record

View additional fields

Figure 24.8 Enter the basic contact information in the Create Contact dialog box.

Save record

Figure 24.9 Clicking the More button in the Create Contact dialog box displays the full record, enabling you to enter additional information.

Manually creating new records

You can manually create new contact records as needed.

To create a contact record manually:

1. If the Address Book window is currently displayed, click the New toolbar icon or press ⌘N.

   or

   Regardless of the part of Entourage that is displayed, you can either choose File > New > Contact or click the down arrow beside the New toolbar icon and choose Contact (**Figure 24.7**).

   The Create Contact dialog box appears.

2. Enter the basic information for the contact (**Figure 24.8**).

3. If you are done entering information, click the Save & Close icon (or click Save & New if you wish to create more records).

   or

   If you want to enter more detailed information, click the More button. The full record for the individual appears (**Figure 24.9**). Enter any other information you like, clicking tabs to view other sections of the record. When you are finished, click the Save toolbar icon.

Deleting Contacts

There are several ways to delete contacts from your Address Book.

To delete contacts:

1. Switch to the Address Book by clicking the Address Book icon in the upper-left corner of the Entourage window.

2. In the address list, select one or more contact records to delete. (You can [Shift]-click to select contiguous records or [⌘]-click to select noncontiguous records.)

3. Click the Delete toolbar icon (**Figure 24.10**), choose Edit > Delete Contact, press [Delete], or press [⌘][Delete].

   A confirmation dialog box appears (**Figure 24.11**).

4. Click Delete to delete the selected contact(s), or click Cancel if you've changed your mind.

✔ Tip

- If a contact record is open in its own window, you can delete it by clicking the Delete toolbar icon, by choosing Edit > Delete Contact, or by pressing [⌘][Delete].

Figure 24.10 Click the Delete toolbar icon to delete the selected record(s).

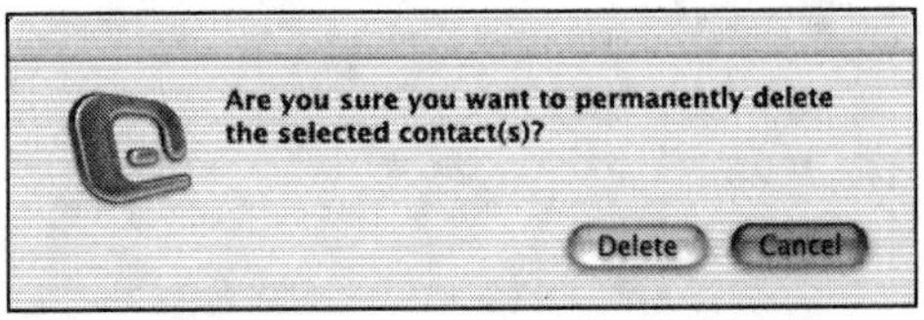

Are you sure you want to permanently delete the selected contact(s)?

Delete   Cancel

Figure 24.11 Record deletions must be confirmed.

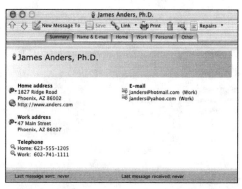

Figure 24.12 Click the various tabs to display and edit the selected person's contact data.

Editing Contact Records

People occasionally move, change jobs, or get new email addresses. You're free to make additions and changes to your contact records.

To edit contact information:

1. Switch to the Address Book.

2. In the address list, double-click the contact you want to edit.

   The person's contact record opens in a separate window (**Figure 24.12**).

3. Click a tab at the top of the window to select the type of information you want to edit, and then make the desired changes.

4. Click other tabs as necessary to make additional changes. When you're through editing, click the Save toolbar icon.

(continues on next page)

✔ Tips

Drag picture file here

■ If you have a Palm or Palm-compatible personal digital assistant (PDA), in the future you will be able to synchronize Entourage data (contacts, calendar events, tasks, and notes) with your PDA. At this writing, however, the required Entourage X conduit does not exist. Check the following Web page for news on the software: www.microsoft.com/Mac/OFFICEX/prodinfo/t_palm.asp.

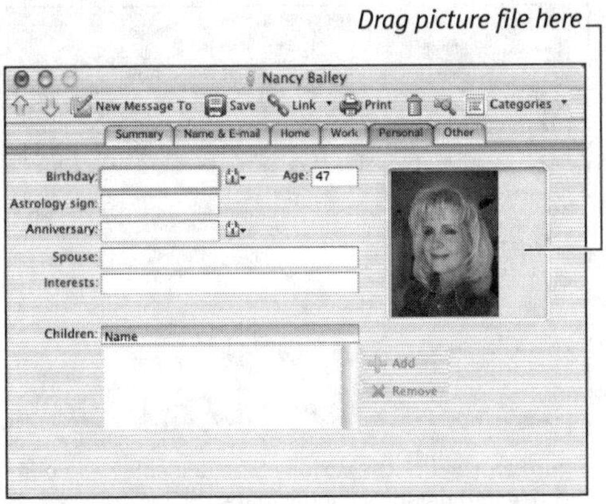

Figure 24.13 You can add a picture of the person by dragging an image file's icon into this area of the contact record.

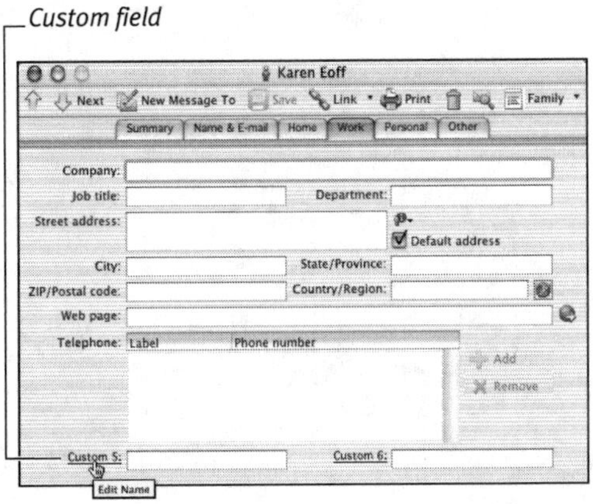

■ To help you better identify people, you can also store a *picture* as part of any contact record. Open the record, click the Personal tab, and drag the file icon for any image file into the gray square (**Figure 24.13**). To remove a picture, drag it to the Trash.

■ Many tabs contain Custom fields. You can rename a Custom field by clicking the underlined Custom label (**Figure 24.14**). Name the field in the Edit Custom Label dialog box (**Figure 24.15**). The new field name is added to all contact records.

Custom field

Figure 24.14 Click a Custom field's label to rename it.

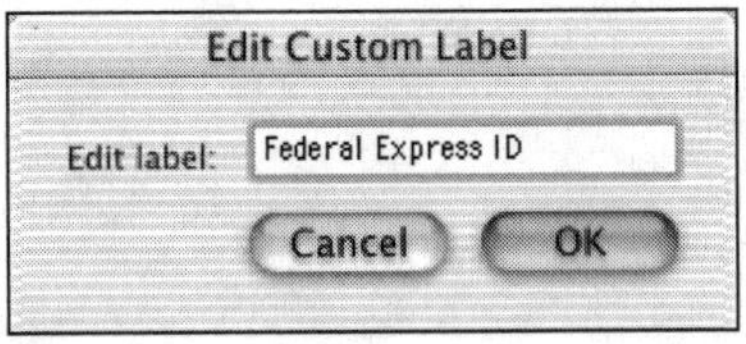

Figure 24.15 Rename the custom field and click OK.

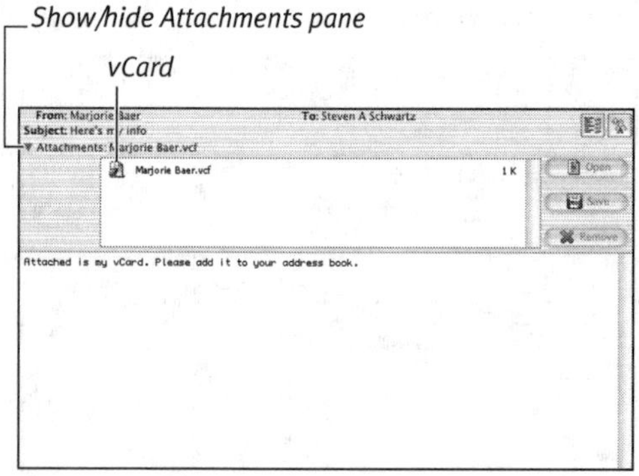

Show/hide Attachments pane

vCard

Figure 24.16 A vCard (.vcf) attachment in an incoming message will be listed in the Attachments pane, like any other attachment.

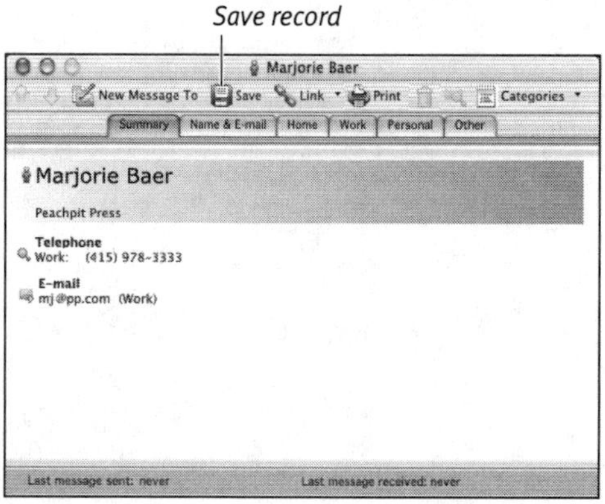

Save record

Figure 24.17 When you double-click a vCard attachment, Entourage automatically displays it as a new record.

Figure 24.18 This is an example of a vCard file icon.

Using Electronic Business Cards (vCards)

Sometimes you may receive electronic business cards (vCards) as attachments to email. You can recognize them by the .vcf filename extension. Entourage can read vCards and create new contact records from them. You can also email any of your contact records to others as vCard attachments.

To add a received vCard to the Address Book:

1. Select the message header in the message list. If necessary, click the Attachments triangle to open the Attachments pane and display the vCard attachment (**Figure 24.16**).

2. Double-click the vCard attachment.

   A new contact record containing the vCard information opens (**Figure 24.17**).

3. Make any necessary changes to the contact data, and click the Save toolbar icon.

   The vCard is added to your Address Book as a new contact record.

✔ Tips

- There's another way to add a received vCard to your Address Book. Open the email message in its own window, switch to the Address Book section of Entourage, and drag the vCard attachment into the address list.

- In some cases, you may receive vCards as files on disk (**Figure 24.18**) rather than as email attachments. To create a new record from such a vCard, open Entourage, switch to the Address Book section, and then drag the vCard file icon into the address list.

To email a vCard to someone:

1. Switch to the Address Book section of Entourage. In the address list, select the contact record you want to send as a vCard.

   You can select your own address or any other record from your Address Book.

2. Choose Contact > Forward as vCard.

   A new email message opens, containing the vCard attachment.

3. Fill in the address information and body of the message. (The subject is already filled in for you, although you are free to change it.) You can add other attachments, if you like.

   The selected address record is included in the Attachments pane as a vCard (**Figure 24.19**).

4. To send the message and the vCard immediately, click the Send Now toolbar icon. If you'd rather just place the message in your Outbox to be sent at a more convenient time, click the Send Later icon.

✔ Tips

- To send *multiple* contact records as vCards, simply select all the desired records from the address list before choosing Contact > Forward as vCard.

- You can also send a contact record as a vCard by dragging the record from the address list into an open email message. (Note that *any* file dragged into an email message is automatically treated as an attachment.)

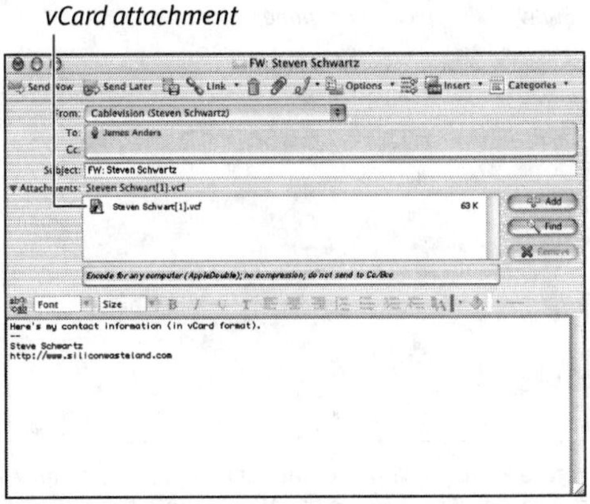

vCard attachment

Figure 24.19 The selected contact record is added as a vCard attachment in a new, preaddressed message.

Selected record

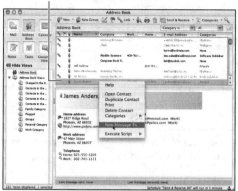

Figure 24.20 One way to initiate creating a message from the Address Book is to Control-click a record in the list and choose New Message To from the pop-up menu.

Addressing Email from the Address Book

In Chapter 23, Email, you learned the most common methods of addressing email. You can also address email directly from the Address Book.

To address email from the Address Book:

1. Switch to the Address Book section of Entourage.

2. In the address list, select the person to whom you want to send the message, and then choose Contact > New Message To.

   or

   Control-click the contact record in the address list and choose New Message To from the pop-up menu that appears (**Figure 24.20**).

   A new message window appears, addressed to the selected contact.

(continues on next page)

Chapter 24

✔ Tips

- If you select multiple contact records in step 2, the message will include all selected people in the To line.

- To rearrange contacts in the To, Cc, and Bcc areas of the address pane, just drag them where you want them.

- You can also address messages by dragging contact records from the address list into the To, Cc, or Bcc area of any outgoing message's address pane.

- Regardless of how you're creating a message, it can be convenient to have the address list displayed when selecting recipients. Open the address pane of an outgoing message and click the Address Book icon (**Figure 24.21**). To add a new recipient, click in the To, Cc, or Bcc area, and double-click the name in the address list. (You can also drag names from the address list into the address pane.)

Address Book icon
(show/hide address list)   *Address list*

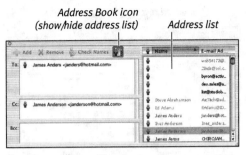

Figure 24.21 When addressing email, you can optionally display your address list.

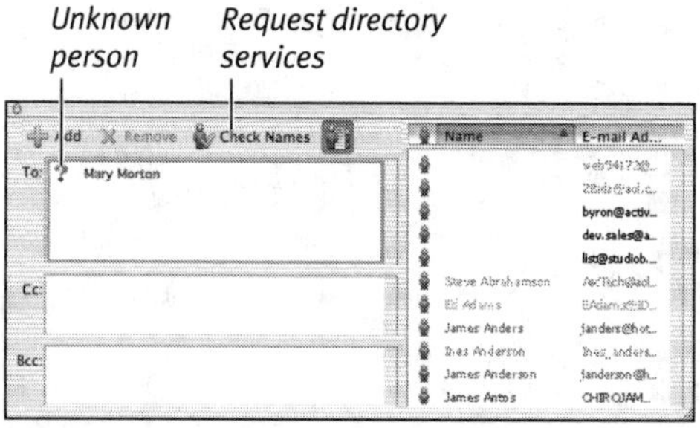

Figure 24.22 If you enter the name of a person who has no contact record and hasn't recently emailed you a message, Entourage marks it with a question mark.

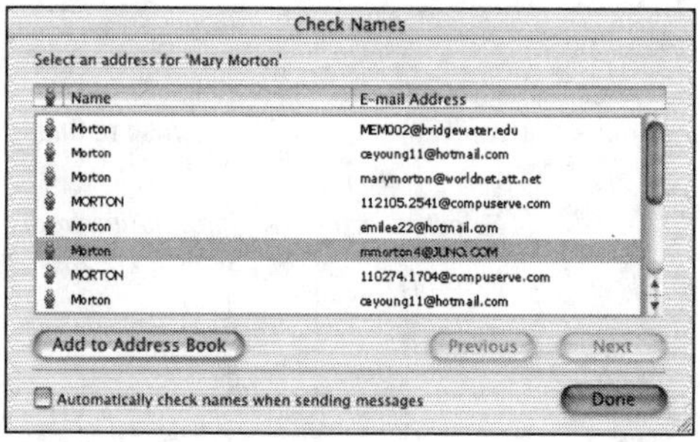

Figure 24.23 Possible matches are displayed in the Check Names dialog box.

Using Directory Services

If you don't have someone's email address, you may be able to find it in a directory service. Entourage supports Lightweight Directory Access Protocol (LDAP) and can consult LDAP servers to search for email addresses. This technique doesn't always work—it requires that you know the person's ISP and directory service (if he or she has registered at all). In a pinch, though, it's worth a try. There are two ways you can search for email addresses: from the address pane of an outgoing message or in the Directory Services dialog box.

To search from a message's address pane:

1. Address an outgoing email message by typing the person's name in the To, Cc, or Bcc area of the address pane.

   If Entourage does not know the person's email address, a green question mark will precede it (**Figure 24.22**).

2. Click the Check Names icon.

   Entourage contacts the default directory service and displays a list of possible matches (**Figure 24.23**).

3. If you see the correct name in the list, select it.

4. *Optional:* Click Add to Address Book to create a new contact record from the selected data record.

5. Click Done to dismiss the dialog box.

   If a record is currently selected, the new email address is substituted for the formerly unknown one. If no record is selected, the unknown address is left unaltered.

To search from the Directory Services dialog box:

1. Choose Tools > Directory Services.

   The Directory Services dialog box appears (**Figure 24.24**).

2. In the Folder List pane, select the directory service you want to search.

3. In the Search for name field, type the person's name.

4. Click the Find button.

   Entourage contacts the selected directory service and displays a list of possible matches.

5. Click a record in the results list, and the available information for it appears in the pane below the list (**Figure 24.25**).

6. If you believe this is the correct person and email address, click the New Message To or Add to Address Book toolbar icon.

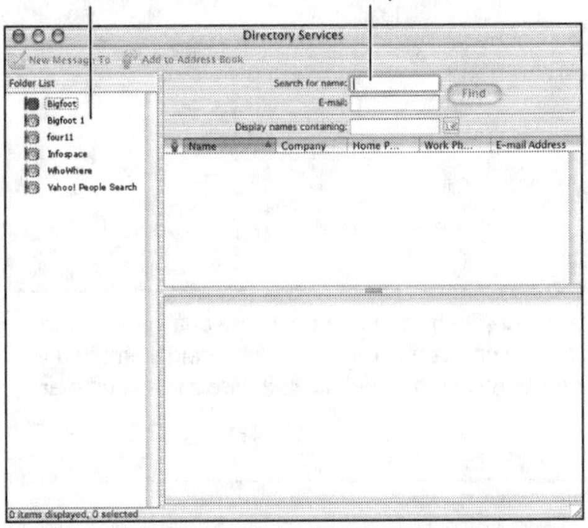

Select a directory service · Enter a name to find

Figure 24.24 Select a directory service to consult (in the Folder List), and enter the name you wish to find.

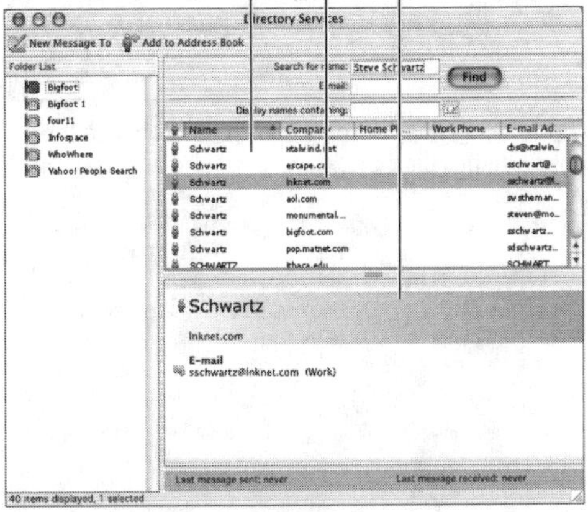

Selected record · Information from selected record

Search results

Figure 24.25 Matching names are returned in a list. Note that you can sort the list by clicking any column heading.

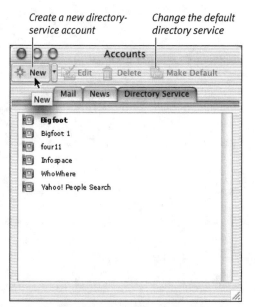

Create a new directory-service account

Change the default directory service

Figure 24.26 To record an additional searchable directory service, open the Accounts dialog box, click the Directory Service tab, and click the New icon.

✔ Tips

- You can add additional directory services as needed. For example, your corporation may have an LDAP server you'd like to use. To add a new LDAP server, click the New icon on the Directory Service tab of the Accounts dialog box (**Figure 24.26**).

- When you're conducting a directory service search from an email message's address pane, Entourage automatically uses the default directory. If you have greater success with another directory service, you can make that one the default. Select its name on the Directory Services tab of the Accounts dialog box, and click the Make Default icon (Figure 24.26).

- If you elected to add a found person to your Address Book, you should edit the person's contact record. Frequently you'll find errors in such records—it may not contain a first name, for example.

CALENDAR

Entourage provides a calendar you can use to record upcoming appointments and events, whether they occur only once or many times. You can schedule reminders for events, send and receive meeting invitations, and view your calendar in a variety of formats. And—when the Entourage conduit is released—you will be able to sync your calendar with any Palm-compatible personal digital assistant (PDA).

Viewing the Calendar

You can change the calendar display in several ways: viewing a day, work week, week, or month at a time; hiding or showing the Tasks pane; or showing only a sequential list of events rather than a calendar. In addition to setting the view, you can select a particular date or range of dates you wish to see.

To change the calendar view:

1. Switch to the calendar by clicking its icon in the upper-left corner of the window, by choosing View > Go To > Calendar, or by pressing ⌘③.

   The calendar and its toolbar are different than they were in Office 2001. Beneath the Folder List is a minicalendar, beside that is the calendar view (showing events for the current day, workweek, week, or month), and to the right is the Tasks pane (**Figure 25.1**).

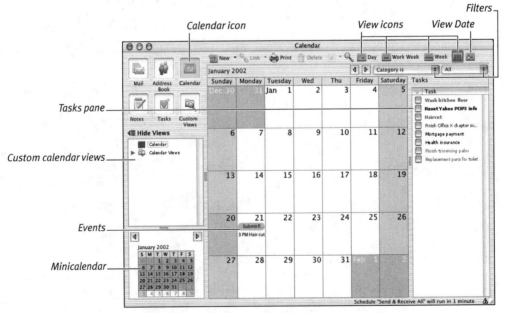

Figure 25.1 To view the calendar, click the Calendar icon.

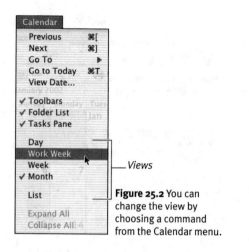

Figure 25.2 You can change the view by choosing a command from the Calendar menu.

— Views

2. To change the view, click the Day, Work Week, Week, or Month toolbar icon.

or

Choose a command from the Calendar menu (**Figure 25.2**).

The current date range is displayed using the new view. A darkened toolbar icon indicates which is the active view.

✔ Tips

■ To view only a list of events for the current view (**Figure 25.3**), choose Calendar > List. To return to a normal calendar view, click a toolbar icon or choose a Calendar command.

■ By default, the Tasks pane is shown only in Month view. You can make it appear in other views by choosing Calendar > Tasks Pane. Choose the command again to hide the pane.

■ You can also display a custom view (in list form) by selecting it from Calendar Views on the left side of the Entourage window (**Figure 25.4**).

Event list

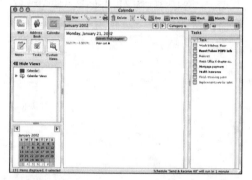

Figure 25.3 Choose Calendar > List if all you'd like to see is a list of events for the selected time period.

Custom calendar views

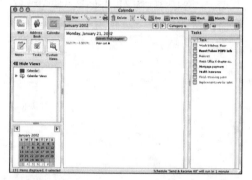

Figure 25.4 To see a particular list of upcoming events, select a custom view.

To view a particular date:

1. To select a date to view, do any of the following:

   ◆ Click the left and right arrows above the calendar window to scroll until the date you want is visible (**Figure 25.5**).

   ◆ Click the left and right arrows above the minicalendar to scroll until the date you want is visible. (Holding down the mouse button over either arrow makes the calendar scroll quickly through the months.) Click the desired date.

   ◆ Choose Calendar > Previous (⌘⬅) or Calendar > Next (⌘➡) to view the previous or next day, work week, week, or month (depending on the currently selected view.)

   ◆ To jump to a specific date, click the View Date icon at the right end of the toolbar or choose Calendar > View Date. In the View Date dialog box that appears, type a date or select one from the pop-up calendar (**Figure 25.6**). Click OK.

   The selected date range is displayed using the view currently in effect.

2. To display the current date, choose Calendar > Go to Today or click the View Date icon and click OK in the View Date dialog box. You can also press ⌘T. (The default date is always today.)

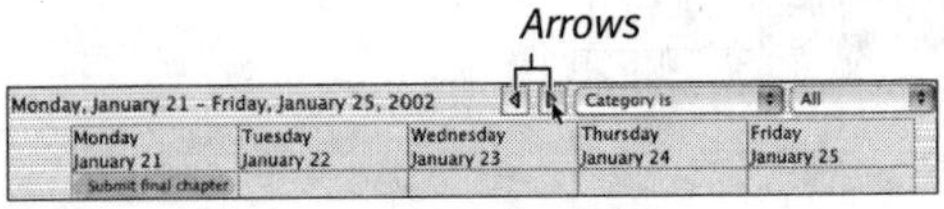

Arrows

Figure 25.5 To advance the calendar or move it backward, click the arrow icons.

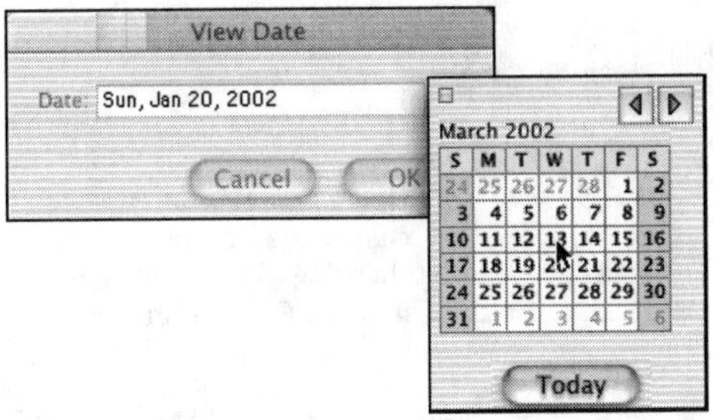

Figure 25.6 You can select a particular date to view by choosing it from the pop-up calendar in the View Date dialog box.

Selected dates

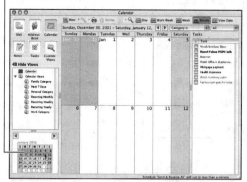

Figure 25.7 To view a particular range of dates (up to six weeks), drag-select the range in the minicalendar.

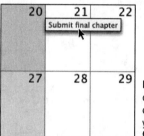

Figure 25.8 If you can't see the full text of an event, hover your cursor over it for a moment.

✔ Tips

- To restrict the calendar to showing a particular range of dates, you can drag-select from one to six weeks in the minicalendar (**Figure 25.7**). Unlike other date-selection methods, this changes the view to match the number of weeks selected.

- In some views, you may not be able to read the full text of an event by just glancing at the calendar. However, if you hover the cursor over the event for a couple of seconds, the full text will be displayed (**Figure 25.8**).

Adding and Deleting Events

As you might expect, there is more than one way to create new calendar events. And when a scheduled event has passed, you can delete it from the calendar.

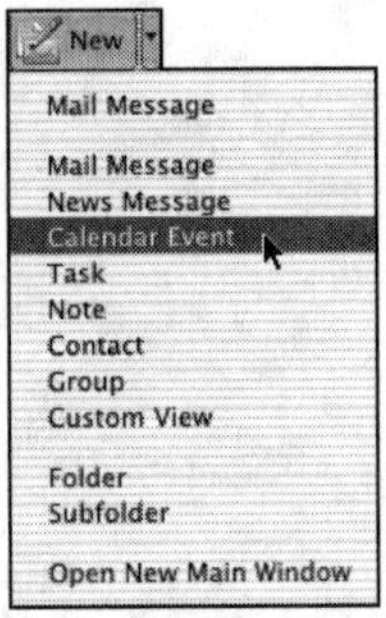

To create a calendar event:

1. Do any of the following:
   - ◆ When viewing the calendar, click the New toolbar icon or press ⌘N. When viewing any other part of Entourage, click the down arrow beside the New toolbar icon and choose Calendar Event from the pop-up menu (**Figure 25.9**).
   - ◆ Choose File > New > Calendar Event.
   - ◆ Double-click the date or time of the event on the calendar.

2. In the event window that appears (**Figure 25.10**), enter the basic information for the event.

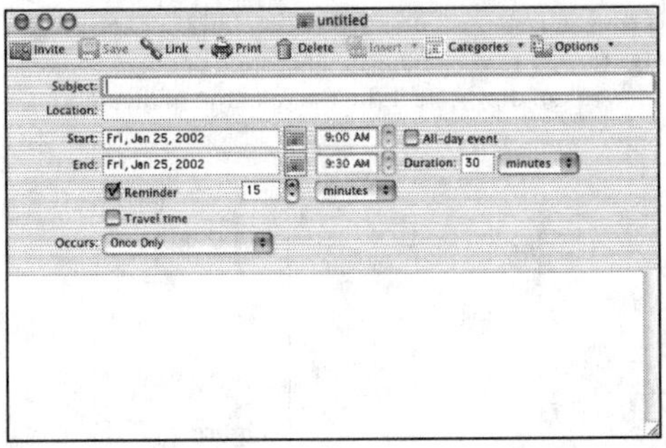

Figure 25.9 To create a new event, choose Calendar Event from the New toolbar icon's pop-up menu.

Figure 25.10 Enter the event information in this dialog box.

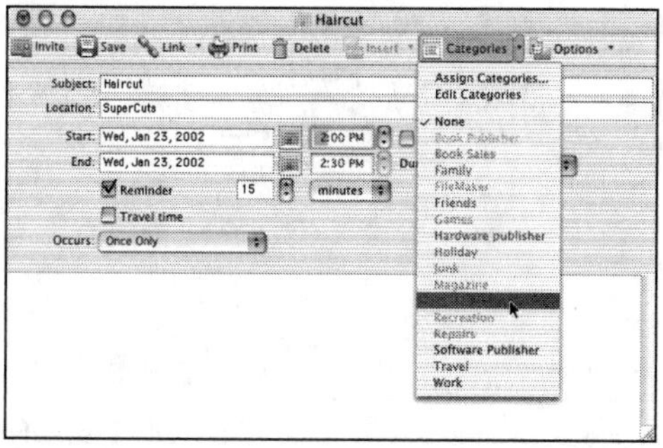

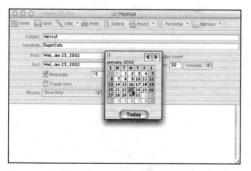

Figure 25.11 Click and hold the Categories toolbar icon to select a category for the event.

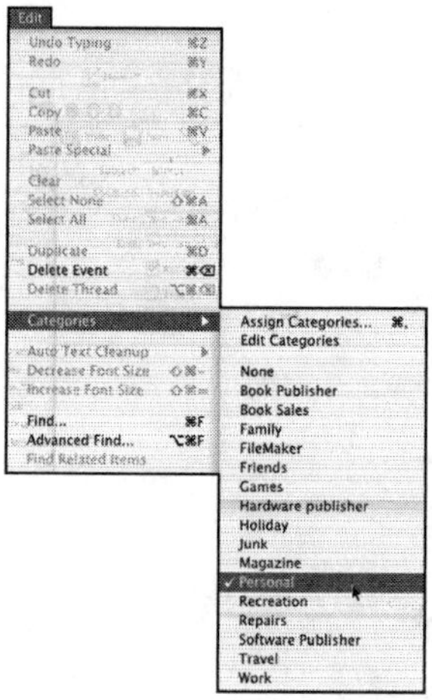

3. To assign a color-coded category to the event, click the Categories toolbar icon (**Figure 25.11**).

or

Choose Edit > Categories, and then choose a category from the submenu (**Figure 25.12**).

4. To set the start or end date, type the date in the appropriate field. Or click the Calendar icon to the right of the field and then click to select a date (**Figure 25.13**).

(continues on next page)

Figure 25.12 You can also specify a category by choosing Edit > Categories.

Figure 25.13 Click the arrows on the minicalendar to scroll to the correct month, and click to select a date for the event.

ADDING AND DELETING EVENTS

5. If this is a recurring event, choose a recurrence schedule from the Occurs drop-down menu. To set a different schedule, choose Custom and then specify the schedule details in the Recurring Event dialog box (**Figure 25.14**).

6. Save the event by clicking the Save toolbar icon, by choosing File > Save, or by pressing ⌘⑤.

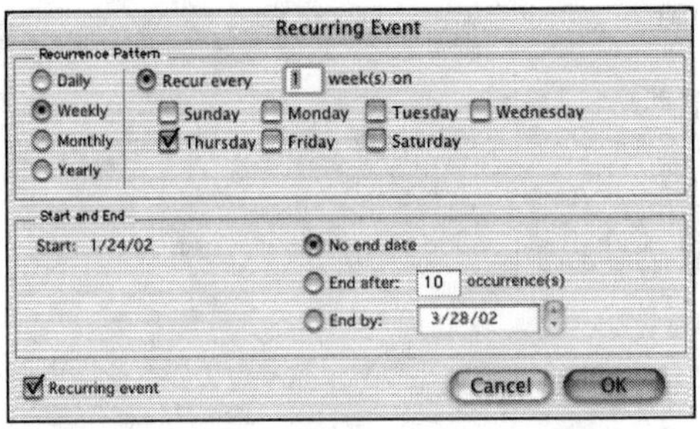

Figure 25.14 If this is a recurring event, you can specify a custom recurrence pattern and an end date for it.

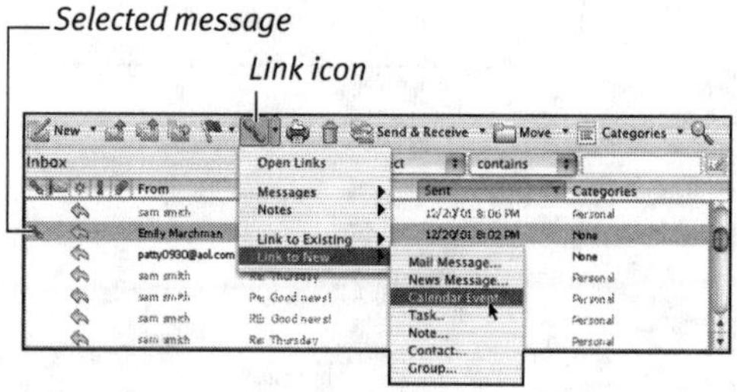

Selected message

Link icon

Figure 25.15 You can link a new calendar event to any selected Entourage item, such as this email message.

To create a calendar event from another Entourage item:

1. Select or open an item, such as an email message or note.

2. Click the Link toolbar icon and choose Link to New > Calendar Event from the drop-down menu that appears (**Figure 25.15**).

3. Enter the information for the calendar event (as described in "To create a calendar event").

To create a calendar event from a date on a contact record:

1. Switch to the Address Book by clicking its icon in the upper-left corner of the Entourage window, by choosing View > Go To > Address Book, or by pressing ⌘2.

2. Double-click the contact record to open it in its own window.

3. Click the Personal or Other tab (whichever one contains the date field you want to add to the calendar).

4. Click the Calendar icon beside the date field, and choose Add to Calendar from the pop-up menu that appears (**Figure 25.16**).

   A new event window opens (**Figure 25.17**), containing the information required to add the date as an annual event.

5. Make any necessary changes, save the event by clicking the Save toolbar icon, and then close the event window.

✔ Tip

- To view events created from contact records (such as birthdays and anniversaries), as well as other annual events you've added to the calendar, click the Recurring Yearly custom view in the Folder List (Figure 25.4).

Calendar icon

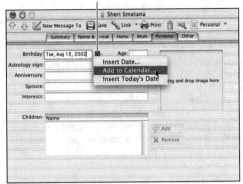

Figure 25.16 To create a calendar event from date field of any contact record, such as this birthday, click the Calendar icon and choose Add to Calendar.

Save icon

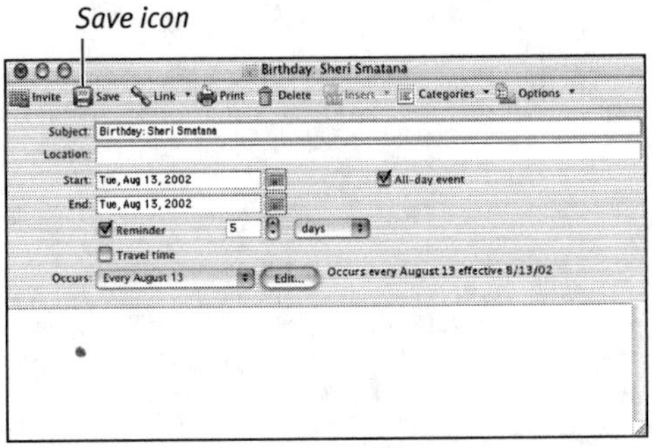

Figure 25.17 A new event is automatically created for the date. Edit it as necessary and click the Save icon.

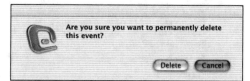

Figure 25.18 You must confirm the deletion of a normal (onetime) event.

Figure 25.19 When deleting a recurring event, you can delete just the selected occurrence or the entire event series.

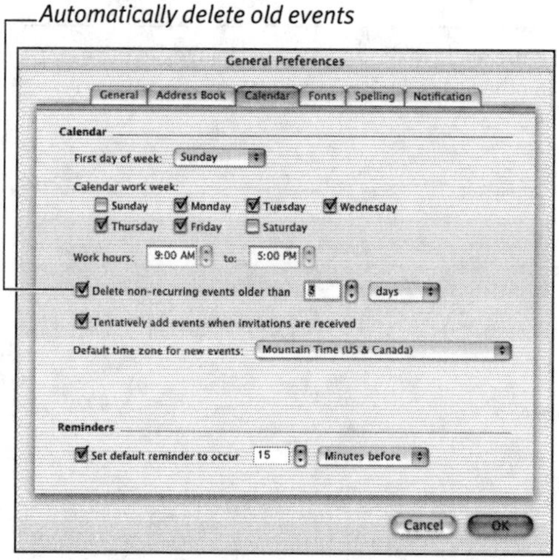

Automatically delete old events

Figure 25.20 Entourage will automatically delete expired events if you set this option in General Preferences.

To delete a calendar event:

1. In the Calendar window, switch to a view that displays the event you wish to delete, and click to select the event.

2. Do one of the following:
   - Click the Delete toolbar icon.
   - Choose Edit > Delete Event.
   - Press ⌘Delete or Delete.

   A confirmation dialog box appears. The specific dialog box you'll see depends on whether this is a onetime or recurring event.

3. If this is a onetime event (**Figure 25.18**), click the Delete button.

   _or_

   If this is a recurring event (**Figure 25.19**), click a radio button to indicate whether you want to delete this and all future occurrences of the event or just this occurrence. Then click OK.

✔ Tips

- You can also Control-click an event in the Calendar window and choose Delete Event from the pop-up menu that appears.

- If an event is open in its own window, you can delete it by clicking the Delete toolbar icon, by choosing Edit > Delete Event, or by pressing ⌘Delete.

- You can instruct Entourage to delete old calendar events automatically. Choose Entourage > General Preferences (⌘;), switch to the Calendar tab of the General Preferences dialog box (**Figure 25.20**), and check the box next to Delete non-recurring events older than _X_ days. Click OK to dismiss the dialog box.

- Be careful when deleting events. There is no Undo command to restore a deleted event.

Modifying Events

You can edit any aspect of a saved event.

To edit an event:

1. Switch to a calendar view that displays the event you want to change.

2. To open the event for editing, do one of the following:
   - Double-click the event.
   - Select the event and choose File > Open Event (or press ⌘O).
   - Control-click the event and choose Open Event from the pop-up menu that appears.

3. If the event you are editing is part of a recurring series, a dialog box appears (**Figure 25.21**). Select an option and click OK.

4. In the event window, make any necessary changes (**Figure 25.22**).

5. Save the edited event by clicking the Save toolbar icon, by choosing File > Save, or by pressing ⌘S.

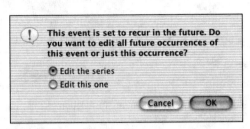

Figure 25.21 When editing a recurring event, you can edit just the selected occurrence or the entire event series.

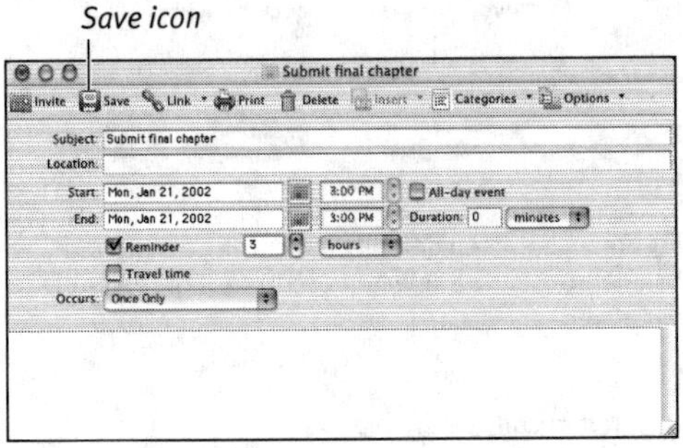

Save icon

Figure 25.22 Make any desired changes to the event and then click the Save toolbar icon.

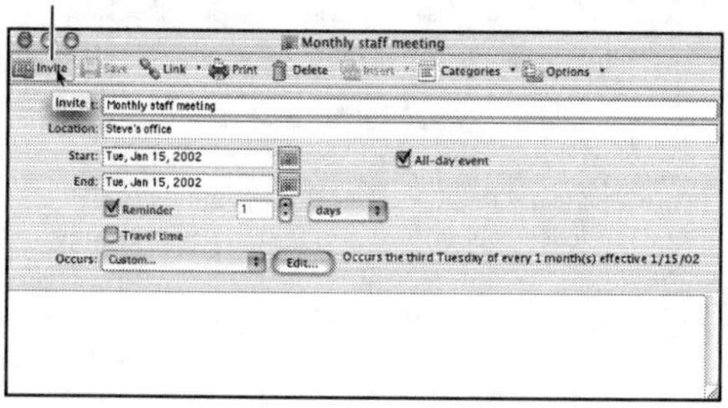

Invite icon

Figure 25.23 To invite others to the event, click the Invite toolbar icon.

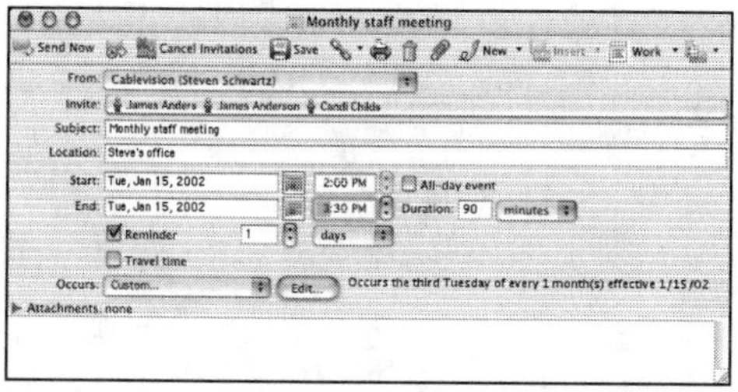

Figure 25.24 Choose the people you wish to invite and specify the event details in this window.

Sending and Responding to Event Invitations

Entourage makes it easy to send invitations to your events via email, as well as to reply via email to event invitations.

To invite others to an event:

1. Switch to the Calendar window, and double-click the event to open it in a separate window (**Figure 25.23**).

   If it's a repeating event, indicate in the dialog box that appears whether you're editing just this instance or the entire event series.

2. Click the Invite toolbar icon.

3. In the address pane, specify the persons to whom you wish to send an invitation.

   When you close the address pane, you can see the event information (**Figure 25.24**).

4. If you have multiple email addresses, click the From drop-down menu to choose the address from which you want to send the invitation.

5. Edit the invitation as necessary.

   To change the event from all day to a specific time span, for example, uncheck the All-day event check box. Note that you can also attach files if you wish.

(continues on next page)

6. Click the Send Now toolbar icon to email the invitation to the designated people.

7. Recipients receive a message in which, if they are using Entourage, they can respond by simply clicking an Accept, Decline, or Tentative toolbar icon. Entourage then relays a response to the person who sent the invitations. Recipients who don't use Entourage can reply with a normal email message.

Figure 25.25 To check recipients' responses to the invitation, click this underlined text in the message window.

✔ Tips

■ Invitation recipients can change their minds at any time by opening the invitation message again and clicking a different response icon.

■ To cancel an invitation you've already sent, double-click the event to open its window and click the Cancel Invitations toolbar icon. Participants receive a cancellation email message.

■ If you're the person who sent out the invitations, you can check the responses by opening the event and clicking the View attendee status underlined text (**Figure 25.25**).

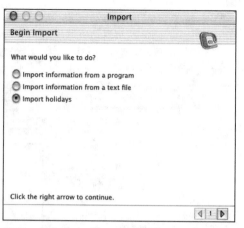

Figure 25.26 On the first screen of the Import wizard, click the Import holidays radio button.

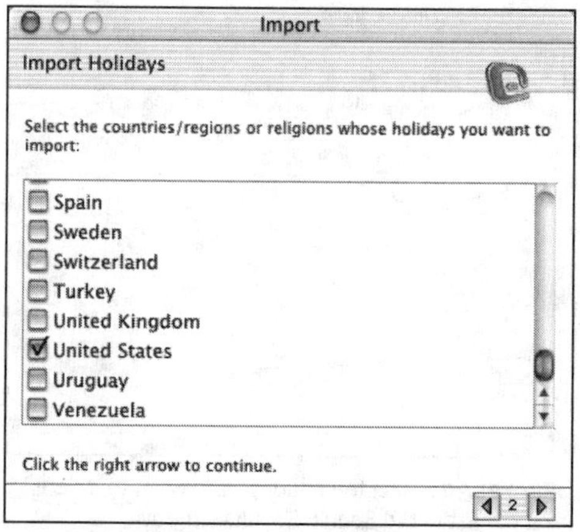

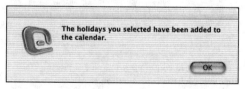

Figure 25.27 Click the check boxes of the countries and religions whose holidays you want to import.

Figure 25.28 The holidays have been added to your calendar.

Adding and Removing Holidays

If you like, you can add country-specific and/or religious holidays to the calendar. The procedure for adding holidays, however, is different from that in Office 2001. You can also decide later to remove all or some of the holidays.

To add holidays to the calendar:

1. Choose File > Import.

   The Import wizard appears (**Figure 25.26**).

2. Click the Import holidays radio button, and then click the right-arrow icon to continue to the next screen.

3. After Entourage finishes building the list of available country-specific and religious holiday sets, make your selections by entering checkmarks (**Figure 25.27**). Click the right arrow to continue.

   The chosen holidays are imported into the calendar.

4. Click OK to dismiss the notification dialog box (**Figure 25.28**), and then click Finish to dismiss the Import wizard.

To remove holidays from the calendar:

1. Switch to the calendar.

2. Choose Edit > Advanced Find or press
   Option ⌘ F .
   The Find window appears.

3. Select only Calendar Events as Item
   Types, and set the criterion as Category
   Is Holiday using the Criteria pull-down
   menus (**Figure 25.29**).

4. Click Find.
   A Search Results window appears, listing
   the found holiday events (**Figure 25.30**).

5. Select the holidays you want to delete.
   (Note that each holiday is listed multiple
   times, representing the different years for
   which it was added to the calendar.)

6. Click the Delete toolbar icon or choose
   Edit > Delete. You can also press Delete
   or ⌘ Delete .

7. Click the Delete button in the confirmation dialog box (**Figure 25.31**).

8. Close the Search Results window.

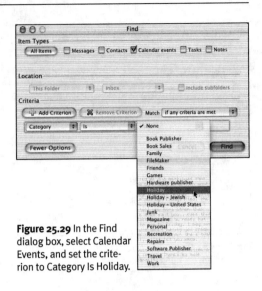

Figure 25.29 In the Find dialog box, select Calendar Events, and set the criterion to Category Is Holiday.

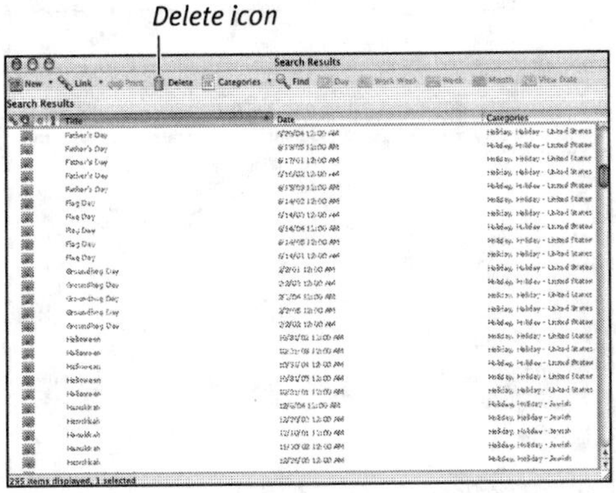

Delete icon

Figure 25.30 Select the holidays you want to delete from the list in the Search Results window.

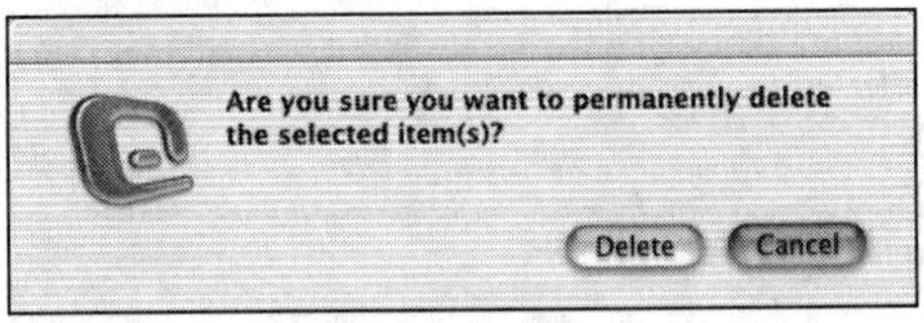

Figure 25.31 To confirm the deletion of the selected holidays, click the Delete button.

ADDING AND REMOVING HOLIDAYS

Holiday   Holiday

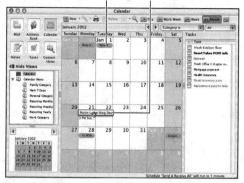

Figure 25.32 Holidays are indicated on the calendar by red ovals.

✔ Tips

- Setting the criterion as Category Is Holidays will find *all* imported holidays. If you imported multiple holiday sets, you can find any one set (for example, Holiday—United States) by setting the search category to that set.

- If you want to delete *all* found holidays, click to select any one of them, choose Edit > Select All, and then perform the deletion.

- You can also remove individual holidays (marked in red on the calendar, as shown in **Figure 25.32**) by selecting and then deleting them as you would any other event.

To-Do Lists (Tasks)

Entourage lets you track to-do items (referred to as *tasks*). You can mark tasks as completed, be reminded of tasks that are due, and connect tasks to other Office documents and Entourage items. You can also set tasks as *repeating*—for example, making a monthly mortgage payment or weekly staff meeting appear in your to-do list at specified intervals.

Viewing the Tasks List

You can view your tasks in several ways, sort them by any important characteristic, and filter the visible list to make it more manageable.

To view the Tasks list:

1. Click the Tasks icon in the upper-left corner of the Entourage window or choose View > Go To > Tasks. Or you can press ⌘5.

   The Tasks list appears (**Figure 26.1**).

2. You can sort the list on any column (except the first) by clicking that column heading. To reverse the sort order, click the same column heading again.

   The heading of the current sort column is shown in blue.

Folder List
Tasks icon
Tasks list

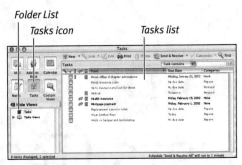

Figure 26.1 Click the Tasks icon above the Folder List to see the Tasks list.

VIEWING THE TASKS LIST

Links
Status (Complete or Incomplete)
Priority
Recurring
Reminder
Clear
Filter text
Filter

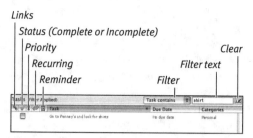

Figure 26.2 You can filter the Tasks list by entering a text string.

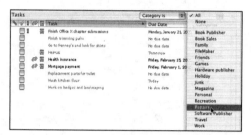

Figure 26.3 You can also filter the Tasks list by choosing a category.

Figure 26.4 Specify which tasks to view by choosing a command from the View menu.

Task custom views
Tasks icon

Figure 26.5 Request a custom view of the tasks list by selecting an icon in the Folder List.

3. You can filter the Tasks list to show only tasks that match a criterion. Do any of the following:

◆ Choose Task contains from the pull-down menu above the Tasks list, and type a string in the text box (**Figure 26.2**). To restore the Tasks list, click the Clear icon.

◆ Choose Category is from the pull-down menu, and choose a category to display (**Figure 26.3**). To restore the Tasks list, click the Clear icon or set Category to All.

◆ Choose a completion command (All Tasks, Incomplete Tasks, or Complete Tasks) or a due-date command (Due Today or Due This Week) from the View menu (**Figure 26.4**). To restore the Tasks list after choosing a completion command, choose All Tasks. To restore the Tasks list after choosing a due-date command, choose the same command again.

◆ In the Folder List, select a custom view by clicking an entry in Tasks Views (**Figure 26.5**). To restore the Tasks list, click the Tasks icon in the Folder List.

Creating and Deleting Tasks

You can create new tasks by adding them directly to the Tasks list or by linking them to other events. When you've completed tasks or you're no longer interested in tracking them, you can delete them from the Tasks list.

To create a new task:

1. To display the Tasks list, click the Tasks icon in the upper-left corner of the Entourage window or choose View > Go To > Tasks. Or you can press ⌘5.

2. Click the New toolbar icon or choose File > New > Task. Or press ⌘N.

   A new task window appears (**Figure 26.6**).

3. Name the task.

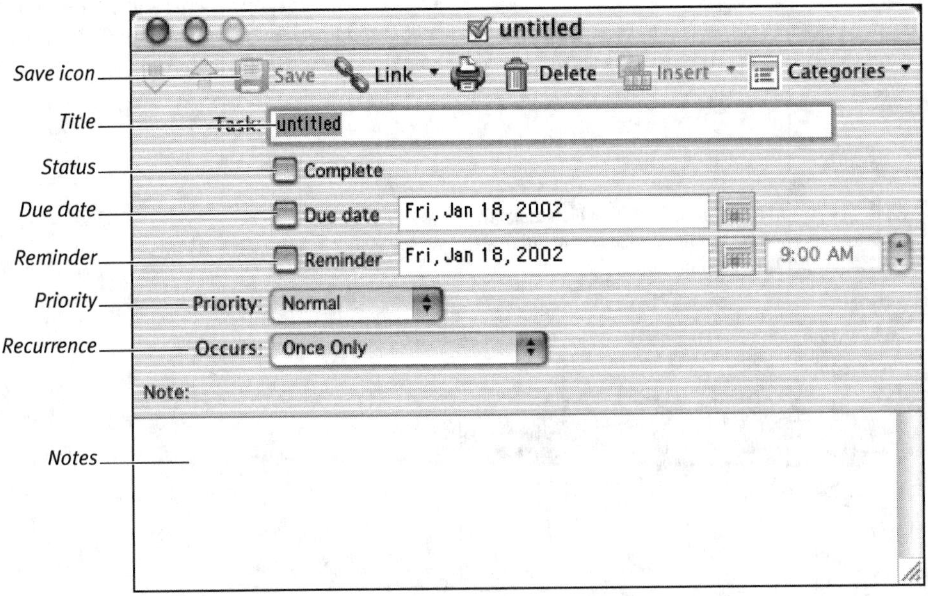

Figure 26.6 Enter information and set options for the new task.

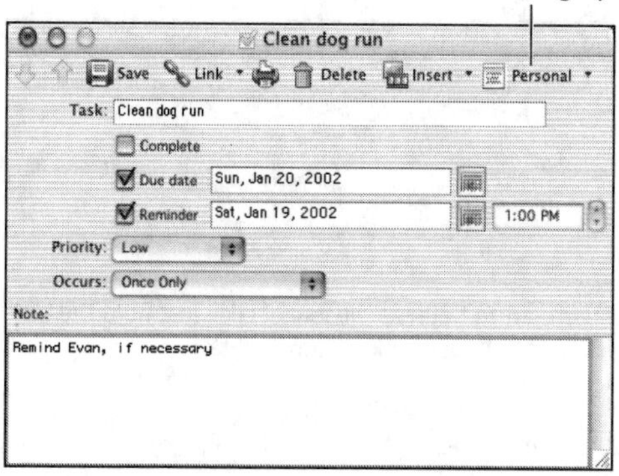

Main category

Figure 26.7 This is an example of a task with a category, due date, reminder, priority, occurrence, and notes.

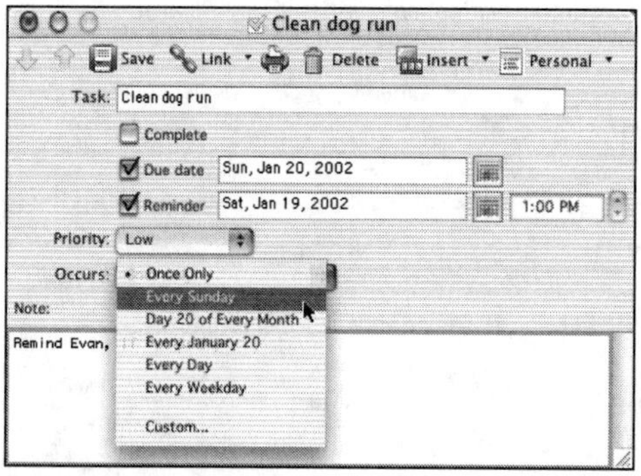

Figure 26.8 Choose common recurrence schedules from the Occurs drop-down menu.

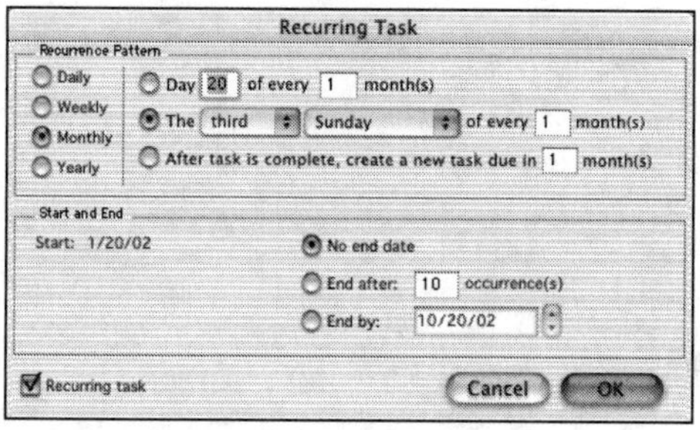

Figure 26.9 Specify more complex recurrence schedules in the Recurring Task dialog box.

4. *Optional:* Choose a category from the Categories pull-down menu, assign a priority, set a due date, schedule a reminder, and/or add a note (**Figure 26.7**).

5. If this is a recurring task, choose a recurrence schedule from the Occurs drop-down menu (**Figure 26.8**).

or

To set a schedule other than the ones listed, choose Custom from the Occurs drop-down menu. The Recurring Task window appears (**Figure 26.9**). Set the recurrence pattern, and then choose an end criterion from the options in the Start and End pane. Click OK.

6. To save the task, click the Save toolbar icon or choose File > Save. Or press ⌘⑤. Close the task window.

The task is inserted into the Tasks list in the current sort order.

CREATING AND DELETING TASKS

To create a new task as a link to another Entourage item:

1. Select or open the Entourage item (an email message or note, for example).

2. Click the Link toolbar icon (**Figure 26.10**), and choose Link to New > Task from the pop-up menu.

   or

   Choose Tools > Link to New > Task.

3. Enter the new task information, and save the task by clicking the Save toolbar icon, by choosing File > Save, or by pressing ⌘S. Close the task window.

   The new task is created, and a link is established between it and the item. The link is indicated by a link icon that precedes both items (**Figure 26.11**). For more information about linking Entourage items, see Chapter 30, Using Programs Together.

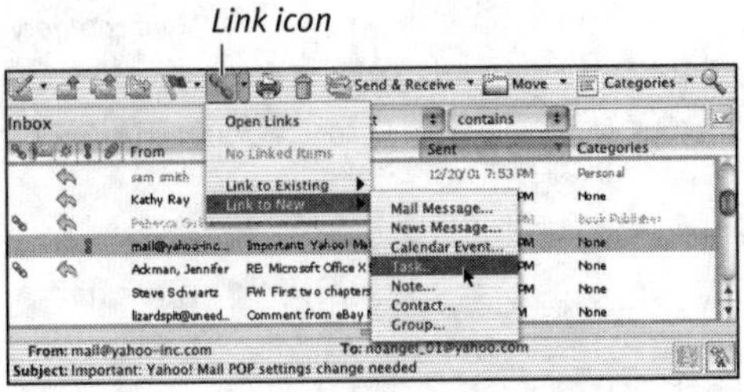

Link icon

Figure 26.10 Select a message, click and hold the Link icon, and choose Link to New > Task.

_Link indicators

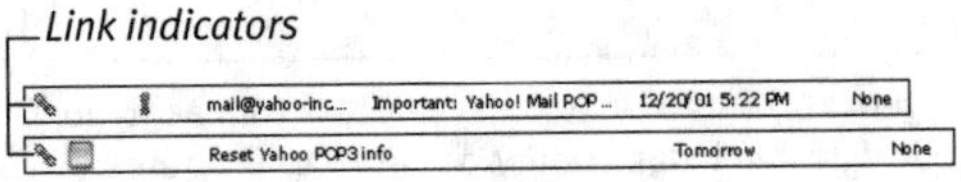

Figure 26.11 After you've created a link, the linked items in the message list (top) and the Tasks list (bottom) are displayed with a link indicator.

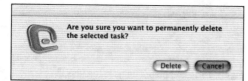

Figure 26.12 You must confirm task deletions.

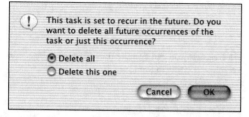

Figure 26.13 You can elect to delete this occurrence only or the entire series.

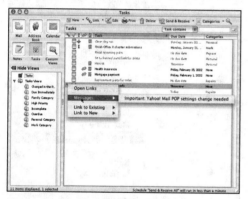

Figure 26.14 To determine what Entourage items are linked to the current item, click its link icon.

To delete a task:

1. Select the task(s) in the Tasks list.

2. Do one of the following:

   ◆ Click the Delete toolbar icon, choose Edit > Delete Task, press [Delete], or press [⌘][Delete].

   ◆ With the task open in its own window, click the Delete toolbar icon, choose Edit > Delete Task, or press [⌘][Delete].

   A confirmation dialog box appears (**Figure 26.12**).

3. Click Delete to delete the task.

4. If the task is a recurring one, a second dialog box appears, giving you the option to delete only this instance or the entire series of tasks (**Figure 26.13**). Click a radio button to indicate your choice and then click OK. (To cancel the deletion, click Cancel.)

✔ Tips

■ To determine what links exist between an item and other Entourage items, click the item's link icon (**Figure 26.14**).

■ You can create tasks from email by selecting a header in the message list and choosing Create Task from Message from the Scripts menu ([Control][T]).

Editing Tasks

You can easily change any aspect of a task.

To edit a task:

1. In the Tasks list, double-click the task you want to edit, or select the task and click the Edit toolbar icon.

   The task opens in its own window.

2. Make whatever changes you like.

3. Click the Save toolbar icon, choose File > Save, or press ⌘S.

✔ Tips

- You can change several task attributes from within the Tasks list, as follows:

  - To change a task's completion status, click the check box that precedes the task in the Tasks list. Completed items are displayed in strike-through text (**Figure 26.15**).

  - To change a task's title, select the task in the Tasks list. Click the title to select it for editing (**Figure 26.16**), make any necessary changes, and press Return or click somewhere else in the Entourage window to save the new title.

  - To assign or change the main category for a task, click the Categories section of any task in the Tasks list and choose a category from the pop-up menu (**Figure 26.17**). Note that since any Entourage item can be assigned multiple categories, choosing a category in this manner assigns it as an *additional* category; previously assigned categories are *not* removed. If that's your intent, choose Assign Categories from the Categories pop-up menu.

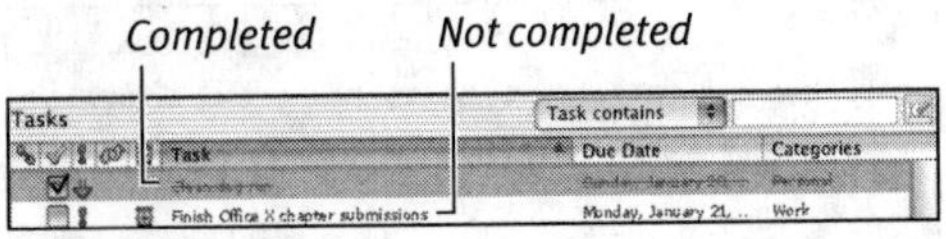

Figure 26.15 Completed items in the Task list are displayed in strike-through text and have a checkmark in the Status check box.

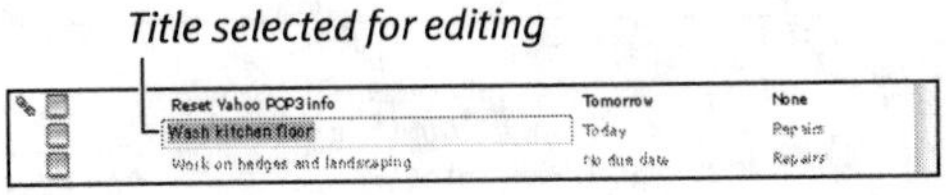

Figure 26.16 You can edit the title of any task by selecting the title in the Tasks list.

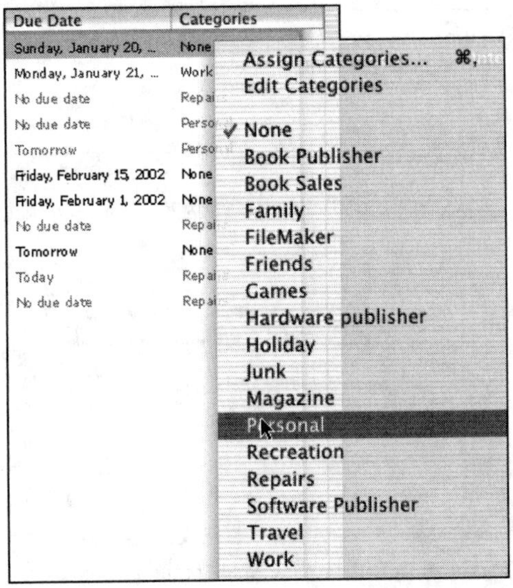

Figure 26.17 To assign a main category to a task, click its Categories entry in the Tasks list and choose a category from this pop-up menu.

- When creating a new task that is similar to an existing one, you may find it quicker to create a duplicate task and then make the necessary edits to the copy. To duplicate a task, select it in the Tasks list and choose Edit > Duplicate Task (or press ⌘D).

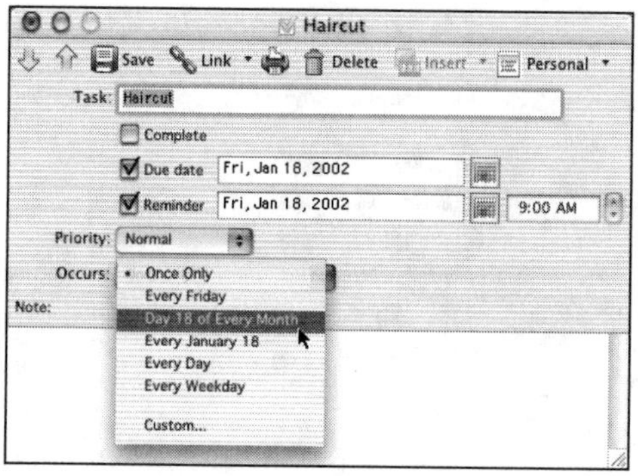

Figure 26.18 Select a recurrence schedule from the Occurs drop-down menu.

Edit recurrence schedule

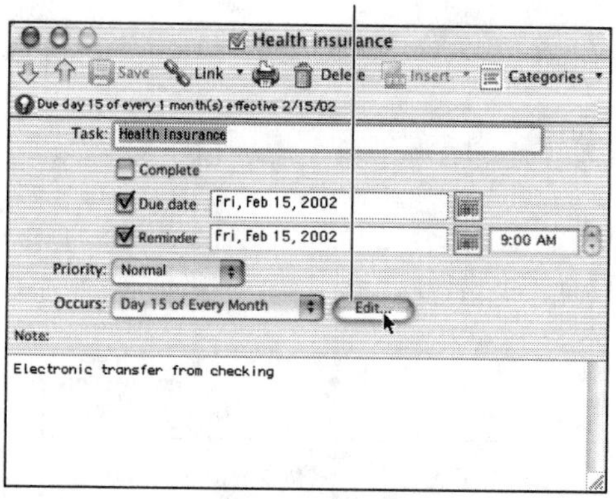

Figure 26.19 To change an existing recurrence schedule to a different custom schedule, click the Edit button.

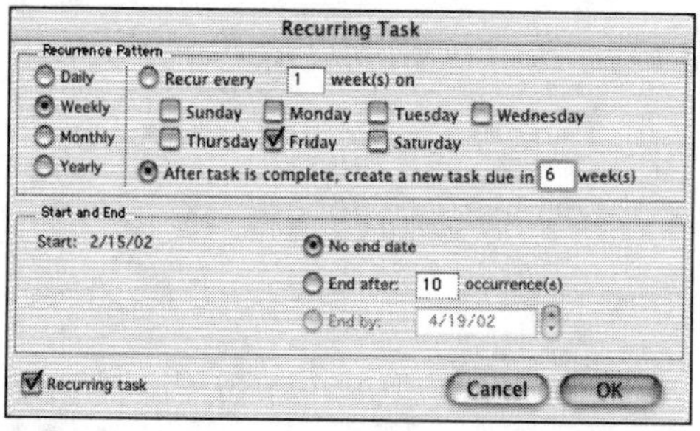

Figure 26.20 Complex recurrence schedules are set in the Recurring Task dialog box. This example shows you how to schedule a haircut every six weeks.

Recurring Tasks

You can set a task to recur at any regular interval, repeating as many times as you like. You can also change a normal task to recurring or vice versa, as well as alter the recurrence pattern for any task

To set a task as recurring:

1. Create a new task (as described previously), or edit an existing task by double-clicking it in the Tasks list.

2. To accept one of the preset schedules, choose one from the Occurs drop-down menu (**Figure 26.18**). Go to Step 7.

3. To specify a different schedule, do one of the following:

   ◆ If this is a new task or an existing non-recurring task, choose Custom from the Occurs drop-down menu.

   ◆ If this is an existing recurring task, click the Edit button (**Figure 26.19**). The Recurring Task dialog box opens (**Figure 26.20**).

4. At the top of the dialog box, specify the recurrence pattern. The options presented vary depending on whether you select Daily, Weekly, Monthly, or Yearly.

5. In the Start and End pane, specify whether the task will recur indefinitely, end after a certain number of occurrences, or end by a particular date.

6. Click OK to close the Recurring Task dialog box.
   The task window reappears.

7. Save the task and close its window.

✔ Tip

■ To stop a task from recurring, open the task window and choose Once Only from the Occurs drop-down menu.

Due Dates and Reminders

Many tasks don't have a specific due date—you just need to wash the car *sometime*, for example. Nevertheless, you can optionally assign a due date and/or schedule a reminder for any task. (Due dates and reminders are independent of each other. Any task can have a scheduled due date, a reminder, both, or neither.)

Setting task due dates

A *due date* specifies when a task must be completed. Unlike an appointment, a due date is associated only with a date, not a time.

To set or modify a task due date:

1. Create a new task or open an existing one.

2. In the task's window, click the Due date check box (**Figure 26.21**), if it isn't already checked.

3. Choose a new date from the pop-up calendar (**Figure 26.22**) or edit the current or suggested date.

4. Save the task and close its window.

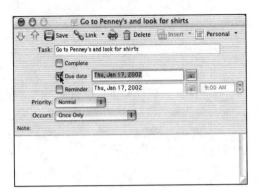

Figure 26.21 To set a due date for a task, click the Due date check box.

Previous month   Next month

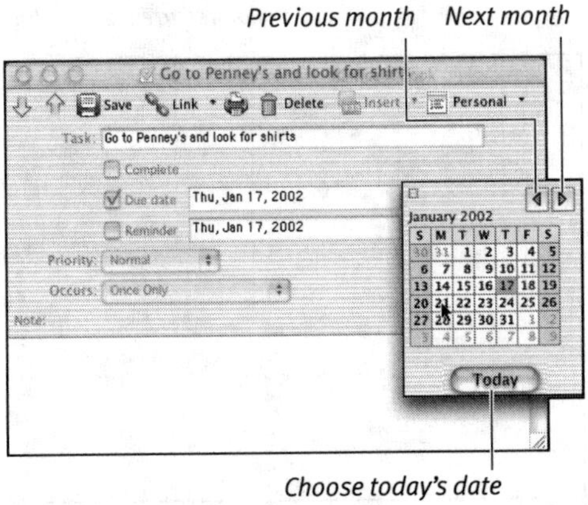

Figure 26.22 You can edit the due date's text or select a date from the pop-up calendar.

Choose today's date

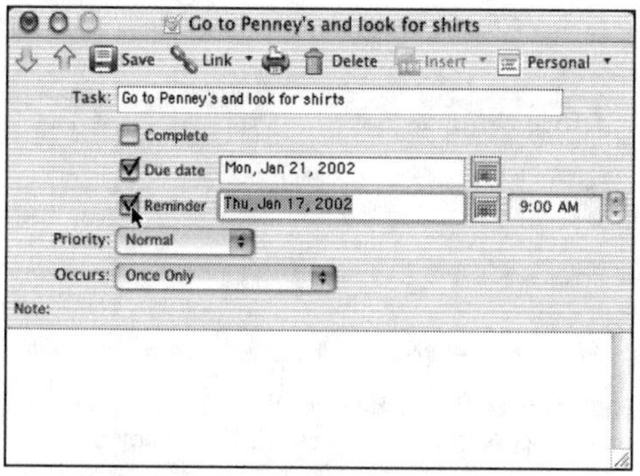

Figure 26.23 To request a reminder for a task, click the Reminder check box, and then set a date and time at which you want to be reminded.

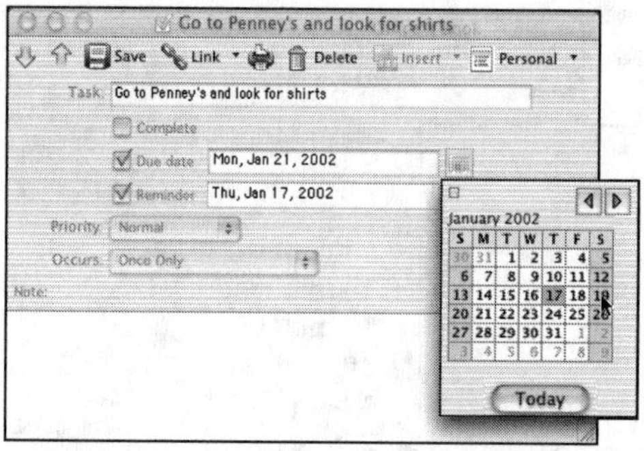

Figure 26.24 As with the due date, you can select a reminder date from a pop-up calendar.

Setting task reminders

Setting a task reminder is different from setting a reminder for a calendar event. Rather than specifying how far in advance you wish to be reminded, you select a specific time at which the task reminder will appear onscreen.

Office X handles reminders—for both tasks and calendar events—using a new, separate program called Office Notifications. This enables reminders to appear onscreen any time your Mac is running, regardless of whether an Office application is running.

To set or modify a task reminder:

1. Create a new task or open an existing one.

2. In the task window, click the Reminder check box (**Figure 26.23**), if it isn't already checked.

3. Choose a new date from the pop-up calendar (**Figure 26.24**) or edit the current or suggested date.

4. Specify a time for the reminder.

   Select the hour, minute, or AM/PM segment of the time. To change the selected segment, click the up- and down-arrow buttons, or type new numbers into the text box.

5. Save the task and close its window.

DUE DATES AND REMINDERS

To respond to a reminder:

1. At the appointed time, the Office Notifications dialog box appears (**Figure 26.25**). If it lists more than one task or event, scroll to select the one to which you want to respond.

2. Do one of the following:

   ◆ To dismiss the reminder so it doesn't reappear, click the Dismiss button.

   ◆ If you've already performed the task, click the Complete check box. Doing so dismisses the reminder and marks the task as complete in the Tasks list.

   ◆ To delay the reminder for 5 minutes (when it will reappear onscreen), click the Snooze button.

   ◆ If you want to be reminded later (from 5 minutes to 1 week from now), hold down the Snooze button and choose a delay interval (**Figure 26.26**).

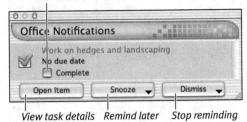

Mark item completed

View task details   Remind later   Stop reminding

Figure 26.25 When a task or calendar reminder is due, Office Notifications presents this dialog box.

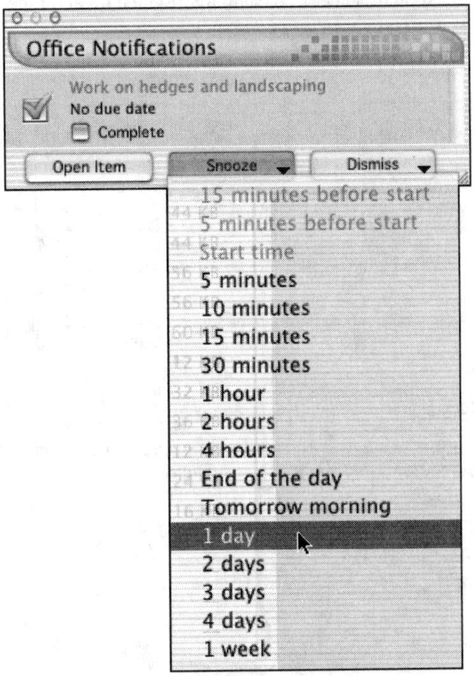

Figure 26.26 Click the Snooze button to be reminded again in 5 minutes (the default) or choose another Snooze time from this drop-down menu.

DUE DATES AND REMINDERS

Office Notifications icon

Figure 26.27 Office Notifications adds its icon to the Dock. The number shows how many current reminders are yet to be handled.

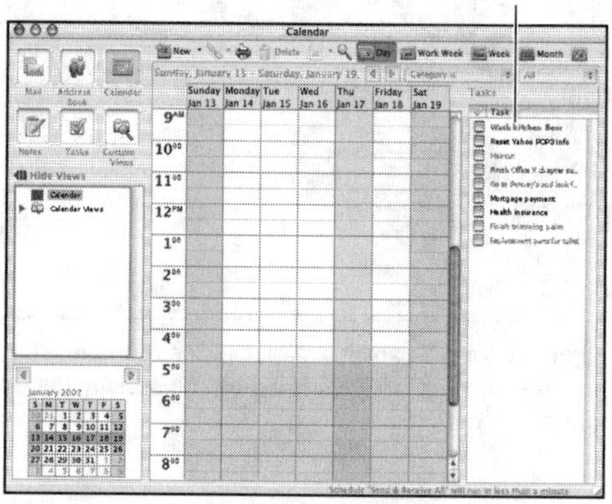

Tasks list

Figure 26.28 The Calendar also displays the Tasks list, but restricts itself to showing only tasks that haven't been marked as complete.

✔ Tips

- If there are multiple reminders to be processed—indicated by the presence of a scroll bar and a number in the icon on the Dock (**Figure 26.27**)—the Office Notifications dialog box remains open until you've responded to each reminder.

- If you want to open the task's window and see its complete details, click the Open Item button.

- You can also view your task list in the Calendar window (**Figure 26.28**). To mark a task as complete, click its check box. To view the details for a task, double-click it.

- Note that even though the task list is displayed in the Calendar window and some of your tasks may have due dates or reminders, tasks are _not_ listed as events on the calendar. This is why it is especially important to decide carefully which items should be created as tasks and which items should be recorded as calendar events.

Marking Tasks Complete

If you mark a task as complete rather than deleting it, the task will still be visible in the Tasks list. This is the appropriate approach when you want to retain a history of a task, as when you're checking off completed project milestones, for instance.

To mark a task as complete:

1. Display the Tasks list by clicking the Tasks icon in the upper-left corner of the Entourage window, by choosing View > Go To > Tasks, or by pressing ⌘⑤.

2. In the Tasks list, click the task's Status check box (**Figure 26.29**) to add a check-mark to it.

   or

   In the Tasks list, open the task in its own window by double-clicking it. Click the Complete check box (**Figure 26.30**), save the task, and close its window.

✔ Tips

- The Status and Complete check boxes work as toggles. To reverse the state of the task (from incomplete to complete or vice versa), click the check box again.

- You can also mark tasks as completed in the Calendar window.

- You can filter the Tasks list to hide the completed tasks by choosing View > Incomplete Tasks. Conversely, to view *only* tasks you have marked as completed, choose View > Complete Tasks.

Status column

Figure 26.29 You can mark a task as complete by clicking its Status check box in the Tasks list.

Status

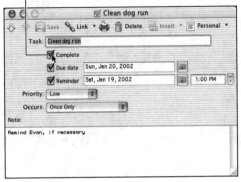

Figure 26.30 You can also mark a task as complete by opening the task in its own window and clicking the Complete check box.

NOTES

Entourage's Notes section is designed as a freeform note-taking utility. You can combine text, images, and hyperlinks in notes, and organize the notes in categories. Unlike most simple note-taking applications, Entourage creates formatted-text notes. Any note can contain multiple fonts, sizes, styles, colors, and paragraph formatting.

Viewing Notes

You can view notes, sort the notes list, and filter the list to see notes that match a particular title or category.

To view a note:

1. To switch to Notes view, click the Notes icon (**Figure 27.1**) or choose View > Go To > Notes. Or you can press ⌘4. The notes list appears in the main pane (**Figure 27.2**).

2. To view a note (**Figure 27.3**), double-click its title.

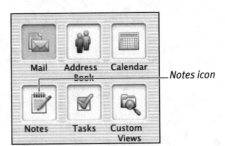

Notes icon

Figure 27.1 Click the Notes icon in the upper-left corner of the Entourage window to see your notes list.

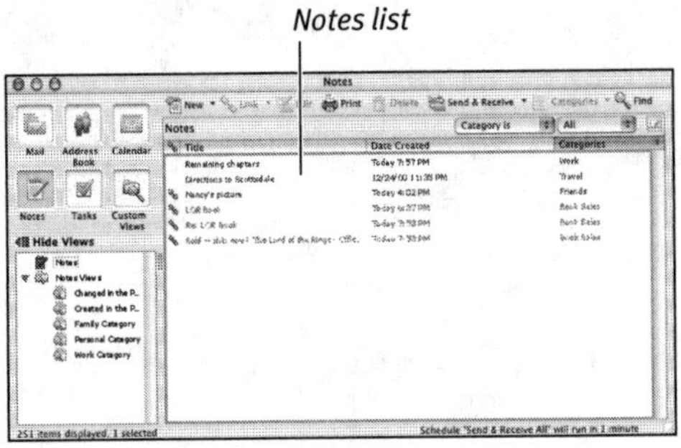

Notes list

Figure 27.2 The notes list is displayed in the main window. Double-click a note title to view the note.

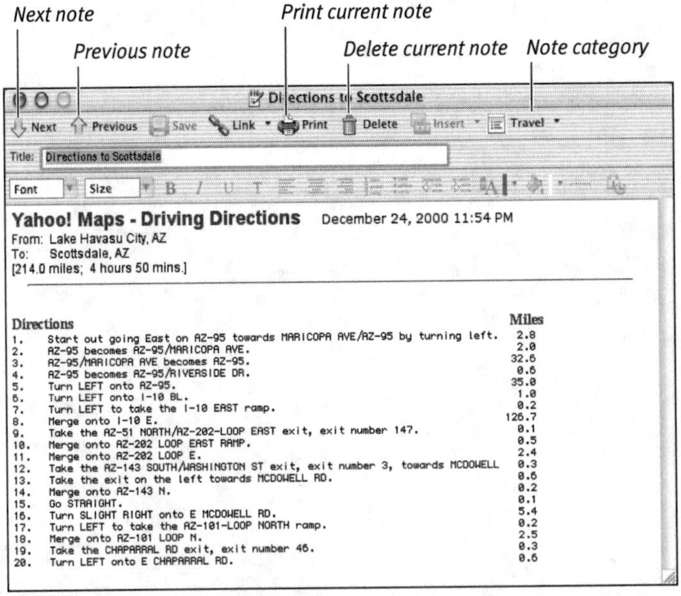

Next note

Previous note

Print current note

Delete current note   Note category

Figure 27.3 To read a note, you must first open it.

VIEWING NOTES

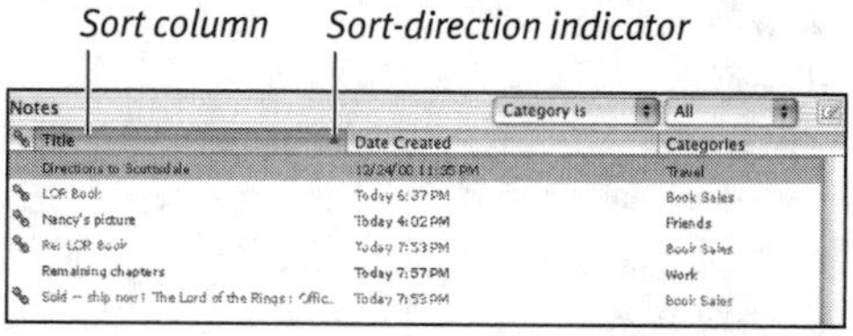

Sort column   Sort-direction indicator

Figure 27.4 Click any column name to sort the notes list by that column.

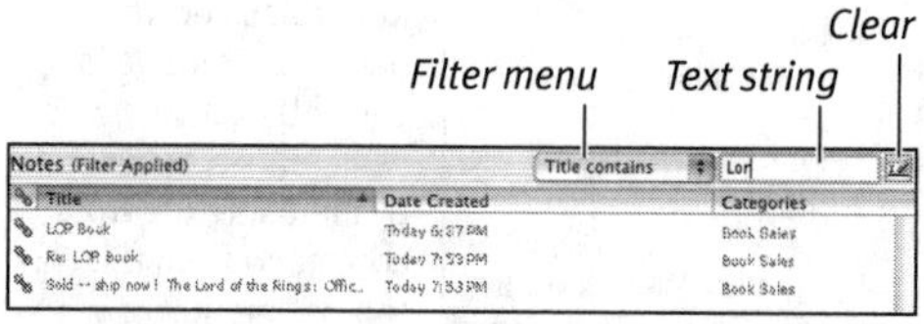

Clear

Filter menu   Text string

Figure 27.5 To restrict the notes list, you can optionally filter it by title or category.

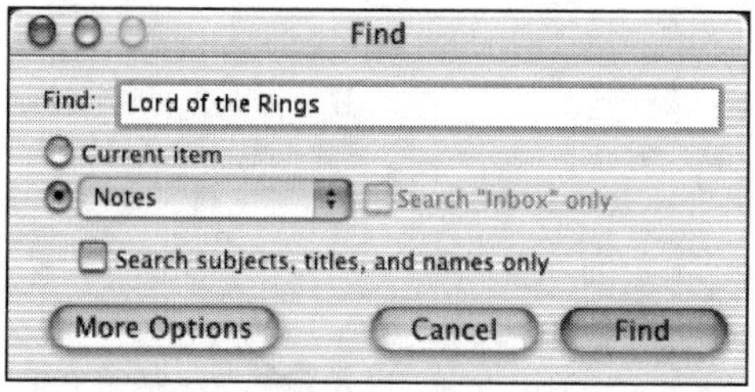

Figure 27.6 For more advanced filtering and selection capabilities, you can perform a Find.

3. You can sort the list by the contents of any column by clicking the column name. To reverse the sort order, click the column name again.

The sort column is indicated by a blue column heading. The sort direction is indicated by the triangle following the column name (**Figure 27.4**).

4. *Optional:* You can filter the notes list to show only titles that contain a particular text string or those to which a specific category has been assigned (**Figure 27.5**).

◆ To filter by title, choose Title contains from the pull-down menu above the notes list, and type a string in the text box.

◆ To filter by category, choose Category is from the pull-down menu, and choose a category from the menu to its right.

✔ Tips

■ To reverse the effects of filtering (to see the entire note list), click the Clear icon beside the filter, set the Category to All, or delete the text in the text box.

■ You can also search for a particular note by clicking the Find toolbar icon and filling in the search information in the Find dialog box (**Figure 27.6**).

■ Once a note is displayed, you can view other notes in the same window by clicking the Next or Previous toolbar icon.

Creating and Deleting Notes

You can create as many notes as you wish. As notes cease to be useful, you can delete them.

To create a new note:

1. To create a new note from Notes view, click the New toolbar icon at the top of the Entourage window, or choose File > New > Note, or press ⌘N.

   or

   To create a new note from any other main view, click the down arrow beside the New toolbar icon and choose Note (**Figure 27.7**), or choose File > New > Note.

   A new note window appears (**Figure 27.8**).

2. Give the note a title and fill in the body of the note by typing, pasting, or dragging and dropping the text. You can optionally assign a category to the note to classify it.

New icon

Figure 27.7
Regardless of what part of Entourage is currently active, you can create a new note by choosing the Note command from this toolbar menu.

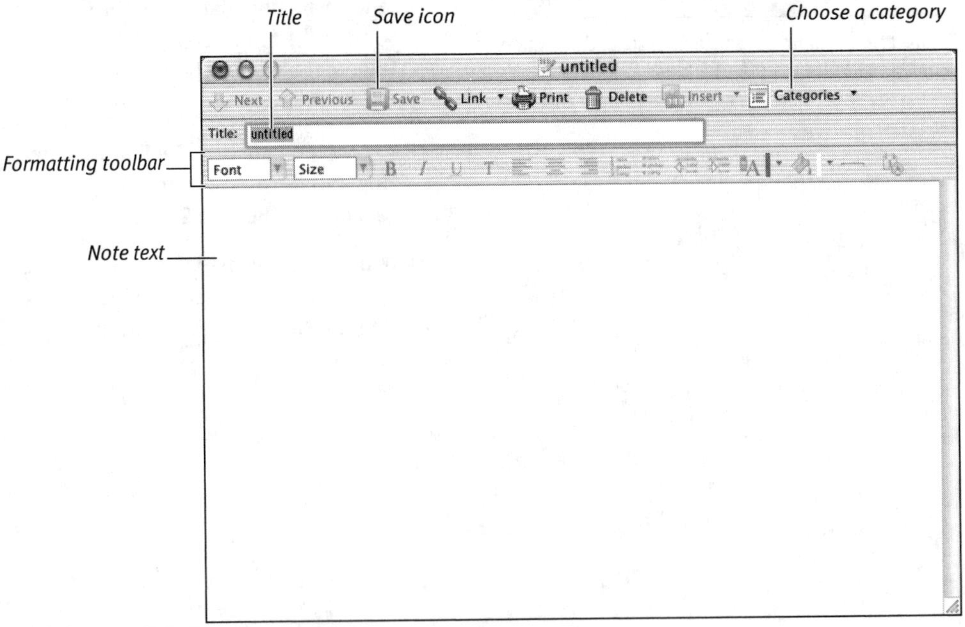

Figure 27.8 A new note window appears.

Scripts menu

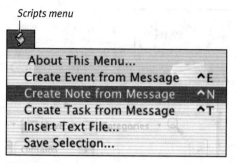

Figure 27.10 You can save the current email message as a note by choosing the Create Note from Message command from the Scripts menu.

Insert

Picture...
Background Picture...
Sound...
Movie...
Hyperlink...

Figure 27.11 You can add pictures, sounds, movies, hyperlinks, and/or a background picture to a note by choosing commands from the Insert toolbar icon.

3. You can use the Formatting toolbar (**Figure 27.9**, below) to format the note's text or choose commands from the Format menu.

4. To save the note, click the Save toolbar icon, or choose File > Save, or press ⌘S.

✔ Tips

■ To save an email message for future reference, you can create a note from it. Select the email message's header in the message list, open the Scripts menu, and choose Create Note from Message (**Figure 27.10**) or press Control N. You can edit the text if necessary.

■ You can add a background color to a note by clicking the Background Color icon on the Formatting toolbar.

■ Notes can optionally contain images, sounds, hyperlinks, movies, or a background picture. Click the Insert icon on the note window's toolbar (**Figure 27.11**) to add one of these items to the current note.

■ You can keep track of important Web site addresses by dragging them from Internet Explorer into a note. You can drag any link you find in the body of a Web page or the current Web page's address from the Address box.

CREATING AND DELETING NOTES

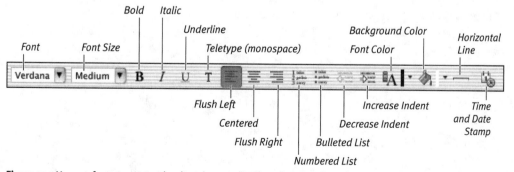

Figure 27.9 You can format note text by choosing commands and options from the Formatting toolbar.

To delete a note:

1. Switch to Notes view and select the note's heading.

2. Click the Delete toolbar icon (**Figure 27.12**) or choose Edit > Delete Note. Or you can press ⌑Delete⌑ or ⌘⌑Delete⌑.

3. In the dialog box that appears (**Figure 27.13**), confirm the deletion by clicking the Delete icon.

✔ Tips

- Note deletions cannot be reversed. There is no Undo Delete command.

- You can simultaneously delete multiple notes. Hold down ⌘ to select additional notes from the notes list, and then perform the deletion as you would for an individual note. Press ⌑Shift⌑ to select multiple contiguous notes from the notes list.

- You can also delete a note that is open in its own window. Click the Delete toolbar icon, or choose Edit > Delete Note, or press ⌘⌑Delete⌑.

Figure 27.12 To delete the current note, click the Delete toolbar icon.

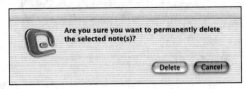

Are you sure you want to permanently delete the selected note(s)?

Delete   Cancel

Figure 27.13 You must confirm any note deletion.

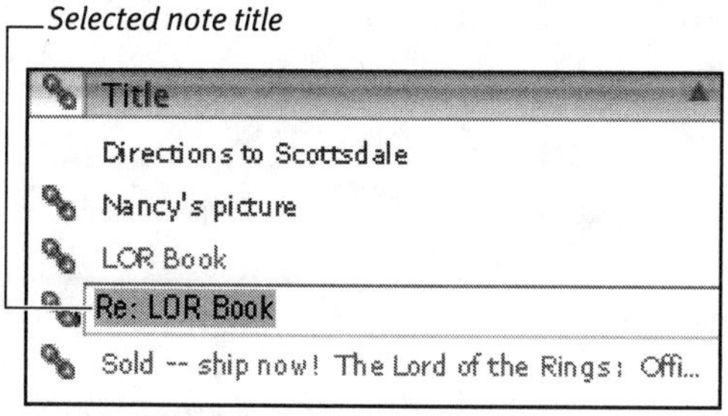

Selected note title

Figure 27.14 You can edit the title of any note by selecting it in the notes list.

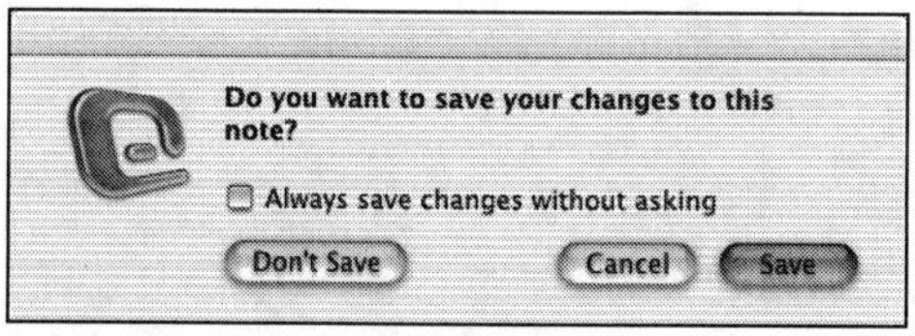

Figure 27.15 If you close a changed note without first saving it, this dialog box appears.

Editing Notes

You can easily change any aspect of a note—including its name.

To edit a note:

1. Switch to Notes view.

2. In the notes list, double-click the note you want to edit.
   The note opens in its own window.

3. Change the note.

4. Click the Save toolbar icon, or choose File > Save, or press ⌘S.

To rename a note:

1. Select the note in the notes list.

2. Click the note's title.
   The title is selected and ready for editing (**Figure 27.14**).

3. Edit the title.

4. Press Return or Enter, or click elsewhere on the page.

✔ Tip

■ If you modify an existing note and attempt to close its window without saving it, a dialog box automatically appears (**Figure 27.15**). Click Save to save the note's changes, click Cancel if you want to resume editing the note, or click Don't Save to close the note and discard all changes. To instruct Entourage to save all changed notes automatically (without forcing you to use the Save command), click the Always save changes without asking check box.

INTERNET NEWSGROUPS

Internet newsgroups (sometimes called Usenet newsgroups) are like computerized public bulletin boards. There are tens of thousands of newsgroups on the Internet, each focused on a particular topic. Messages—resembling email messages—are posted to newsgroups, and anyone with access to the newsgroup can read them. If you respond to a message you've read, your reply is posted along with it. Some newsgroups include *binaries* (files associated with messages, similar to email attachments) that are available for downloading.

Creating a News-Server Account

To use Entourage for working with news-groups, you need access to a news server that uses Network News Transfer Protocol (NNTP). Your Internet Service Provider (ISP) is likely to have one. Check its sign-up instructions for the name of its news server. If your ISP doesn't offer newsgroups, you can use a search engine to locate one of the many free public news servers (visit www.google.com, for example, and search for "public news servers"). There are also Web-based news servers, such as groups.google.com, but you view these in a Web browser, not in Entourage.

To set up a news-server account in Entourage, you'll need the name or IP (Internet Protocol) address of a news server to which you have access. In some cases, you may also need a user name and password. Once you have the necessary information, you're ready to set up Entourage as your newsreader.

To create a news-server account:

1. Choose Tools > Accounts.

   The Accounts window appears.

2. Click the News tab (**Figure 28.1**).

3. With the News tab open, click the New icon to create a new account.

   The Account Setup Assistant appears (**Figure 28.2**).

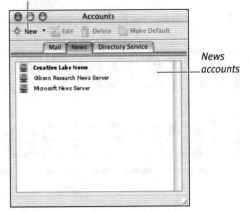

Create a new account

News accounts

Figure 28.1 The News tab of the Accounts window displays the names of all news servers you have set up.

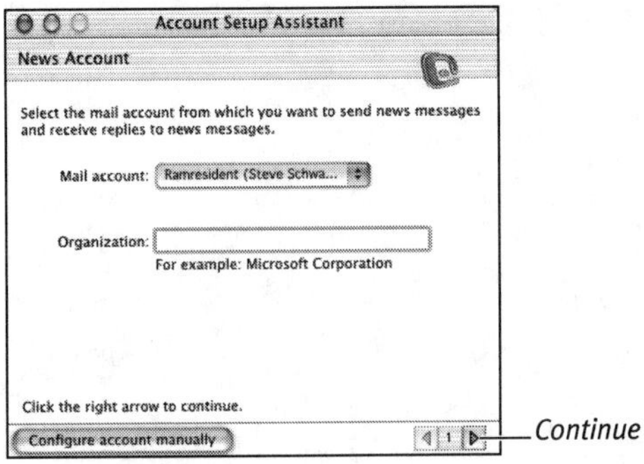

Continue

Figure 28.2 Choose a reply-to email address from the Mail account list, and enter an organization name (if you wish).

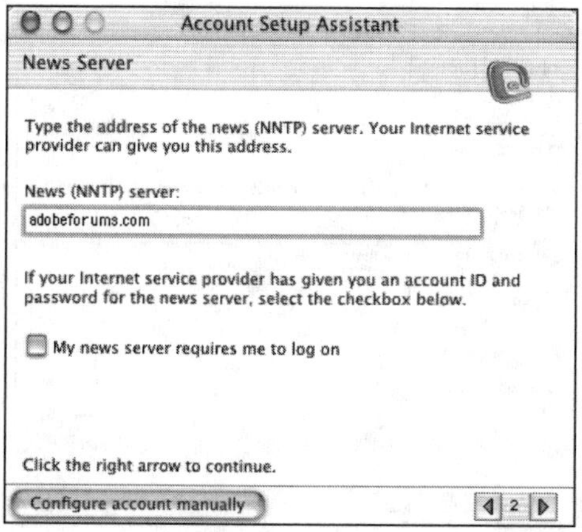

Figure 28.3 Enter the name or IP address of the news server.

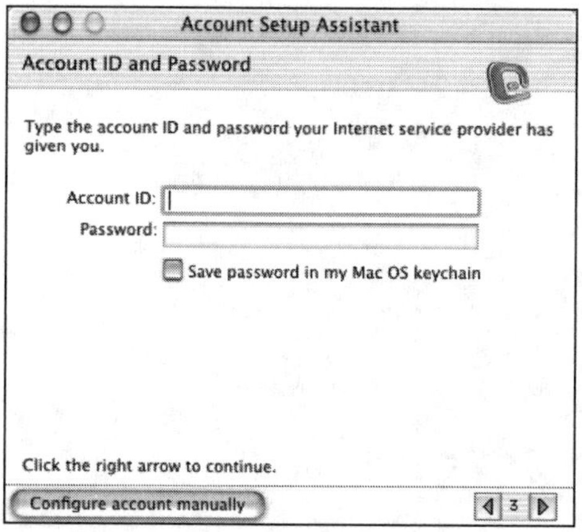

Figure 28.4 If you are required to use them to log on, enter your account ID (user name) and password.

4. People who reply to your newsgroup posts can respond to your email address and/or post a public reply on the newsgroup. If you've defined multiple email accounts in Entourage, pull down the Mail account menu and choose the address you want to use for receiving newsgroup replies.

5. The header information included with your posted messages can include an organization with which you're affiliated. You can opt to enter its name in the Organization text box. Click the right-arrow button to continue.

6. Enter the name or IP address of the news server to which you want to connect (**Figure 28.3**).

7. If the server requires you to enter a user name and password, check My news server requires me to log on. Click the right arrow to continue.

8. If you indicated that a user name and password are required, enter them here (**Figure 28.4**). To have the password automatically entered each time you access the news server, check Save password in my Mac OS keychain. Click the right arrow to continue.

(continues on next page)

9. On the final screen (**Figure 28.5**), enter a name for the news-server account, and then click Finish.

   The news-server account appears in the Accounts list and the Folder List.

✔ Tips

- To add other news servers, repeat these steps for each account. Your default news account is displayed in bold in the Accounts list. To set a different default, select the account and click Make Default (Figure 28.1). Note that you can also *delete* accounts here.

- To get you started using newsgroups, an account is automatically created for the Microsoft News Server, which hosts Microsoft's product-related newsgroups. To use this news server, all you have to do is specify an email account to use as your reply-to account (as explained in Step 4).

- People who send junk email (spam) often collect the email addresses of people who post messages to newsgroups. To avoid receiving unwanted email in your primary account, consider using Hotmail or another free email account as your reply-to address.

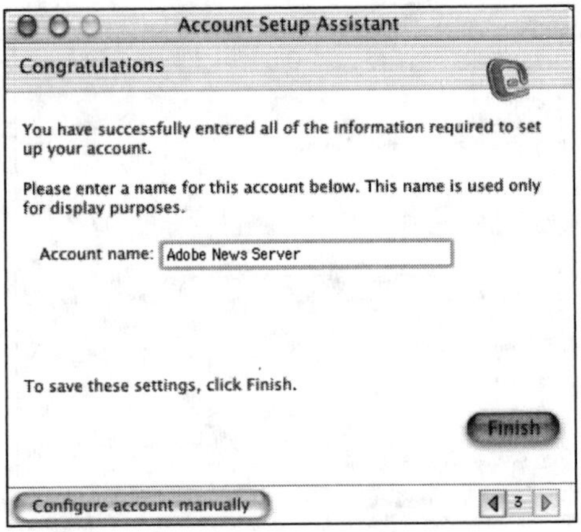

Figure 28.5 Name the account and click Finish. The name will identify the news server in your Folder List (Figure 28.7).

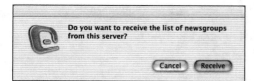

Figure 28.6 Click Receive to download the newsgroup list from the server.

Viewing Newsgroups

Once you have at least one news-server account set up, you can download the list of newsgroups available on that server. You can also specify the newsgroups you'd like to read regularly.

To view the newsgroups on a server:

1. Click a news-server name in the Folder List.

2. If this is the first time you've selected the news server, Entourage will ask if you want to receive the list of the newsgroups that server carries (**Figure 28.6**).

3. Click the Receive button.

   The list of available newsgroups will appear in Entourage's right pane (**Figure 28.7**). It may take a while to receive the entire list, depending on the speed of your Internet connection and the number of newsgroups the server offers.

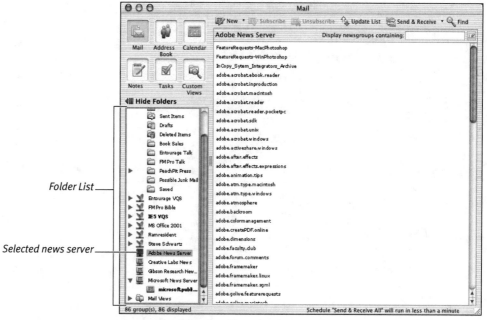

Figure 28.7 The list of newsgroups appears.

Updating the Newsgroup List

The newsgroups available on any given news server can—and often do—change over time. If it's been a while since Entourage last downloaded the list of newsgroups on a server, you can refresh that list.

To update the list of newsgroups on a server:

1. Click the news-server account in the Folder List.

2. Click the Update List icon on the toolbar or choose View > Get New Newsgroups.

   If no new newsgroups have been added, you will be informed (**Figure 28.8**). Otherwise any new newsgroups will be added to the list.

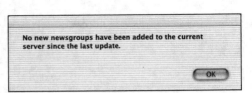

Figure 28.8 If there are no new newsgroups, this message appears.

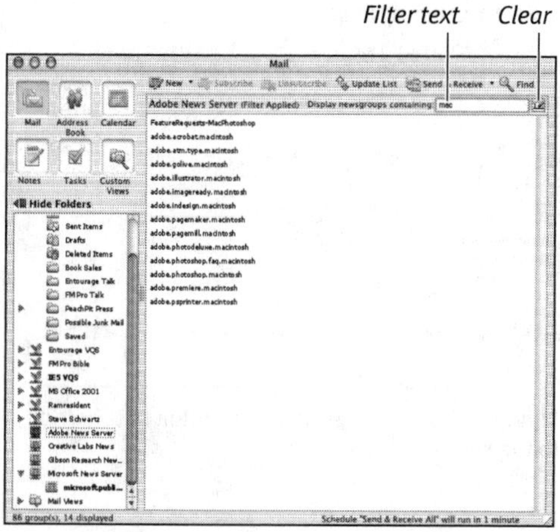

Filter text   Clear

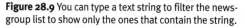

Figure 28.9 You can type a text string to filter the newsgroup list to show only the ones that contain the string.

Filtering the Newsgroup List

Many news servers carry thousands of newsgroups, and it can be a daunting task to find a particular one. Entourage lets you filter the list of newsgroup names.

To filter the list of newsgroup names:

1. Click the name of the news-server account in the Folder List.

2. Type a search string in the box labeled Display newsgroups containing, above the newsgroup list.

3. Only newsgroups that contain the search string in their titles are displayed (**Figure 28.9**); all others are temporarily hidden.

   To restore the complete list, click the Clear icon or delete the text in the text box.

Subscribing to Newsgroups

If you find some newsgroups you'd like to read regularly, you can subscribe to them. This isn't the same as subscribing to a magazine; you don't receive anything automatically. And subscribing to a newsgroup doesn't add you to a list anywhere, as subscribing to an email mailing list does. Subscribing simply makes it easier to follow a newsgroup by adding its name to the Folder List (beneath the news server), as well as displaying its name in bold in the newsgroup list. You can also filter the list to show only those newsgroups to which you subscribe.

To subscribe to newsgroups:

1. Click the news-server account in the Folder List.

2. Select a newsgroup in the right pane to which you want to subscribe.

3. Click the Subscribe icon on the toolbar (**Figure 28.10**) or choose Edit > Subscribe. Or you can Control-click the newsgroup name and choose Subscribe from the pop-up menu that appears.

   The newsgroup name is added to the Folder List beneath the server name.

To view only subscribed-to newsgroups:

1. With a news server's newsgroup list displayed, choose View > Subscribed Only.

   Names of newsgroups to which you haven't subscribed are hidden (**Figure 28.11**).

2. To see the entire newsgroup list, choose View > Subscribed Only again.

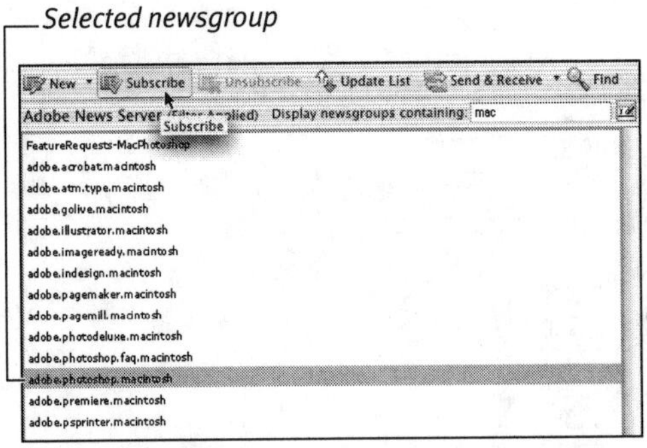

Selected newsgroup

Figure 28.10 Click the Subscribe button to subscribe to the selected newsgroup.

Figure 28.11 Only subscribed-to newsgroups remain visible. Their names are displayed in bold and color.

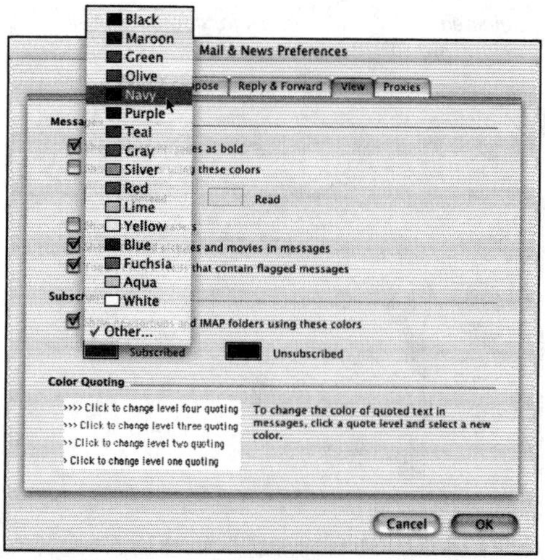

Figure 28.12 Click the Subscribed icon to display this pop-up color list, and then select a new color.

To unsubscribe from a newsgroup:

1. Click the news-server account in the Folder List.

2. Select the newsgroup from the list in the right pane.

3. Click the Unsubscribe toolbar icon (Figure 28.10) or choose Edit > Unsubscribe. Or you can (Control)-click the newsgroup name and choose Unsubscribe from the pop-up menu.

✔ Tip

■ Names of newsgroups to which you have subscribed appear in bold and color in the newsgroup list. A Preference setting determines the specific color. To change the color, choose Entourage > Mail & News Preferences, click the View tab, click the Subscribed color box, and select a new color from the pop-up list (**Figure 28.12**).

Managing Newsgroup Messages

Once you have set up a news-server account, retrieved the list of newsgroups, and found a newsgroup you'd like to read, the next step is to retrieve the current list of messages (also known as *posts*) and read the ones that interest you. Older messages are periodically deleted from the news server to make room for new ones. Messages are usually updated several times a day.

To manage the current list of messages in a newsgroup:

1. If you subscribe to the newsgroup, click its name in the Folder list.

   The initial list of message headers for the newsgroup appears in the upper-right pane (**Figure 28.13**).

   or

   If you don't subscribe to the newsgroup, select the news server in the Folder List and then double-click the name of the desired newsgroup in the right pane.

   The list of message headers appears in a new window.

2. If additional, older messages for this newsgroup are available on the server, you can retrieve the next batch by clicking the More toolbar icon or choosing View > Get More News Messages.

3. You can sort the messages in the message list by clicking any but the first column head (Online Status). Clicking the same column head a second time reverses the sort order.

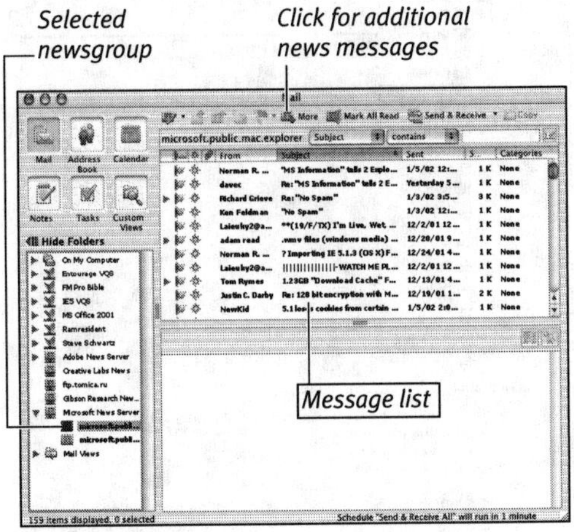

Selected newsgroup

Click for additional news messages

Message list

Figure 28.13 Current message headers for the selected newsgroup appear in the message list.

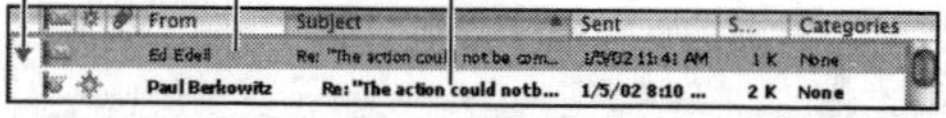

Thread indicator   *Original message*   *Reply*

Figure 28.14 In Threaded view, click any triangle to reveal replies to the initial message.

✔ Tips

■ To make it easier to follow a particular message conversation (called a *thread*), choose the View > Threaded command. This groups every original message with all responses to it. A triangle in the first column indicates that there are replies to that particular message. Click the triangle to reveal the replies (**Figure 28.14**). Click it again to hide the replies.

■ To simultaneously reveal or hide all replies in the message list when in threaded view, choose View > Expand All or View > Collapse All.

Reading Messages

When Entourage displays the message list for a newsgroup or updates the list, it downloads only the message headers—not the message body or attachments. After you've selected one or more message headers, Entourage downloads their text.

To read a message:

1. Click the message header to view the message text in the Preview Pane (**Figure 28.15**).

   or

   Double-click the message header to open the message in its own window (**Figure 28.16**).

2. To read additional messages, do any of the following:

   ◆ Click another message header in the message list.

   ◆ Choose View > Next (⌘]) or View > Previous (⌘[).

   ◆ Click the Next or Previous toolbar icon (only available when you're reading messages in a separate window).

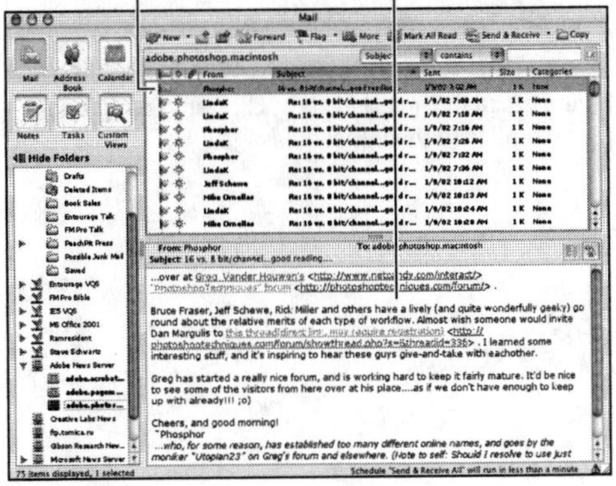

Selected message header   *Message text*

Figure 28.15 Click a message header in the list to read the message in the Preview Pane.

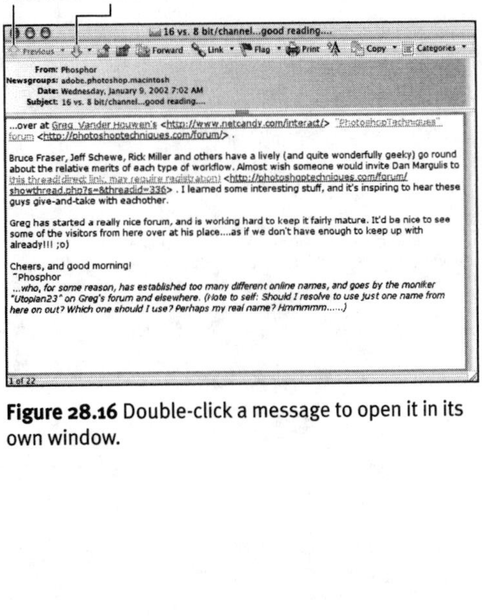

Previous   *Next*

Figure 28.16 Double-click a message to open it in its own window.

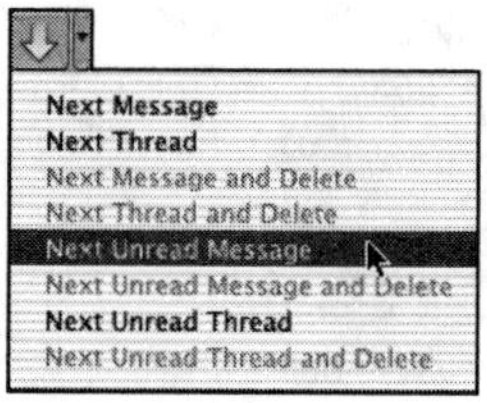

Figure 28.17 Click the down arrow beside the Next or Previous toolbar button for more options.

✔ Tips

- You can also use the cursor keys to select messages to read. Press → and ← to expand or collapse a thread, and press ↓ and ↑ to read the next or previous message. Note, however, that any message the cursor touches—even momentarily—will be downloaded.

- When reading messages in a separate window, you can click the down arrow beside the Next or Previous toolbar icon to reveal a menu of other message-navigation choices (**Figure 28.17**).

- You can scroll through lengthy messages by holding down Spacebar or scroll up by pressing Shift Spacebar. When you reach the end of a message, you can press Spacebar to jump to the next unread message in the message list.

- You cannot *delete* newsgroup messages as you can email. However, you can set the message list to display only messages you haven't read by choosing View > Unread Only. To revert to seeing the entire list, choose the command again.

- You can also select the headers of messages you want to ignore and mark them as read by choosing Message > Mark as Read (⌘ T). Then set the view to Unread Only to hide these messages in the message list.

READING MESSAGES

Posting to Newsgroups

You can post messages to newsgroups by either replying to an existing message or posting a new one. It is common courtesy—and in your own best interest—to read the messages in the newsgroup for a while before posting anything. Also make sure to read the FAQ for the newsgroup, which should be posted at regular intervals. The FAQ—if one exists—usually explains what constitutes an appropriate posting. Messages the group's regular participants deem inappropriate are likely to be on the receiving end of *flames* (attacking or insulting messages).

To reply to a message:

1. Select a message in the message list to view it in the preview pane, or double-click the message to open it in its own window.

2. To post a reply, do one of the following:

   ◆ To post a reply to the newsgroup, click the Reply to Newsgroup toolbar icon (**Figure 28.18**) or choose Message > Reply. Or you can press ⌘R.

   ◆ To send an email message to the author of the newsgroup post, click the Reply to Sender toolbar icon or choose Message > Reply to Sender. Or press Option⌘R.

   ◆ To post a reply to the newsgroup *and* send an email message to the author, choose Message > Reply to All or press Shift⌘R.

   A new message window opens (**Figure 28.19**), containing a copy of the message to which you are replying. The message is preaddressed to the newsgroup, the author, or both, as appropriate.

Reply to Sender   Reply to Newsgroup

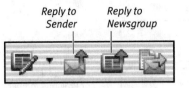

Figure 28.18 Click Reply to Newsgroup to post a reply to the newsgroup.

— Original message
Newsgroup   Author's email address

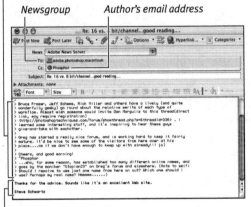

— Reply

Figure 28.19 A new, preaddressed message opens.

3. Delete any of the original message text that's irrelevant to your response. (You should quote the part of the message to which you're replying).

4. Add your comments in the body of the message.

5. Click the Post Now or Post Later toolbar icon at the top of the message window. (If one of the icons is missing, expand the message window to display it.)

   or

   Choose Message > Post Message Now (⌘Return) or Message > Post Message Later (Shift ⌘ Return).

To post a new message to the group:

1. Open the newsgroup list to which you want to post a message by selecting it in the Folder List or by double-clicking it in the news server's newsgroup list.

2. Click the New toolbar icon or choose File > New > News Message. Or you can press ⌘N.

   A blank message window opens, pread-dressed to the newsgroup (**Figure 28.20**).

3. Add other desired recipients to the address field (additional newsgroups go in the To line and email recipients go in the CC line), enter a subject, and type the body of the message as you would an email message (see "Sending Mail and Files" in Chapter 23, Email).

4. *Optional:* You can add attachments just as you would with an email message. It is polite to compress attachments to save retrieval time for the recipients.

5. *Optional:* You can click the Use HTML icon on the Formatting toolbar (Figure 28.20) to toggle between unformatted and formatted text, or you can choose Format > HTML. Be aware, however, that many people use text-only newsreaders and may find formatted text virtually unreadable.

6. When you're done composing your message, click the Post Now or Post Later toolbar icon.

   or

   Choose Message > Post Message Now (⌘Return) or Message > Post Message Later (Shift ⌘ Return).

Server   Newsgroup

Use HTML

Figure 28.20 Compose the new message in the window that opens.

Show/hide attachments pane

Attachments pane

Save the selected attachment(s)

Figure 28.21 The Attachments pane appears after the message is downloaded from the server.

Downloading Files from Newsgroups

Attached files show up in newsgroup message headers as attachments, just as they do in email messages. However, the paper-clip icon does not appear in the message header in the Attachments column until you've clicked the message header and downloaded the message. You can usually tell if a message contains an attachment by its size: anything over a few kilobytes is almost certain to include an attachment. After you've previewed or opened a message, you can handle its attachments the same way you would in email (see "To manage attachments in received email" in Chapter 23). Newsgroups that actively promote messages with attachments (such as pictures, movies, or song files) often include the word *binaries* in their name.

To download a file from a newsgroup:

1. Click the news-server account in the Folder List.

2. Select the newsgroup in the Folder List or double-click the newsgroup's name in the newsgroup list.

3. Select or double-click the header of a message that contains an attachment.

   After your Mac downloads the message and attachment(s) from the news server (this can take a while), the Attachments pane appears (**Figure 28.21**).

   (continues on next page)

4. Select the attachment and click the Save button beside the Attachments pane.

The Save Attachment dialog box appears (**Figure 28.22**).

5. Navigate to the disk and folder in which you want to save the file, and then click Save.

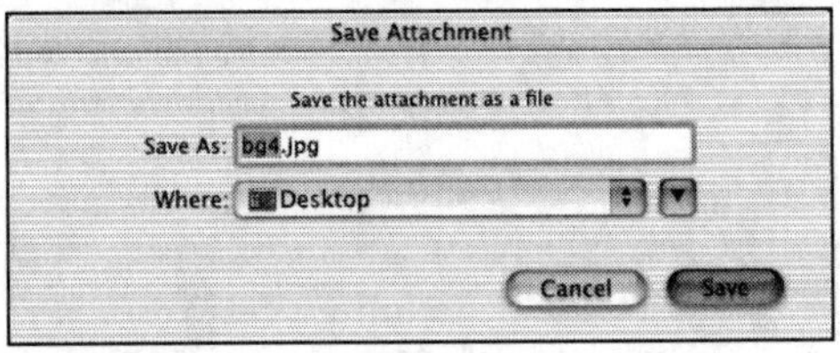

✔ Tip

■ Picture attachments that are in a format Entourage supports (such as JPEG and GIF) appear as pictures in the body of the message.

Figure 28.22 Select a destination disk and folder, and then click Save.

Part VI: Combining the Applications

COPYING, EMBEDDING, AND LINKING

Office lets you easily share information between its applications. The three main methods are to copy, embed, or link information from one application to another. This chapter covers the basics, while Chapter 30, Using Programs Together, explains the specifics of sharing information between Office applications.

The simplest method is to *copy and paste* or *drag and drop* information from one application to another. For example, you can copy Excel data and paste it into a Word document. The data becomes part of the Word document as an editable table. Similarly, after switching to Slide Sorter View in PowerPoint, you can drag a copy of a slide into a Word document. Data added via the copy-and-paste or drag-and-drop method becomes a part of—and is saved with—the destination document.

If you want to maintain a link between the original data or object and the new document, you can use *embedding* or *linking*. The difference between the two procedures lies in where the data is stored. Embedded data becomes part of the destination document, making it transportable. Linked data, on the other hand, is stored only in the original document and is *referenced* by the destination document. Thus, linking is an excellent choice for working with files on a network.

Using Drag and Drop

The easiest way to move something from one application to another is by using drag and drop. Dragging and dropping *between* applications works just like dragging and dropping *within* an application. Arrange the document windows of the two applications so you can see them both. Then drag selected text or an object from one application window to its destination in the other application's document window. **Table 29.1** lists the types of items you can drag and drop between applications.

To drag and drop an object:

1. Arrange the document windows of the two applications so you can see both the source object and its destination.

2. Select the object or text—in this example, a worksheet range (**Figure 29.1**).

Table 29.1

Common Objects to Drag and Drop	
Word	Selected text or a table
Excel	A cell, a cell range, graphics, or a table
PowerPoint	A slide from Slide Sorter view

Selected cell range

Figure 29.1 Using drag and drop, you can copy a selected cell range from an Excel worksheet into a Word document.

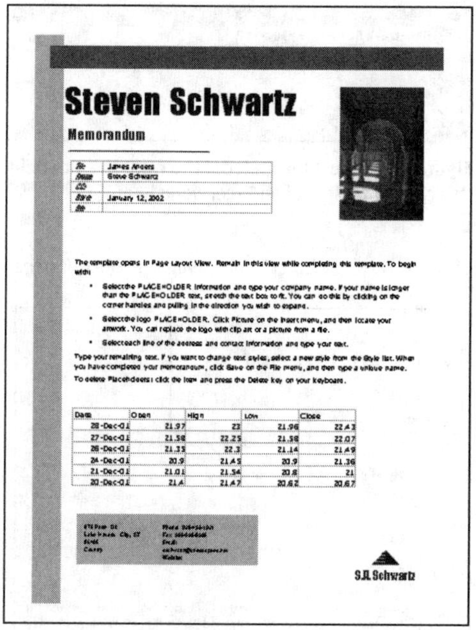

Figure 29.2 Drag the Excel object into the Word document.

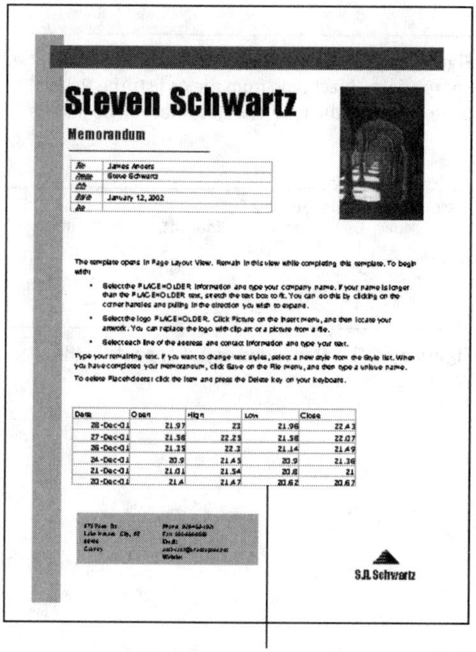

Dragged data

Figure 29.3 The dragged Excel data appears in the Word document as a new table.

3. Drag the border of the object or text to the destination in the other window (**Figure 29.2**).

4. Release the mouse button (**Figure 29.3**). The object or text appears in the destination document.

✔ Tips

■ To accomplish a drag and drop, you may need to resize the two document windows and rearrange them onscreen.

■ When you drag and drop an item, it becomes embedded in the destination application. The copy will not reflect any changes made to the original material unless you establish a link. See "Linking Objects" later in this chapter.

■ You are free to modify the object or text in the destination document.

■ If you hold down (Option)(⌘) as you drag an object between applications, a pop-up menu allows you to either copy or move the object (moving destroys the original object).

Embedding an Object

An *embedded object* is one that is copied or moved from its source application to a target application. All data for the object is copied to the target application. As a result, if you move the target file to another computer, the object will be moved, too. Objects that are copied and pasted or dragged and dropped also become embedded.

This section covers how to embed an existing object in a target application, as well as how to create an embedded object from scratch. The examples embed an Excel object in a Word document, but the procedures are the same for the other applications.

To embed an existing object:

1. Select the object or text in its source application (**Figure 29.4**).

2. Choose Edit > Copy or press ⌘C.

3. Switch to the target application (Word, in this example), and click to set the destination for the object.

   The embedded object will appear at the insertion point.

4. Choose Edit > Paste Special.

   The Paste Special dialog box appears (**Figure 29.5**).

5. Select the item labeled as an Object (in this instance, the Microsoft Excel Worksheet Object). Make sure Paste is selected, and then click OK.

   The embedded object appears in the document (**Figure 29.6**).

To create an embedded object:

1. Click to set the destination for the object.

   The embedded object will appear at the insertion point.

	A	B	C	D
1	Student Scores - Quiz 12			
2	Jones, J.	Abrams, B.	Edwards, S.	Smith, Y.
3	1	1.1	1.55	2
4	2	1	2	1
5	3	2	4	5
6	4	3	5	2

Figure 29.4 Select the material you want to embed (in this case, a portion of an Excel worksheet).

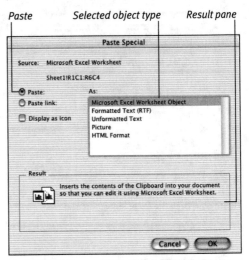

Paste · · · Selected object type · · · Result pane

Paste Special

Source: Microsoft Excel Worksheet

Sheet1!R1C1:R6C4

○ Paste: As:
○ Paste link: Microsoft Excel Worksheet Object
                  Formatted Text (RTF)
☐ Display as icon Unformatted Text
                  Picture
                  HTML Format

Result
Inserts the contents of the Clipboard into your document so that you can edit it using Microsoft Excel Worksheet.

Cancel   OK

Figure 29.5 In the Paste Special dialog box, select the appropriate object type from the As list. The Result pane indicates the type of object that will be inserted.

Student Scores - Quiz 12			
Jones, J.	Abrams, B.	Edwards, S.	Smith, Y.
1	1.1	1.55	2
2	1	2	1
3	2	4	5
4	3	5	2

Figure 29.6 The embedded object appears in the Word document.

Object

Object type:

Microsoft Equation
Microsoft Excel Chart
Microsoft Excel Worksheet
Microsoft Graph Chart
Microsoft Organization Chart
Microsoft Word Document
Microsoft Word Picture

☐ Display as icon

Result

Inserts a new Microsoft Excel Worksheet object into your document.

From File...   Cancel   OK

Figure 29.7 Select Microsoft Excel Worksheet as the type of object you want to create.

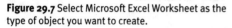

Figure 29.8 Create the new object—in this instance, a formatted Excel worksheet.

Student Scores - Quiz 12			
Jones, J.	Abrams, B.	Edwards, S.	Smith, Y.
1	1.1	1.55	2
2	1	2	1
3	2	3	5
4	3	5	2
2.50	1.78	2.89	2.50 Average
10.00	7.10	11.55	10.00 Total

Figure 29.9 The embedded object appears in the destination document.

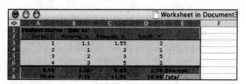

Figure 29.10 The object opens in an untitled document in the application in which it was originally created.

2. Choose Insert > Object.

   The Object dialog box appears (**Figure 29.7**).

3. Select the desired type of object and click OK.

   The appropriate Office application opens and a new, blank document appears.

4. Create the object (**Figure 29.8**).

5. *Optional:* Save the object document by choosing File > Save Copy As.

6. Close the object document.

   The object appears in the document in which it was inserted (**Figure 29.9**).

To edit an embedded object:

1. Double-click the object (in this example, the worksheet embedded in the Word document).

   or

   Select the object and choose Edit > *object type* > Edit. (The command may be worded Edit > Worksheet Object > Edit or Edit > Document Object > Edit, for example.)

   The source application launches, and the object appears in a new, untitled document window (**Figure 29.10**).

2. As you modify the object, the changes automatically appear in the embedded object, too. When you are finished editing, close the untitled document window and return to the original document.

   It is *not* necessary to save changes when editing an object. Any changes you make to the object are automatically conveyed to the document in which the object is embedded.

✔ Tip

■ You can elect to view the embedded object as an icon. To do this, check Display as icon in the Object dialog box.

Linking Objects

When you link rather than embed an object, the object remains in the original application's document. A *copy* of the object—linked to the original—is displayed in the second application. Think of the copy as representing the linked object; it is merely a reference to the original. Any changes made to the original object also appear in the linked copy.

You create linked objects using the Copy and Paste Special commands. The object is updated whenever you reopen the destination file. In addition to (or instead of) automatically updating a link, you can also manually update a link.

The example below shows how to link an Excel chart into a Word document.

To link an object:

1. In the original document, select the object to link (**Figure 29.11**).

2. Choose Edit > Copy or press ⌘C.

3. Open the document in the target application (in this example, Word), and click where you want the object to appear.

4. Choose Edit > Paste Special.

   The Paste Special dialog box appears (**Figure 29.12**).

5. Click the Paste link radio button, select the object to link, and click OK.

   The linked object appears in the destination document (**Figure 29.13**).

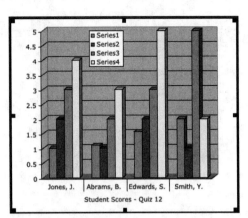

Figure 29.11 Select the object you want to link—in this case, an Excel chart.

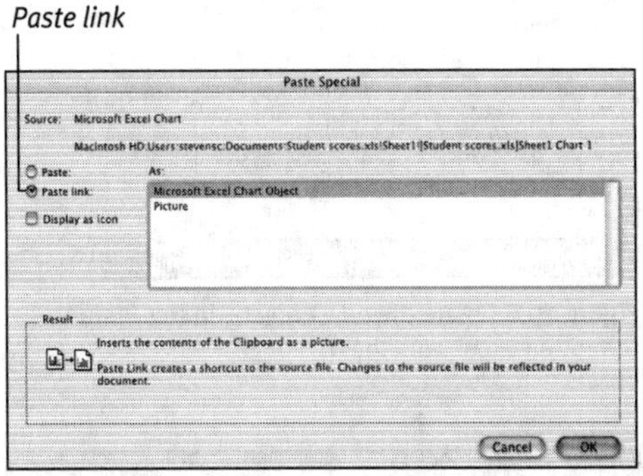

Paste link

Figure 29.12 Click the Paste link radio button, select the specific object type, and click OK.

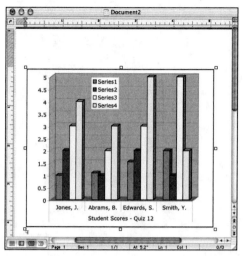

Figure 29.13 The linked Excel object appears in the Word document.

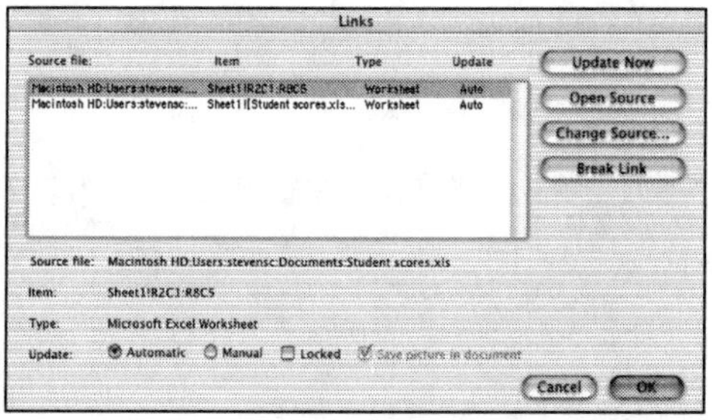

Figure 29.14 In the Links dialog box, click Update Now to update the selected link automatically.

✔ Tips

- You can double-click a linked object (in the destination document) to edit the original object.

- When you open a document containing links that automatically update, the links are checked for any necessary updates.

To update a link manually:

1. Choose Edit > Links.
   The Links dialog box appears (**Figure 29.14**).

2. Select the link from the list and click Update Now.
   The linked object is updated.

3. Click OK to close the Links dialog box.

✔ Tips

- To set the link so that it updates *only* when you click Update Now, set Manual as the Update option.

- To change a linked object into an embedded object, select the link and click the Break Link button.

USING PROGRAMS TOGETHER

Separately, each Office application is impressive. But when combined, they form a powerful system for sharing information.

As shown in Chapter 29, Copying, Embedding, and Linking, you can copy a table of numeric data from Excel into a Word document—to add some relevant numbers to a memo, for instance. To ensure that future changes to the Excel numbers automatically flow to the table in the Word document, you can link the data between the documents.

See Chapter 29 for detailed information on copying, dragging and dropping, embedding, and linking material. This chapter provides some additional examples of ways to share data between Office applications and also explains how to link Entourage items to Office documents.

Combining Word and Excel

Word and Excel work well together, especially when you're creating Word documents that display structured numerical data. Chapter 29 explained how to copy and link Excel data into Word documents. In this section, you'll learn how to do the reverse—copy a Word table into an Excel worksheet. Later in this chapter, we'll cover copying text from Word into Excel and PowerPoint.

To copy a Word table into Excel:

1. In Word, click any cell within the table you intend to copy.

2. Choose Table > Select > Table.
   The table is selected (**Figure 30.1**).

3. Choose Edit > Copy or press ⌘C.

4. Switch to Excel, and select the cell in which the Word table will start.

5. Choose Edit > Paste or press ⌘V.
   The Word table is pasted into the Excel document. Adjust the column widths as necessary to display fully the contents of each column (**Figure 30.2**).

✔ Tips

- A table copied in this manner is fully editable within Excel. The data maintains no link to the Word document.

- To expand a column so it displays the longest text string, double-click the right edge of the column head—to the right of the letter *E* (**Figure 30.3**), for example.

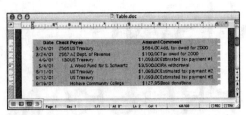

Figure 30.1 To select your table in Word, click any cell of the table and then choose Table > Select > Table.

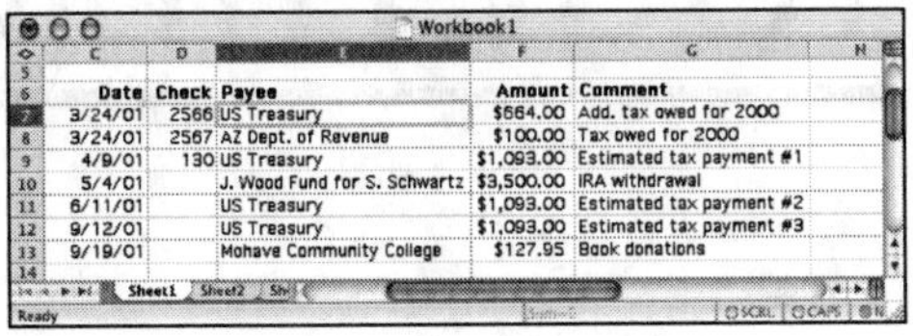

Figure 30.2 The Word table appears in the Excel document.

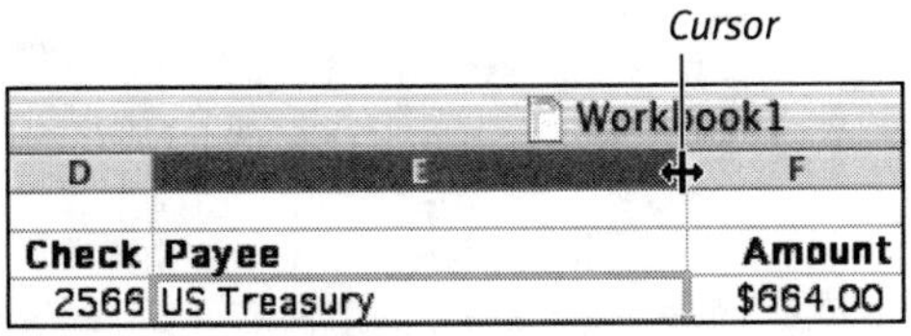

Cursor

D	E	F
Check	Payee	Amount
2566	US Treasury	$664.00

Figure 30.3 To reset a column width to match the longest cell entry in the column, double-click the right edge of the column head.

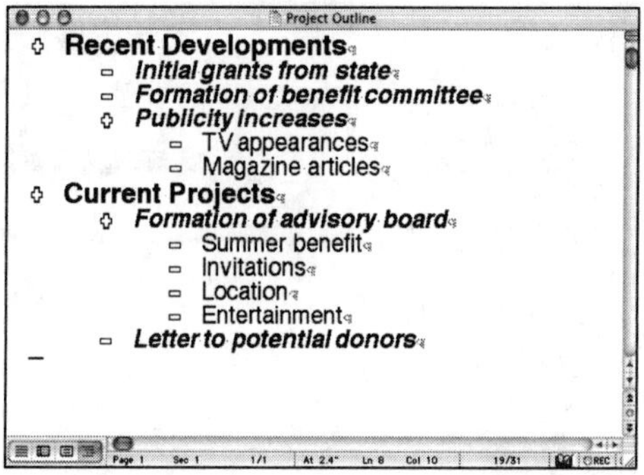

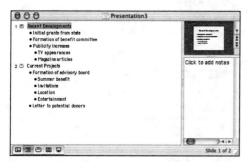

Figure 30.4 Create a presentation outline in Word.

Figure 30.5 The Word outline appears as a new presentation in PowerPoint.

Combining Word and PowerPoint

You can use Word and PowerPoint together to create documents. This section covers importing outlines from one application to the other. It also explains how to copy meeting minutes from PowerPoint into Word.

You can also copy text from Word and paste it into the documents of any other Office applications. We'll discuss that in the next section, "Copying Text from Word to Excel or PowerPoint."

To use a Word outline file in a PowerPoint presentation:

1. Create and save a presentation outline in Word (**Figure 30.4**).

   Each Heading 1 paragraph will become the title of a new slide. Heading 2 paragraphs will become first-level text.

2. Choose File > Send To > Microsoft PowerPoint.

   PowerPoint launches and the Word outline appears as a new presentation (**Figure 30.5**). No link is maintained to the original Word outline.

✔ Tips

- Generating the outline in Word allows you to use Word tools, such as the thesaurus. Most people find writing and editing easier to do in Word than in PowerPoint.

- If heading styles haven't been applied to the paragraphs in Word, PowerPoint uses the paragraph indentations to determine the presentation's structure.

To copy a presentation outline to a Word document:

1. Switch to Outline View in PowerPoint (**Figure 30.6**).

2. Choose File > Send To > Microsoft Word. The PowerPoint outline opens as a new Word document (**Figure 30.7**).

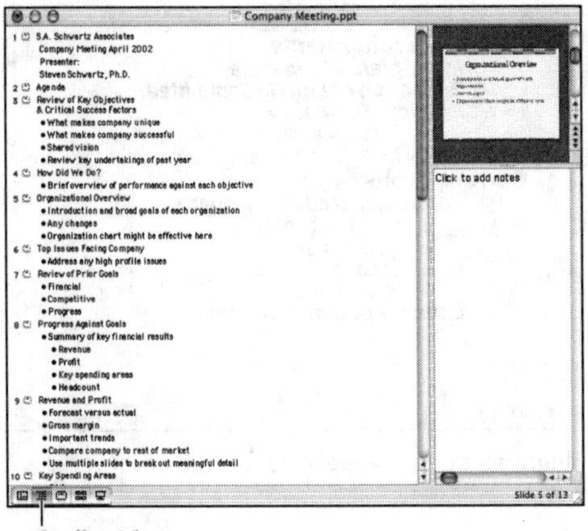

Outline View

Figure 30.6 Create or open a PowerPoint Presentation, and switch to Outline View.

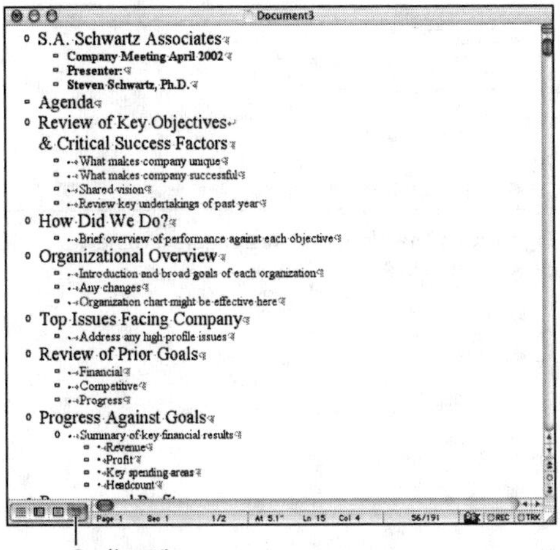

Outline View

Figure 30.7 A new Word document opens with the PowerPoint outline in it.

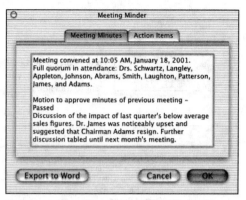

Figure 30.8 To transfer the contents of the Meeting Minder dialog box into Word, click the Export to Word button.

To copy Meeting Minder notes into a Word document:

1. In PowerPoint, choose Tools > Meeting Minder.

   The Meeting Minder dialog box appears.

2. Enter or edit your meeting notes and action items (**Figure 30.8**).

3. Click the Export to Word button.

   A new Word document opens that contains the meeting notes and action items (**Figure 30.9**).

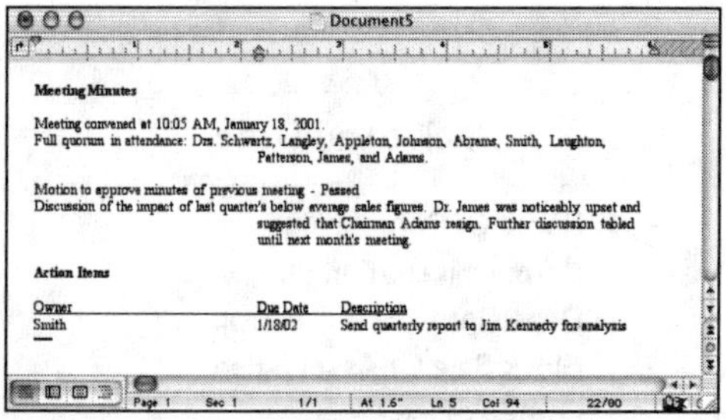

Figure 30.9 The meeting minutes and action items appear in a new Word document.

Copying Text from Word to Excel or PowerPoint

You can copy text from Word into Excel or PowerPoint via copy and paste or drag and drop.

To copy text from Word or PowerPoint:

1. Arrange the Word document window so you can also see the Excel or PowerPoint document window.

2. In Word, select the text you want to copy (**Figure 30.10**).

3. Choose Edit > Copy (⌘C). Paste the text into an Excel cell or a PowerPoint slide by choosing Edit > Paste (⌘V).

   or

   Drag the text to a destination cell in Excel or onto a slide in PowerPoint (**Figures 30.11** and **30.12**).

   The text is copied to the destination.

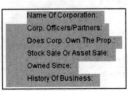

Figure 30.10 Select (or copy) the Word text you want to transfer.

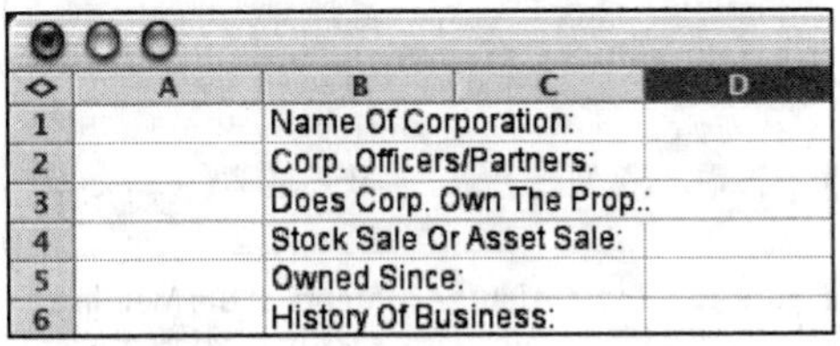

	A	B	C	D
1		Name Of Corporation:		
2		Corp. Officers/Partners:		
3		Does Corp. Own The Prop.:		
4		Stock Sale Or Asset Sale:		
5		Owned Since:		
6		History Of Business:		

Figure 30.11 Drag or paste the selected text into an Excel cell.

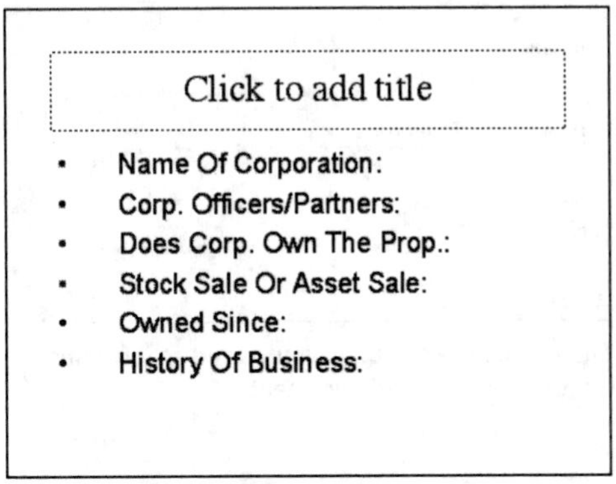

> Click to add title
>
> - Name Of Corporation:
> - Corp. Officers/Partners:
> - Does Corp. Own The Prop.:
> - Stock Sale Or Asset Sale:
> - Owned Since:
> - History Of Business:

Figure 30.12 You can also drag or paste it into a text placeholder on a PowerPoint slide.

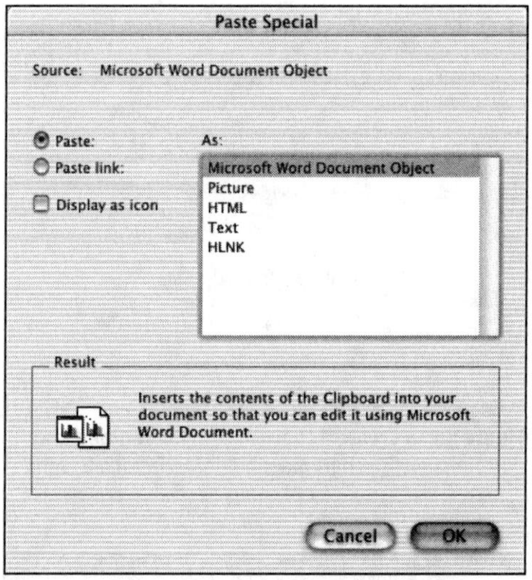

Figure 30.13 Using the Edit > Paste Special command, you can transfer copied Word text as an object.

✔ Tips

■ Formatting, such as font, size, and style, is also copied and will appear in the Excel worksheet. In PowerPoint, however, the formatting of the destination placeholder text determines the font size.

■ In Excel, pasted Word text frequently overflows the cell. Expand the cell width or enable text wrapping for the cell, if necessary.

■ Excel attempts to mimic the paragraph formatting of copied Word text. A tab within a paragraph is treated as an instruction to place the text in the next cell; a return is treated as an instruction to move down to the next row.

■ You can also paste Word text as a floating object. In Excel or PowerPoint, choose Edit > Paste Special and select Microsoft Word Document Object as the format (**Figure 30.13**). The result is an embedded text object that is editable in Word.

COPYING TEXT FROM WORD

Combining Excel and PowerPoint

Excel and PowerPoint can share information, too. You can copy and paste material from either application into the other. You can also import Excel files into a PowerPoint presentation.

To create a PowerPoint chart from imported Excel data:

1. Create a chart slide in PowerPoint, and double-click the "Double click to add chart" placeholder (**Figure 30.14**).

   Graph launches (**Figure 30.15**).

2. If you want the imported data to begin in any cell other than the upper-left corner of the datasheet, click to select the starting cell.

3. Choose File > Import File.

4. Select the Excel file you want to import, and click Choose.

   The Import Data Options dialog box appears (**Figure 30.16**).

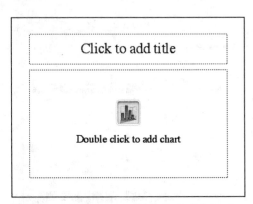

Figure 30.14 Create a chart slide in PowerPoint and double-click the chart placeholder to launch Graph.

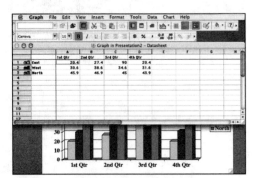

Figure 30.15 Graph opens, displaying sample data and a temporary chart.

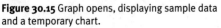

Figure 30.16 Select which sheet to import. By clicking the appropriate radio button, you can import the entire worksheet or a particular cell range.

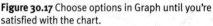

Figure 30.17 Choose options in Graph until you're satisfied with the chart.

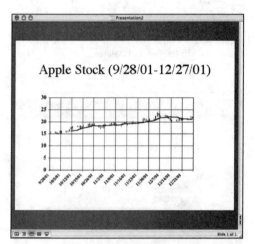

Figure 30.18 Quit Graph. The finished chart appears on the PowerPoint slide. If you later need to alter the chart, double-click it on the slide.

5. Select the sheet to import, specify the range (if you want to import only part of the worksheet), and click OK.

6. Edit and rearrange the data as necessary.

7. Select a chart type from the Chart Type drop-down palette on the toolbar or choose Chart > Chart Type.

8. Format the chart elements as you wish (**Figure 30.17**). When the chart is satisfactory, choose Graph > Quit & Return to *presentation name*.

The finished chart appears on the slide (**Figure 30.18**).

✔ Tip

■ You can consolidate data from several worksheets by repeating the import procedure to different destination cells. Be sure to remove the checkmark from Overwrite existing cells in the Import Data Options dialog box.

COMBINING EXCEL AND POWERPOINT

To link Excel data to a PowerPoint chart:

1. Create a chart slide in PowerPoint, and double-click the "Double click to add chart" placeholder (Figure 30.14). Graph launches (Figure 30.15).

2. Switch to Excel, and select the cell range you want to use to create the chart (**Figure 30.19**).

3. Choose Edit > Copy or press ⌘C.

4. Switch to Graph, and select the datasheet cell in the upper-left corner.
   This is where the Excel data will appear.

5. Choose Edit > Paste Link.
   The data appears in the datasheet (**Figure 30.20**).

6. Edit and rearrange the data as necessary.

7. Select a chart type from the Chart Type drop-down palette on the toolbar or by choosing Chart > Chart Type.

8. Format the chart elements as desired. When the chart is satisfactory, choose Graph > Quit & Return to *presentation name*.
   The finished chart appears on the slide (**Figure 30.21**).

✔ Tips

- If the Excel data includes totals, make sure not to select them when importing the data. (Totals normally aren't included in charts.)

- As long as Graph is running, the PowerPoint chart will reflect any changes made to the data in Excel. Otherwise, to update the link, double-click the chart on the PowerPoint slide. Graph launches and automatically updates the figures based on the current version of the Excel worksheet.

Selected cell range

	A	B	C	D	E	F
1	2001 Sales	Qtr. 1	Qtr. 2	Qtr. 3	Qtr. 4	
2	North	6.20	9.20	12.00	4.00	
3	East	2.00	3.03	2.24	2.00	
4	South	1.28	6.00	1.73	1.32	
5	West	4.00	9.40	3.97	3.32	
6						

Figure 30.19 In Excel, select the cell range you want to link.

	A	B	C	D	E
	2001 Sales	Qtr. 1	Qtr. 2	Qtr. 3	Qtr. 4
1	North	6.2	9.2	12	4
2	East	2	3.03	2.24	2
3	South	1.28	6	1.73	1.32
4	West	4	9.4	3.97	3.32
5					
6					

Figure 30.20 Choose Edit > Paste Link to add the copied data to the Graph datasheet.

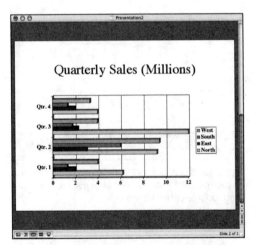

Figure 30.21 After you complete the chart and quit Graph, the chart appears on the PowerPoint slide.

COMBINING EXCEL AND POWERPOINT

Selected contact record

Link icon

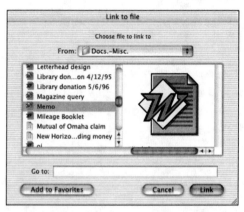

Figure 30.22 Select the contact record, click the Link toolbar icon, and choose Link > Link to Existing > File.

Figure 30.23 Select the desired document from the Link to file dialog box.

Link indicator

Figure 30.24 The link indicator appears beside the contact name in the Address Book. To open the linked document, click the indicator and choose the file from the pop-up menu.

Linking Entourage Items

In Entourage, you can link files, calendar events, or notes to any other item in Entourage. Links in Entourage are useful when you're planning meetings, for example. You can link a document pertaining to the meeting to a contact record in your Address Book. This enables you to open the document directly from the Address Book, as shown in the following example.

To link an Entourage contact to an Office document:

1. In Entourage, switch to the Address Book by clicking its icon in the upper-left corner of the window, by choosing View > Go To > Address Book, or by pressing ⌘2.

2. Select the record in the contact list.

3. Click the Link toolbar icon and choose Link > Link to Existing > File from the pop-up menu that appears (**Figure 30.22**).

   The Link to file dialog box appears (**Figure 30.23**).

4. Select the file to which you want to link the contact information, and click Link.

   A link indicator appears beside the contact name in the Address Book, showing that the contact is linked to a file or an Entourage item.

   To view the linked file later, click the link indicator in the person's record and choose the linked file from the pop-up menu that appears (**Figure 30.24**).

✔ Tips

- You can link Entourage items to files created in *any* application—not just Office.

- You can also link notes, calendar events, and tasks to any document, as well as to each other.

- When a link ceases to be useful, you can break it. Click the link icon and choose Open Links from the pop-up menu that appears (Figure 30.24). The Links To dialog box appears, listing all links to the selected item. Select the link to break (**Figure 30.25**), click the Remove Link toolbar icon, and close the dialog box.

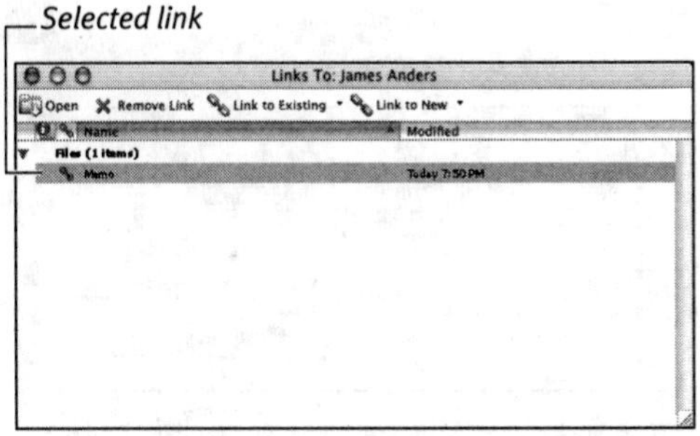

— Selected link

Figure 30.25 You can break a link by selecting it in the Links To dialog box and clicking the Remove Link toolbar icon.

INDEX

C

INDEX

WWW.PEACHPIT.COM

Quality How-to Computer Books

Visit Peachpit Press on the Web at www.peachpit.com

- Check out new feature articles each Monday: excerpts, interviews, tips, and plenty of how-tos

- Find any Peachpit book by title, series, author, or topic on the Books page

- See what our authors are up to on the News page: signings, chats, appearances, and more

- Meet the Peachpit staff and authors in the About section: bios, profiles, and candid shots

- Use Resources to reach our academic, sales, customer service, and tech support areas and find out how to become a Peachpit author

About

News

Books

Features

Resources

Order

Find

Welcome!

Peachpit.com is also the place to:

- Chat with our authors online
- Take advantage of special Web-only offers
- Get the latest info on new books